26 '71

P9-AFI-606

JACK LONDON REPORTS

Jack London Reports

WAR CORRESPONDENCE,

SPORTS ARTICLES,

AND MISCELLANEOUS WRITINGS

Edited by King Hendricks
and Irving Shepard

DOUBLEDAY & COMPANY, INC., GARDEN CITY, NEW YORK, 1970

Library of Congress Catalog Card Number 69–12212
Copyright © 1970 by Irving Shepard and King Hendricks
All Rights Reserved
Printed in the United States of America
First Edition

CONTENTS

INTRODUCTION

After London's death, George Sterling, California poet, wrote a eulogy for the San Francisco *Examiner* in which he said:

> . . . London is destined to surge triumphantly above race and time. Already he is, as indicated by his friend, Upton Sinclair, the literary representative of our land in Sweden, Germany and Russia. This, however, is but a beginning; a genius so flaming, so passionate, so sincere and catholic is not to be circumscribed by the bourns of prejudice and nationality.

Sterling's prediction has come true. Even now, barely half a century after London's death, his novels, short stories, and essays are read by the scholars and the laymen, the leaders and the led throughout the entire world. They have been translated into more than fifty languages and millions of copies have been printed and sold. He is no longer looked upon as merely a teller of tales but as an interpreter of the ideals and desires of mankind.

He was a man of many facets: sometimes brutally frank, sometimes tender and compassionate, but always honest and sincere. His friends were many and heterogeneous, ranging from hoboes and convicts to the greats and near greats of his time. If an unknown high school girl asked him to criticize a story and give some hints for improvement, he took time to answer the letter and evaluate the paper. Or, when he learned of an impending execution of some revolutionaries in Japan, he took time to lodge a protest with the Japanese ambassador. He had no patience for hypocrisy or sympathy for mediocrity. He hated man's injustice to man as he hated man's cruelty to animal. And this very hatred all too frequently brought upon him the condemnation of his contemporaries.

His genius was universal. Through his reading he encompassed the best thoughts of his cultural heritage. In his own adventurous living he came into contact with the problems and motivations of people from the Alaskan gold mines, the working classes of America (the privileged and the underprivileged), the humble peasant of Korea, the lepers of Molokai, the natives of the South Sea islands, and the intelligentsia of America and Europe. From this background of reading and human contact his perceptive mind and his indomitable will forged more than a hundred and fifty short stories and essays and nineteen full-length novels, and, as he once said, a "mountain of letters," in a period of seventeen years.

Jack London was born in San Francisco, January 12, 1876, at a time when the city was a haven for men of every description—the city by the Golden Gate—gateway to the Pacific and the Orient; the city of the Barbary Coast; the city just emerging from the frontier where the necessity for and the actions of the Vigilantes were fresh memories.

In his earliest years he knew at first hand the perils of poverty and insecurity. At the age of fifteen he became an oyster pirate. Oyster pirating was illegal. It was carried on by young hoodlums, for the most part, who hovered around the wharves and the bars of Oakland. At night, in small boats, these men would raid the privately owned oyster beds of the lower part of San Francisco Bay and sell their products in the morning to the city markets. The pirates could make anywhere from twenty to two hundred dollars per raid. The money and the adventure appealed to London. He bought a sloop of his own from a character known as French Frank. It was his first adventure and he proved his metal. His prowess and his daring earned for him the respect of his comrades and the title of "The Prince of the Oyster Pirates."

Oysters, however, were not the only object of the pirates on the bay. Other groups, including Chinese and Greeks, were engaged in illicit traffic in shrimps and salmon. An officer of the fish patrol suggested that London join the side of law enforcement. That he did. His services as a law-enforcement officer were brief—because in 1893, at age seventeen, he signed on a sealing vessel, the *Sophie Sutherland*, as an able-bodied seaman.

He was a youngster among seasoned tars and he knew it. He knew that he must hold his own in every situation, working or brawling. But he was no fledgling in rough company; his strength and daring served him again as it had among the oyster pirates and he became a fully accepted member of the crew. There is another side of London that must be noted if we are to understand him as a writer. He was a prodigious reader. In spite of his poverty, his activity, and his associates, he always read. Aboard the *Sophie Sutherland* he read such books as *Madame Bovary* and *Anna Karenina*, which he managed to procure before he left Oakland.

His return from the sea came at an unfortunate time. The country was in the depths of a depression because of the financial panic of 1893. Jobs were hard to get and wages were low. His own family was in dire distress. He went to work, at the only job he could find, in a jute mill at a wage of ten cents an hour for a ten-hour day. Here he saw the American labor scene at one of its lowest ebbs. Children, some crippled, some diseased, working in humid, crowded, noisy conditions, were earning perhaps two dollars for a sixty-hour week. He left the jute mills to work as a coal heaver at a wage of thirty dollars a month with one day off.

One day his mother called his attention to an announcement of an essay contest in *The Morning Call* (San Francisco). London wrote "Typhoon Off the Coast of Japan" and submitted it. It won first prize and was printed November 12, 1893, over the signature of John London.

During the next year (1894) he published two items: "An Old Soldier's Story" in the May issue of *Evenings at Home* (Oakland) and "Old Baldy" in the September issue. He also submitted a story to the *Youth's Companion*, what we do not know, but among his rejection notices in the Henry E. Huntington Library in San Marino, California, is a form letter from the *Youth's Companion* addressed in longhand to John London, Esq., and with a postscript, in the same longhand, which reads: "We are very sorry that this narrative does not seem quite adapted to the *Companion*." It was signed simply "The Editors."

Sometime later he abandoned the name of John for all purposes and signed his letters and his manuscripts simply "Jack London." (Occasionally, when he added postscripts to his letters, he initialed them J.G.L.) On October 10, 1899, before the publication of "An Odyssey of the North" in *The Atlantic Monthly* and the collection of short stories *The Son of the Wolf*, by Houghton Mifflin, the editors of *The Atlantic* wrote to him and asked if Jack London were his real name or a *nom de plume*. The letter read in part: ". . . We should much prefer to substitute on the title page of *The Atlantic* your real name, and in the former case we venture to suggest the use of the more frequent form of the Christian name—John seeming to us better suited than Jack to literary purposes."

Jack replied that the name "had stood him on the trail, in the snows, in hunger and in plenty and he did not propose to go back on it at this late date."

The depression of 1893 deepened in 1894. Thousands of men were unemployed. Such leaders as Coxey in Ohio and Kelly in San Francisco organized the unemployed into armies for a march on Washington. London heard of Kelly's plans and decided to join his contingent. Kelly arranged with the railroad for free transportation for his army and announced the scheduled departure as April 6. However, when London arrived in the afternoon, he found the Army had left in the morning. This did not deter him—he "jumped" a freight and followed, determined to join Kelly at the earliest possible moment. He rode the blinds, or unlocked freight cars; he carried on a running battle with railroad men and police officers; he begged for food from the back doors of residences and found all too frequently that he had better luck in the shanties of the poor than he did in the comfortable homes of the well-to-do. He finally caught up with Kelly at Chautauqua Park in Iowa. The citizens of Iowa at first were sympathetic toward the marchers, and for a short period of time food and clothing were available. However, the period of opulence was brief, and when the "Industrial Army" began to starve, its members deserted in droves. London was among the deserters.

Again he was on his own as a hobo. He made his way, via freight cars once more, to Chicago, to Washington, and to New York before the summer's end. A brush with the law in New York started him on his way again and a few days later he was picked up for vagrancy in Niagara Falls, sentenced to jail at hard labor for thirty days, and sent to the Erie County Penitentiary. Now he was to see another side of life—the inside of a prison. He saw men whipped, tortured, and beaten to death. He became the friend and confidant of hardened criminals, listened to their yarns, their gripes and their philosophies, all of which became a part of the literary luggage that he was later to draw on. Once released, he crossed into Canada and after some months and three thousand miles of travel on Canadian railroads, mostly on freight trains, he arrived in Vancouver, where he signed as a seaman on a coastwise craft and worked his way back to San Francisco.

The experience "on the road" was a turning point in his life. He saw, and lived, the life of the underprivileged at its worst. He mingled with men who were physically strong and capable of productive labor but to whom society or social conditions denied any opportunity. He realized how insecure was the man who depended for his subsistence upon brawn, and decided he must have an education.

The results were twofold: he returned to school and he became a socialist. He was nineteen years old. He entered the Oakland High School, and while here he published five pieces in the school paper, *The Aegis*. But he soon found the pace too slow and took instead five weeks in a cramming school in preparation for the entrance examinations of the University of California. He studied at the university one semester before conditions in his family forced him once more into the labor market. He found a job in a laundry. The work was hard, the hours were long; and he had no time to read, to think, or to write. He wanted to write—he knew he could. He wanted more adventure, and the discovery of gold in the Klondike presented to him the opportunity. In 1897 he joined the throng of goldseekers bound for Alaska.

In the Yukon, London found an entirely different milieu and atmosphere. The men he met were not the oppressed castoffs of society; they were men of strength and courage in a boom environment looking for riches and adventure. The weak dropped by the wayside and returned to the States; the strong went over Chilkoot Pass into the vast wilderness beyond, where the challenge was great and the stakes were high. It was just the right situation for his adventurous spirit. When the Indians demanded too high a price to carry his supplies over the pass, London and his three companions carried them—eight thousand pounds of supplies—over the pass in ninety days. When boats which were needed to carry the supplies over rivers and lakes were not

available, or priced too high, he and his men built their own
—two, *The Belle of the Yukon*, and *Yukon Belle*. Where other
men failed to negotiate the rivers, particularly the rapids, London
succeeded; but in spite of his hard labor and determination
winter caught his party seventy miles from their goal, Dawson,
and forced them to spend some months in an abandoned cabin
halfway between Stewart River and Henderson Creek.

Failure to find gold and an attack of scurvy ended his Yukon
journey. He returned to San Francisco in the summer of 1898—
a little older, a little wiser, and if possible a little more im-
poverished; but he had garnered something—knowledge and experience—that was destined to bring him both fame and fortune.

It is safe to assume that upon his return from the Yukon
in July 1898 he turned to writing with serious intent. On the
seventeenth day of September he wrote a letter to the editor of
The Bulletin (San Francisco) asking if he would be interested
in an article describing his trip from Dawson to St. Michaels.
The editor wrote a negative reply on the bottom of London's
letter and returned it. Jack's wife, Charmian London, later added
another note: "This was Jack's first letter to an editor."

Also at this time London began to keep a record of the
materials he submitted for publication. He kept this record in
notebooks which he called *Magazine Sales*. There are four of
these: No. 1 dates "From 1898 to May 1900," No. 2 "From
May 1900–Feb. 1903," No. 3 "From Feb. 1903–Feb. 1909," and
No. 4 from February 1909 until his death. The first two are particularly significant because they reveal his struggle as a young
writer.

In these records he listed the title, the number of words, the
name of each magazine or newspaper to which he sent an item,
dates of submission, trailers (by this he meant letters of inquiry
if the reply from the editor was not received in a short time),
date (if accepted), date of publication and payment received.
Some were never accepted and after a number of rejections,
varying from three to twenty, he wrote "Retired."

The initial date of his first entry was September 21, 1898,
four days after his letter to the *Bulletin*. It was entitled "From
Dawson to the Sea" and reads:

Outing	Sept. 21/98
Trailer	Dec. 6
Trailer	Jan 29/99
Finally returned	Feb. 18/99
Revised --------------------	3720 words
Examiner	Mar. 18/99
Western Press	Mar. 24/99
Buffalo Express	Apr. 12/99
Trailer	May 18/99
Accepted	June 1/99
Published	June 4/99
Sent for copies	June 7/99
Received copies	June 19/99
Dunned --------------------	July 18/99
Received $10.00	July 29/99

The second entry, "The Devil's Dice Box," was made two days later:

McClure's	Sept. 23/98
Munsey's	Oct. 18/98
Bacheller Syn	Nov. 14/98
Lippincott's	Jan. 3/99
Gray Goose	Feb. 17/99
Donahoe's Magazine	Mar. 31/99
Illustrated American	Apr. 26/99
Carter's Monthly	May 11/99
(To be changed)	
Retired	

This was the beginning of a period of feverish activity. The *Magazine Sales No. 1* carries one hundred and one entries—short stories, essays, poems and six jokes—submitted to more than a hundred and twenty publishing agencies including newspapers, farm journals, short story magazines, and such magazines as *The Atlantic Monthly*. The record shows four hundred and ten rejections. Forty-four items were rejected two hundred and forty-seven times, while the other fifty-seven received only one hundred and sixty-three rejections. This would indicate, what many critics have felt about London, a wide disparity in the quality of his work. The payments varied from fifty cents, for joke no. 1, to two hundred dollars for a prize-winning essay, "What a Community Loses by the Competitive System," (published by *Cosmopolitan*, November 1900). The total sales of the period September 1898 to May 1900 amounted to $1826.25, an average of less than a hundred dollars a month.

On November 10 (1898) he sent "To the Man on Trail" to *Overland Monthly*. It was accepted and printed in the January (1899) issue. Sometime later London received five dollars for it. On November 13 he submitted "A Thousand Deaths" to *Black Cat*. The editor accepted it and offered him forty dollars. It was published in the May (1899) issue. In the *Magazine Sales* entry London wrote: "First money I ever received from a magazine for a story."

This was a very important event for London. He had conceived the idea that he could, or should, make two cents a word for his stories. "A Thousand Deaths" was four thousand words in length. *Black Cat* would pay him forty dollars if he would reduce it to two thousand printed words—two cents a word. His dream had come true.

Perhaps the most significant entry in *Magazine Sales No. 1* was "An Odyssey of the North" (12,250), which reads:

McClures	May 24/99
Atlantic Monthly	June 10/99
Will accept if shorten by 3000 words	July 29/99
Reduced to 10,000 words (Returned to Atlantic Monthly)	Aug. 1/99
Accepted	Aug. 25/99
Proofsheets received	Oct. 11/99
Letter relative to my name	Oct. 16/99
Advance Sheets	Oct. 30/99
Received $120.00 & one year's subscription	Oct. 30/99
Published	Jan. 1900

While the rate was only slightly more than a cent a word, it opened the way for his first book publication. *The Atlantic Monthly* was an affiliate of Houghton Mifflin Co. who published a collection of his stories under the title *The Son of the Wolf* in April 1900. Before his death in 1916, London would see forty-three more volumes—novels and collections of stories and essays—published; and five, complete at the time of his death, would be published within four years.

The *Magazine Sales No. 2* (May 1900 to February 1903) is a different story. First, London did not send out as many items, only sixty-four. Second, while he received many rejections, two hundred and five, most of the items were published, sixty-one to be exact, which left only three to be retired. The total income for these sixty-one items was $3727.03. Third, as the preceding figure indicates, the rate of pay was considerably higher, ranging from ten dollars for "The Sickness of Lone Chief" (*Outwest*, September 1902) to one hundred and sixty dollars for "The League of Old Men" (*Brandur Magazine*, October 1902). *Youth's Companion* paid him fifty dollars for "To Build a Fire" (May 1902). Later London wrote a second version of "To Build a Fire" and sold it for four hundred dollars to *Century Magazine*, who published it in August 1908.

After its publication R. W. Gilder, the editor, complained to London that he had sold him a story which had previously been published. London explained that the first version was a juvenile story but "I was worried by the inadequate treatment I had given the motif . . . and resolved to take the same motif and handle it for men." Gilder was apparently satisfied with London's explanation.[1]

While there are one hundred and one entries in *Magazine Sales No. 1* for a period of nineteen months and only sixty-four in *Magazine Sales No. 2* for a period of thirty-four months, the latter was by no means a period of inactivity for London. Many of the stories printed in magazines went into book form. McClure, Phillips and Company published a collection under the title of *The God of His Fathers* in May 1901; Macmillan, who published thirty-nine of his forty-nine books, brought out another collection, entitled *Children of the Frost*, in September 1902; J. B. Lippincott Co. published his first novel, *A Daughter*

[1] For treatment of this see *Studies in Short Fiction*, Fall 1967, "Jack London's Twice-Told Tale," by Earle Labor and King Hendricks. The first version of the story is an appendix to the article.

of the Snows, in October 1902; and the Century Co. his juvenile book, *The Cruise of the Dazzler,* in October 1902. A few months later (July 1903) Macmillan issued his great classic, *The Call of the Wild.*

One might question the veracity of London's manuscript records—six hundred and forty-four rejections in slightly more than five years—but for the fact that most of the slips and letters have been preserved and are on deposit in the Huntington Library. There are five hundred and fifty filed in one box and some others in the correspondence files. Many of these are undated, but a check against the manuscript records established rather definitely that they belong to this period. (Also later rejections came in the form of personal, not form, letters.) Not only are many of the earlier ones not dated, many cannot be identified as to title of item or name of company. One publisher used a two-by-four card upon which was printed in bold face RESPECTFULLY DECLINED, nothing more. Some editors wrote short notes giving reasons for rejection. Often these were undated, unsigned, and with no reference to the title rejected. For instance, one wrote: "I have more Mss. than I can possibly find time to read, and you ask me for remuneration. I can only tell you that I can buy no materials from any one."

Another wrote in longhand, on a piece of brown wrapping paper: "This type of story is *absolutely impossible* for us. Try *Vanity Fair* or *Town Topics.* It is in their line. We want clean stories of love or incident." One from the *Century Magazine,* no signature and no title identification but dated September 6, 1902, reads: "Capital piece, but falls outside our range by the unrelieved tragedy of it."

During this early period of his writing activity, in April 1900, he married Elizabeth (Bessie) Maddern. She bore him two daughters, Joan and Bess.

In July 1902, London received an offer from the American Press Association to go to South Africa and write a series of articles on the Boer War and political and economic conditions in the British colonies. When he arrived in New York, however, he found that plans had changed. Instead of going to South Africa he went to England, where he lived for some weeks in the slum district of London, from which experience he wrote *The People of the Abyss*.

In 1904 he went to Korea as a newspaper correspondent to cover the Russo-Japanese War. Three important events occurred in 1905. He was divorced from Bessie, married to Charmian Kittredge, and made his first purchase of land of what was to become his thirteen-hundred-acre Beauty Ranch in the Valley of the Moon, Sonoma County, California. He said that he bought the ranch "mostly for its beauty and for a place to live and write," but it was to be something more—it became a challenge—a challenge to develop better stock and to improve farming methods in order to increase agricultural productivity.

One day, after having read Captain Joshua Slocum's book, *Sailing Alone Around the World*, he suggested to Charmian such a voyage in a forty-foot craft. The adventurer in Charmian responded, and after many disappointments in preparing for the voyage they sailed out of San Francisco harbor in April 1907 into the vast Pacific with a crew of four: Roscoe Eames, who knew nothing of navigation, as navigator; Bert Stolz, a Stanford student who had no knowledge of engineering, as engineer; Martin Johnson, later famous as a big game hunter, who couldn't cook, as cook; and a young Oriental as cabin boy.

The trip took them to such places as Hawaii, the Marquesas, Tahiti, Pitcairn Island, the Solomon Islands, and Australia. The Londons returned to San Francisco in July 1909, after twenty-six months filled with excitement, frustrations, illness, and hard work. The story is best told by London in *The Cruise of the Snark* and by Charmian in *The Log of the Snark*, which was published in England in two volumes entitled *Voyaging in the South Seas* and *A Woman Among the Head Hunters*.

Despite engine troubles, crew troubles, tropical climate and disease, London continued to write his thousand words a day. In a period of twenty-six months (April 1907 to July 1909), he wrote the equivalent of eight volumes, including his novels *Martin Eden, Adventure,* and *Burning Daylight,* and a number of short stories and essays.

The last six years of his life were filled with frustrations, disappointments, and tragedy. In 1910 Charmian's second child died at birth. The death was a severe blow to London because

he had had such an ardent desire to have a son and realized
now that it could never be. In 1913 he became involved in a
lawsuit over his copyrights, the outcome of which could have
been disastrous to him and to all other writers. The Balboa
Amusement Company, which had produced a moving picture
of *The Sea Wolf*, maintained that writers did not own the
copyright to a story once it was published in a magazine. The
case was costly to London in time, money, and energy. Fortunately, for all writers, London and his colleagues won and
established a precedent that clarified copyright laws.

One of London's lifelong dreams was to build a house
of his own. This he did in 1913 and called it the Wolf House.
When it was almost finished (August 22) it burned—apparently
the work of arsonists.

The year before his death he became involved in a water
right suit which troubled him because it involved people who
were near and dear to him, and a few months before his death
his famous shire stallion, Nueadd Hillside, died. These were only
a few of the major troubles during these years, troubles that
might have dismayed a weaker man, but the indomitable will
of London prevailed.

He continued to write. In 1912 he signed a contract with
Cosmopolitan to supply a short story every month and one
novel a year for serialization. Actually he completed ten novels
(seven of which were published before his death, three post-
humously) and five volumes of short stories.

And he contined to adventure. He and Charmian would fre-
quently take a cruise of the bay in their yacht, *The Roamer*.
In 1911 they took a four-horse driving trip through northern
California and Oregon. The following year they traveled from
Baltimore to San Francisco, around the Horn, on a windjammer.
When the Mexican troubles brewed in 1914, he went to Vera
Cruz as a war correspondent for *Collier's*.

After his return from Mexico his health began to fail. He
developed uremia. In 1915, and again in 1916, he went to Hawaii
in hopes of improving his physical condition but to no avail.

At the time of his death on November 22, 1916, he was one
of the highest paid writers in America and one of the most
popular. For two or three decades his popularity declined, but

after World War II he began to come into world recognition. He has been the subject of biographies and critical articles; a number of his stories have been printed in special collections and anthologies; most of his novels have been reprinted; Arthur Calder-Marshall, one of England's noted critics, wrote of *John Barleycorn* "a literary masterpiece, not merely the greatest book Jack London wrote, but, seen in its true setting, one of the most poignant documents of our century, a fortuitous work of inhibited and tortured genius."[2]

Perhaps the best picture of London's place in the world of letters regarding the large volume of work, the wide international interest, and the critical attention is seen in an excellent bibliography recently published.[3] It is divided into two parts.

Part one lists London's writings as published in collections, anthologies, periodicals, newspapers, etc., in both English and foreign languages. The *Morning Press* of Pleasant Hill, California, March 26, 1969, carries an article about Mrs. Joan London Miller (London's oldest daughter) in which occurs the statement: "Another explosion of interest in his [London's] writings occurred in the 40's which led to books being translated into 55 different languages, including Vietnamese."

Part two lists the writings about London; books, pamphlets, articles, theses, and reviews in both English and foreign languages. The bibliography contains 2450 entries.

Under date of September 5, 1969, Professor Hensley C. Woodbridge wrote to us concerning the continuation of the work on the bibliography and pointed out that a number of items have appeared in such places as the *Jack London Newsletter*, *American Literary Realism* and a Russian bibliography mentioned in vol. II no. 2 of the *Jack London Newsletter*. Also theses and dissertations in progress may add a number of items. Professor Woodbridge stated, "In brief had I known what I know now about 2,500 more items could have been added to it."

[2] *The Bodley Head Jack London*, edited, with introduction, by Arthur Calder-Marshall, London, Bodley Head, 1964, vol. 2.
[3] *Jack London: A Bibliography*, compiled by Hensley C. Woodbridge, John London, and George H. Tweney, The Talisman Press, Georgetown, California, 1966, p. 422.

PART ONE

War
Correspondence

LETTERS FROM KOREA TO CHARMIAN

By the end of 1903 Jack London's fame as a writer was definitely established. During the year he published eighteen stories or essays in journals and newspapers, and three books: The Call of the Wild, The Kempton-Wace Letters, *and* The People of the Abyss. *At the end of the year he had finished* The Sea Wolf. *Also during this year he and his wife Bessie were separated.*

When trouble developed between Russia and Japan, the San Francisco Examiner *asked London to go to Japan and Korea as a war correspondent. In a letter to Cloudesley Johns, dated January 7, 1904, he wrote:*

> Sail today for Yokohama. Am going for *Hearst*. Could have gone for *Harper's*, *Collier's*, and the New York *Herald*—but *Hearst* made the best offer.

He sailed on the S.S. Siberia along with a number of other correspondents, including Captain Lionel James, London Times; *Percival Phillips, London* Daily Express; *Sheldon Inglis Williams, artist for London* Sphere: *O. K. Davis, New York* Herald; *Frederick Palmer and R. L. Dunn, for Collier's, and Collier's veteran war photographer, James H. Hare. Five days later, January 12, he became twenty-eight years old.*

The day before he sailed, he completed the manuscript of The Sea Wolf, *which was to be serialized by the* Century Magazine *and published in book form by The Macmillan Company. During his separation from Bessie he had become a close friend to Charmian Kittredge and he left to her and George Sterling the responsibility for proofreading the copy from* Century Magazine *and The Macmillan Company.[1] Also, he set up a correspondence with Charmian Kittredge in which he recorded day to day events and experiences which he did not often include in the* Examiner *articles. We have used here only the portions of the letters that have a bearing upon his activity as a war correspondent.*

[1] London's handwritten copy of *The Sea Wolf* was in a steel vault in San Francisco during the earthquake and fire. It was damaged and, although marred, it is on deposit, along with all of London's other holograph manuscripts (except for *The Call of the Wild*) in the Henry E. Huntington Library in San Marino, California.

S.S. *Siberia*, Jan. 13/04

Somewhat weak and wobbly, but still in the ring. Came down with a beautiful attack of La Grippe. Of course, didn't go to bed with it, but spent the time in a steamer chair, for one day half out of my head. And oh, how all my bones ache, even now! And what wild dreams I had!

Honolulu is in sight, and in an hour I shall be ashore mailing this, and learning whether or not there is war.

Am, Grippe excepted, having a nice trip. The weather is perfect. So is the steamer. Sit at the Captain's table, and all the rest—you know.

S.S. *Siberia*, Jan. 15/04

Well, we sailed yesterday from Honolulu. Am still miserable with my Grippe, but getting better. Had a swim in the surf at Waikiki. Took in the concert at the Hawaiian Hotel, and had a general nice time.

Had some fun. I bucked a game run by the Chinese firemen of the *Siberia*, and in twenty-five minutes broke three banks and won $14.85. So, you see, I have discovered a new career for myself.

The war correspondents, the "Vultures," and a jolly crowd. We are bunched up at the Captain's table, now that the passenger list has been reduced by the lot who left at Honolulu. In fact, the trip to Honolulu had three bridal couples which sat at the upper end of the table. This is a funny letter—the correspondents are cutting up all around me; and just now I am being joshed good and plenty.

S.S. *Siberia*, Jan. 20/04

Quite a time since I last wrote. You'll wonder why. Well, know that I am the most fortunate of unfortunate men. The evening of the day we left Honolulu I smashed my left ankle. For sixty-five sweaty hours I lay on my back. Yesterday I was carried on deck, on the back of one of the English correspondents. And to-day I have been carried on deck again.

The smashed ankle is the misfortune; the fortune (which has prevented me from writing you) is the crowd of friends I seem to have collected. From six o'clock in the morning till eleven at night, there was never a moment that my stateroom did not have at least one visitor. As a rule there were three or four, and very often twice as many. I had thought, when the accident happened, that I should have plenty of time for reading; but I was not left alone long enough to read a line.

I am looking forward with interest to the sixth day, when, if the surgeon does not change his mind, I may put my foot to the deck and try to walk with the aid of crutches.

Of course, what you want to know is what the smash consists in. I was jumping and coming down from a height of three feet and a half. I landed on my left foot—having "taken off" with my right. But my left foot did not land on the deck. It landed on a round stick, and lengthwise with the stick. Stick about diameter of broom-handle. Of course, my foot went up alongside of my leg. My ankle was strained on one side, sprained on the other. That is, the tendons on the inside were stretched and ruptured, the bones on the outside ground against each other, bruising themselves and pinching the nerves—result, an irresistible combination.

Now I have two weak ankles. I fear me I am getting old. Both my knees have been smashed, and now both my ankles. It might be worse, however. What bothers me just now is that I don't know just how bad this last ankle is. Absolute rest, in a rigid bandage, has been the treatment, so not even the surgeon will know till I try to walk on it.

Don't worry because I have let my worry out in this letter. Anyway, I'll be able to write you later, before we make Yokohama, and let you know more. I hope the report will be promising.

S.S. *Siberia,* Jan. 21/04

You should see me to-day. Quite the cripple, hobbling around on a pair of crutches. I can't stand on the ankle yet, but hope to be able to walk by the time we make Yokohama. To-day is Thursday, and we expect to arrive next Monday morning. I hope war isn't declared for at least a month after I arrive in Japan—will give my ankle a chance to strengthen.

All hands are very good to me, and I might say I am almost worn out by being made comfortable. I am in for a game of cards now, so more anon.

S.S. *Siberia*, Jan. 23/04

Yesterday I dragged about on crutches to the boat deck and to tiffin, and to bed. To-day I have ventured without crutches. But I walk very little—just from stateroom to boat deck.

A young gale is on, but the *Siberia* is behaving splendidly. P.S. The young gale is still growing.

S.S. *Siberia*, Jan. 24/04

Just packing up. Shall be in Yokohama at six to-morrow morning. Ankle is improving. Am walking (very slowly, and limpingly, and carefully), without crutches. I just missed breaking the leg—so you can see what a twist it was. Hope the war holds off for a month yet.

Thursday, Jan. 28/04

If you can read this. The train is joggling, and the temperature inside the car is 40. I am on the express bound for Kobe—where, on Jan. 31, if not sooner, I expect to get a steamer for Korea. I am bound for Seoul, the capital. Was pretty busy in Yokohama and Tokio. Arrived Monday, and have been on the jump until now, though this writing looks as though I were still jumping.

Ankle is getting better very slowly.

I called, and called, and called, for your letter which should have come on the same steamer with me. But no letter to date. Either it is lost or it missed the steamer.

Jan. 29/04

You should have seen me plunging out of Kobe this morning, myself and luggage in three rickshaws, with push-boys and pull-boys and all the rest, and racing to catch the express for Nagasaki. No steamer out of Kobe till Feb. 3rd, so am going to try my luck at Nagasaki, twenty-two hours ride on the train and no sleeping car.

Weather is warmer down here. It was bitter cold up Yoko-hama-way.

Have caught beautiful glimpses of the Inland Sea to-day, the sea whereon you and I shall soon be sailing. I think, however, we'll say in May at the earliest—spend summer in Japan, and winter say in India.

If I do not refer to war doings, know that there is a censor-ship, and cables, etc. are held up.

Shimonoseki, Feb. 3/04

Still trying to sail to Chemulpo. Made an all-day ride back from Nagasaki to Moji to catch a steamer, Feb. 1 (Monday). Bought ticket, stepped outside and snapped three street scenes. Now Moji is a fortified place. Japanese police "Very Sorry," but they arrested me. Spent the day examining me. Of course, I missed steamer. "Very sorry." Carted me down country Monday night to town of Kokura. Examined me again. Committed. Tried Tuesday. Found guilty. Fined 5 yen and camera confis-cated. Have telegraphed American Minister at Tokio, who is now trying to recover camera.

Received last night a deputation from all the Japanese news-paper correspondents in this vicinity. Present their good offices, and "Very sorry." They are my brothers in the craft. They are to-day to petition the judges (three judges sat on me in black caps) to set up mock auction of camera, when they will bid it in and present it to me with their compliments. "Very uncertain," how-ever, they say.

Expect to leave for Chemulpo on the 6th or 7th inst.

On board junk, off Korean Coast
Tuesday, Feb. 9, 1904

The wildest and most gorgeous thing ever! If you could see me just now, captain of a junk with a crew of three Koreans who speak neither English nor Japanese and with five Japanese guests (strayed travelers) who speak neither English nor Korean—that is, all but one, which last knows a couple of dozen English words. And with this polyglot following I am bound on a voyage of several hundred miles along the Korean Coast to Chemulpo.

And how did it happen? I was to sail Monday, Feb. 8th., on the *Keigo Maru* for Chemulpo. Saturday, Feb. 6th, returning in the afternoon from Kokura (where my camera had been returned to me)—returning to Shimonoseki, I learned *Keigo Maru* had been taken off its run by the Jap. Government. Learned also that many Jap. warships had passed the straits bound out, and that soldiers had been called from their homes to join their regiments in the middle of the night.

And I made a dash right away. Caught, just as it was getting under way, a small steamer for Fusan. Had to take third class passage—and it was *native* steamer, no white man's chow (food) even first class and I had to sleep on deck. Dashing aboard in steam launch, got one trunk overboard but saved it. Got wet myself, and my rugs and baggage, crossing the Japan Sea. At Fusan, caught a little 120 ton steamer, loaded with Koreans and Japs, and deck load piled to the sky, for Chemulpo. Made Mokpo, with a list to starboard of fully thirty degrees. It would take a couple of hundred of such steamers to make a *Siberia*. But this morning all passengers and freight were fired ashore, willy nilly, for Jap. Government had taken the steamer to use. We had traveled the preceding night convoyed by two torpedo boats.

Well, fired ashore this morning, I chartered this junk, took five of the Jap. passengers along, and here I am, still bound for Chemulpo. Hardest job I ever undertook. Have had no news for several days, do not know if war has been declared—and shall not know till I make Chemulpo—or maybe Kun San, at which place I drop my passengers. God, but I'd like to have mouthful of white-man's speech. It's not quite satisfying to do business with a 24-word vocabulary and gesticulations.

Thursday, Feb. 11/04

On board another junk. Grows more gorgeous. Night and day traveled for Kun San. Caught on lee-shore yesterday, and wind howling over Yellow Sea. You should have seen us clawing off —one man at the tiller and a man at each sheet (Koreans), four scared Japs, and the fifth too seasick to be scared. Of course, we cleared off, or you wouldn't be reading this.

Made Kun San at nightfall, after having carried away a mast and smashed the rudder. And we arrived in driving rain, wind cutting like a knife. And then, you should have seen me being made comfortable last night—five Japanese maidens helping me undress, take a bath, and get into bed, the while visitors, male and female, were being entertained (my visitors). And the maidens passing remarks upon my beautiful white skin, etc. And this morning, same thing repeated—the Mayor of Kun San, the captain of the police leading citizens, all in my bed-room, visiting while I was being shaved, dressed, washed, and fed.

And all the leading citizens of the town came down to see me off, and cheered me, and cried "Sayonara" countless times.

New junk, manned by Japanese—five—and not one knows one word of English, and here I am adrift with them on the Korean coast.

No white man's news for a long time. Hear native rumors of seafights, and of landing of troops, but nothing I may believe without doubting. But when I get to Chemulpo, I'll know "where I'm at."

And maybe you think it isn't cold, traveling as I am, by junk. The snow is on the land, and in some places, on North slopes, comes down to the water's edge.

And there are no stoves by which to keep warm—charcoal boxes, with half a dozen small embers, are not to be sneered at—I am beside one now, which I just bought for 12½ cents from a Korean at a village, where we have landed for water.

Saturday, Feb. 13/04

Still wilder, but can hardly say so "gorgeous," unless land-scapes and seascapes, seen between driving snow squalls, be gor-geous. You know the tides on this Coast range from 40 to 60 feet (we're at anchor now, in the midst of ten thousand islands, reefs and shoals, waiting four hours until the tide shall turn toward Chemulpo—30 ri, which means 75 miles-away).

Well, concerning tides. Yesterday morning found us on a lee shore all rocks, with a gale pounding the whole Yellow Sea down upon us. Our only chance for refuge, dead to leeward, a small bay, and high and dry. Had to wait on the 40 ft. tide and we waited, anchored under a small reef across which the breakers broke, until, tide rising, they submerge it. Never thought a sampan (an open crazy boat) could live through what ours did. A gale of wind, with driving snow—you can imagine how cold it was. But I'm glad I have Japanese sailors. They're braver and cooler and more daring than Koreans. Well, we waited till eleven A.M. It was twixt the devil and the deep sea—stay and be swamped, run for the little bay and run the chance of striking in the surf. We couldn't possibly stay longer, so we showed a piece of sail and ran for it. Well, I was nearly blind with a headache which I had brought away with me from Kun San, and which had been increasing ever since; and I did not much care what happened; yet I remember, when we drove in across that foaming bar, the white water showing reefs and shoals clear across, that I took off my overcoat, and loosened my shoes—and I didn't bother a bit about trying to save the camera.

But we made it—half full of water—but we made it. And maybe it didn't howl all night, so cold that it froze the salt water.

All of which I wouldn't mind, if it weren't for my ankles. I used to favor the right with the left, but with the left now smashed worse than the right, you can imagine how careful I have to be (where it is impossible to be careful) in a crazy junk going thro' such rough weather. And yet I have escaped any bad twists so far.

Junks, crazy—I should say so. Rags, tatters, rotten—something always carrying away—how they navigate is a miracle. I wonder if Hearst thinks I'm lost.

Monday, Feb. 15/04

Oh, yes, we waited four hours! When four hours had passed, wind came down out of the north, dead in our teeth. Lay all night in confounded tide-rip, junk standing on both ends, and driving me crazy what of my headache.

At four in the morning turned out in the midst of driving snow to change anchorage on account of sea.

It was a cruel day-break we witnessed; at 8 A.M. we showed a bit of sail and ran for shelter.

My sailors live roughly, and we put up at a fishing village (Korean) where they live more roughly, and we spent Sunday and Sunday night there—my five sailors, myself—and about 20 men, women and children jammed into a room in a hut, the floor space of which room was about equivalent to that of a good double-bed.

And my foreign food is giving out, and I was compelled to begin on native chow. I hope my stomach will forgive me some of the things I have thrust upon it—filth, dirt, indescribable, and the worst of it is that I can't help thinking of the filth and dirt as I take each mouthful.

In some of these villages, I am the first whiteman, and a curiosity.

I showed one old fellow my false teeth at midnight. He proceeded to rouse the house. Must have given him bad dreams, for he crept in to me at three in the morning and woke me in order to have another look.

We are under way this morning—for Chemulpo. I hope I don't drop dead when I finally arrive there.

The land is covered with snow. The wind has just hauled ahead again. Our sail has come in, and the men are at the oars. If it blows up it'll be another run for shelter. O, this is a wild and bitter coast.

Chemulpo, Tuesday, Feb. 16/04

Just arrived. Am preparing outfit—horses, interpreter, coolies, etc., for campaign into the North toward the Yalu and most probably into Manchuria.

Chemulpo, Feb. 17/04

Am preparing to advance north—campaign to the Yalu and perhaps into Manchuria. I shall accompany. Am busy getting interpreters, coolies, horses, saddles, provisions, etc. Only four outside newspapermen here. The rest, a host, cannot get here.

Grand Hotel, Seoul, Feb. 24/04

Am starting in five minutes for the North. Have been about crazy trying to outfit and start:
    3 pack ponies
    2 riding horses
    1 interpreter (Jap.)
    1 cook (Korean)
    2 mapus (Korean grooms).

Ping Yang, March, 4/04

Have made 180 miles on horseback to this place. I shall be able to ride a little with you when I return, for it appears there are months of riding before me. I have one of the best horses in Korea—was the Russian minister's at Seoul before he went away.

Very little chance to write these days—am not writing enough for the *Examiner* as it is. Worked to death with the trouble of traveling.

Have received no more letters from you nor anybody.

Am pulling North soon for Anju and maybe the Yalu. Am now in the midst of accounts with correspondents, interpreters, mapus and what not, so cannot think. I do not know when I shall ever be able to write you a real letter—lack of time.

But I'm learning about horses—last two days traveled 50 miles a day, and I was saddle-sore and raw.

Am living in a Japanese hotel crammed with soldiers. Only three of us (1 English correspondent [Macleod]—1 American photographer [Jones]). Am ordering whiskey just now for them.

March 4/04

I think as to the quietness, strictness and orderliness of Japanese soldiers it is very hard to find any equals in the world. If it were our boys they would have gone lightheartedly to all the places and we would surely have heard for many a time about them kicking up a row, but such things never happen in Japanese and it is wonderful how they keep so orderly. Therefore no citizen in the town has any fear at all about them and women, bar, property and all the rest are quite safe. It is well known fact that in last China-Japanese war the Japanese troop on every occasion paid for articles got off citizens and they are still continuing this method now. You will hear from all Koreans that "if they were Russians what might have happened!" I have never seen even a single Jap soldier who got drunk or acting violently, yet its infantry is perfectness itself, as can be judged by our General Allen's saying that the Japanese infantry excels anyone else in the world. In fact, although each of them carries the necessary things weighing 42 pounds on the march the sign of distress never can be found on any of them. None bend forward, none stoop their body, none fall behind from the company, none to be seen re-arranging the strap, none to be attracting notice by making disagreeable noise caused by the carrying of articles not properly put on, and its orderliness and perfectness of company is just the same as with that of each individual. With no fault on individual and no delay on the work, they go straight on the aim. Japanese is the race who can produce real fighting men, and its infantry is simply superb. But, on the other hand the cavalry, I think, is not the department they are well acquainted with, it seems something funny to our eyes. The horses are small and strong but they cannot be compared with ours, and the riding style is also very unseemly, holding the rein mostly with one hand, either with right or left. All the horses are untrained stallions, therefore when they start to fight each other, they cannot be managed by Japanese hands very well. For instance, few days ago when their horses started to fight each other at the front of hotel they were only separated by hand of General Allen after great difficulty. But they are also soldiers, so I think the day will come, ere long, when they are able to ride on good Russian horses by capturing them, and then not take trouble by savageness of their horses anymore.

Poval Colli, March 8/04

How the letters have roused me up! Furthermore, they have proved to me, or, rather, reassured me, that I am a white man.

As a sample of many days, let me give to-day. Was forbidden departure by Gen. Sasaki at Ping Yang—argued it out through interpreters—vexations, delays drive me mad. Should have started at 7 A.M. Scarcely started to load pack horses, when summoned by Japanese Consul—more interpreter—distraction—successful bluff—pull out late in afternoon.

Arrive at this forlorn village; people scared to death. Already have had Russian and Japanese soldiers—we put the finishing touch to their fright. They swear they have no room for us, no fuel, no charcoal, no food for our horses, no room for our horses, nothing—no grub for our mapus and interpreters. We storm the village—force our way into the stables—capture 25 lbs. barley hidden in man's trousers—and so forth and so forth, for two mortal hours—chatter and chin-chin to drive one mad.

And this is but one of all the days. One can scarcely think whiteman's thoughts, as I write this, the horses are breaking loose in the stable—native horses are fiends, and I have desisted writing long enough to stir up the mapus.

I read your letters in the saddle as I rode along to-day, and it reminded me of a letter of mine you once read in the saddle. And the horse you were astride of was named Belle. The horse I was astride of to-day is named Belle. I named her. She is as sweet and gentle as yours, and she is the only sweet and gentle horse in Korea. She is an Australian barb, and have I told you she was the Russian minister's at Seoul? She is gigantic compared with all other horses in Korea—Chinese, Japanese, and Korean horses—and excites universal wonder and admiration.

As I write this a cold wind is blowing from the North, and snow is driving. Also, before my door are groaning and creaking a hundred bullock-carts loaded with army supplies and pushing North.

My interpreter comes in with his daily report. Manyoungi,[1] my Korean cook and interpreter, comes in with tea and toast. Dunn sends down half a can of hot pork and beans—and there are a thousand interruptions.

Sunan, Wednesday, Mar. 9/04

Here we are—captured and detained, while the wires are working hot between here and Ping Yang and Seoul. I mean captured by Japanese soldiers who will not let us proceed North to Anjou. And five more vexatious hours have just elapsed—chin-chin and delay galore.

As I write this, a thousand soldiers are passing through the village past my door. My men are busy drawing rations for themselves and horses from the Army.

Red Cross ponies, pioneers, pack horses loaded with munitions and supplies, foot soldiers, are streaming by. Captains are dropping in to shake hands and leave their cards, and then going on.

IMPORTANT. ANOTHER VEXATION!

Just caught five body lice on my undershirt. That is, I discovered them, Manyoungi picked them off, the while he interpreted for me an invitation from a Korean nobleman to come to his place and occupy better quarter! The nobleman looked on, while the lice were caught and I changed my clothes. Lice drive me clean crazy. I am itching all over. I am sure, every second, that a score of them are on me. And how under the sun am I to write for the *Examiner* or write to you!

Intermission—the horses, stabled within ten feet of me, have been kicking up a rumpus—kicking, biting, stampeding my Belle and my three other horses—and broken legs would not be welcome just now. I am advised to get my life insured.

[1] London brought Manyoungi to the States as a houseboy. He served London until the *Snark* voyage in 1907.

And the troops stream by, the horses fight—mapus, cook and interpreter are squabbling 4 feet away from me. And the frost is in the air. I must close my doors and light my candles.

A Korean family of refugees—their household goods on their backs, just went by.

[*London enclosed the following*]

Japanese Consulate,
March 9/04

To Mr. Jack London;
Sir:
I have the honor to inform you by the order that you would stay here until our Land Forces under Major General Sasaki proceed for the North.

Yours truly,
(signed) C. Chinjo,
Jap. Acting Consul.

[*London wrote:*]

This is one of many commands not heeded. This was issued yesterday at Ping Yang. I am now North of that city and in advance of General Sasaki.

The first command, had I obeyed it, would have held me in Tokio to this day, where are 50 other correspondents who did heed. I am prepared, however, to be held up by Japanese scouts at any moment and be brought back to Ping Yang. But it's all in the game. I am the only correspondent this far in advance. With me is Dunn, a photographer for *Collier's Weekly*. In Ping Yang are two other correspondents—and that is all the regular correspondents in Korea at present moment.

Sunan, March 11/04

Have just returned from a ride on Belle—doesn't that strike you familiarly? North I may ride for a hundred yards, and when I come thundering up at a lope the Japanese guard turns out on the run, presenting bayonets to me in token that I may proceed no farther. East, West, and South I may ride as far as

I wish, but North, where fighting is soon to begin, I may not go. Nor may I go until I receive permission from Lieut-General Inouye, commander of the 12th Division of 12,000 men, and just now at Seoul, a couple of hundred miles to the South.

Your two letters I received several days ago were brought up, horseback, from Seoul. As I write I look out my door and a dozen feet from where I am sitting, see Belle munching away at her barley ration which I have drawn for her from the Army. She *is* a joy! I am my own riding teacher. I hope I don't learn to ride all wrong. But anyway, I'll manage to stick on a horse somehow, and we'll have some glorious rides together.

Sunan, March 12/04

You needn't worry about my welfare. The Japanese are taking very good care of me. Here I am, 40 miles from the front, and here I stay. The only other newspaperman who reached this far, Dunn, has gone back. So I'm farthest north of all the correspondents. Furthermore, no others may now pass out of Ping Yang.

[Charmian wrote on her copy of this letter]
He quotes several short poems from the Korean—and comments: "These are sweet, are they not? They are the only sweet things I have seen among the Koreans!"

Ping Yang, March 16/04

Here beginneth the retrograde movement. Have been ordered back 50 li[1] from Sunan to this place. Am now ordered back 540 li from this place to Seoul—the Japanese are disciplining us for our rush ahead and the scoop we made—and they are doing it for the sake of the correspondents who remained in Japan by advice of Japanese and who have made life miserable for the Japanese by pointing out that we have been ahead gathering all the plums.

540 li to Seoul and 540 li back=1080 useless li I have to ride, plus 100, (Sunan and return)=1180 usless li. Well, I'll become used to the saddle at any rate.

[1] Li—Chinese unit equal to about one-third of a mile.

Seoul, March 18/04

Just arrived, fired hence from the North. Pull out on a little side jump to Wei-hai-wei to-morrow morning early. Learn that a bunch of letters is chasing around after me up at Ping Yang. Shall get them a week hence when returning from Wei-hai-wei.

Seoul, Korea, March 29/04

Here I am, still in Seoul, assigned to the first column but not permitted to go to the Front. None of the correspondents at front. All held back by Japanese, and in this matter we are being treated abominably.

I have decided that I shall remain away no more than a year. Ten months from the time I left San Francisco, I shall cable Hearst to send out another man to take my place at the front—if I've got to the front by that time.

Since writing you from north of Ping Yang at Sunan, I have not only received not one letter from any one else, but not one letter from you. You, at least, have my miserable letters to the *Examiner* to read. Have never been so disgusted with anything I have done. Perfect rot I am turning out. It's not war correspondence at all, and the Japs are not allowing us to see any war. Photographs inclosed taken at table upon which I am writing this.

Grand Hotel, Seoul, Korea, April 1/04

And still no mail. I'll never go to a war between Orientals again. The vexation and delay are too great. Here I am, still penned up in Seoul, my 5 horses and interpreters at Chemulpo, my outfit at Ping Yang, my post at Anjou—and eating my heart out with inactivity. Such inactivity, such irritating inactivity, that I cannot even write letters.

Mark you, while inactive, I am busy all the time. What worries is that I am busy with worries and nothing is accomplished. Never mind, I may not ride beautifully or correctly, but I'll wager that

I stick on and keep up with you in the rides we are to have together in the years to come.

Just now I'm riding all kinds of Chinese ponies, with all kinds of saddles, in all kinds of places (and some of the ponies are vicious brutes). I was out yesterday, without stirrups, and loped all over the shop [sic] with another fellow, down crowded streets, narrow streets, crooked streets, over sprawling babies for the ponies are hard-mouthed and head-strong (a thousand shaves), and live to tell the tale.

> Letter received from Mr. James, Chemulpo, at this time.

Dear London:

Your mare and the ponies are well looked after. Only a little influenza in her and she wants a lot more exercise. She is quite fat.

Chin-chin, old chap.

> Yours as a Sourdough,
> (Signed) James.

[*London's interpreter, K. Yamada, added:*]

For you don't returned within long time there happened trouble yesterday that I has been arrested to Japanese gendarme as reporting military secret to you and after 10 hours examined several questions, I could come back to my boarding house. Received telegram and I shall do your order.

> Y.ff'ly (affectionately?!)
> (Signed) K. Yamada.

If you don't come back I can't help plenty troubles.

[*London comments upon the foregoing two communications as follows:*]

These two letters, on same sheet, is indicative of some of my troubles. Here I am, compelled to remain in Seoul, my horses at Chemulpo. My interpreter, K. Yamada, left in charge of horses, arrested. My mare with influenza, and suffering from "hay-belly," which James mistakes for being with foal. Hay I had sternly for-

bidden, for I had learned effect on mare. James (an Ex-Klon-
diker) and making a dash for Chemulpo, I asked to take a look
at my horses.

Seoul, Korea, April 5/04

I'm going out to ride off steam now on a jockey saddle and a
spanking big horse, and if we don't kill each other we'll kill a
few native babies or blind men. Had the horse out yesterday—
hardest mouth—took half a block to bring it to a walk and half
a dozen to hold it when I got off to pay a call. How I stuck on I
don't know—but I never took the reins in both hands a la
Japanaise, nor did I throw my arms around his neck. Oh, I'm
learning, I'm learning. I never had time in my life to learn to
play billiards, but I'm learning now. I never had time to learn to
dance, but if this war keeps on I'll learn that, too—only the missionaries don't dance, and the *Kresang* (Korean dancing girls)
can't dance because the Emperor's mother is dead and the Court
is in mourning.

To-morrow night I give a reading from *Call of Wild* [sic] before foreign residents for benefit of local Y.M.C.A.—and I give it
in evening dress!!! Custom of the country and I had to come to
it. In Japan, however, one has to have a frock coat and top hat
—imagine me in a Prince Albert and a stovepipe. Any way, if
Japan wins this war the Japs will be so cocky that white people
will be unable to live in Japan.

Here's the horse, and I go. Say, I have learned a new swear-
word (Korean), "Jamie." Whenever you want to swear just say
"Jamie" softly, and people won't know you are swearing.

O Pay, Korea, April 16/04

In the saddle again and riding long hours. Roads are muddy.
Was putting Belle in up to the shoulders as darkness fell last
night. Have breakfast eaten and am under way at 6 A.M. It is
now 9:30 P.M., and I have just finished supper and am going
(in about one minute) rather tired to bed.

Anjou House, April 17/04

Plugging along in the race for Japanese Headquarters. Four men ahead of me, but expect to overhaul them though I am bringing my packs along and they are traveling light. The rest of the bunch is left in the rear.

Beautiful long hours in the saddle, and beautiful mud. Had Belle in up to her shoulders more than once to-day.

Am prouder than a peacock, for I am able to keep her shoes on her, to tighten them when they get loose, and to put on a shoe when she casts and loses one. Of course, it is cold-shoeing, but they *work!* they *work!*

Wiju, April 24/04

Well, I didn't overtake the four men ahead of me, though I caught up with them when they were stopped farther back along the road, and arrived here with them, where we shall stop for some time.

Now, to business. As I understand it, Macmillans expect to bring out *The Sea Wolf* late this fall. I shall not be able to go over the proof-sheets. And you must do this for me. I shall write Macmillans telling them this and asking them to get into communication with you. In the first place, before any of the book is set up in print, you must get from them the original MS in their possession. Much in this MS will have been cut out in the *Century* published part. What was cut out I want put back in the book. On the other hand, many GOOD alterations have been made by you and George [Sterling],[1] and by the *Century* people— these alterations I want in the book. So here's the task—take the Macmillan MS, and, reading the *Century* published stuff, put into Macmillan MS the good alterations.

Furthermore, anything that offends you, strike out or change on your own responsibility. You know me well enough to know that I won't kick.

[1] Californian poet and London's very close friend whom he called "Greek."

Headquarters 1st Japanese Army
Manchuria, May 6/04

I am well, in splendid health, though profoundly irritated by
the futility of my position in this Army and sheer inability
(caused by the position) to do decent work. What ever I have
done I am ashamed of. The only compensation for these months
of irritation is a better comprehension of Asiatic geography and
Asiatic character. Only in another war, with a whiteman's army,
may I hope to redeem myself. It can never be done here by any
possibility.

Headqrs. First Jap. Army,
Feng-Wang-Cheng,
Manchuria, May 17/04

I have so far done no decent work. Have lost enthusiasm and
hardly hope to do any thing decent. Another war will be required
for me to redeem myself, when I can accompany our army or
an English army. Well, time rolls on. In six weeks the rainy
season will be here. The chances are that I'll pull out for some
point in China where I can get in touch with a cable.

Do you know—beyond my camera experience at Moji (mailed
before the War) I do not know whether the *Examiner* has
received one article of mine (I have sent 19) or one film (and
I have sent hundreds of photographs).

Headqrs. First Jap. Army,
Feng-Wang-Cheng,
Manchuria, May 22/04

My heart does not incline to writing these days. It could only
wait, for I am hungry to be where you are, and disgusted at being
here. War? Bosh! Let me give you my daily life.

I am camped in a beautiful grove of pine trees on a beautiful
hill-slope. Near-by is a temple. It is glorious summer weather. I
am awakened in the early morning by the songs of birds. Cuckoo
calls through the night. At 6:30 I shave. Manyoungi, my Korean

boy, is cooking breakfast and waiting on me. Sakai, my interpreter, is shining my boots and receiving instructions for the
morning. Yuen-hi-kee, a Chinese, is lending a hand at various
things. My Seoul mapu is helping in the breakfast and cleaning
up generally. My Ping Yang mapu is feeding the horses.

Breakfast at 7. Then try to grind something out of nothing
for the *Examiner*. Perhaps go out and take some photographs,
which I may not send any more for the Censor will not permit
them to go out undeveloped and I have no developing outfit
or chemicals with me.

I am at liberty to ride in to headquarters at Feng-Wang-Cheng,
less than a mile away. And I am at liberty to ride about in
a circle around the city of a radius little more than a mile.
Never were correspondents treated in any war as they have
been in this. It's absurd, childish, ridiculous, rich, comedy.

In the afternoon, the call goes forth, and we (the correspondents) go swimming in a glorious pool—clear water, over our
heads, plenty of it. It all reminds me of Glen Ellen. A campfire
at night, whereby we curse God, or Fate, and divers peoples and
things which I shall not mention for the Censor's sake, and the
day is ended.

Disgusted, utterly disgusted.

I have this day written the *Examiner* that in a month or six
weeks (at outside) I shall pull out of the country and go to
some place where I can get in direct cable communication
with them; that my position here is futile; that there is no reason
for my continuing here, and that, unless arrangements have been
made for me to go on the Russian side, I shall return to the
United States—unless they expressly bid me remain.

May 22, 1904

Now I don't think it is possible for them to make arrangements for me to go on the Russian side, so, as you read this I
may be starting on my way back to the States, to God's Country,
the Whiteman's Country! Who knows? Who knows? At any rate,
believe me, the year in Japan and the Inland Sea is settled
and done for. It would take a many times bigger salary than I
am receiving to persuade me to put in the year in Japan much

less pay for the year out of my own pocket. In the past I have preached the Economic Yellow Peril[1]; henceforth I shall preach the Militant Yellow Peril.[2]

And just imagine the Censor reading all this, and reading this, too, which I am penning. Not a letter; not a line. I know not what is happening.

If I write not often, it is because I cannot write. I have no heart, no head, no hand, for anything. In preposterous good health, but ungodly sick of soul. You may next hear from me, cabling from some Chinese port: "Am coming."

THE JAPANESE-RUSSIAN WAR

It's not war correspondence at all, and the Japs are not allowing us to see any war . . .

(see letter to Charmian, March 29)

London had three encounters with the Japanese Military command. The first one he relates in his first article to the Examiner. *The second offense occurred about March 16 when some of the correspondents were allowed to go north to Sunan. London went beyond Sunan to Ping Yang where he was picked up by the Japanese Military police and returned to Sunan and from there to Seoul where he was imprisoned for a few days. The third incident occurred late in May. London's mapu (Manyoungi) complained that a Japanese mapu was stealing fodder which had been allotted to Manyoungi. An argument followed; the Japanese mapu became insolent and, according to an account given to Charmian later, made a threatening gesture. London knocked him down. Immediately the other correspondents present realized the seriousness of the situation. The incident was reported to Major General Fuji (Kuroki's chief of staff), who ordered London arrested and held for court-martial. The news, of course, got to Tokyo and Richard Harding Davis wired T. R. Roosevelt, President of the United States. Apparently President Roosevelt took immediate action because a few days later London was called*

[1] See "The Yellow Peril," page 340.
[2] See "If Japan Wakens China," page 358.

into General Fuji's quarters where he gave his account of the fracas. The court-martial was canceled, London was released from prison and a few days later left Korea for Yokohama and home.

While the San Francisco articles may not, as London said, be war correspondence they do give some vivid pictures of behind-the-line scenes and become to us today particularly significant because of our present involvement in Korea.

Perhaps some of London's frustrations developed from the rigid regulations set down by the Japanese First Army for war correspondents. London brought a copy home with him which we include:

REGULATIONS FOR PRESS CORRESPONDENTS

Art. 1. All the press correspondents with this Army shall act according to these regulations.

Art. 2. The general affairs concerning press correspondents shall be under the management of Adjutants, and their supervision and the inspection of their correspondence shall be under the Staff Department.

Art. 3. Press correspondents shall be commanded by the supervising officer, obey the orders of the Army Head-quarters, and act according to the instructions given by it.

Art. 4. Press Correspondents should look and behave decently, and should never do anything disorderly.

Art. 5. Press correspondents should take care not to do anything harmful to the troops and never enter the office rooms of the Head-quarters.

Art. 6. When thought necessary by the Army Head-quarters, press correspondents may be attached to some of the Army's detachments, in which case press correspondents shall be commanded by the commander of that detachment or by the supervising officer and obey his orders.

Art. 7. Press correspondents shall not go about in the battle field except at the time and place shown by the supervising officer or the detachment commander.

Art. 8. All the correspondence of press correspondents (including their reports, private letters, telegrams, etc.) must be inspected by the supervising officer before sending. The supervising officer, after inspecting such correspondence shall seal (if enveloped) and stamp "passed inspection" upon the envelope, the note paper, or the telegraph application paper, and then give it back to its sender.

The name of the correspondent and of the press he represents must always be written on the envelope or the front page of the report.

Art. 9. Correspondence without the inspector's stamp is not allowed.

Art. 10. Correspondence in a foreign language may in some case be requested to accompany its Japanese translation, or the kind of language to be used may be limited.

Art. 11. Correspondents must pay particular attention to the following items:

    1. Things liable to disturb the public peace or to dispirit the troops should not be written.

    2. Only the facts of the past may be written in regard to the actions of troops and never the things to happen in future or of mere supposition.

    3. Strength of our troops, their numbers, their locations, and the time and place of despatching correspondence must not be written, unless it is allowed by the supervising officer.

Art. 12. One representative shall be chosen each among the Japanese and the foreign correspondents. These representatives are to go between the Head-quarters and the correspondents in regard to matters concerning the correspondents in general.

Art. 13. These regulations are to be applied to the interpreters and servants of press correspondents.

THE FIRST ARMY HEAD-QUARTERS.

In the Korean articles we have used London's date lines because, perhaps of troubles in transmission, the articles were printed much later and not always in sequence. On the other hand, the Collier's *articles were printed soon after they were written and in sequence, so for these we have used the publication dates.*

HOW JACK LONDON GOT IN AND OUT OF JAIL IN JAPAN

SHIMONOSEKI, Wednesday, February 3. — I journeyed all day from Yokohama to Kobe to catch a steamer for Chemulpo, which last city is on the road to Seoul. I journeyed all day and all night from Kobe to Nagasaki to catch a steamer for Chemulpo. I journeyed back all day from Nagasaki to Moji to catch a steamer for Chemulpo. On Monday morning, in Moji, I bought my ticket for Chemulpo, to sail on Monday afternoon. To-day is Wednesday, and I am still trying to catch a steamer for Chemulpo. And thereby hangs a tale of war and disaster, which runs the gamut of the emotions from surprise and anger to sorrow and brotherly love, and which culminates in arrest, felonious guilt and confiscation of property, to say nothing of monetary fines or alternative imprisonment.

For know that Moji is a fortified place, and one is not permitted to photograph "land or water scenery." I did not know it, and

I photographed neither land nor water scenery; but I know it now just the same.

Having bought my ticket at the Osaka Shosen Kaisha office, I tucked it into my pocket and stepped out the door. Came four coolies carrying a bale of cotton. Snap went my camera. Five little boys at play—snap again. A line of coolies carrying coal—and again snap, and last snap. For a middle-aged Japanese man, in European clothes and great perturbation, fluttered his hands prohibitively before my camera. Having performed this function, he promptly disappeared.

"Ah, it is not allowed," I thought, and, calling my rickshaw-man, I strolled along the street.

Later, passing by a two-story frame building, I noticed my middle-aged Japanese standing in the doorway. He smiled and beckoned me to enter. "Some chin-chin and tea," thought I, and obeyed. But alas! it was destined to be too much chin-chin and no tea at all. I was in the police station. The middle-aged Japanese was what the American hobo calls a "fly cop."

Great excitement ensued. Captains, lieutenants and ordinary policemen all talked at once and ran hither and thither. I had run into a hive of blue uniforms, brass buttons and cutlasses. The populace clustered like flies at doors and windows to gape at the "Russian spy." At first it was all very ludicrous—"capital to while away some of the time ere my steamer departs," was my judgment; but when I was taken to an upper room and the hours began to slip by, I decided that it was serious.

I explained that I was going to Chemulpo. "In a moment," said the interpreter. I showed my ticket, my pass-port, my card, my credentials; and always and invariably came the answer, "In a moment." Also, the interpreter stated that he was very sorry. He stated this many times. He made special trips upstairs to tell me he was very sorry. Every time I told him I was going to Chemulpo he expressed his sorrow, until we came to vie with each other, I in explaining my destination, he in explaining the state and degree of his emotion regarding me and my destination.

And so it went. The hour of tiffin had long gone by. I had had an early breakfast. But my appetite waited on his "In a moment" till afternoon was well along. Then came the police examination, replete with searching questions concerning myself, my antecedents, and every member of my family. All of which information was gravely written down. An unappeasable interest in my family was displayed. The remotest relatives were hailed with keen satisfaction and placed upon paper. The exact ascertainment of their antecedents and birthplaces seemed necessary to the point at issue, namely, the snaps I had taken of the four coolies carrying cotton, the five little boys playing and the string of coal coolies.

Next came my movements since my arrival in Japan.

"Why did you go to Kobe?"

"To go to Chemulpo," was my answer. And in this fashion I explained my presence in the various cities of Japan. I made manifest that my only reason for existence was to go to Chemulpo; but their conclusion from my week's wandering was that I had no fixed place of abode. I began to shy. The last time the state of my existence had been so designated it had been followed by a thirty-day imprisonment in a vagrant's cell![1] Chemulpo suddenly grew dim and distant, and began to fade beyond the horizon of my mind.

"What is your rank?" was the initial question of the next stage of the examination.

I was nobody, I explained, a mere citizen of the United States; though I felt like saying that my rank was that of traveler for Chemulpo. I was given to understand that by rank was meant business, profession.

"Traveling to Chemulpo," I said was my business; and when they looked puzzled I meekly added that I was only a correspondent.

Next, the hour and the minute I made the three exposures. Were they of land and water scenery? No, they were of people. What people? Then I told of the four coolies carrying cotton, the five small boys playing and the string of coal coolies. Did I stand with my back to the water while making the pictures? Did I stand with my back to the land? Somebody had informed them that I had taken pictures in Nagasaki (a police lie, and they sprang many such on me). I strenuously denied. Besides

---

[1] A reference to his experiences as a tramp in 1894. He records these in his book *The Road*. He was arrested in Niagara for vagrancy and sentenced to thirty days in the Erie County Penitentiary.

it had rained all the time I was in Nagasaki. What other pictures had I taken in Japan? Three—two of Mount Fuji, one of a man selling tea at a railway station. Where were the pictures? In the camera, along with the four coolies carrying cotton, the five small boys playing and the string of coal coolies? Yes.

Now, about those four coolies carrying cotton, the five small boys playing and the string of coal coolies? And then they threshed through the details of the three exposures, up and down, back and forth, and crossways, till I wished that the coal coolies, cotton coolies and small boys had never been born. I have dreamed about them ever since, and I know I shall dream about them until I die.

Why did I take the pictures? Because I wanted to. Why did I want to? For my pleasure. Why for my pleasure?

Pause a moment, gentler reader, and consider. What answer could you give to such a question concerning any act you have ever performed? Why do you do anything? Because you want to; because it is your pleasure. An answer to the question, "Why do you perform an act for your pleasure?" would constitute an epitome of psychology. Such an answer would go down to the roots of being, for it involves impulse, volition, pain, pleasure, sensation, gray matter, nerve fibers, free will and determinism, and all the vast fields of speculation wherein man has floundered since the day he dropped down out of the trees and began to seek out the meaning of things.

And I, an insignificant traveler on my way to Chemulpo, was asked this question in the Moji police station through the medium of a seventh-rate interpreter. Nay, an answer was insisted upon. Why did I take the pictures because I wanted to, for my pleasure? I wished to take them—why? Because the act of taking them would make me happy. Why would the act of taking them make me happy? Because it would give me pleasure. But why would it give me pleasure? I hold no grudge against the policeman who examined me at Moji, yet I hope that in the life to come he will encounter the shade of Herbert Spencer and be informed just why, precisely, I took the pictures of the four coolies carrying cotton, the five small boys playing and the string of coal coolies.

Now, concerning my family, were my sisters older than I or

younger? The change in the line of questioning was refreshing, even though it was perplexing. But ascertained truth is safer than metaphysics, and I answered blithely. Had I a pension from the government? A salary? Had I a medal of service? Of merit? Was it an American camera? Was it instantaneous? Was it mine?

To cut a simple narrative short, I pass on from this sample of the examination I underwent to the next step in the proceedings, which was the development of the film. Guarded by a policeman and accompanied by the interpreter, I was taken through the streets of Moji to a native photographer. I described the location of the three pictures of the film of ten. Observe the simplicity of it. These three pictures he cut out and developed, the seven other exposures, or possible exposures, being returned to me undeveloped. They might have contained the secret of the fortifications of Moji for all the policemen knew; and yet I was permitted to carry them away with me, and I have them now. For the peace of Japan, let me declare that they contain only pictures of Fuji and tea-sellers.

I asked permission to go to my hotel and pack my trunks—in order to be ready to catch the steamer for Chemulpo. Permission was accorded, and my luggage accompanied me back to the police station, where I was again confined in the upper room listening to the "In a moments" of the interpreter and harping my one note that I wanted to go to Chemulpo.

In one of the intervals the interpreter remarked, "I know great American correspondent formerly."

"What was his name?" I asked, politely.

"Benjamin Franklin," came the answer; and I swear, possibly because I was thinking of Chemulpo, that my face remained graven as an image.

The arresting officer now demanded that I should pay for developing the incriminating film, and my declining to do so caused him not a little consternation.

"I am very sorry," said the interpreter, and there were tears in his voice; "I inform you cannot go to Chemulpo. You must go to Kokura."

Which last place I learned was a city a few miles in the interior.

"Baggage go?" I asked.

"You pay?" he countered.

I shook my head.

"Baggage go not," he announced.

"And I go not," was my reply.

I was led downstairs into the main office. My luggage followed. The police surveyed it. Everybody began to talk at once. Soon they were shouting. The din was terrific, the gestures terrifying. In the midst of it I asked the interpreter what they had decided to do, and he answered, shouting to make himself heard, that they were talking it over.

Finally rickshaws were impressed, and bag and baggage transferred to the depot. Alighting at the depot at Kokura, more delay was caused by my declining to leave my luggage in the freight office. In the end it was carted along with me to the police station, where it became a spectacle for the officials.

Here I underwent an examination before the Public Procurator of the Kokura District Court. The interpreter began very unhappily, as follows:

"Customs different in Japan from America; therefore you must not tell any lies."

Then was threshed over once again all the details of the four coolies carrying cotton, the five small boys playing and the string of coal coolies; and I was committed to appear for trial next morning.

And next morning, bare-headed, standing, I was tried by three solemn, black-capped judges. The affair was very serious. I had committed a grave offense, and the Public Procurator stated that while I did not merit a prison sentence, I was nevertheless worthy of a fine.

After an hour's retirement the judges achieved a verdict. I was to pay a fine of five yen, and Japan was to get the camera. All of which was eminently distasteful to me, but I managed to extract a grain of satisfaction from the fact that they quite forgot to mulct me of the five yen. There is trouble brewing for somebody because of those five yen. There is the judgment. I am a free man. But how are they to balance accounts?

In the evening at the hotel the manager, a Japanese, handed me a card, upon which was transcribed: Reporter of the "Osaka

Asahi Shimbun." I met him in the reading-room, a slender, spectacled, silk-gowned man, who knew not one word of English. The manager acted as interpreter. The reporter was very sorry for my predicament. He expressed the regret of twenty other native correspondents in the vicinity, who in turn, represented the most powerful newspapers in the empire. He had come to offer their best offices; also to interview me.

The law was the law, he said, and the decree of the court could not be set aside; but there were ways of getting around the law. The voice of the newspapers was heard in the land. He and his fellow correspondents would petition the Kokura judges to auction off the camera, he and his associates to attend and bid it in at a nominal figure. Then it would give them the greatest pleasure to present my camera (or the Mikado's, or theirs) to me with their compliments.

I could have thrown my arms about him then and there—not for the camera, but for brotherhood, as he himself expressed it the next moment, because we were brothers in the craft. Then we had tea together and talked over the prospects of war. The nation of Japan he likened to a prancing and impatient horse, the Government to the rider, endeavoring to restrain the fiery steed. The people wanted war, the newspapers wanted war, public opinion clamored for war; and war the Government would eventually have to give them.

We parted as brothers part, and without wishing him any ill-luck, I should like to help him out of a hole some day in the United States. And here I remain in my hotel wondering if I'll ever see my camera again and trying to find another steamer for Chemulpo.

P. S.—Just received a dispatch from the United States Minister at Tokio. As an act of courtesy, the Minister of Justice will issue orders to-day to restore my camera!

P. S.—And a steamer sails to-morrow for Chemulpo.

TRIP TO PING YANG[1]

February 26th — "Buy everything in sight and get ready to start for Ping Yang."

[1] See also *Jack London's Tales of Adventure*, edited by Irving Shepard. Hanover House, 1956.

Thus was I greeted as I landed at Chemulpo. It was the first mouthful of white-man's speech I had had in eight days, during which time I had been traveling with a native crew up the Korean coast in a sampan, or open fishing boat.

The speaker was one of the two non-local newspapermen on the spot. I made the third. Fifty or more were expected at any moment from Japan, as soon as they could find a ship to carry them—hence the advice.

"I've been here two weeks and am all ready to strike out," he added, "horses, coolies, interpreters, everything."

War had been on for a week, though I learned it now for the first time. I had been badly poisoned with charcoal fumes, and my mind was in a daze. I could scarcely identify myself with people and houses and white-men's chow, yet I proceeded to outfit. The trip had to be performed on horseback. I did not know how to ride. Jones, who had advised me, and Macleod, the second newspaperman, proceeded to teach me.

Their method was illuminating—for the mob of mapus (grooms), rickshawmen, coolies and passersby, before the Grand Hotel. Jones and Macleod were mounted on mild, medium-sized Chinese ponies. For me they procured a stallion. He was splendid-looking. My heart thrilled as I looked at him. I felt very proud. I failed to see anything significant in the fact of the two mapus holding his head. I mounted. The mob laughed and scattered. The mapus loosed their hold, and away I went.

But I did not go like an arrow from a bow. Rather was my course that of a boomerang charged with unlimited energy and speed. I curved back and forth, circled about, plunged into snow banks, knocked other people's horses out of my path (which was a path other people could not divine), and cut up scandalously.

But it was not my fault. All I tried to do was to make the horse go straight ahead, and all I succeeded in doing was to stick on. Other horses bit at mine. He bit back, reared on his hind legs, his teeth snapping, striking with his forelegs and pawing the air.

"Say, old man, do it this way!" Jones shouted at me.

I had no breath left in me to thank him, but my steed responded. His forefeet just missed the small of Jones' back. Jones circled his horse about. Mine followed, striking with his forefeet and biting. Jones beat him over the face and nose with a whip. I hauled with all my strength on the reins. I hauled vainly, for Jones ran away after Macleod. I followed, plunged off the beaten path into the soft snow, and flurried about like a hailstorm. Two mapus made a rush and swung onto my horse's head, and I slipped off and got out of the way. I looked at my watch. The performance had lasted four minutes, yet I could have staked my life that it had lasted twenty minutes. Every bone and muscle was aching and sore. I was breathing heavily. My heart was going like a Waterbury. It was a cold morning —several degrees above zero—yet the sweat was starting from every pore; I could feel it trickling down my back, and my face was wet as from a shower bath.

"You take the horse," suggested Macleod to Jones, "and let him get on your horse."

Jones shook his head, and my stallion pranced back to the hotel between two mapus, who looked anything but happy.

"What you need, old man, is a mild, sweet-tempered animal," said Jones.

The remark was superogatory. It was the thing I had expressly stipulated just previous to beginning the lesson.

And all this preliminary to going off to see the Russians and Japanese fight.

"Anyway," said I, "that horse is one of the things in sight which I shall not buy."

I engaged an interpreter—provisionally. I know not what happy thought led me to make the engagement provisional, for his conversation was excellent. He was a Japanese, and he had memorized it all!

When the bargain was concluded he delivered himself of his last sentence: "I wish to go with you to the war with all my heart."

He had reached the end of his rope, and five minutes later I had to borrow Jones' interpreter in order to understand what my interpreter was talking about.

"You need a mapu," said Jones, "also a boy."

A mapu is a groom, whose ordinary wage is four to six dollars a month and who finds himself.

I declined engaging a mapu until I should find the mild, sweet-tempered horse; but a boy was a necessity, and Mr. Emberly, proprietor of the hotel, said he had just the man. Manyoungi was his name, and he came to work for me for $17.50 and find himself—a liberal wage.

He dressed in European clothes, with a white shirt, stand-up collar, tie, studs, and all complete, and he talked English better, far better, than my provisional interpreter, and he was Korean. Not only did he know how to work himself and achieve results, but he possessed the miraculous faculty of getting work out of other Koreans. For the first time the hotel boys built a fire in my room and brought hot water before I was dressed and away. And for the first time the fires they built burned.

Having secured me such a gem of a boy, I concluded that Mr. Emberly was just the man to get me a horse—mild and sweet-tempered. So I listened to him and went off with him to see Mr. Brown, chief of the Korean Customs.

Mr. Brown had two horses. We looked at them. One stamped fierily. "I need a horse; I shall take that one," said Mr. Emberly. "Of course, he's too lively for you," he added.

I quite agreed. The second horse I fell in love with on first sight. The prettiest head and gentlest eyes I had ever seen in a horse. It allowed me to pet him, rubbed his neck against me, whinnied, and begged for more petting.

"Is he all right?" I asked. "You know I know nothing about horses."

"Just the horse for you," was the reply. I bought him. Next morning he was brought around to the hotel. Frazier, a gentleman jockey and steeplechase rider, took him for a canter. General Allen[2] looked on.

"Splendid motion," said he. "The easiest riding horse of all, and the hardiest."

"Well set up," said Frazier. "Will endure more than either Macleod's or Jones'."

Again I was proud over a horse. I mounted, and this time rode away. I rode into Seoul, and as I rode I noticed the horse sheered constantly to the right.

[2] Henry T. Allen (1859–1930), military attaché (1890–1895) in Russia. Organizer and head of the Philippine Constabulary. Apparently in Korea as an American military representative.

"Carries a weather helm," I said to myself and thereafter rode with the helm hard aport. The resulting course was approximately straight ahead, but it struck me that the manner of obtaining it was not precisely the proper thing.

I determined to see how far this predilection to the right would carry him, so I hauled the helm amidships and waited. At once the sheer to the right began, and to the right yawned a ten-foot ditch.

"Surely he will give over when he gets to the edge," I thought, and steeled my soul to endure his daring. He dared the edge, the very edge. In fact he was falling into the ditch when I luffed him out of it to port.

And with helm to port I navigated the narrow, crowded streets of the capital of Korea. I marvel at it, when I look back upon it—bulls and bullock carts, trains of Korean pack-ponies, soldiers afoot and ahorse, a swarm of children, apathetic Koreans too lazy to get out of the way, blocked traffic, jams, plunging and rearing of many horses—most of them stallions, and never a collision.

It was not till I turned homeward that the first collision occurred. It was on Legation street, just beyond the Palace, and it was deliberate. To the right, instead of a yawning ditch, was a frowning wall. I put the helm amidships to study the sheer. The horse sheered, plump into the wall, sideways, and brought up with a resounding thump. I passed my hand in front of his eye. It never fluttered. A minute later, walking, he butted head-on into a wall. He was blind, stone blind. I wonder if the derivation of the phrase "stone blind" had anything to do with horses and stone walls?

In the afternoon I rode in a rickshaw. Also I discharged my interpreter, who had become wholly unintelligible, and hired another. His name was Yamada, and he had been Jones' interpreter, but he had resigned because Jones addressed him as "boy." I engaged always to call him "Mr. Yamada," whereupon he looked very pleased and asked me for an advance of two months' salary.

"Macleod and I start on Monday," said Jones. "Will you be ready?"

It was Sunday. Likewise it was Japanese, Chinese and Korean

New Year, and shopkeepers and artisans had given over work and were busy with a celebration scheduled to last anywhere between six days and as long as their money held out.

"Impossible," I answered. "I'll meet you in Ping Yang."

"We're all ready, you know," said Jones, "or we wouldn't mind waiting for you."

I saw Macleod. He said he was all ready to start.

I alone was unprepared, so I went off to be vaccinated, and not only was I vaccinated but I bought a horse from the doctor —one of the Russian Minister's horses which he had left behind when he hurriedly departed. It was a splendid animal, had been imported from Australia, and was as cheap as a Chinese pony, while several times as large. In fact, the girths of the saddle which I had bought for my blind horse would not go half way around.

I returned in glee to the hotel to find that three Korean pack-ponies had been purchased for me. But before I ratified the purchase I assured myself that they were at least not blind. Also I learned that Macleod and Jones, who were all ready, would not be ready until Tuesday, where-upon I went out and bought a horse for my interpreter—I beg his pardon, I mean Mr. Yamada.

I was now the owner of five horses, and two mapus were engaged to take care of them. Then came the rush, in which Manyoungi, the gem of boys, was my savior. He worked like a demon, and had everybody else working. Everything was to be bought—saddles, bridles, blankets, hitching straps, nose bags, rope lashings, spare sets of horseshoes all around, horseshoer's tools, pack-saddles, extra girths, canned goods, rubber boots, mittens, caps, gloves, clothes, flour, cooking utensils, shoes, candles, and all the thousand and one articles necessary for a campaign which might extend into Manchuria. And it was New Year's!

Tuesday found Macleod and Jones not yet ready, and Wednesday found Jones outfitting from canned goods which I was lightening from my packs, and Macleod delayed and unable to start until Thursday. So my pack-ponies were the first to take the highroad north through Peking Pass; and that night, at the

end of fifty li, found Jones sans boy, sans mapus, sans everything and dining with me.

But I am proud possessor of the horse of horses. It is a little
Korean pony scarcely larger than a Newfoundland dog. I verily
believe I could tuck it under my arm and walk away with it. The
first day I found it loaded with the heaviest pack. Under the
mountain of luggage I could see only its tail and its patient little
feet which went pit-a-pat, pit-a-pat throughout the day.

"This will never do," I said. "It is cruel. To-morrow, Manyoungi, you must put a light pack on that little pony (you see it is
the smallest of the lot), and ride it yourself."

It is the wise custom for the boy to ride, so that at the end of
the day he will be fresh enough to make camp and cook dinner.

Next day Manyoungi rode the pony. He weighed 120 pounds
and he rode on a pack weighing 130 pounds, while the pack-
saddle weighed at least twenty pounds more—270 pounds in all.
The pony weighed possibly 350 pounds, and yet all day it kept
up with our riding horses. Whenever we broke into a lope, it
loped after us, whinnying all the while. Nor could Manyoungi
hold it back. He tried with the reins and his strength, and he
tried with the Korean language and his imagination, but the
pony trotted, loped, or walked always at our heels.

Jones and I decided that it would be dead by the time we
made camp. But I changed my mind that night at feeding time,
when it kicked and plunged and bit the other larger ponies till
it had its own food and half their share to boot, to say nothing
of the best place to sleep and the most room. Jones is now trying
to buy it, and I am trying to decide whether or not I shall
ride it if something happens to my own horse. Jones' principal
objection to this is that both my feet will drag on the ground,
and I half believe him. To-morrow I shall mount it and find out
for myself. Perhaps I may be able to tuck my feet up a little.

ADVANCING RUSSIANS NEARING JAPAN'S ARMY

PING YANG, via Seoul, March 2.—The Russians are boldly and
fiercely pushing forward their advance south of the Yalu river.
Their Cossacks are scouting far in advance of the main body
through Northern Korea.

Three hundred Russians have seized Anju, which is about 45 miles from Wiju, the port declared open by Korea. Wiju is some 25 miles from Ping Yang, where the first great battle of the war between China and Japan was fought. There has been no attempt by the Japanese as yet to dislodge the daring advance guard of the Russians at Anju. The country between Anju [and] Ping Yang is very mountainous, and campaigning there will be conducted under the greatest difficulties. But as the Japanese are in force here a collision cannot be long deferred. How far behind the Russian advance is the main body of the invading army is not known here, but fleeing Koreans declare the invaders are in great force.

The Koreans make no effort to check the Russian advance, but regard the invaders as desperate enemies. As a consequence they are fleeing in fear and some of the scenes of suffering are equal to the horrors of De Quincey's "Flight of a Tartar Tribe."

Ping Yang is in a state of panic so far as the natives are concerned. The Koreans seem to feel that this is to be a great battle ground again. Ten thousand of them already have fled the city and others are leaving hourly. From further north, in the direction of the Yalu, tens of thousands of refugees have been driven out. The fear of the Russians have become a blinding terror.

But, beyond the fear of the Russians, there is no anti-foreign feeling in Northern Korea. Tales of Russian cruelties are spreading rapidly through the native population, and these tales have inspired the mad scramble southward. The Koreans seem to have no fear of the Japanese and are seeking safety behind the Japanese lines.

Another move in the advance of the Russians is the seizing of the Korean telegraphs, thus cutting off both Wiju and Yuen San as well as Ping Yang from telegraphic communication with Northern Korea. Evidently this was to keep from the Japanese definite news of the Russian invasion.

There is almost certain to be some fierce skirmishing within a few days between the outposts of the armies.

But, with all the blood letting, conditions in all Northern China are extremely critical. The troops and the people have been incited by the placards pasted on all the walls grossly exaggerating the Japanese successes, and calling on the Chinese to rise and wipe out the Russians. These placards are particularly numerous and sensational in the Tartar city of Yuan Shih Kai.

The Russians fear an advance of the Chinese army and the cutting of the Trans-Siberian railway by them. Fifteen thousand of China's most efficient troops are at Shan Hai Kwan, on the northern frontier. These troops are being reinforced daily. They are well drilled and armed with modern weapons. They represent the flower of the Chinese army.

In this formidable force are many turbulent leaders who are urging an advance on the Russian line of communication. But the Viceroy has issued an order that the slightest effort to incite rebellion or sedition will be punished by death. With all this, it is the general fear here that the neutrality of China cannot long be maintained. The slightest thing is apt to start an uprising, and once there is an outbreak there is sure to be an effort to attack the Russians in the rear.

Foreigners in Pekin and Tientsin declare that there will be no distinction as to nationality in the massacres which would be attempted if the war agitators once get the upper hand. The cry will again be, "Kill the foreign devils."

Consequently all the nations are preparing for emergencies. There are 2,000 American and European troops at Tientsin and 1,500 more guarding the legations here at Pekin. But in a general uprising these would have to look to their lives.

Minister Conger[1] said to me that the Chinese authorities are determined to maintain neutrality and order, but in times like these they have the greatest difficulty in controlling the troops and the populace. He thinks trouble is possible, and that it will come on the slightest provocation.

VIVID DESCRIPTION OF ARMY IN KOREA

SEOUL, March 4. — To the Korean the Japanese occupation is a source of ineffable joy.

The first war prices obtained increase day by day and the coolie, Mapu and merchant are equally busy amassing money

[1] Edwin Conger (1843–1907), onetime Minister to Brazil, appointed Minister to China in 1898.

which will later be squeezed from them by the master class, which is the official class.

Just now the officials and nobles are anxious and frightened, while the poor, weak Emperor knows not where to turn. He cannot elect to fly nor to remain in his palace, so in the meantime he graciously decrees whatever the Japanese politely intimate they would like to have, as, for example, when he turns his soldiers out of their barracks in order that the Japanese soldiers may be made comfortable.

At Chemulpo all is bustle and excitement, but perfect order rules. There is no confusion, no delays and no blocking of traffic. Daily transports from Japan arrive, drop anchor in the outer harbor and men, horses, mountain artillery in strings, towed by launches, cross the inner harbor to the shore and depart by train to Seoul, twenty-seven miles away. It is the last time in a long while that the men will lift up their legs and let steam carry them to their destination.

From Seoul begins their 180-mile march north to Ping Yang and from Ping Yang still north.

Through the snowclad Korean mountains their way leads to Wiju, on the river Yalu, where the Russians are waiting for them.

I doubt if there be more peaceable, orderly soldiers in the world than the Japanese. Our own soldiers, long ere this, would have painted Seoul red with their skylarking and good-natured boisterousness, but the Japanese are not boisterous. They are deadly serious.

Yet no one of the civilian population is afraid of them. The women are safe; the money is safe; the goods are safe. The Japanese established a reputation in 1894 for paying for whatever they took and they are living up to that reputation.

"But if they were the Russians"—say the Koreans, and the Europeans and American residents ominously shake their heads. I have yet to see one drunken Japanese soldier. Not one disorderly nor even boisterous one have I seen—and they are soldiers.

I may quote General Allen in saying, "The infantry is as splendid as any in the world. They will render a good account of themselves."

They march along without apparent effort under their forty-two pound kits. There is no stooping forward, no slouching, no lagging nor does one see a man continually adjusting straps and pads or hear tin cups rattling or accouterments clattering. As it is with their organization as a whole so with it as a unit. The man is everything. He works smoothly. Above all he works toward an end.

The Japanese are a race of warriors and their infantry is all the infantry could possibly be; but it cannot be said that the Japanese are a race of horsemen. Their cavalry would appear ridiculous to a western eye. The horses are small and strong, it is true, but not fit for comparison with our own steeds. But do the Japanese know how to manage their horses? It is a common thing to see them riding with the rein in either hand, while practically all of them sit in their saddles most uncouthly.

Nearly all of the horses are stallions. There are constant fights among the beasts, and the men are quite helpless when it comes to managing them. It required an American General the other day, General Allen, to rush in and break up a fight among the stallions in front of the Seoul Hotel. Several cavalrymen present knew not what to do and were ineffectually trying to prevent their horses from destroying one another.

But to the infantry too much praise cannot be given. However, the cavalrymen, afoot or ahorse, are men, and fighting men, and anyway, ere long, they soon may be astride large Russian horses.

ROYAL ROAD A SEA OF MUD

PING YANG, March 5.—If age and history are to be taken into account, it is a royal road that leads out of Seoul through the gap of Pekin Pass. North it leads half the length of the Peninsula to the Yalu, and then, sweeping westward, rounds the head of the Yellow Sea and finally arrives at Pekin. Up the length of this road and down have passed countless Chinese imperial envoys in splendor of tinsel and barbaric trappings.

Indeed a royal road, and yet, to the western eye and judgment, a bog hole and a travesty of what he has understood "road" to mean. The least rain and it is a river of mud. Horse and rider must beware on its crazy bridges, and large opportunity is given a steed to break a leg anywhere along its length. It is a dirt road to begin with, and the Korean method of repairing it is to shovel in more dirt. I use "in" advisedly, for too many a weary mile of it is worn far down beneath the level of the rice fields on either side.

Yet up this quagmire the Japanese are shoving their troops and supplies with a patience and speed which is, to say the least, commendable. The infantry I passed was walking eighty li a day—roughly, twenty-five miles. When the ice goes out of the bay at Chemulpo the troops may be landed there, and when the Tai-tong river clears itself of ice they can be towed up by steam launches to Ping Yang.

I felt like an army all by myself as I rode out of Seoul and took the Pekin road. My outfit, loaded on three Korean ponies (the latter scarcely larger than Newfoundland dogs), was cared for by two mapus, or grooms. On the lightest-loaded pony, perched upon the summit of the pack, road Manyoungi, my Korean cook, interpreter, treasurer, manager and what not. On a Chinese pony rode my Japanese interpreter, Mr. Yamada, while I rode the horse which the Russian minister had been wont to ride before his hasty departure from Seoul.

Then there was Jones, with his interpreter, mounted on Chinese ponies, and his packhorses and the packhorses of Macleod, who was himself to overtake us with his Korean and Japanese interpreters. All told, we numbered seventeen horses—a puzzling parcel to deposit in chance livery stables along the way. And stables were a necessity, first because of the impossibility of carrying horse food or of grazing horses at night in the snow, and second because Korean ponies are only fed on cooked beans and soup, piping hot. No explanation is given, except that in this way they have been fed all their lives. Nor, for that matter, are they ever given water to drink. The soup at mealtime suffices.

The road was crowded with cavalry, infantry and stores. Pack trains and huge bullock carts plodded along, and long lines of coolies, clad in white sweeping garments and burdened with rice, toiled through the slush and mud. On the left cheek of each coolie a scarlet or purple smear of paint advertised his employ with the Japanese army transport.

Possibly the strangest feature was the incongruous white garments worn by these coolies, and, for that matter, by all

Koreans. The effect was like so much ice drifting on the surface of a black river. A stalwart race are the Koreans, well-muscled and towering above their masters, the "dwarfs" who conquered them of old time and who look upon them to-day with the eyes of possession. But the Korean is spiritless. He lacks the dash of Malay which makes the Japanese the soldier that he is.

The Korean has finer features, but the vital lack in his face is strength. He is soft and effeminate when compared with the strong breeds, and whatever strength has been his in the past has been worked out of him by centuries of corrupt government. He is certainly the most inefficient of human creatures, lacking all initiative and achievement, and the only thing in which he shines is the carrying of burdens on his back. As a draught animal and packhorse he is a success. And yet, I am confident —ay, willing to lay odds—that my own breed can beat him at his own game; that my own breed, from what I have seen of it in the West and North, can outwalk him, outpack him, and out-work him at coolie labor. In this latter connection I may state that three coolies are required to work an ordinary shovel. As one may see in Seoul any day of the year, one coolie steers the shovel by the handle, and two other coolies, sometimes three, furnish the motive power by means of ropes upon which they drag.

My two mapus—and they struck me a little better than the average—required an hour to put the loads on the ponies, and then spent the rest of the day trying to keep the loads from falling off. The simplest act requires half an hour of chin-chin and chatter before it can be performed, and if left alone the Korean would prefer giving a day to the preliminary discussion. About the only way to break up this discussion is vociferate "Os-saw!" which means hurry up, and to threaten to pull his topknot or break his head.

For the Korean is nothing if not a coward, and his fear of bodily hurt is about equal to his inaction. The creation of any word in a language denotes need for that word. The lack of quickness and the need for it has given to the Korean vocabulary a score of words, at least, among which may be mentioned Pat-pee, Ol-lun, Soik-kee, Oil-ppit, Koop-hee, Ning-kom, Bal-lee and Cham-kan. And though Kipling has well said that one musn't hustle the East, these are the first words the white man learns.

The following instance, culled from Pekin road, gives a good comparison between the East and the West. The scene has three actors—a mapu, a white man and a kicking Chinese pony. The mapu had attended horses all his life and he was thirty years of age and past. He knew nothing but horses, thought nothing but horses, was half horse himself. The white man had had ten days' experience with horses, no more, and most of which ten days had been spent in getting knowledge, not of horses, but mapus. The horse had bitten, kicked and squealed all his life.

The white man wished to know the condition of the horse's shoes. This was the mapu's business, but the white man had already learned that whatever was the mapu's business the mapu knew nothing about. So he directed the mapu to examine the horse's feet. Mapu said feet and shoes were all right. White man ordered three times, through an interpreter. Fourth time interpreter re-enforced order with a threatening flourish of his riding whip. Mapu gingerly lifted one forefoot and then the other.

Back feet were all right, he insisted, and several additional orders and flourishes of whips were needed before he proceeded to the hind feet. His method of procedure was in keeping. He squatted in the mud a dozen feet to the rear and after peering profoundly for a minute declared that all was well with the hind feet. As the feet were buried in the mud to the fetlocks the white man doubted the report.

More orders and bellicose persuasion, and the mapu, like a man going to his death, approached the dreaded hind feet. His approach was from the head, and he patted the horse with a tentative, trembling hand. The horse grew nervous, no doubt wondering what new and terrible atrocity was being meditated. After three minutes of this the mapu had approached the hind leg, while the horse was trembling, as frightened as the man.

Then the horse kicked and the mapu leaped for life. A crowd had gathered, which began to jeer and guy the mapu, who however, was not to be shamed into the deed. It was a crowd of mapus, and the crowd was invited by the white man to lift the dreaded hind foot, whereupon the crowd showed signs of panic and fell back.

Then the West asserted itself. The white man knew nothing about horses, and probably the only thing to be said in his favor was that he was not a Korean. He walked up to the horse, patted it roughly a couple of times and reached for the foot. Not only did he reach for it, but he got it. The next instant he was flung clear by the consequent kick.

Now the white man was as badly scared as the mapu. But he was a white man. He went right back to the foot. The horse kicked, but the white man insisted, and after some time the horse grew tired and the foot lifted. It is true the horse, instead of supporting itself on the other leg, leaned its body over on the man's bent back. But the man, instead of standing out from under, held on to the foot and held the horse up. He likened himself to Atlas, and he held until the horse, finding that nothing terrible was happening, resumed the perpendicular. After that the mapu was persuaded into lifting the other hind foot. The horse did not even attempt to kick and the shoe was found broken in two and one half missing.

This rather extended account of a trivial affair has been given to show concretely the inefficiency and helplessness of the Korean. What is true of the mapu in this affair is true of the race in all its affairs. It doesn't know how, it doesn't try to learn how, it doesn't care. In a day, what of the broken shoe, the horse would have been limping. The Korean race and government have been limping for centuries and will continue to limp until some first-class, efficient mapu takes hold, lifts the feet and puts the shoes in shape.

The Asiatic is heartless. The suffering of dumb brutes means nothing to him. Returning to the subject of mapus, for mapus are an important item on the Pekin road, it were well to advise any prospective traveler to have an eye to his horses during feeding time and during all feeding time. He may order feed and see it put under his horses' noses; but if he goes out of the stable for a minute and returns he will find no feed under his horses' noses. The mapus will have stolen it. If left alone the mapus will continue stealing the food till a horse cannot stand of itself, must less carry a pack or a man. Then they will inform the white man and owner, "Horse sick." Inquiry as to the cause of sickness will elicit the usual voluble Asiatic expression of ignorance.

To shoe a pony the size of a calf the Korean must throw it on the ground. A broken back is no uncommon result, but what of that? The Korean will say he is very sorry. In short, the first weeks of a white traveler on Korean soil are anything but pleasant. If he be a man of sensitive organization he will spend most of his time under the compelling sway of two alternating desires. The first is to kill Koreans, the second is to commit suicide. Personally, I prefer the first. But, now consider myself fairly immune and have reasonable hopes of surviving the trip.

The Japanese may be the Britisher of the Orient, but he is still Asiatic. The suffering of beasts does not touch him. The following case is in point and I am sure that the like would not occur with our cavalry or the cavalry of any Western power.

The day was bitter cold. A cruel north wind was blowing and the spattering mud froze wherever it struck. Jones and I had overtaken and were passing a troop of cavalry. The curious nervousness and excitement of a horse attracted our attention.

Mud to the weight of fully twenty pounds had frozen in a solid lump to the end of his sweeping tail. Had the tail been tied up in the first place this would not have happened. As it was, at every step the twenty-weight of mud swung forward between its hind legs, striking the legs on the shinbones. As a result the horse lifted its feet high in order to try and step over the object which administered the blow. It was walking over its own tail, frantic with fear.

We told the man to tie it up or to cut it off, and for the latter purpose offered a large and sharp-bladed knife. But he smiled commiseratingly at us for our anxiety and solicitude and for what he probably termed arrant idiocy, and rode on, the frozen mud, the size of a workman's dinner pail, banging the horse's shinbones at every step and the horse vainly trying to step over it. The man was only a common soldier after all, but where was the officer?

AMERICANS PRAISE JAPAN'S ARMY

PING YANG (Korea), March 5. — The Japanese soldiery and equipment seem to command universal admiration. Not one dissenting voice is to be heard among the European and American residents in Korea. On the contrary, favorable comparison is made with our own troops and the troops of Europe.

Dr. Wunsch, a German resident of Seoul and a man of military experience, was unmeasured in his praise of the "little brown men," the "dwarfs," as the Koreans have called them from old time. What Dr. Wunsch especially remarked was the lack of noise in the issuing of orders on the part of the officers. As he put it, there were practically no sounds at all. The Japanese soldiers executed maneuvers apparently without command. At least there were none of the bellowing of commands such as he had been accustomed to in his own experience.

American and British army officers, pleased though they are with the conduct of the men, are especially concerned with the equipment and commissariat. Confessing that their own soldiers would not be so quiet and orderly, they go on to enlarge upon the equipment of the men, and upon the whole system of transporting them, provisioning them and getting them to the front.

In the first place, food, luggage and everything in the way of baggage which must be carried with an army are done up in packages which can easily be handled by individuals unaided, and which, if needs be, can be carried on the backs of men. So there are no army wagons nor army mules. Pack horses and coolies do the work; and, though many Korean bullock carts have been put into service, there is no necessity for them.

The rice, which is the staple food, is done up in sixty-pound sacks. One coolie can carry a sack all day over the most rugged country. Two sacks go to make the load of a Korean pony, and from three to four sacks the load of a Japanese pony. Meat is put in one-half pound tins, eighty of which tins are incased in a box. One horse under three of these boxes carries one meat ration for a company. Four horses carry a meat ration for a battalion.

A sheet-iron cylinder, carried in sections, constitutes a camp stove. This stove is twenty-seven inches high and thirty inches in diameter. In this the fire is built and into it is fitted a sheet-iron kettle. Into this, in turn, is fitted a perforated kettle in which the rice is cooked—and cooked without scorching. One kettle will cook rice for one hundred men. Eight or nine such kettles will suffice for a battalion.

Sodium sulphate in tins is part of the soldier's outfit. It is to be doubted, in a country so fearfully unsanitary as Korea, if a drop of healthy drinking water can be found. So the sodium sulphate, in little flannel sacks, is placed in boiling water to precipitate the impurities, and the "little brown man" is thus given a larger opportunity of dying on the battle field and of killing Russians ere he dies. Certainly, so far as Japan is concerned, it is more economical for its soldiers to be filled with lead than with fever germs.

In small cotton bags, weighing little and occupying less space, are emergency rations. This ration is made of rice, boiled and then dried in the sun till each grain has shrunk to the size of a pinhead. Each soldier carries six of these rations in his knapsack. On a pinch they would suffice him for days; and always it must be remembered that rice is to the Japanese what bread is to us, and butter and meat to boot.

The soldier's kit is light and complete. Including 120 rounds of ammunition, it weighs 42½ pounds. The kit of the American soldier weighs 55 pounds. I may quote General Allen as saying that the Japanese infantry is as well equipped as any in the world.

The soldier's mess pan is after the German pattern—aluminum and blackened on the outside. It will hold two rice rations, which, cooked in the morning, he may carry with him for the day. The water bottle, likewise of aluminum, holds a full pint.

There are two methods of carrying the kit. First, is the European knapsack on the back; second, and probably the better, is the American banderole—the blankets rolled and twisted over the shoulder and about the body.

In connection with this is a sort of narrow bag, open at both ends, six inches wide and four feet long, made of blue cotton drill, which likewise crosses the shoulder and winds about the body.

In Seoul was to be observed a rather curious thing—a revival of the old navy grog. Twenty gallons of saki (the Japanese wine made from rice) were distributed each day to a battalion. But I learned that only in Seoul was this grog-ration to be distributed. Once on the field the soldiers would have to content themselves with their boiled water purified by sodium sulphate.

A battalion varies in strength between eight and nine hundred men. Each battalion has a pack train of 180 ponies. This constitutes its camp transport and immediate provisions for a few days.

In addition to this, there is the regimental train, variable in size and composed of coolies, bulls, ponies, carts and anything that can move and carry weight.

Behind all this is the etappe service, or relay stations, the function of which is to keep food and munitions moving in a constant stream to the front from the base of supplies. This service is of the most vital importance. When it fails the soldiers at the front must break ground and fall back.

Everything depends on the firing line, but the firing line depends on the etappe service.

The Japanese army rifle is a trifle less than thirty caliber. One thousand four hundred and forty rounds of ammunition weigh 110 pounds; and in such quantities are packed into ammunition boxes. Two of these boxes compose a load for a pack pony. Chains at each end of the box loop on corresponding hooks on the pack saddle, so the loading and unloading of the ponies is simple and expeditious.

These ponies supply the firing line when the soldiers are fighting. Eighteen ponies will give each man of a battalion seventy additional rounds.

Returning to the opening paragraph, a slight emendation must be made. The praise for the conduct of the Japanese soldiers is not quite universal. The Koreans are beginning to grumble—that is, the people—and they have reason to grumble, though through no fault of the Japanese. The Koreans complain that goods are taken from them by the soldiers, for which they receive no pay.

The true inwardness of the situation is this: The Japanese military authorities requisition so much food and forage for which they pay a fair price. But the deal goes through the hands of the Korean officials. Now, the Korean official can give the Occident cards and spades when it comes to misappropriation of funds. The Oriental term for this is "squeeze." Centuries of practice have reduced it to a science, and in Korea there are but two classes—the squeezers and the squeezees. The common people, of course, as all the world over, are the "squeezees."

When the Japanese military authorities want food for the soldiers the Korean officials demand and receive from each family, say, two measures of rice. The Japanese soldier eats the rice, the Korean people furnish the rice, the Japanese Government pays for the rice and the Korean officials pocket the money.

The Koreans make another complaint. The soldiers take their chickens and eggs and do not pay for the same. The Koreans are a poor people, and this is really a severe hardship upon them; but, on the other hand, what soldier under the sun has ever done otherwise? Ever since war began and man domesticated the fowl, chickens and eggs have been considered lawful loot, and so long as man shall be irrational enough to fight wars, that long will the stomach and the ethnics of the soldier remain unchanged.

COSSACKS FIGHT THEN RETREAT[1]

PING YANG, March 5.—The first land fight!

The first contact of the Japanese and Russians on the land and the first powder actually burned by the land forces occurred at Ping Yang on the morning of February 28th.

A scouting party of Russian Cossacks, crossing the Yalu at Wiju, had ventured 200 miles south into Korea to get in touch with the Japanese and discover how far north they had penetrated.

Three Americans escorting women from the mines of the American concession, fifty miles east of Anjou, encountered the scouting party of Cossacks at Anjou, on the main Pekin road. They traveled with the troop for a day and described the Cossacks as splendid looking soldiers, perfect horsemen and mounted on sturdy Russian ponies.

As an instance of the discipline of the men the following is related: One of the Americans had given a trooper the makings of a cigarette. The soldier, sitting in the saddle, had just begun

[1] See also *Jack London's Tales of Adventure*, edited by Irving Shepard. Hanover House, 1956.

to roll the cigarette when the command was given for them to break into a gallop. Away fluttered tobacco and rice paper as the soldier instantly obeyed.

The Cossacks had not the slightest idea of where they would pick up with the Japanese, and each village was a possible and probable ambuscade. Approaching a village, they dismounted and spread out, and in this order they entered, with their horses between them and the houses.

But no Japanese did they encounter till they reached the ancient walled city of Ping Yang, the scene of the slaughter of the Chinese by the Japanese in 1894 and a city whose written history leaps boldly back into the centuries before Christ. Here in the pleasant valley beyond the walls of Ping Yang the Cossacks, twenty in number, ran upon five Japanese cavalry. A race resulted, the Cossacks pursuing and only giving over when met with a hot fire from the wall.

To Company 7 of the Forty-sixth regiment of infantry, Twelfth division of the Japanese army, belongs the honor of firing the first shots on the land. Fourteen men of this company, under command of First Lieutenant C. Yoshimura, ensconced upon the crumbling battlement, had watched the chase as it led up to them. At 700 meters (about 2,300 feet) distance, time 9:30 A.M., they opened fire.

The Cossacks promptly whirled their horses and rode away. Thirty shots were fired in all, to which the Cossacks made no reply. They had fulfilled their errand of finding the Japanese and wisely entertained no idea of capturing Ping Yang.

It is remarkable that none was killed or wounded by such short range fire. The Japanese explain it by the fact that they were afraid of hitting their own fleeing cavalry. They aver, however, that two Cossacks were seen to dismount from evidently wounded horses and lead them away. So Russian blood was shed in the first land engagement, even if it was only horse blood.

Lieutenant C. Yoshimura gave the command to fire and was the only officer present, though my first details were obtained from a brother officer, Lieutenant Y. Abe, who called upon me in my quarters in a Japanese hotel, and whom I entertained in the Japanese fashion—the only fashion available.

We sat on the matting floor of my room, shoes off, drinking tea and saki and eating pickled onions with chopsticks. Between us was the customary hibachi with its few glowing coals, and into it was dropped the ashes from endless cigarettes. The Japanese are inveterate cigarette smokers, and politeness demands that they shall be fed to one's visitors. Which is all very well, but which is rather hard on the poor correspondent, far from his base of supplies.

Lieutenant Abe, by the way, is a typical officer of the new Japan. For all his European uniform and close-cropped beard, he was Oriental. His legs were folded under him to the manner born, and he was very comfortable, while my legs sprawled out awkwardly and required constant shifting to prevent going to sleep, and I was decidedly uncomfortable.

A graduate of the military academy at Tokio, he knew French and English and Chinese, and was studying German at the present moment. After the war was over, he informed me, he was scheduled to return to the academy and take post-graduate courses in military science.

The Japanese are surely a military race. Their men are soldiers, and their officers are soldiers. I called upon Captain Kauchiba of the Pioneers who lives in the room adjoining mine. He was a very busy man, just now having charge of the construction of the bridge across the Tai-tong river and of the Ping Yang fortifications.

He sat on the floor in the midst of a mass of correspondence, maps and plans. Orderlies came and went with innumerable reports, messengers arrived and were dispatched—all serving to punctuate our brief conversation. Between us was the hibachi, cigarettes were offered, and tea ordered. The wall was lined with military chests, of a size convenient for pack ponies. Saddle bags, belt and saber hung on the wall. There was no table. All his work was done on the floor.

His men had marched up on Seoul averaging twenty miles a day; and on my inquiring about sore feet he reluctantly admitted that some of his men were suffering, but added immediately that they were so fired with love of country that sore feet would not matter when it came to fighting the Russians. So far as the Russians were concerned, there was no such thing as sore feet, was his way of putting it. Some few of them might be in poor condition for marching, but all were in good condition for fighting.

I was in search of horseshoes and departed after a brief ten minutes with a letter to an officer of cavalry. Also, I carried with me Captain Kauchiba's promise of an additional set of shoes from himself. In all such matters of help and advice the Japanese officers have shown themselves uniformly courteous and kind, and though they are busy men they always have a minute to spare for the stray correspondent seeking help of some sort or other.

OVER THE PEKIN ROAD ON THE WAY TO THE YALU[1]

PING YANG. March 7, 1904.—On the Pekin Road.

This Pekin Road has been described as a river of mud. This is not quite correct for it is true only in the day time. In the night it turns to a river of ice, while on the north side of every pass the road remains sheeted with ice all day long.

And on these ice-sheets, pitching down at a slope of from 15 to 30 degrees is where a man leads his horse and prays, first, that the horse will not break its legs, and next, that it will not fall upon him. Not only must the man look out for his horse behind him and above him and in imminent likelihood of falling upon him and crushing him; but he must look out for his own footing. For it must be borne in mind that it is glare ice, hard as adamant, and that its pitch makes it many times more slippery than a polished floor.

The combination of a slipping man and a slipping horse is not a happy one, while the combination of many slipping horses and men, in a long string, brings out the sweat alike on man and beast. I shall not soon forget such an ice-slope we climbed at the rear of a column of infantry. The men were sprawling right and left. Slipping became contagious. Macleod, in front of me, after mad gyrations, went down. A soldier picked him up and promptly went down himself. My feet were inclined to move in divers simultaneous directions, and the resultant was

[1] See also *Jack London's Tales of Adventure*, edited by Irving Shepard. Hanover House, 1956.

precarious equilibrium maintained at hazard and by miracle. But poor Belle, my horse, had four feet sliding in many simultaneous directions; and behind her and under her was Jones and his horse, both slipping and floundering, the former shouting each time Belle threatened to fall back upon him. As Belle threatened every moment, his shouting was continuous.

"Watch out! Your horse is breaking its legs!" was his burden. Then it changed to "Look at her shoes!"

I looked. She was pawing and scrambling wildly, and at each impact of a foot with the ice I could see the shoe itself move and slide on the foot as well as on the ice. When we gained the summit—and there was no stopping till we did— all her shoes were loose and two could be pulled off by hand, while Macleod's horse had no shoes at all on its hind feet.

Jones pushed on with the packs, and Macleod and I led our horses. Five li farther on we encountered a village filled with soldiers. As luck would have it our interpreters were ahead or behind, but we showed our credentials, also a letter written in Japanese by Minister Hiyashi, and were most courteously treated by the officers. One trim young lieutenant, astride his horse, unbuckled his saddlebags and drew forth a horseshoe.

"Well, all I can say is that I have learned something about war," said Macleod.

And so had I. Bernard G. Shaw's chocolate cream soldier may be true of Europe, but it is not true of Japan. The officers of Nippon certainly do not carry confectionary in their saddlebags and holsters. But there were no farriers, and while we stamped our feet in the cold for three hours waiting the arrival of the next detachment of cavalry, we resolved that henceforth we would carry horseshoes in our own saddlebags, also that we would become farriers ourselves.

We started out after dark, the hoofs of our horses ringing out sharply on the frozen roadbed, and at the end of ten li caught up with Jones. He had found quarters in a village of six houses, where one hundred soldiers had been billeted, and right valiantly had he held our room. There was just space in it for our three camp cots side by side, yet it would have accommodated a dozen soldiers packed on the floor. He had been ordered by an officer a number of times to vacate, and a number of times all our goods had been carted into the street. The Korean mapus and interpreters, mortally afraid of the "dwarfs," had begged him, after each eviction, to go on to the next village; but Jones figured that the next village was equally crammed with soldiers, and each time our goods were thrown out he had ordered the trembling mapus to carry them back.

And here arises a question of ethics. Was Jones justified, and were we, as sharers in the night's shelter, justified in occupying the house? The house might be called ours by rights of possession; it might be called the soldiers' by right of occupation of the country. On the other hand, how about the Korean who owned it? Anyway, Macleod and I were grateful to Jones and our sleep was sound.

To keep shoes on our horses was the great problem. In the first place, our horseshoes were whiteman's horseshoes, about which the Korean farriers knew nothing. And as their knowledge of their own kind of shoes was the accumulated wisdom of centuries, it was beyond the wildest flights of imagination to dream that they could learn anything about whiteman's shoes inside several centuries more. In the meantime we could scarcely afford to wait.

Next, the farriers of the Japanese army seemed to have no luck in shoeing our horses. Every day they were putting on shoes for us, and every day the shoes were coming off. It made us sigh for a good American smithy, and it made us lead our horses into Ping Yang at the end of the first hundred and eighty miles.

Here I bought several pounds of horseshoe nails from Mr. Graham Lee, an American missionary. Through the same missionary I managed to get hold of a Korean blacksmith who agreed to make two sets after the pattern of Belle's shoes, and who promptly got drunk upon receipt of so extensive an order. But Mr. Lee wrestled with him and I ultimately obtained the sets. Also, a set of ready made shoes from a Captain of Pioneers, and another set from a cavalry captain quite fixed me up. Hereafter I travel with a complete set in my saddlebags, likewise with a hammer, pinchers, and a wedge of iron for clinching the nails. And if Belle survives the ordeal, I shall surely learn something of the farrier's trade.

But horses' feet were not the only feet that suffered on the Pekin Road. Sore-footed soldiers were pretty much in evidence. They trailed along for miles behind every marching company and battalion. And few miseries are greater than sore feet of men on the march. Each step is torture, and they must go on, step by step, all day long. If they could only lie down and rest till the sores were healed, all would be well; but on they must go, step by step, each step hurting anew the lacerated flesh.

To them paradise would sum itself up in cessation of movement; and doubtless they dreamed of their Buddhist Nirvana through the long hours of tramping. At any rate they dreamed as they marched, for nothing could rouse them. The sound of our flying hoofs made no impression upon them. And when we zig-zagged through a bunch of "sore-feets" they did not scatter. Not the least effort did they make to get out of the way when our horses came in contact with them in thrusting past. They were too far gone, like seasick persons, to care. It was easier to be run down than to make a quick effort to leap aside. We did not run any down, but it was through no virtue of care on their part.

As we were traveling faster than the army we were continually overtaking the "sore-feets" who straggled in the rear of every detachment of infantry. The majority had discarded their knapsacks, which they heaped upon the backs of coolies impressed for the service. Many of them discarded the army shoe of stiff leather, and went back to their native gear, the soft straw sandal. And some I saw with a piece of stiff cloth under the sole of the foot, the foot naked, trudging along through the freezing mud. But this was the breaking-in process. There will be few "sore-feets" after they have marched half a thousand miles.

There were other breaking-in processes along the road, as instance at Hwang-ju, where the Korean inhabitants were broken in to the expediency of giving lodgings and horsefood to white-men, and to the inexpediency of stealing from whitemen. Hwang-ju is an ancient walled-city of an estimated population of 30,000, beautifully situated on the right bank of the Nam-chlion River. Macleod and Jones had traveled 140 li that day, crossed the great Tong-sun pass in the late afternoon, journeyed on in the darkness through 20 li where there were no villages because of fear of the native mountain robbers, and arrived, horses and men exhausted, at Hwang-ju. I, as usual, was pushing along behind, delayed by a loose horseshoe.

Hwang-ju has 30,000 people who live in houses, yet not one room would they rent to Macleod and Jones, nor one ounce of beans or barley would they sell for the horses. The weary men and jaded horses were led back and forth over the town. There was endless chin-chin but no chow, while there were frequent invitations to go on to the next village, "ten li more."

This phrase, "ten li more," has a peculiarly irritating effect on Jones. He avers that he has heard nothing else since he entered the country, and that he has heard it so often and under such exasperating circumstances that he is going to write a book on Korea and entitle it, "Ten Li More." When he found himself, with Macleod, finally led to the gate, and invited, with the objectionable phrase appended, to go on to the next village, he balked.

If 30,000 people would not sell shelter, what was to be expected of a small village? Jones declined to move on, Macleod seconded him. They negligently transferred their revolvers from one pocket to the other, and it would have done Isabella Bird Bishop's[2] heart good to see the transformation. It would have atoned for much which she suffered at the hands of inhospitable and insulting Koreans. At once heads were put together, there was quick whispering, and in two minutes horses and men were in comfortable quarters.

Later in the night I arrived rousing all Hwang-ju with my yells as I rode through its streets seeking my party. Luckily, I was without an interpreter, and so escaped knowledge of the many invitations doubtlessly extended to continue on my way "ten li more." So I rode and yelled and woke the town, till I heard the welcome voice of Jones' interpreter, and found Jones and Macleod stretched out on the floor of a miserable Korean room and waiting chow.

We had left our packs behind and were making a dash for Ping Yang. Our camp cots were with the packs, and a rug

[2] English traveler, writer, and founder of a hospital and orphanage in Japan, Korea, and China during the years of 1894 to 1897. Elected a fellow of the Royal Geographical Society in 1892. Published at least nine books between 1856 and 1859, mostly travelogues.

apiece was our portion; and our commissary was exhausted. No milk, little sugar, no bread, a little tea, and dirty, half-cooked native rice was the menu; and the rice was eaten without sugar, which later went into the making of a lot of whiskey toddy. And then we had no more whiskey.

In the morning we awoke to a still more limited menu and to the fact that two blankets had been stolen off our horses. The house-master knew nothing. This was ascertained after an eternity of chin-chin. The house-master was very sorry. A second eternity of chin-chin was required to extract this information, and after a third eternity we learned that the house-master could do nothing to recover the blankets.

Our horses were saddled. We were ready to start. We expressed our wrath by appropriate vociferation and gesture, and thrust the house-master out in quest of the stolen property. It was a cold, raw morning, and I do not remember ever seeing a more pitiful and miserable specimen of humanity than that same house-master as he stood, irresolute and helpless, in the middle of the street, hands thrust for warmth into either voluminous sleeve, shoulders stooped, eyes weazened and appealing and deprecating, his whole bearing and expression that of a man passively and fearfully awaiting death by slow torture.

But the fear of death sprang up in another man's heart. We sent for the head-man of the neighborhood, a well-dressed individual with the rotund indications of material prosperity. Him we addressed through an interpreter something in this fashion: "Two blankets have been stolen. We hold you responsible. We want, not chin-chin, but blankets. We give you five minutes to find them. If at the end of five minutes they are not forthcoming, we will stand you in the corner there on that heap of refuse, and give your men five additional minutes to find the blankets. And then, if they are not found, we will take you with us to Ping Yang, and . . ."

We never finished that final sentence, but left what horrid fate awaited him at Ping Yang to his own imagination. His first five minutes were fruitless, and we stood him in a corner on the refuse. Then began the search of his men. Under his direction it was feverish. They turned everything topsy turvy. All Hwang-ju had arrived to look on. I was beginning to wonder how we could possibly back our bluff if it failed, or save our

faces, when a shout went up. An enterprising coolie had unearthed the missing blankets from a hiding-place not a dozen
feet away.

But in Korea it does not pay to be enterprising. For the
coolie's discovery was the signal for a general onslaught upon
none other than himself. Macleod's interpreter was the first
to get him, and he got him by the top-knot. Blows and kicks
were rained upon him, the while he protested to high heaven
and Hwang-ju. High heaven did not hear, but Hwang-ju was
delighted.

In the meantime I was busy with the head-man. In my innocence I had thought he was rushing to attack the interpreter,
and to make life livable on the Peking Road one must back
up his interpreter. So I shoved the head-man back into his
corner. I shoved a little too sharply, for he lost his footing. Yet
I had done his intention, not himself, an injustice. In reality,
he had leaped forward to join in the beating being given his
coolie.

But why under the sun the coolie was beaten passed my comprehension for the moment. It was certainly Asiatic—a conception that the weak, by wreaking hurt upon the weaker, would
propitiate the strong. By the time I had got this through my
head, Ming-yang, the Korean interpreter, had the head-man by
the top-knot. I was delighted. Assembled Hwang-ju was astounded. The state of mind of the head-man was something
beyond words, so was his top-knot when Ming-yang had done
with him.

"Tell him that fifty more white men, just like us, will arrive
in half an hour," said Jones, as we mounted our horses.

"If you do, in twenty minutes there won't be a single inhabitant left in Hwang-ju," said Macleod.

And, heedful of his warning, we rode away, our consciences
salved with the knowledge that we had withheld the full measure
of our wrath and not depopulated a flourishing city of 30,000
souls.

TRANSLATOR TROUBLES

POVAL COLLI, March 8. — In Korea every item in one's outfit is a
worry all by itself. Five horses mean twenty horseshoes, and

twenty horseshoes mean twenty worries about which no one will worry but onself. One mapu (groom) is harder to manage than a boy's reform school, and I verily believe it is easier to be President of the United States than to manage two mapus. And of the thousand and one worries on the Pekin Road I have given but twenty-two. I may well make it twenty-three by including the interpreter.

Mr. K. Yamada is my interpreter. He is a Japanese and he speaks as good English as the average interpreter, while his knowledge of Korea gives him an added value. Also, he knows enough French to explain to a raiding Russian officer, should the contingency arise, that I am only a harmless newspaper correspondent. I have no way of testing his French, but I hope it will not hang fire at the vital moment, as his English is wont to do.

I remember once hearing a description of a police court scene in which an Italian witness is testifying through an interpreter. A question has been asked by the court.

"Wobble, wobble, wobble, gobble," says the interpreter.

"Gobble, gobble, gobble, wobble," says the witness.

This continues back and forth for ten minutes. Then the interpreter turns to the court with the remark "The witness says 'yes.'"

I did not appreciate it at the time, but I do now. Not only is it true of our interpreters, but the very converse is true. Sitting with Mr. Yamada and interviewing a Japanese officer, I have put a simple question, requiring yes or no for an answer, and listened to "Gobble, wobble, wobble, gobble" for fifteen minutes before the answer forthcame. Also I have talked for five minutes, carefully and deliberately elaborating an important and fairly subtle statement into elementary English, and have had Mr. Yamada make a single "gobble wobble" to the officer and then say to me, "He understands."

The chief difficulty with a Korean interpreter is to get him to do any thinking, even for himself. But the chief difficulty with a Japanese interpreter is to head him off from doing your thinking as well as his own. Also the Japanese interpreter is Asiatic. He no more understands a white man's mental processes than a white man understands his. So long as his work consists in expressing one's desire for a horseshoe or a night's lodging, all well and good. But the instant the interpreter is called upon to express an abstraction, confusion and cross-purposes begin. He cannot comprehend the point of view, and at once he begins to do your thinking for you, and the worst of it is that you will not be aware of it for some time, perhaps never. The thoughts become as elusive and scattered as the players at blindman's buff. In addition the players are rapid-change artists and are blindfolded themselves. You are "it," but you do not recognize a thought when you catch it. It was your thought the moment before, but in the intervening moment something happened to it. It has become another thought. But you do not know it, and you wander haltingly through the shifting phantasmagoria till the interview is ended and you go away with a definite conclusion in your head. You will act upon this conclusion and at the end of the week discover that it is all wrong; that all you have based upon it is wrong; that you are still "it" and must try again.

Each evening Mr. Yamada brings me a written report for the day. Such a report has just come in for to-day, and I append it with the proud assertion that I understand every word of it. Also, I challenge the reader to say the same when he has finished reading it.

"Report, Monday 8th March cloudy (about 45 degree.)

"We started Pyng Yang at about 2:30 P.M. after called major general and the consul, thanking kindly advise for our party.

"P. S. we has visited major general Sasaki about our movement from Pyng Yang. General says; there no danger at all for you go down Anju (Anju is city but is smaller than Pyng Yang and there are staying Japanese cavalry and infants as the spy) but I want advise you that you will better to go down until my information, and so we beg to stay more Pyng Yang under the general advise but we can't do that for a reason as we are correspondent and we don't like to spend so much money without pleasure and nothing news.

"We started Pyng Yang disputing the advise for purpose place Anju.

"Passing Kalga village (10 Ri from Pyng Yang, Kan-fugi (5 Ri) Wolpongie (5 Ri) and arrived Poval-Colli village at about 5:30 P.M. so we walked (25 Ri) to-day.

"We saw Japanese cavalries spys at Paval villages, and they

told some secret about war there is no Russian soldiers beyond Anju but sometimes will find few his spies (of cause Cosack cavalry).

"At 4 P.M. snow came down but very little and our troop were good condition.

"We expected lieut-general K. Inouye as the commander of the province division. When he reach down to Anju, certainly the fight shall begin with Russia."

If the army censor dows not consider this narrative of Mr. Yamada's a betrayal of military secrets, there is a likelihood that it will go through. If he does consider it a betrayal, the censor at least will have added to his wisdom concerning the matter of interpreters.

TRAVEL IN KOREA

SUNAN, March 10, 04. — To travel in Korea in peace-time is not particularly easy, but in war-time it becomes a pretty serious proposition. In the first place, one has to get to Korea. Japan was not overwhelmingly anxious that correspondents should get to Korea in time for the beginning of hostilities. Her officials recommended the correspondents to remain in Japan till permits to accompany the army were issued. Many lingered. And to this day of writing, so far as is known here in Korea, they are still in Japan.

At least, they are not in Seoul nor Ping Yang nor with the Japanese advance northward on the Pekin Road. War was immediately preceded by a withdrawal of all vessels scheduled to sail from Japanese to Korean ports. I managed to get a third-class passage on the last vessel which departed. Her anchor was up and she was steaming out of Shimonoseki when I boarded her in a launch.

And from her I was put ashore at Fusan, at the extreme southeastern extremity of Korea. The day was Sunday. On the previous day a couple of Russian transports had been captured just outside the harbor. With this information, though no one knew of any official declaration of war, I pulled out on a cockleshell of a coasting steamer; but was thrown ashore bag and baggage, with all the passengers—I was the only white man aboard—at Mokpo.

The same day found me in a Korean sam-pan and heading up the west coast of Korea. Now a sam-pan is a tiny open fishing-boat with sails made of grass, or straw, and with sails and running-gear so rotten that even a cat's paw is bound to carry something away. Tuesday night found me in Kunsan. The naval battle had been fought at Chemulpo, and at that port I arrived six days later, in another sam-pan. The masts and funnels of the sunken ships greeted me as I entered the harbor.

The naval fight was a week old. War had been declared for about the same length of time. It had been preceded by fifteen weeks of preliminaries, and yet I found in Chemulpo and Seoul but three correspondents, Lewis, of Nagasaki; Mackenzie, for the London *Daily Mail*, and Dunn, for *Collier's Weekly*. I made the fourth. And there were no more arriving. The only ships coming in were war vessels and transports. And none of us would have been on the spot had we heeded the advice of the Japanese officials.

Next, as we lingered in Seoul, we were advised by the Japanese Minister and generals to remain there until the Headquarters Staff should arrive. Daily soldiers passed out through Peking Pass and took the road to the north toward the seat of war, and daily we were importuned and warned to remain. But the Headquarters Staff did not appear, nor did our permits to accompany the army appear.

The only thing to do was to go, permit or no permit, and three of us shoved on 180 miles to Ping Yang. On the way we overtook and passed General Sasaki, who begged us to remain with him.

At Ping Yang the acting Japanese Consul sent for us individually and warned us against continuing northward. General Sasaki arrived and he insisted that we should not go on. Yet from neither could we get anything definite, while we had in mind always the Chino-Japanese War,[1] wherein, by similar tactics, all but two or three men were inveigled into missing about everything that happened. The few that succeeded in seeing anything, had succeeded by virtue of the fact that they had shoved on. Also, they must have had a fair comprehension of the Oriental mind.

[1] August 1894–April 1895.

Mackenzie fell by the wayside. Most anxious of the three of us to push on at once north to Anju, he allowed himself to be persuaded by General Sasaki and deported on a side-trip to the seaport of Chemulpo. Dunn and I persisted. The Consul said that the Japanese feared for our safety. We replied that we had come to see the fighting. To this the answer was that the Russians had fallen back from Anju and were retreating upon Wiju, nearly a hundred miles farther away. If this were so, we demanded, how could there be danger on the road to Anju? The Consul smiled and talked about other things.

General Sasaki—and a splendid, soldierly man he is—said it would be better if we remained with him until he started north. When would he start north? He did not know, but if we would travel with him we would be afforded every convenience, such as food for ourselves and horses, extra pack animals, spare riding horses if anything happened to ours, and information galore. He even promised me fresh horses along the way to Anju in case of fighting at that point, and information the moment he received it of said fighting. Anju was 190 li away, and he told me I could make it over the bad road in a day and a night of hard riding. Meanwhile, I wondered how much of the fight would be left for me to see by the time I got there.

At another interview we asked straight out if he would give us permission to go on. This he declined. "Then will you order us to remain in Ping Yang?" was our next query. This he refused to do. And there we were—nothing definite.

"Then we shall start today," we informed him.

"If you do, I shall not be responsible for you," was his rejoinder.

We explained that he need not worry about our safety, and that what we were worrying about was our responsibility to our employers; that if he did not command us to remain in Ping Yang it was our plain duty to start northward at once.

And so it ended—or shall I say, began? Before we had the packs on our horses an urgent summons was received from the Consul. And while the packs continued to go on we threshed the whole thing over again with him. Would he command us to remain. He would not. Then we undertake to be responsible for our own lives. But scarcely had I passed out of the West Gate than my interpreter overtook me with a letter from the Consul.

It was as ambiguous as all our interviews. Nothing definite. We were neither permitted to go on, nor commanded to stay back.

The day, Tuesday, was nearly gone, and we camped at Poval village 25 li along the road. Wednesday morning I received a letter from a Korean messenger. He had left Anju on foot. The letter stated that a body of Cossacks had appeared at Pak Chun, 30 li north of Anju, and that a fight with the Japanese scouts was imminent.

Ten li farther on we were held up by an infantry captain in this half-deserted village of Sunan. He had received orders by field telephone from Ping Yang to detain us. And here we are, with orders for the pack horses to be ready at seven tomorrow morning and wondering if we are to be allowed to proceed.

Incidentally, I had my bit of fun with the captain. He informed us that the Japanese and Russian scouts had had a brush and that one Japanese had been killed. Where he did not say, and, true to Asia, he was quite indefinite about it.

"Tell him it took place at Pak Chun," I told the interpreter to say to him.

And he was wide-eyed with astonishment. He had just received the news himself by the field wire. He knew we had no means of getting information over the wire. No messengers could have traveled the intervening distance on foot. Then how had we learned it. We did not inform him, and I guess he is puzzling about it yet.

Such is one phase of the trouble of traveling in Korea in wartime. Another, for instance, is the finding of accommodation at night, and the farther we win north the greater it becomes. The villages are nearly deserted, the few remaining inhabitants frightened out of the little wits they ever happened to possess. Scouting Cossacks have passed through, taking what they needed. The Japanese have passed through. And we arrive, a totally different and remarkably wonderful breed of which the very worst is to be expected.

Last night at Poval is a fair example. We rode in with our ten riding and pack horses. Dunn (who has hitherto figured as Jones), and myself, with our followers, making ten persons. There were ten houses in Poval, but not room for a single horse, we were told. Ten li more we would find a horse stable. "Ten li more"

is a red flag to Dunn, and at once turns him into an angry bull
—a very angry bull. His charge is directed against the nearest
entrance to a walled enclosure, and in a trice he is inside in the
midst of a stable the existence of which seems to have never been
known to the inhabitants. But there is no horse food.

"Paw-ree isso!" we shout.

"Paw-ree oopso!" they reply.

"Paw-ree auso!" we rejoin.

The which dialogue is as follows:

"Have you any barley?"

"We have no barley."

"Get barley quickly."

It is a dialogue which we have conducted so often that we
can now say it backward in our sleep or begin at the middle and
repeat both ways at once.

Leaving Dunn to extract twenty-five pounds of barley from
the baggy trousers worn by the nearest man, I start off with
Manyoungi, my Korean factotum, in search of sleeping quarters.
By this time the inhabitants are shouting "Ten li more," in every
mood and tense. Doors have to be brushed open, owners thrust
aside, and interiors inspected. Withered, naked-breasted beldames
shriek curses at us. Men, old and young, do everything except
fight, and a multitude of dogs begin barking and growling at us.

"Son of a toad," is the most frequent appellation I receive,
and to the Koreans it is a pretty bad one, for they are ancestor-
worshippers and it smirches my ancestors.

Pandemonium (spl?) reigns. Interpreters are in search of
houses themselves. The uproar is deafening, the chin-chin endless. Every mapu has a dozen quarrels on his hands, while the
villagers are desperate. When we have hit upon the houses of our
choice the packs are carried in. The cooks take possession of the
kitchens.

And then, presto, all is changed. The villagers learn that we
pay for what we get. Barley and beans appear, enough for a
cavalry regiment. Brush wood and charcoal arrive. Chickens and
eggs are resurrected from all manner of hiding places. And the
villagers, amiable and smiling, surround us, anxious to do small
services and content in return to satisfy their curiosity by staring

at us. In the morning they are loth to have us depart, and are left somewhat richer by having known us.

In every country in the world money is a vexatious problem. Likewise in Korea, but with this difference: in other countries the vexation is to get the money, in Korea the vexation does not arise until after the money is got. Without money, all is serene, as soon as it arrives, one's troubles begin.

To commence with, one arrives in Seoul. His money is in American gold. One dollar of it will buy two Japanese dollars —yens, they are called. He is elated. His capital has doubled. One thousand dollars has become two thousand dollars. He makes purchases. His Japanese paper and silver are taken everywhere. And then one day he awakes to the fact that half his purchases have been price-listed in Korean coinage, and that he has been paying Japanese dollars for Korean dollars, which is to say that each transaction of that nature has involved a loss of roughly 33⅓%.

No one ever saw a Korean dollar. Nevertheless, a Korean dollar is worth less than a Japanese dollar; and though one does not handle Korean dollars, one loses money by them. One hundred Japanese cents will buy, or would buy, say, 150 Korean cents. When I was in Seoul, 100 Japanese cents would buy one 140 Korean. I sent my interpreter down to Chemulpo to buy. Had he bought the evening he arrived he would have received 154. He waited till next day for a better price, but the market slumped and he bought at 148.

Japanese coinage can only be used in the treaty ports and capital. Outside these half dozen cities Korean coinage must be used. The unit of Korean coinage is the Chinese cash. It is a round piece of copper with a square hole punched through it. The square hole enables it to be strung on strings. A stout pack horse can carry about fifty American dollars worth of cash. An afternoon's shopping would require a couple of coolies to carry the money. To pay a debt of two or three thousand dollars would require several pack-trains, while all that a robber could carry away on his back would not constitute a serious loss to the one robbed.

But the nickel saves the day, or partially saves it. Several months journey in the country would be impossible without it. Five cash make one 5-pun piece—a round copper coin, unpunched and rarely seen. Five 5-pun pieces make a nickel. This nickel is the largest coin in circulation. All nickels are counterfeit. Everybody knows they are counterfeit, but only the clumsy counterfeits are rejected, and then, only by the poorer people. In fact, the nickel itself makes so bulky a coinage that it is counted as infrequently as possible. The way of the country around Seoul and Chemulpo is to wrap it up in rolls of paper of 50 nickels each. If you owe a man five dollars you give him two rolls. You do not count it. He does not count it. You did not count it when you received it, nor will he count it when he pays it out.

When I left Seoul for the north I took with me fifty dollars (American) worth of nickels for my traveling expenses. Fifty American dollars bought 100 Japanese dollars, which, in turn, bought 148 Korean dollars. The 148 Korean dollars, in bogus nickels, weighed forty pounds. And with the forty pounds of nickels, I took with me the satisfying conviction that I had mastered the mysteries of Korean coinage.

Alas and alack, I had just entered upon my novitiate. At Ping Yang a missionary, Mr. Koons, proved it to me.

"What do you mean by Korean dollars?" he demanded. "I do not understand the term."

"A Korean dollar," I said proudly, "is 100 Korean cents. One and forty-eight-one-hundredths Korean cents makes one Japanese cent. Two Japanese cents make one American cent. Q. E. D."

Mr. Koons looked at me pityingly. "Sit down, old man," he said, "and let me explain it to you. To commence with, you're all wrong and must begin all over."

I sat down.

"The unit of Korean coinage is a yang."

"By yang you mean cash," I interrupted, with laudable desire of expediting matters.

He shook his head sadly.

"Then what is a yang?" I asked humbly. "I am at your feet. Elucidate."

He elucidated.

"A yang is 4 nickels."

"Twenty Korean cents," I again interrupted.

"I tell you there is no such thing as a Korean cent." His voice slightly rose, and I could see he was irritated. "A yang is the unit, and henceforth, if you wish to get along you must use only yang, speak only yang, think only yang."

I was anxious to show that I possessed some intelligence, so I said, "Yes, I understand now if 4 nickels make one yang, 5 yang make one dollar."

He threw up his hands in despair. "How often must I tell you there is no such thing as a Korean dollar?"

I subsided, and begged him to proceed.

"That is all," he said.

"Four nickels make one yang," I recited. "The yang is the unit, the yang is everything."

He nodded his head delightedly.

"Can I buy nickels farther north than Ping Yang?" I asked.

"No," was his depressing reply, "and furthermore, that stuff won't be worth a cent up there. Nobody will look at it."

By "that stuff," he meant the Japanese paper money in my pocketbook.

"Then what am I going to do?" I queried helplessly. "I may be gone with the troops for months. I have two mapus, a cook, and interpreter. I have five horses. My daily expenses are heavy —in nickels. I shall need a dozen ponies and half a dozen more mapus to carry my money for me and that will increase my daily expenses, so that I shall have to get still more mapus and pack horses."

"In the south, your situation would be just as you state it," said Mr. Koons. "But in North Korea it is different. You must buy silver dollars."

"But I thought there were no Korean—" I began.

"Hold on, old man, take it easy. These are Japanese silver dollars. Just listen to me. You buy them and they will be taken in all the large villages in the north—if there are any villagers left to take them."

"How much do they weigh?" I asked.

"Let me see," he calculated; "100 silver yen weigh six pounds."

"Then will you buy me 18 pounds of them, and a few pounds of nickels?"

I handed him $300 in Japanese paper. He looked at it in amazement.

"Just now," he said, "it will require 430 paper dollars to buy 300 silver dollars."

"But the paper dollars are gold dollars," I protested. "They are backed by gold."

"But the silver dollars are not money at all," he retorted. "They're so much silver, that is all. They're bullion. Besides, you don't lose anything."

"Hold on," I interjected. "I have followed you carefully and closely. I thought I understood and now you tell me that when I pay 430 gold dollars for 300 silver dollars that I am not losing anything. Let me hold my head and think for a while."

"But don't think too long," he smiled. "This war is depreciating Japanese paper. You are losing money every moment that paper remains in your hands."

"I do not understand, but I believe you," I said. "I have faith in what you say. I put myself and my money into your hands. Buy, and buy now, 300 silver yen."

"You'll have to buy at about 750," he said.

"Seven fifty what for what?" I asked.

"Why 750 cash per paper yen for each silver yen which is rated at 1000 cash."

"But I thought the yang was the unit," I said, "I had just begun to speak yang, to think yang and dream yang, and now you hurl me back to cash.

"But never mind," I added hastily. "Don't try to explain. I know I am a dunce. Buy, and buy now, before this paper becomes worthless."

And he sent out to a Christian money-lender to buy. It was evening, and I departed to my quarters. My interpreter met me with a beaming countenance. Had I heard the news. What news? Why that an order had been issued from Tokio commanding that the army note should circulate at 10 yang to the yen, which was equivalent to 1000 cash.

"But how about the gold paper?" I demanded.

"Eleven hundred and twenty-five cash to each yen," was the answer.

And I was selling 430 yen at 750 when I could be receiving 1125!

I wanted to stop the deal, but it was too late.

"You haven't lost anything," Mr. Koons explained to me.

"I trust—I believe—I have faith—" I murmured sympathetically.

"Just wait and see, old man," he said sympathetically.

I waited. I waited five days. And then, in spite of the government's fiat, Dunn bought at 620.

"So you see, I was right," said Mr. Koons.

And then we went to dinner.

"You were lucky in buying when you did," said Dr. Moffett. "Last January I bought at 1180. You bought at 750; Mr. Dunn bought at 620; and between you you have bought so much that if you tried to buy any more the yen would fall to 500."

"That is all the army note is worth now in Ping Yang," said somebody else.

"There are notices posted on the gates of the city," said another, "that the army note will be redeemed at Pong-san at 10 yang to the yen. —Which is 1000 cash," was added for my benefit.

Pong-san was but fifty miles south, yet the same note, in Ping Yang, was circulating at 500 cash.

"We do not know—cash or yang at Un-san," said an Englishman just down from the mines at the place, which was about ninety miles north of Ping Yang. "We reckon Korean money in dollars and cents."

Mr. Koons looked at him, and he looked at Mr. Koons.

"I have faith—I believe," I found trembling on my lips, and had just time to shut them and keep the words in.

So I left Ping Yang with 18 pounds of silver yens and 30 pounds of nickels in my treasure-chest. Every time I heft the weight of it, I feel rich, but how rich I cannot tell for the life of me. I do not know what anything costs me—at least in intelligible terms. I pay 15 Korean cents for three eggs. I know that that means 3 nickels, three-quarters of a yang, or 75 cash. But what three-quarters of a yang, or 75 cash are equivalent to in terms of American coinage is beyond me. I am short on writing paper and dare not sit down to figure it out. Besides, I don't think I could figure it out in a paper factory.

And anyway, I have faith and believe, so what's the good of figuring it out?

HOW THE HERMIT KINGDOM BEHAVES IN TIME OF WAR

SUNAN, 50 li north of Ping Yang. March 12/04.

Here at the village of Sunan, some sixteen miles north of Ping Yang and on the main Pekin Road which leads straight to the Russians, I wait and wait for permission to go onward. East I may ride, and west and south, as far as I please; to the north I may ride a hundred yards, and then a Japanese guard turns out and warns me back.

Sunan, and it must have contained four or five thousand inhabitants, is practically deserted. Already the doors and windows have begun to disappear, and inside the houses are quite bare.

A captain, with a company of men, is in charge of the town; and each day it is his duty to make arrangements and billet the soldiers which arrive each night from the south and push on next morning into the north. Naturally, the houses thus occupied by the never-ending procession of troops have been abandoned by their owners.

But the rest of the villagers have fled as well, even those living on the outskirts. Ten years ago, when the Chinese came down the self-same road, the villagers learned what occupation by soldiers meant. This time the Russian scouts came down and went back, and the Japanese are going up; while the villagers are hitting the high places for their hiding-places in the hills.

Each day the men trickle back along the foot-paths to have a "look see" and to carry away more of their household goods. As they took the most valuable first, and continued to do this, their loads are now quite bulky, being composed of rolls of matting, great earthenware pots and jars and such things as planks and the iron-work used in their houses. Some are even carrying away their doors and windows. When the Chinese were in Sunan they burned such things in their campfires.

The next salient characteristic of the Korean after inefficiency, is curiosity. He likes to "look see." *Koo-kyung* is his word for it, and a *koo-kyung* is to him what plays, lectures, sermons, horse-shows, menageries, excursions, picnics, and what not are to us. And in this he has one advantage over us—it comes cheaper. To the Korean a "look see" is the sum of all delight. The most trivial thing or event is sufficient to hold him for hours, and for hours he will stand or squat, just looking and seeing.

The Sunanites, now that they have carted away their goods and chattels, and having learned that the Japanese soldiers will not harm them, come back each day from their retreats for a *koo-kyung*. And it is a perpetual *koo-kyung*. Soldiers and supplies are continually coming by, and between whiles they have me.

I live on the main street in a deserted house of which I have taken possession, and all day long there is a rapt and admiring audience before my door. It is like a Japanese play, because it lasts all day. The curtain never rings down. Korean houses are so made that for light and air the doors must be opened. Mine are open, and it keeps Manyoungi, my Korean factotum, on the jump to force the crowd back so that light and air may come in.

I am certain if I charged a penny a "look see," that I should more than clear expenses; and I am equally certain that a head charge of a nickel would yield a handsome dividend on the capital invested in this trip by Mr. Hearst. The first of the audience arrives before breakfast and in wonder and amaze watches me turn out and wash. With the explanation that the Korean does not wash, his wonder and amaze will be understood.

Each doing of mine is duly noted and before nightfall is spread to the remotest recesses of the hills. Some of my actions are greeted with shouts and exclamations. There is a constant discussion going on as to why I do this or that; but my star performance is shaving. When Manyoungi brings the hot water and I lather my face the street blocks up. The marching troops have to force their way through; it is like a street in front of a metropolitan newspaper when the election returns are being posted.

I no longer live an obscure and private life. All my functions, from eating to sleeping are performed in public, as, for instance, yesterday, when I became aware of a suspicious itching of the skin and approached the doorway for better illumination. Manyoungi helped me in the quest, and as we sought for signs of

vermin, a man in the fore front of the audience began to talk
to Manyoungi. I thought he had experience in the matter and
was giving advice. But no, for Manyoungi said to me: "This
man Korean nobleman. Him very kind. Wantee you go live
his house. Very clean house."

I looked. He was clad in spotless white, his face was washed,
and his rounded lines showed all the evidences of prosperous
eating. His house, I learned, was a long distance off the main
road, which would not do at all; and while I changed my
undergarments I courteously declined the invitation. But it was
the most intimate interview with a nobleman I ever had in my
life.

In the middle of the day, when the sun tempers the bite of
the wind which sweeps down from across Siberia, it is my custom
to go for a ride. First, I ride north my allotted hundred
yards for the pleasure of having my guards turn out and warn
me back. Then I turn to the east, following the trend of the
village, and ride to Captain Teshima's quarters. Captain Teshima
is my jailer, and he is "very sorry" for me, as everybody has
been "very sorry" for me ever since I struck Japan. I know half
a dozen words of Chinook, and he speaks French; so I fall
back on my interpreter in order to learn the state of Captain
Teshima's feelings for me.

He is constant, at any rate, for each day he is equally sorry
for me, and he is as courteous as he is sorry. He gives me rations
for my horses, and rice and soy (sauce) and beef for my men—
also, any information he is at liberty to divulge.

I learn to-day that all other foreigners and correspondents
are being held back in Ping Yang. And as Dunn has gone
back to Ping Yang to wake the dead in an effort to get permission to proceed, I am here in Sunan alone and farthest
north. Also, I heard to-day that there was a likelihood of Dunn's
being unable to return even to Sunan. It all depends upon
whether or not he can get a pass from General Sasaki.

From Captain Teshima's I ride to the field telephone station,
which is located in a deserted temple. And after a visit to the
Red Cross doctor I turn eastward again past abandoned yamens
and temples and through the silent suburbs. No smoke curls

up from the houses, and the only life in evidence is a host of prowling, snarling dogs.

The Korean dog is a wolf-dog. Here and there will be found a strain of European stock, but through it all the wolf runs, and it is the wolf characteristics which predominate. The wolf has to predominate if the dog is to survive; for the Korean is Asiatic, and as such knows little of sympathy and kindness, and towards dumb beasts none at all. He eats his dogs, not only when he is hungry but when he wishes to titillate his stomach with a delicacy. Young dog in the spring is to him what spring lamb is to us, and old dog is just common, every day mutton.

As like as peas are many of the dogs to the sled-dogs of the Klondike, and here in the deserted streets of Sunan may be duplicated all the slight differentiations of the Klondike breed. Here also is the prototype of the Hudson Bay dog, somewhat larger than the Klondike dog, heavier, chestier, and shorter-furred.

The country, as far as the eye can see, is equally deserted. No peasants bend their backs in the fields or gather fuel from the wooded slopes. But the paths through the hills have been churned into bogs by the feet of the fugitives. Here and there, like forlorn ghosts in their white wrappings, may be seen strings of men drifting back to town for their *koo-kyung* and for any stray doors or windows which may be lying about.

But the center of things, the seething life, is to be seen on the street where I live. It is the Pekin Road, twenty-feet wide between the houses, and everything passes my door. In the afternoon I set up my photograph gallery, and the audience of Sunanites becomes perturbed, excited, and delighted. The perturbation is individual, the excitement and delight belong to the mass. The poor wight I pitch upon for my victim comes in fear and trembling to the gleeful shouts of the crowd, and each selection is hailed with a shout from all save the one selected.

One married man I was compelled to hold while the camera was snapped by proxy. He squirmed and twisted, the tears washing white channels through the coating of dirt on his face and thereby making his expression of fear the more ghastly. But this particular married man was only ten years old; yet he was a man, for no male is a man in Korea until he is married. A man is a boy, if he be a bachelor (spl?), and must wear his hair down his back; while a boy is a man, if he be married, even though no more than five or six years of age, and it is his privilege to wear his hair in a top-knot on the top of his head.

Manyoungi has quite entered into the spirit of my photography, and fares forth enthusiastically to capture any specimen I desire. Yesterday a Korean refugee, with a child and household goods on his back, drifted into Sunan, bound south. Manyoungi seized upon him forthwith, and man and boy howled and cried for very life. Between sobs the man assured me that he had done no wrong, that he was a mere nobody, a poor man who had no money, nothing. But his howls and tears redoubled when I put the camera on him, for he took the glittering mechanism for some terrible instrument of death.

Not always is Manyoungi's zeal so successful. Another refugee he captured had a child on his back the head of which was covered. Manyoungi drew the blanket back, exposing at the same time the child's face and a case of smallpox in the extreme stage. The blanket was drawn up hastily and the specimen passed on unrecorded.

At night-fall, the *koo-kyung* over, the main body of the audience disperses; but still stream by the soldiers, bullock-carts, horse-trains, and coolies. And late at night, as I crawl between my blankets, I hear the jarring of wheels and creaking of leather, the lowing of tired bullocks, squalling of ponies, curses and yells of drivers, and the crunch, crunch, crunch of hoof and sandaled foot on the frozen mud—bound north all, man and beast, to where the Russian lies in wait.

THE SUFFERINGS OF THE JAPANESE

SUNAN, March 13.—The French medical authorities estimate, upon mobilization of the French army, that after the first two weeks of marching fully 100,000 men will be in the hospitals —this being due to sore feet and breakdown from exhaustion and exclusive of those disabled by wounds. So, even before the actual fighting begins an unusually fair share of suffering is the soldier's lot. The softer the men and the greener, the greater the suffering.

Napoleon in his last days complained of his last conscripts

drawn from exhausted France: "They block my roads with their carcasses." In fact, the modern warrior is a different creature from the warrior of old time—as different as modern warfare is different from the warfare of old time. There is nothing to-day to compare with the running regiments of the Zulus, which carried no baggage and killed their own wounded; with the Mongols, mounted on shaggy ponies, their great toes thrust into looped straps for stirrups, their baggage the clothes and arms on their backs; nor with our own Viking forebears, who went out to ravage fair coasts with little more than a few casks of water in their narrow, sharp-beaked galleys.

Life was simple in those days, and war was simple. There were no preliminaries. The first intimation was the cry of the watchers on the towers or the flare of signal fires along the coast. The fighting immediately followed. But to-day, owing to the changed conditions of society and warfare, it takes a very long time to get a war officially started, and an equally long time to get the combatants together. This last is due, not to the vastness of modern armies, but to the enormous outfits which must be carried with them.

Granted that an army can live off the country, it dare not cut loose from its base because it would soon have no powder or shell or cannon balls. In ancient warfare the energy which drove home death was generated in a man's body directly from the food he had eaten. He cut his bow from the nearest wood and strung it from the tail of the horse he rode or from the hide of the bullock he killed for his last meal. Did it become necessary to besiege a city, he built his battering rams and catapults on the spot and for ammunition gathered stones from an adjacent hillside. But to-day the energy which drives home death is generated by the chemists in large factories and must be carted about by the soldiers who are to use it, while shrapnel and shell are not to be gathered from hillside until after the battle is over. Here, in Korea, six weeks have passed since the landing of the Japanese soldiers and one scout has been killed; nor is it likely that another six weeks will see any considerable bodies of Russian and Japanese soldiers locked in combat. Yet the men on both sides will be as busy as nailers getting ready to make preparations to fight.

And as the conditions of warfare have changed, so have the conditions changed which make the soldiers. The conscript of the Twentieth Century is a totally different man from the man-at-arms of the middle ages whose business was fighting and who engaged in wars that lasted sometimes beyond his life time. The conscript of to-day lives a peaceable, industrious life, and has never heard war's alarms until the moment he is jerked from out his little pigeon-hole and hurled onto the field of battle. He is practically unused to hardship, and is certainly untrained to long marching with a heavy knapsack on his back. And further, his nervous and moral fiber, so far as endurance and bloodshed are concerned, is soft and flabby when compared with the professional soldier.

It is because of these things that the French hospitals would be filled with 100,000 exhausted and crippled men within two weeks after the mobilization of the army; and it was with this in mind that I selected as most opportune for a visit the surgeon's busy day. Sunan was occupied by several hundred men of the Twelfth Division. Their function was to guard the line of communication and to be broken in to the work of soldiers. Several hours of each morning and afternoon they spent in rough field drilling. They sought shelter on their stomachs, bellied forward through muck and mire, charged imaginary Russians on distant hilltops, retreated in precipitate order, raced across the rice fields, leaped ditches or floundered through, and scaled the most inaccessible places in sight. It brought the sweat out on them and caused them to breathe heavily. In short, it was pretty severe work for they were mainly reserves, with a sprinkling of regulars, and throughout the drill they carried their knapsacks on their backs.

When the afternoon's work was over they were permitted to call on the surgeon. I called at the same time, and found him, with his assistant and a clerk, squatting on the floor of a room which measured seven by eight. The men waited outside until their names were called by the clerk. The large majority were regular cases, for they were in the book and they held tickets for admittance. For two hours I squatted at the surgeon's shoulder and watched. There was little stomach trouble, and that little caused by cold alone, and dysentery. A few had colds and were given powders, of which a heap, paper-wrapped, lay on the floor. The surgeon, in reply to my query as to what per cent had gone into hospitals since the landing at Chemulpo, said: "About nothing per cent."

But the sore feet! Fully 90 per cent of the cases were of that nature. And such sore feet! There were open sores, on which the burdened men had walked day after day. Such sores, anywhere from the size of a ten-cent piece to a half dollar, were open with hard edges and filled with proud flesh. Here, on the side of the heel, a square inch or so of skin was off. There, on the sole of the foot, would be a great callous place of the nature of a hundred corns massed into one. And the next man would exhibit a little toe, quite deformed and shapeless, or a hole in a toe into which another toe had worked nearly to the bone. At least half the men had both feet sore, and some had as many as six or eight separate sores.

Throughout it all the doctor kept up a running fire of advice and witticism. To one, whose request to be relieved from duty was denied, he said: "Before you were merely a reserve, now you are a soldier. Your feet hurt because you are unused to walking. Walk skillfully hereafter and they will cease to hurt." To another, upon whom a decidedly painful operation was performed and who had to be held by his comrades: "Why do you cry? A soldier does not cry. You are going to fight the Russians." The man ceased squirming and composed his face. To another: "Why do you come to war if you make trouble over a little thing like this?"

These men, used to the straw sandal all their lives, had been summoned to join their colors and to incase their feet in the harsh leather boot of the West. Not only this, for many of the fits were bad, or rather, there were many misfits. And yet again, the whole leg and foot action of a man who has worn sandals is different from that which comes of wearing boots. And even if the boots had fitted the feet, the very action of the feet and the legs alone would have chafed and lacerated.

It was obvious that the poor "sore feets" in the first march of 200 miles must have yearned for the pliant sandals to which they had been accustomed. But it was a vain yearning for sandals were prohibited under severe penalties. A man would, however, after his feet had been knocked up by the boots, receive permission from the surgeon to relapse into sandals.

Of course the fact that the men were reserves argues that they were unskilled in taking care of their feet; and the taking care of feet is a little science by itself which is not learned in a day. The Japanese had tramped solidly on day after day on their festering feet, making no effort to relieve the chafes and pressures, and not even washing the dirt from the sores. As the surgeon complained, accustomed as they were at home to frequent baths, they had neglected their bodies from the time they began marching.

In this connection a number may be instanced with bad sores on their bodies. These, the surgeon explained, had been caused by the chafe of belts and knapsacks and the lack of washing; and in the matter of bathing his advice to the men was continuous. He informed me that he had also advised the higher army officers that it would be expedient to arrange baths for the men wherever it was possible.

If my feet were half as bad as those of the soldiers I saw I am sure that I should elect to remain on my back for a day or so to give the misused tissues a chance to renew themselves. But next morning I beheld the "sore feets" charging across the paddy fields and up to the crest of mountains bearing what to many of them must have been excruciating pain. So one pays the penalty of being a twentieth century soldier, of being unpracticed in the science of footgear and of being compelled to carry his destroying energy in heavy cartridge boxes slung outside his body instead of inside in the arm and shoulder muscles.

And in the afternoon, after torturing their feet for additional hours, they returned to the surgeon for fresh patching up. And with adhesive plasters, wads of cotton and simple medicines he patches. A pleasing operation, this patching, and one that recommends itself to the intelligence. And yet—how shall I say?— there seems another side to it. Here is man, a rational creature, a creator of wonder and of beauty, and of marvels. He has enslaved the blind elements and forced them to do his work for him, weighed the sun as a grocer might weigh sugar and measured the distances between the stars more correctly than the Korean measures between villages, while in the matter of ethics he has achieved equally remarkable results and determined with keenness and precision what is right and what is wrong in the social relations of men.

Having done these things, he devotes his intelligence to the manufacture of machines of destruction, to systems of government and taxation which will enable him to equip himself with many of these machines and to use them. Also, he takes a man and instructs him in the humanities of medicine and surgery. This man becomes skilled in the alleviating of pain and the mending of injuries. And this man, with a lot of other men and with many machines of destruction, are dispatched to Korea to travel up the Pekin Road to Manchuria. His business is to see that the other men undergo the minimum of pain consequent upon such a journey. The object of this is to enable them to reach Manchuria, with their machines of destruction, in condition to inflict the maximum of pain upon some Russians they expect to find there. In brief, he mends the men that they may mar other men. The Russian surgeons, on the other hand, are doing precisely the same thing. The most striking difference between men and dogs is that of nationality. The difference between war and a dog fight seems to be one of machines to kill and surgeons to make well. The ends are the same, to kill, to kill swiftly and to kill to the uttermost.

DR. MOFFETT[1]

SUNAN, March 13, 1904. — At Ping Yang lives Dr. Moffett, an American missionary. He has lived there a long time. Also, he has a native name, and I am glad that I learned it. "Mah-mok-sah" is the Korean rendering of "Moffett," and it is a word to conjure with.

On the road to Sunan a Korean messenger, bound south, delivered a letter to me from the American mines at Un-san. He could not speak a word of English; nor could I of Korean. "Ping Yang?" I queried, with appropriate gestures indicating interrogation and prospective journeying. He nodded his head. I handed him a letter. "Dr. Moffett, Ping Yang," I said. He

[1] This must have been written as an article for the San Francisco *Examiner* but apparently did not reach the editor. Our copy was taken from a holograph which is in the Henry E. Huntington Library.

looked blank. I repeated it, with gestures of one syllable. He looked blanker. Then we stood in the middle of the muddy road and stared in mutual blankness. The cold north wind whistled by, with a flurry or two of snow. I looked vainly down the reaches of the Pekin Road for Manyoungi, my gem of Korean boys with whom pigeon English always achieved results. He was behind, I knew not how many miles, with the pack-horses.

Then I turned upon that Korean messenger and wrestled with him. He wrestled back. I increased the number and simplicity of my gestures. He gesticulated back. We contorted our faces, wrote Odysseys on the air with our wildly waving arms, and in the throes of a great desire for understanding broke simultaneously into speech. I matched his Korean with my English. He vied with me. We shouted, and, again, lapsed into periods of attentive silence. I gave up in despair and started on my way. His thirst for knowledge must have been severe, for he followed me entreatingly. I stopped my horse and we gathered together and wrestled it all over again.

He gave up and started south. I called after him pleadingly, shouted commandingly, and we closed in a third bout. As we assumed expressions of regret preliminary to our final parting, I suddenly remembered my notebook and that therein I had inscribed Dr. Moffett's native name. I pulled the book out eagerly, but the man regarded me with skepticism. He knew, past all doubt, that I was unintelligible. He had proved it. He turned to go, but I caught him by the arm and held him till I found the place, and then I said, slowly and carefully and distinctly: "Mah-mok-sah."

Infinite comprehension dawned upon his face, and there flooded over it waves of happiness like unto that of angels. I knew it was all right and gave him the letter. It went through that very day; and thereafter, not alone in my notebook, but on the tablets of my memory, I carried the magic name, Mah-mok-sah.

It is a sympathetic bond capable of connecting me with half the Koreans I encounter. Yesterday I rode over the snow-clad hills to the east on a foot path churned knee-deep with mud by the refugees from Sunan. Shrewdly sheltered in an elbow of the hills I found a tiny village. The children fled at sight of me, without doubt considering me a Russian; while the elders, after a while, crept timidly forth—a sort of committee of safety, I took it, for anxiety was writ large on their faces and by meek gestures I was invited to leave.

I caught the eye of the chief elder, and said, "Mah-mok-sah."

At once into his face came that familiar dawn of infinite comprehension. He opened his arms to me. So did the village. I was invited to dismount and to enter the houses to be entertained. My horse was entertained. They were loth to have me depart, and when I finally did tear myself away the whole village turned out to guide me on a short cut back to Sunan.

From which experience, and divers others, I am driven to conclude that Dr. Moffett has no need to be ashamed of his own name, while of avoiding pride in his Korean name his need must be great indeed.

To-day I had a visitor. It was the chief elder of the tiny village in the elbow of the hills. He removed his shoes and came in and squatted down on the mat before me.

"Mah-mok-sah," he said. It was a word to conjure with both ways, for it warmed the cockles of my heart and I sent for Manyoungi.

The frightened Sunanites were beginning to come back, my visitor told me. Or, at least, a small percentage of the men were returning to their forsaken homes. At first they had been struck and kicked by the soldiers; but the officers had issued orders against this and the ill-treatment had promptly ceased. Also, the Sunanites were beginning to make money.

Yes, the Japanese paid for everything, but the people were just learning how to gather to themselves the profits. Previously the officers had bought through the "Number One Man," who had obtained the supplies from the villagers but pocketed the proceeds. Or, to be exact, he had paid them about thirty cents on the dollar and kept the difference.

"Number One Man" was Manyoungi's English equivalent for magistrate. A most detestable magistrate he was, named Pak-Choon-Song, a *yang-ban* or nobleman, and a robber. Now all *yang-bans* are robbers. The people expect them to rob. They have never known anything else than robbery on the part of their rulers. But there are degrees of robbery—"squeeze" is what they call it. A fair squeeze is legitimate. A magistrate who robs within reason is loved by his people, and when he departs elsewhere they select a suitable spot near the city entrance and erect a monument in honor of the temperateness with which he robbed.

But such a man was not Pak-Choon-Song. While I interviewed the chief elder a mob of Sunanites crowded my doors and backed him up in the charges he made. They were unanimous in asserting that Pak-Choon-Song kept seventy per cent of all moneys due them for goods sold to the Japanese officers. Yes, it was true, they were receiving their money now, but that was because they were dealing directly with the Japanese. On the other hand, and up to very recently, they had been robbed grievously by Pak-Choon-Song, and after the Japanese went away they were going to rise up and kill him.

As Manyoungi translated the woes of his people, I could see him growing angrier and angrier, his swarthy skin made more swarthy as the hot blood rose in his face.

"Much poor people," he said suggestively. I took no notice. "Very much poor people," he added a little later.

But I kept him busy translating the chorus of woe and complaint which rushed in through both doors upon me. Finally, unable longer to restrain himself, he spoke straight out: "Master go see Number One Man."

What faith he had in my power and nerve I know not; but in his short life he had learned, what all Asiatics learn, that justice is a characteristic belonging peculiarly to the white man, and that from the white man only is it obtainable. His eyes did not drop. He looked straight into mine, and in the look there was challenge as well as request.

I did not reply at once, but turned to Mrs. Isabella Bird Bishop's book on Korea. On page 86 therein I read her description of a visit she had once paid to a Korean magistrate and which was a sample of the treatment she received from all magistrates.

"One attendant, by no means polite, took my *kwan-ja* to the magistrate, and very roughly led the way to two small rooms, in the inner one of which the official was seated on the floor, surrounded by a few elderly men. We were directed to stand at the opening between the two rooms, and behind us pressed as many of the crowd as could get in. I bowed low. No notice was taken. An attendant handed the magistrate a pipe, so long that it would have been impossible for him to light it for himself, and he smoked. Mr. Miller hoped that he was in good health. No reply, and the eyes were never raised. Mr. Miller explained the object of the visit, which was to get a little information about the neighborhood. There was only a very curt reply, and as the great man turned to one of his subordinates and began to talk with him, and rude remarks were circulating, we took leave, with the usual Korean phrases of politeness, which were not reciprocated."

I laid the book down. Manyoungi was still looking at me, and the challenge had not died out of his eyes—keen black eyes in which I knew I dared not lose prestige. Besides, there was Mrs. Bishop. I might at least avenge her. Also, here I was cooped up in the desolate village of Sunan by order of His Imperial Japanese Majesty's Minister of War, unable to proceed the matter of a few miles to the firing-line, and decidedly bored by my own society.

"Manyoungi," I said, and I began to practice what I imagined was the pompousness of a *yang-ban*, "Manyoungi, go to Number One Man's house. Catch Number One Man. Tell him I come in two hours and that he must wait for me. If he no wait tell him I get very much angry. Understand?"

Manyoungi was transfigured. His face shone like the full moon. "Yes, master," he said exultantly, "I very much understand. I go now."

And he went, splitting the crowd at the door like the stem of a ship cutting a sea.

"Oh, Isabella Bird Bishop," I thought, "if you had only sent such a summons how different your treatment might have been!" But that was ten years back, and she had had no invading army at her heels. Decidedly her treatment would have been different.

Two hours later I walked up to the *yamen* of Pak-Choon-Song. It was beautifully located on rising ground overlooking Sunan, but was in a sad state of disrepair. Everything had gone to rack and ruin, including the erstwhile rudeness of the now and exalted flagstones of a courtyard as like as two peas to the one described by Mrs. Bishop. The torn paper was fluttering from the lattice windows and the lacquer and paint were scaling off. And to two precisely similar small rooms was I led, in the inner one of which sat Pak-Choon-Song upon the floor.

It was strangely familiar. I had seen it all before—through Mrs. Bishop's eyes. There were the elderly men surrounding the magistrate, the unrecognizing, unseeing, and supercilious hauteur of that worthy, and the crowd pressing in on my heels. But some of the things Mrs. Bishop's eyes had seen I resolved mine should not see; so, to prevent being posted like a dime museum freak in the opening between the two rooms, I promptly walked over and sat down on the cushions beside Pak-Choon-Song.

The attendants were aghast. Pak-Choon-Song, for all his studied indifference, could not forbear stealing an apprehensive look at me out of the corner of his oblique eyes. He did not speak. Manyoungi was standing and being shouldered by the crowd, more of which had jammed in. In his head was the ferment of a new idea, the Western idea of the rights of man. In his head were mutiny and revolt. In his head, though dimly perhaps, were the ideas of Revolutionary France. In his head were hatred for the *yang-ban* class and defiance. But in the soul of him was the humility of generations, a thing not to be downed in a day by any idea of the head. I do verily believe that his humble demeanor was as much reflex action as that of the new-born fly-catcher bursting its head through the shell and snapping its beak at the first passing insect.

I wondered if he was going to funk, and ordered him to sit down—an unheard of proceeding in the presence of so exalted a personage as a heaven-born *yang-ban*. He looked about him dubiously and fearfully.

"Sit down," I said sharply. He sat, but in doing so made obvious effort to occupy the least space possible.

"Tell them to get out," I said, pointing at the crowd.

Manyoungi talked to them in a respectfully subdued voice, and the sight of their going seemed to help him pull himself together.

"Tell them to get out," I said, pointing at the elderly men who surrounded Pak-Choon-Song in a sort of body guard.

And oh, if only Mrs. Isabella Bird Bishop had been there to see them go!

"Tell him I have come to see him," I said—and it was quite

to the point, for so far he had been superbly unaware of my existence and of the fact that I was present. Upon this intimation Pak-Choon-Song looked in my direction and officially discovered that I was there. He was a large man, nearly six feet in height as I afterward learned and his body looked comfortably dimensioned under its spotless white robes. He was full-featured and bearded, and towered above me as he sat there on the floor. What of his size and mien and spotless robes in so tiny a room he seemed for all the world a tenderly cherished joss in some temple sanctuary. His hands were white and soft as a woman's, and I am sure he was flabby; while his face had that sickly whiteness of a swarthy skin sheltered for a lifetime from the rays of the sun.

He asked if my health was good. I reciprocated, and for five minutes we outdid each other in politeness. In the end the victory fell to him. It always does. There is no coping in such things with the Asiatic and all the while his heavy-lidded eyes studied me with that species of cunning which is best described as Oriental or vulpine.

I enquired about the advent of the Russian scouts, their retreat, and the subsequent advent of the Japanese. He was voluble in his replies, and the time passed. Manyoungi, whose head, by now, had again dominated his soul, grew impatient.

"Master," he suggested, "you speak Number One Man him catch very poor people's money. Him keep allee time no give. Very poor people, very much poor."

I explained that I would work around to it, and went on. Yes, Pak-Choon-Song had furnished the Japanese soldiers with fuel and rice and forage for their horses, and he had been paid for the same. Where had he obtained the fuel, rice, and forage? From the people. Then why did he not pay the people the money which belonged to them?

Manyoungi was like a wrathful angel as he translated the question. His voice, no longer subdued, rang like a trumpet in the tiny room. He sat up erect, and his sunburned face grew dark.

Pak-Choon-Song glowered at me in speechless anger. Of course, it must be understood that directness is as repulsive to the Oriental mind as the violation of every one of the Ten Commandments is to the Occidental. Besides, I had begun by being so beautifully indirect, and then to spring this most brutal, point-blank directness upon him! He would have looked reproach at me had he not been so angry. He glanced about him and made as though to call his attendants, while I wondered what kind of a fight Manyoungi could put up and wished fervently that Mrs. Bishop could be looking on.

But the times had changed. Who or what I was, or what were my powers, Pak-Choon-Song did not know. He knew only that I was a visitant in the chaos of war, that his authority was not what it once was, and that I was mystery and to be feared.

His anger faded away to helplessness. The lines which years of authority had put into his face likewise faded. He began to talk to Manyoungi, in soft insinuating tones. He talked and talked. The insinuating tones sank into a seductive crooning. Waiting, I nearly dozed off to sleep. And the upshot of it all was that he pleaded not guilty and that I was mistaken, that I did not understand.

"What you think?" I asked Manyoungi.

"I think him lie," was the reply.

I explained the condition of the poor people to Pak-Choon-Song. I drew harrowing pictures of their poverty and suffering and demonstrated that a squeeze of seventy per cent was more than they could stand.

Pak-Choon-Song was very sorry for the poor people. I asked for some more substantial expression of his sorrow than mere words. Pak-Choon-Song did not understand. I grew immediately afraid. "I do not understand" is the impregnable citadel of the Oriental. When once he has retreated to it, everything is up. There is nothing in the universe capable of dislodging him. So I hastened to cut off Pak-Choon-Song's retreat. I looked very severe, and Pak-Choon-Song looked at me, while I explained very minutely every detail of the process of giving back to the people the seventy-per-cent squeeze.

He said he understood, and he promised faithfully that every cent of it would be returned. There was nothing more to be said. The mission was accomplished. I arose to go. A swarm of attendants appeared. Pak-Choon-Song himself saw me to the door, and he saw me through the door, and through two more rooms, and down the steps, and across the courtyard to the outer gate, and at the top of the last flight of stairs bade me an obsequious goodbye.

But so far as concerned the return of the seventy-per-cent squeeze, I knew, and Manyoungi knew, and Pak-Choon-Song knew and we all knew one another knew, that Pak-Choon-Song intended nothing of the sort.

Examiner WRITER SENT BACK TO SEOUL

SEOUL, Korea, March 28.—A war is like a tea party—whoever gives it runs it, and the guests must smile and be polite, no matter how bored they may be. At present Japan is running the war, with Russia a lagging assistant, while the correspondents are trying to smile and be as polite as they can. They began to arrive in Japan early in January, and here, at the end of March, the majority of them are still in Japan. They are still in Japan because their kind hosts, the Japanese, have not yet given them permission to proceed to the front.

There are no signs that such permission will be given them anywhere in the near future, but they are an optimistic lot, these correspondents, and they still cherish the belief that they will arrive at the front in time for the finish. In the meantime they are wined and dined by their hosts and spend the rest of their time in receiving dispatches of the following nature from their papers: "Why no Tokio news?" "What is the matter with the Tokio service?" "Why no news from the front?"

Every little while—so I am given to understand—they get together and pass resolutions. Then they proceed in a body to one or another of the Japanese officials who are guiding their destinies, and a conversation like the following takes place:

Correspondents: "General So-and-So, we have held a meeting and decided that we must proceed immediately to the front."

General So-and-So: "By the way, the Japanese newspaper men are getting up a dinner for you."

Correspondents: "When may we proceed to the front?"

General So-and-So: "This dinner is six days off."

Correspondents: "We have made up our minds, permission or no permission to leave Japan."

General So-and-So: "You will all wear evening dress at the dinner."

Correspondents visibly angry.

General So-and-So: "And by the time the dinner takes place we will have news for you concerning your departure."

Correspondents go away mollified and encouraged, and when six days are past and the dinner is dined, the thing is repeated and they find themselves lingering on in Tokio for another dinner.

And at last, when even Asiatic indirection can no longer hold them, they are promised, definitely, that on a certain date they will receive their permits. The day arrives, the permits are received, but—the permits are the first of a string of permits. Attached to each permit is a slip which attests its worthlessness until further permits are obtained.

There is the matter of assignment, for instance. What good is a general permit to accompany the army when one lacks the assignment to a particular column of that army? A few more weeks and a few more dinners, and the assignments are obtained, and then—well, the correspondents are still in Tokio, in possession of permits and assignments, and waiting for the permit of permits, the final permit, which will allow them to go to the front. And somewhere down dim and apparently interminable vistas of dinners the more hopeful of them believe that they catch the vague loom of the final permit.

It may be wondered why I, a war correspondent, am writing all this, not about war, but about war correspondents. The explanation is simple. There is no war, so far as I am concerned, to write about. Seoul has become a backwater. The little flurry of war it experienced has passed on into the north. And here I remain, assigned to the first column, an army which has been in Korea nearly two months, and which is even now fighting in the north, and which I may not join until the permit of permits, the final permit, is given me. In military parlance, I am in Seoul under instructions from the War Department and awaiting further instructions.

And there are others in Seoul in like predicament. While we are geographically nearer the seat of war than those in Tokio, from the point of knowing what is taking place we are even farther away than the humblest citizens of the United States or Europe. We are in a backwater. We know nothing. We have no daily paper filled with telegrams from all the world, and when we do get a little war information it is already ancient history to the rest of the world.

It is true, we made a dash for the front—three of us. Luckily for us, we escaped from Japan before war was declared and in various ways arrived in Chemulpo—Dunn and McKenzie arriving in time for the naval fight, while I was still hammering up the west coast of Korea in a sampan. The rest of the correspondents, overpersuaded by their kind hosts, politely lingered and dined in Japan. That was two months ago. They are still dining.

When the first troops left Seoul to march north, Dunn, McKenzie, and I started out, leaving directions for our permits to follow us, and thereby hung the string by which the War Department had hold of us, and also by which the dining correspondents of Tokio had hold of us.

Ignoring endless dissuasion from the army officers we encountered, we managed to make the first 180 miles to Ping Yang. There McKenzie was dissuaded, and Dunn and I headed valiantly northward for Anju, Wiju and the Yalu, only to be stopped and held at the village of Sunan.

And this is how it was: The dining correspondents at Tokio said to their hosts: "Here we are. We have been very polite. These other men are at the front, three of them. They are very impolite, yet see how their impoliteness has been rewarded. You must recall them. If you do not recall them we, too, shall become impolite and dine no more."

Upon hearing this dire threat, the War Department pulled the string and ordered us back for our permits. But the chief spokesman for the dining correspondents, a canny man who missed his vocation when he failed to become a statesman, attempted a little coup all by himself. Loudest in demanding our recall, and at the very moment his voice was at its topmost pitch, he secretly dispatched a subordinate with orders to catch up with us and if possible to keep on going. Thus, in the game of war correspondence, he played to win either way.

Ordered back to Ping Yang, we met the subordinate just arriving; and the next order in the retrograde movement included him, and I loaned him a horse to ride the fifty miles down to the coast at Chinnampo. Here with the ice barely out of the harbor, the bay was filled with transports and troops were being rushed ashore. But we had no time to see; we were in full retreat. The Japanese Consul, turning a deaf ear to the complaints of the captain, held a coasting steamer all afternoon and long after dark until he saw us safely on board and steaming out of the harbor, our backs to the seat of war and our faces heading south-ward to the backwaters of Chemulpo and Seoul.

And here we wait, while the war goes merrily on, wondering when the permit of permits is to arrive. We are less fortunate than our Tokio brethren. There are no dinners here—only gorgeous uncertainty and a hotel proprietor who raises the rates every little while and calls it a war price.

JAPANESE SUPPLIES RUSHED TO FRONT BY MAN AND BEAST

WIJU (Korea), April 21.—For days we had forced our horses along a road which swarmed with white-clad coolies. Their shoul-ders were stooped forward, their faces bent toward the ground, their backs burdened with rice and fish, soy and saki, and all the food supplies of an Oriental army. The villages were deserted. All doors and windows were missing and the houses appeared blank and sightless, mutely protesting against the general devas-tation. Here and there, along the road, old men and women and children sold food to the toiling coolies; and it was even possible, by proper skirmishing and fair purchase, to obtain beans for our pack-horses from the secret granaries among the hills.

And then one day, late in the afternoon, there came a change. We had dismounted and were leading our horses up the steep slope of a pass between two valleys, when a long line of horse carts, each horse led by a soldier, poured down upon us from the summit.

The thousands of Korean coolies had given place to the regular army transport. We drew our horses to one side among the rocks and waited for the line to pass. And we waited and continued to wait while the sun went down and twilight came on. But the line thickened instead of ceasing. Hundreds of pushcarts poured down in the midst of the horsecarts. Each pushcart was manned by three soldiers, and they brought the carts down so fast and thick that it was beyond us to count them.

And still they poured down from the summit of the pass, horsecarts and pushcarts, soldier-drivers, officers and occasional cavalrymen. It was but one train of many transport trains, and for the first time one began to get a true conception of what the feeding and munitioning of an army means; also we were over-joyed with knowledge of the fact that at last, after months of endeavor, we were approaching our goal.

Finally, in desperation, we forced our horses into the living stream, whenever it thinned a trifle, and slowly stemmed it to the summit. It was easier going down against it on the other side, and in the darkness we rode into the large town where we were to spend the night.

But the town was filled with soldiers. Every inch of floor space in every house was occupied. The Korean kitchen (in relation to the rest of the house) is a hole in the ground; yet every kitchen was filled with tired soldiers. So we urged our weary horses on into the darkness, and ten li farther along made ourselves lords and masters of a deserted village.

Next day, early a-saddle, we found the road as far as the eye could see across the valleys, from pass to pass and the crests of the passes, gorged with baggage trains, coming and going in double lines. There were squads of cavalry and detachments of infantry, officers mounted and officers afoot, parties of the Red Cross outfit, bunches of pioneers drifting along and repairing the road, men of the telegraph corps at work on the military wires, coolies, bullock carts, pack bullocks, trains of the little indomitable Korean ponies, tiny braying jack-asses, squealing horses—and down through it all a lone Chinese from Manchuria, looking neither to the right nor left, but heading southward with in-curious eyes and expressionless face for a land where peace still smiled.

There were not two roads, nor three, but many. Right sternly was the beautiful valley marred and scarred by the feet of war—dykes and ditches were broken down, the paddy fields churned into muck and scored with great grooves by the wagon wheels, and everywhere the patient toil of the peasant people was stamped into the earth and destroyed. And always one received, gazing into the faces of the men who had done these things, an impression of strength. Yellow peril became a tangible thing, shaped itself in the intellect, and remained to be pondered, and pondered, and be pondered yet again.

April 22. — I stood on the summit of Wiju Castle in a sort of summer pavilion and tried to convince myself that I was gazing out upon what Captain Okada was pleased to term "the theatre of war." "I am all of a tremble with excitement," confessed a correspondent beside me, a man who had been through a dozen campaigns. But for myself I was curiously apathetic.

There was nothing stirring to be seen. Below me, and seen across the battlement of Wiju's outer wall, lay the wide valley of the Yalu—a stretch of sandy flats separated by various channels of the river. From the farther banks rose the mountains of Manchuria. And that was all. The stage was empty.

It was a dreamy, peaceful day. Well does Korea merit its ancient name, Chosen—land of the morning calm. There was not a breath of air, the land shimmered in the heat and the valleys and distant mountains were vague and indistinct in the blue, summer haze. Nothing moved in all that wide expanse, and the peace and quietness of it conveyed not a hint of war.

FIGHTING AT LONG RANGE DESCRIBED

WIJU, April 30.[1] — Long-range fighting is all very well. It is a splendid example of the extent to which man has risen above his natural powers and of the knowledge he has gained in flinging missiles through the air. It is a far cry from the sling with which David went into battle to the modern field gun; and yet, such is the paradox, the sling and hand-wielded weapons of David's time, expenditure of energy being taken into consideration, were a hundred or so times more deadly than are the civilized weapons of to-day. That is to say, the hand-wielded weapons of that ancient day more simply and immediately accomplished the pur-

[1] This article was printed in the San Francisco *Examiner* on Sunday, June 5, 1904, with the following introductory statement: "Mr. London is one of the seven correspondents representing press associations and great newspapers of the world with the first Japanese army corps."

poses they were made to serve than do the weapons of to-day. Which is to say, in turn, first, that the hand-wielded weapons killed more men, and, second, that they killed more men with far less expenditure of strength, time and thought. To kill men to-day requires harder work, harder thinking, harder inventing and longer time. The triumph of civilization would seem to be, not that Cain no longer kills, but that Cain has to sit up nights scheming how he is to kill.

Take the present situation on the Yalu. On one side of a river winding through a smiling valley are a lot of Russians. On the other side are a lot more Japanese. The Japanese wish to cross. They wish to cross in order to kill the Russians on the other side. The Russians do not wish to be killed, so they prepare to kill the Japanese when they attempt to cross. It is quite impersonal. They rarely see each other. To the right, on the north bank, are some Russians who are hammering away at long distance at some Japanese who are hammering back from the islands in the river. A Japanese battery on the south bank, to the right, begins flinging shrapnel into the Russians. Some four miles away to the left, at a diagonal course across the river, a Russian battery shells this Japanese battery with an enfilading fire. This will never do. From the Japanese center a battery shells the Russian battery. Nor will this do, either. From the Russian center a battery begins hurling shells clear over a high mountain at the battery on the Japanese center. The Japanese battery on the right ceases shelling the infantry on the Russian side. And so it goes, Russian left battery changing its fire to Japanese center, Russian center changing its fire to Japanese right battery.

The net result of all this, measured in terms of killing, is practically nil. The thing effected was that each side prevented the other side from killing. The Russian right infantry was bent upon killing the Japanese infantry on the island. The Japanese right battery made the Russian infantry quit shooting and hunt cover. The Russian left battery made the Japanese right battery quit trying to kill the Russian infantry. The Japanese center battery made the Russian left battery quit trying to kill the Japanese right battery. And so on, and so on, in a sort of five-cornered duel, wherein many men and guns were engaged, much powder was burned, much intelligence exercised and no body hurt.

Of course, on the other hand, a tactical advantage may have been gained by the Japanese which strengthened their strategic movement. Now, what is a strategic movement? A strategic movement, I take it, is the manipulation of men and war machinery in such a way as to make the enemy's position untenable. An untenable position is one wherein the enemy must either surrender or be all killed. But no commander, unless he blunders, remains in an untenable position. He promptly gets out and hunts a position which is tenable. With much strategical labor he may be driven out of this, when he seeks a third. This continues, not indefinitely, but until he is cornered in the last of all tenable positions possible for him to occupy. Then the original proposition is made to him: Surrender or be killed. Of course, he surrenders. It is the same old time-worn proposition of the highwayman, "Money or your life." A traveler so addressed is usually in an untenable position, and very naturally yields up his money. A nation, when its army is finally caught in an untenable position, does just the same thing, yielding up either fat provinces, commercial privileges or a money indemnity.

At least, this is modern warfare to the mind of this layman. Whether it be with small bodies of men, large armies or groups of armies, the strategic end is the same, namely, to get men and war machinery in an untenable position, where all will be destroyed if all is not surrendered. Here, for instance, on the Yalu, are two armies opposing each other. The Japanese army, by good strategy, may make the position of the Russian army untenable and compel it to fall back. On the other hand, a second Japanese army may land to the westward, somewhere on the gulf of Liao Tung, render untenable the position of a second Russian army, which it might encounter thereabouts, and thus, being on the flank of the Russian army on the Yalu, render the position of that army untenable.

But it is the long-range fighting which makes modern warfare so different from ancient warfare. In David's time a General did not know that his position was untenable till both sides got together with the hand-wielded weapons, and then it was too late to retire, for the killing had commenced. The only men killed in

twentieth century warfare, supposing a General to be neither a
fool nor a blunderer, are those killed by accident. "Accident" is
used advisedly. Bullets have their billets, but very few bullets
have the billets intended for them, and very few soldiers see the
proper billets when they are firing their bullets. The theory seems
to be to pump lead at the landscape in such quantities that there
are bound to be some lucky accidents. While so far as shell and
shrapnel fire goes, it is the sheerest accident that a man is killed
by such means.

Certainly, if men remained in the open, they would be killed.
So would they be killed if they stood up and emptied their rifles
at each other at five hundred yards. When shrapnel begins to
fly they seek the reverse slopes, where they are quite safe.

The ratio, in warfare, of men killed to energy expended is far,
far smaller than that of men killed in house burglaries and hold-
ups, the prize ring or the football field.

When warfare was simple and weapons were crude, the killing
was on a large scale. The men got together at close range in
those days, and the battles were decisive. Even up to nearly the
close of the nineteenth century decisive battles were still possible.
As late as the Civil War the enemy could be got on the run and
chased off the battlefield. But that is not likely to happen in
future years—at least in battles between civilized peoples. The
beaten army will merely retire, and the victorious army will occupy the field at about the same rate of speed. It will have dis-
lodged the enemy by long-range fighting, and the enemy, by the
same long-range fighting, will prevent it from sweeping the field
and making the defeat a crushing defeat. The beaten army's
position will have been rendered untenable, and it will retire to
take up another and tenable position. Killing decided ancient
warfare; the possibility of being killed decides modern warfare.
In short, the marvelous and awful machinery of warfare of to-day,
defeats its own end. Made pre-eminently to kill, its chief effect
is to make killing quite the unusual thing.

When the machinery of warfare becomes just about perfect,
there won't be any killing at all. When one army gets the drop
the other army will throw up its hands and deliver the valuables
of which it is custodian. And in that day, the soldier boy's farewell

to his mother will be just about the same as his farewell to-day when he goes off for his summer vacation.

GIVE BATTLE TO RETARD ENEMY

ANTUNG (Manchuria), May 1.—It is patent that the Russians never intended to make a determined stand on the Yalu. At no time did they have many men on the north bank, and it is obvious that their intention was stubbornly to retard the Japanese advance, and so gain time for whatever preparations were being made behind them in the depths of Manchuria.

On the afternoon of April 29th the Russians set fire to the customs house and the various villages and farm houses on the islands in the river bed and retreated to the north bank. The Japanese were at last ready to cross, after having been delayed for weeks and compelled to make the most elaborate preparations. To the east lay a division, to the west a second, while a third division held the center at Wiju. The islands in the river were occupied—some peaceably, and some after slight skirmishes, bridges were built and being built across the different channels, and many places up and down the Yalu pontoons were ready to be strung together and swung across, and batteries, which the Russians had never succeeded in unmasking were hidden everywhere.

The correspondents were well in the dark as to these secret preparations. Everything was secret, the landscape fairly bristled with secrets, and, with the exception of stolen peeps at a couple of batteries, they had no knowledge where the guns were located. The area of their movements was something like two miles square. They might ride into Wiju in a party under the guidance and control of the supervising officer, but they were not permitted to ascend the heights of Wiju, overlooking the position of the center.

The supervising officer had conducted them on the first trip to the summer pavilion on the top of Wiju Castle, but the trip was never repeated. The supervising officer had made a mistake, and allowed them a closer view of the Yalu than they were to have been permitted. Nor were they allowed to approach the Yalu on the right or left, their glimpses of that stream being caught from distant hill tops well in the rear.

The burning of the island villages and the customs house was the first intimation that the crossing of the Yalu was imminent. On the same evening rations for the servants and interpreters were issued for three days by the quartermaster, and the correspondents were bidden to repair in a body to the quarters of the supervising officer at 5:30 next morning. It was too late for them to give the secret away. Before their dispatches would get out to the world (five days in transit) the Yalu would be crossed.

The morning of April 30th was hazy. The sun shone dimly, and the distant valleys and canyons seemed filled with the smoke of some vast conflagration. But this cleared away with the growing day, and the valley of the Yalu lay before us. Half a mile in front of us was Wiju Castle, on the summit of which, adjoining the summer pavilion, was a field battery of six guns. To the right, where a farm house topped a hill, we knew there was another battery. To the left we had a military-secret inkling of a couple more batteries, and that was all. We were more in the dark concerning the Japanese position than the Russians themselves, lying quietly on the opposite bank.

The Japanese were quiet, too. From Antung, down the river, came the occasional boom of a distant gun. Seven o'clock, eight o'clock, nine o'clock, and nothing had happened. In the valley beneath us and between us and the batteries were massed the reserves. Arms were stacked, knapsacks discarded, and the men were lying on the reverse slope, sheltered against shell fire, mostly asleep, stretched out in long windrows, their dark blue uniforms blotted against the pale brown of last year's dried grass. Cooks were at work in the bottom of the valley; men were shoeing horses, and pack trains were moving along the military road which threaded the sheltered valley parallel to the river.

In a little ravine several soldiers were digging a spring, and another soldier, back from foraging amongst the hills, burdened with sprays of white blossom, had stopped to gossip with them.

At 10 o'clock the Japanese battery on the right fired the first gun. Following the report was a sound as of the violent ripping of a vast sheet of cloth, as the shell tore through the atmosphere and sighed away in the distance. Two miles away, across the river and to the right of Tiger Hill, there was a bright flash, a puff of smoke and a dust-cloud rose where the flying shrapnel tore the earth.

After that the report of the bursting shell was borne to the ear. Gun after gun opened up, right along the line to the Japanese left, where, from Kin-tei-lao island, in the middle of the river, unexpected batteries of field guns and howitzers unmasked. These batteries the Japanese had advanced from the south bank the previous night under cover of darkness.

The Russians replied with two batteries—one from behind Tiger Hill, the other from a conical hill on the Russian right, near to the village of Kuel-ian-ching. For half an hour this artillery duel continued, no visible damage being done to the Japanese. A few shells fell here and there amongst the reserves at our feet, but not immediately amongst them.

At 10:30, when the lull came in the firing, a farm house flamed up to the right of Tiger Hill. By the time a second house was flaming our glasses made out the several Russians who were responsible. Whenever one emerged from a house the burning thatch quickly showed his handiwork. The Russians were retiring.

At this time a dark line, thin as a hair, was observed crawling along the base of the rugged mountains which rise to the eastward on the Manchurian shore. This line was hugging the shore and moving westward toward the burning houses and Tiger Hill. The Japanese had effected their lodgment on the north bank. The Mikado's troops were in Manchuria. They were the men of the East Division, who had crossed on pontoons the preceding night.

It was plain that they had met with no opposition and were meeting with no opposition, else they would not have been strung out in a thin line for miles. The Russians in process of retiring had not contested their crossing, and what was then the execution of their flanking movement.

Soon they began to swarm up the steep mountains—precipitous mountains, they might be called. The line crept up the slopes and over the brows till the head lost itself to the northward. The Russian battery behind Tiger Hill peppered it with a few ineffectual rounds of shrapnel, and in return was roundly hammered by the batteries of the Japanese right and center.

It was preparing to retire, and voiced its farewell by suddenly turning loose on the battery in front of us, adjoining the summer pavilion. That battery promptly went out of business. Not that it had to go out, but it had no cause to endure needless punishment. The gunners sought shelter in the casemates. The glasses showed the six guns deserted. Not a man was in sight, and the Russians could have shelled till Doomsday without injuring a soul. A few of their shells went clear over and burst in the houses of Wiju.

In the meantime they were being enfiladed by the batteries on the Japanese right, and when they ceased fire they ceased fire for good, withdrawing their battery up the opening in the mountains made by the Ai-ho river. At once the deserted battery in front of us sprang into life, and the Japanese farewell went shrieking over Tiger Hill and up the mouth of the Ai-ho to the retreating Russians.

To the west, on the Russian right, the battery on the conical hill opened on the Japanese batteries on Kin-tei-lao island and gave them a thorough shelling. The white sand was flung into great fountains, and the whole island seemed afire, so much smoke was there from the bursting shells.

In return the whole Japanese fire was concentrated on the conical hill, shrapnel and common shell, till the hill, in turn, resembled a smoldering mountain. The Russians could scarcely stand by their guns under such a rain, and their guns were silenced. And then, in the very thick of it, one gun spoke again and continued resolutely to speak for some time.

Then all guns ceased. The day was over. On the north bank remained only a few thousand Russians and one battery, and beyond a doubt the battery would withdraw during the night. The 30th of April was nearing its close. The morrow was the 1st of May. The Yalu was waiting to be crossed.

During the night the Japanese threw their whole force upon the islands. The three divisions, generally supposed to be strung out along the river front for a matter of fifty miles, were concentrated upon the immediate front at Wiju. The strategy, experts declared, was perfect. The center division, on the center, was to storm the front. The west division, on the left, and the east division on the right and already lodged and away over the hills, were ready to strike the enemy's flanks.

But there was no sign of the enemy, and first he must be searched for with shell and shrapnel, this in lieu of cavalry, the operation of which was impractical on a river bed divided into many islands by various channels.

The search was vain. The hills were explored for miles with the death-dealing, noisy missiles, but no Russian gun replied. They had no guns with which to reply. Their battery had withdrawn and was then on the Pekin Road in full retreat.

From the outer wall of Wiju we watched the searching artillery fire and the thin Japanese lines beginning to move across the open sand. Their batteries worked vigorously, their lines drew closer to the ridge and conical hill where Russian guns had thundered the previous day. Closer, still closer, and the north shore silent, when suddenly, at half-past 7, there arose a rowdy bubbling sound, like water boiling in a pot.

The foremost Japanese line, on the naked sand under the conical hill, broke back for cover. The specks of men, at regular distance, running back could be clearly seen, and as they ran gaps formed in the line, the distance became irregular and the specks diminished in number. The Russians had opened fire. The rowdy bubbling was the reports of the rifles of the thousand or so men left behind to cover the Russian retreat.

The Japanese never stopped nor hesitated. Twice they reinforced their line, advancing at the double across the shelterless sands, the while every gun of every battery worked at fever heat shelling the ridge and conical hill till at times the Russian position was literally obscured by the smoke of bursting cannon shell and shrapnel.

The Japanese are so made that nothing short of annihilation can stop them. Patriotism is their religion and they die for their country as the martyrs of other peoples die for their gods. The thin lines in front of the conical hill swung to the left, where men of the west division were already crossing a ford. To the right another ford was being crossed, the men streaming darkly into the water and out again and up the slope.

Here, at 8:15, on what was the Russian left, was broken out the first Japanese flag, fluttering white, like a tiny handkerchief, as its bearer climbed higher and higher. Only a few minutes later the flag of Japan was broken out on the Russian right.

All firing ceased. The white flag of Japan mounted higher and higher on the bare road along the crest of the ridge. The immediate battle was over, and the Japanese spectators beside us on the wall of Wiju were shouting "Banzai!"

But the Russians had failed to reckon the dash and swiftness of the Japanese. On right and left the pursuit was taken up by the Japanese, while the reserves of the center division, fresh, took up the chase hot-footed. Their cavalry was not used. And then was given a spectacle which must have brought a grin to the stern features of the God of War—artillery, drawn by horses over good roads, where no rain had fallen for days, pursued and overtaken by men on foot!

And the Japanese did it. They caught two batteries and a battalion at a place called Hamatan, and forthwith stormed the position from the left, front and right. It cost them 300 casualties, but they got the guns.

And now for the battle in retrospect, from a tyro's point of view. The question of frontal attack arises. Why did the Japanese make this frontal attack? Their casualties for the day were, by their own figures, 1,000 men. Was it necessary to lose all these men? I think not. On the night of April 29th the East division effected a lodgement on the Manchurian shore. On April 30th these men were seen streaming over the hills away from the river. They were meeting with no opposition. The Russians were withdrawing.

Behind these men of the East division was the Yalu. They controlled its fords and bridges whereby they had crossed. The whole first army could have crossed after them without the loss of a life. The main body of the Russian had withdrawn, leaving only a thousand or so entrenched on and near the conical hill.

Had the Japanese army crossed on the heels of the East division on the night of April 30th, or even in the early morning of May 1st, they would have flanked the Russian detachment, and one of two things would have happened—either the Russian detachment would have been surrounded and compelled to surrender or it would have retreated with all the attendant risk of being cut to pieces. In either case there would have been practically no Japanese loss, and in either case the end would have been the same. Manchuria would have lain open before them.

Yet the Japanese elected to make the frontal attack, and in the face of the dictum of military experts that frontal attack in ordinary instances is suicide, and that, in instances, where numbers heavily preponderate, a fearful cost must be paid. Certain I am that no European or American commander would have ordered this attack when the crossing to the right was open and uncontested.

But the Japanese are Asiatics, and the Asiatic does not value life as we do. The generals of Japan have no press of populace at home to harp at the cost of victory, while they do have at home a press and a people clamorous for victory, splendid victory, and never mind the cost.

On the other hand, there may have been other factors which made this victory by frontal attack a desirable thing. The prestige of Japan had appreciated all over the world because of the remarkable successes of her navy at Port Arthur. And yet the world wagged its head dubiously and said:

"Wait till we see what Japan does on land." Perhaps it was to settle this doubt and to gain at the outset land-prestige equal to its sea-prestige that prompted Japan to make a frontal attack across the naked sands of the Yalu. It certainly demonstrated that its soldiers have dash and go, and it took four hundred Russian prisoners, twenty-eight guns, and some baggage.

What the Russian loss was in killed and wounded has not yet been ascertained. The cost to Japan was one thousand men killed and wounded. It was the price Japan paid, and doubtless, considered well to pay.

There is a still further consideration. The doubtful old world had shaken its head and said:

"The Japanese are Asiatic. Hitherto they have fought only Asiatics. But what showing will they make when they go up against our own kind, the white kind of the earth?"

The Japanese have been very sensitive to this, and they have been fiery to prove themselves fit from the white man's point of view by facing white men. To prove themselves fit at the very start was enormously to add to their own prestige and enormously to make Russia "lose face" in the eyes of other Asiatic peoples.

All these factors tend to justify the Japanese in accepting the slaughter of a needless frontal attack. Japan has proved its soldiers desperate and intelligent fighters, and has proved itself fit to face white men in anger. Nevertheless, I do not believe that the sum of these promptings would have been sufficient cause for a white commander to hurl his troops forward on such a frontal attack. I am confident that a white commander who did so would not find justification for the act in the eyes of his people at home.

Apropos of this being fit to face white men, I rode across the Yalu into Kuel-ian-ching. I passed the Japanese dead and wounded on the road and found myself thrilling gently to the horrors of war. And now, mark me, I had been traveling for months with Asiatic soldiers. The faces were Asiatic faces. The skins were yellow and brown. I had become used to a people which was not of my kind. My mind had settled down to accepting without question that the men who fought had eyes and cheek bones and skins different from the eyes and cheek bones and skins of my kind. It was all a matter of course, the natural order of things.

And thus I rode into Kuel-ian-ching. Into the windows of a large Chinese house I saw many Japanese soldiers curiously peering. Reining up my horse at a window, I too, curiously peered. And the sight I saw was as a blow in the face to me. On my mind it had all the stunning effect of the sharp impact of a man's fist. There was a man, a white man, with blue eyes, looking at me. He was dirty and unkempt. He had been through a fierce battle. But his eyes were bluer than mine and his skin was as white.

And there were other white men in there with him—many white men. I caught myself gasping. A choking sensation was in my throat. These men were my kind. I found myself suddenly and sharply aware that I was an alien amongst these brown men who peered through the window with me. And I felt myself strangely at one with those other men behind the window— felt that my place was there inside with them in their captivity, rather than outside in freedom amongst aliens.

Sad, as I had not been sad all day, I turned and rode down the Yalu to the Chinese city of Antung. On the way I saw a Pekin cart drawn by Chinese mules. Japanese soldiers marched with the cart. It was the gray end of day, and the cart was burdened with gray—gray blankets, gray jackets, gray overcoats. On either side, from amidst this mound of gray, bristled the fixed bayonets of Russian rifles. On top of the mound of gray was a head of hair like my own and a white forehead. The rest of the face was covered. But from the rear projected a naked foot and leg. It was the leg of a man who must have stood over six feet, and it was white. It moved up and down with the joggling two-wheeled cart, beating ceaseless and monotonous time as it drew away in the distance.

Later I saw a Japanese soldier astride a Russian horse. He exhibited a Russian medal; on his feet were a Russian officer's boots; and somehow my mind reverted to the white foot beating time on the joggling Pekin cart.

In the headquarters at Antung a Japanese in civilian clothes addressed me in English. He did all the talking, and he talked of the victory. He was beaming. Not a hint of the thoughts in my own mind had I breathed to him, and yet he said at parting:

"Your people did not think we could beat the white. We have now beaten the white."

The word "white" was his own, as the thought was his own, and as he spoke leaped into my eyes a vision of the white foot beating time on the Pekin cart.

JAPANESE IN INVISIBLE WAR

ANTUNG, May 2.—The call came at 4 o'clock, April 26th, and we tumbled out of our beds, crying to each other in the darkness and stumbling along the road to Wiju. From our right and up the Yalu came the steady poppy-ti-pop of rifles, with occasional volleys, and to this we listened while we gazed down into the well of blackness where the Yalu lay.

As dawn broke in the east the blackness stratified into ink and silver—the ink the tips of the low-lying hills, the silver the night-mist still lingering over the water. At 5 rifle firing

opened heavily on our left and by 6 we could distinctly see
black specks of men appearing and disappearing amongst the
willow brush which striped the sandy surface of Ran-shi island
with green and white. North of Ran-shi island ran one of the
three branches of the Yalu; on the north side of this branch
stood the village of Chong-kain-die and the Korean custom
house in a red-brick compound, both of which places were occupied by the Russians. The black specks appearing and disappearing amongst the willow brush of Ran-shi island were the
Japanese.

This was the battle—a river bed, a continuous and irregular
sound of rifle firing over a front of miles, a few black moving
specks. That was all. No Russians were to be seen. With all the
hubbub of shooting no smoke arose. No shot was seen to be
fired. The black specks disappeared in the willows. The hubbub
of firing continued. Smoke filtered through the air, but the
enemies who hurled death at each other were not visible.

It might be a war of ghosts for all that eye or field-glass could
discern. The sandy islands were virtually bare of cover. The village
of Chong-kain-die and the custom house were devoid of life.
No banners fluttered, no smoke curled from the chimneys, no
living creatures moved or showed in the open spaces between
the houses. Only the sun blazed down over all, the west wind
blew up from the sea, and the rifles cracked from the empty
island and the empty village.

In the foreground, directly at our feet, a bridge was being
built across the south branch of the Yalu. The thump of timber
came to our ears. Korean coolies in white, Japanese soldiers
in dark, toiled upon it. There was no battle so far as they were
concerned. It was in their day's work to build a bridge and they
were building it. They passed back and forth upon the completed portion, carrying beams upon their shoulders, beams and
men and bridge sharply silhouetted against the surface of the
Yalu. In the rear a train of pack horses was being disburdened
of planks carried fresh-sawn from the mountains. A little farther
to the rear, behind a low hill on the outskirts of Wiju itself and to
our right, perhaps 500 reserves were clustered. They were about
a thousand yards distant, and we could see their number being

added to by sightseeing members of the Imperial Guard, who crossed an open field from their quarters in Wiju.

And still the invisible battle went on. The custom house and village of Chong-kain-die baked in the blazing sunshine. It was almost beyond comprehension that so forsaken-looking a place should be receiving, enduring and repelling attack. True, there was the sound of rifle firing; but whence did it come? One only knew that from out there somewhere in the midst of the river there was a crackling sort of sound. It was "out there somewhere," nor could it be more definitely located.

From down the Yalu, many miles down, came the dull reports of heavy field guns. The firing on the right died away into occasional splutters. The firing on the left re-doubled. Bang! Somewhere in front of us a gun had been fired! Half a score of field glasses searched the landscape. A piece of mountain artillery, it was declared. But where was it? Bang! The glasses roved, vainly everywhere. Again bang! and yet again bang! And the glasses discovered nothing. There was much conjecture. As Ambrose Bierce once said, we tried to judge its location by the "configuration of the landscape." And, so judging and testing, a glass caught a flash from the ridge of Tiger Hill, a rocky promontory jutting out from the Manchurian shore.

The flash was taken by a watch. Twelve seconds later the report reached our ears. Since sound travels 1,020 feet per second, said the experts, the gun must be 12,240 feet away, or something like two and one-third miles. The rifle firing sprang up again on the right, continued on the left, and the Russian gun banged from Tiger Hill; while in front, at our feet, Japanese and Koreans calmly went on bridge-building.

For fifty minutes the gun on Tiger Hill played its part, and was then withdrawn. The firing on the right died away and ceased. The firing on the left died away and ceased. No more sound arose save the thumping of the timbers where the bridge-building went on. The west wind blew, the sun rose higher, and in the midst of the silence a squadron of Cossacks,— black dots upon the sand,—rode out from behind the tail of Tiger Hill. They were trotting, but so far away were they that they seemed to crawl as they veered toward the Manchurian shore in the direction of the village of Kuel-ian-ching. But one

man, alone, walked his horse along the river bank. He walked
his horse, and never broke it from a walk, through the stretch
where the invisible fighting had been thickest, in the direction
of the custom house. We looked for the firing to open up
again. We looked for a single shot, perhaps, from some Japanese
sharpshooter. But the silence remained unbroken. The lone rider
walked his horse along the front of the village, into which he
turned before reaching the custom house.

The squadron of Cossacks was lost to sight. Japanese reserves,
hitherto hidden, were marching back into Wiju. The fight demonstration, skirmish, battle, or what ever it might be called, was
over. The correspondents departed, sleepy and hungry, for camp
and breakfast. Only remained three of us, the bridge-builders,
the reserves behind the hill, and a pack train toiling out with
planks from Wiju to the bridge.

We three remained because our boys had brought our horses
and were even then cooking breakfast behind the crest of the
hill on which we lay. We were sprawling drowsily in the sunshine when the reports of three guns, in rapid succession,
aroused us. There was a shrill trilling or whistling. Above the
bridge floated three puffs of smoke, and the bridge-builders
had quit work. They were racing madly for the shore. More
rings of smoke appeared about them. In more places than one
the river was lashed white as though some giant had tossed into
it a handful of rocks from a distant hilltop. And by timing the
flashes we knew it was the Russians throwing shrapnel from a
Manchurian hilltop four miles away.

Came a lull, and one of us dispatched his boy back to camp
for a camera. Later he cursed him, for he had mistaken his
way and was galloping into Wiju. The kettle was boiling,
saddles were off and horses were grazing, when the whistling
and screeching of the shells began again. They burst in the air
above Wiju, they burst in the houses in Wiju, they burst beyond
Wiju, they burst among the reserves behind the hill at our
feet, and they burst in the midst of the pack train.

A house flamed up. The reserves scattered under the shrapnel
which burst directly above them. The pack train was disrupted,
ponies losing their planks as they ran away, and an officer's

horse, riderless, galloped up the hill to us, while one of us cried, "Oh, my God! And my poor pony in the thick of it!"

And that was really all. The day's fighting was over. The west wind blew sweetly and the sun was at the zenith when we rode down into the town to the burning house. The pack train had been gathered together and was already toiling back again to the riverside. A string of Red Cross stretchers, burdened with wounded men, passed us in a narrow street. Soldiers were gossiping in the alleyways or sleeping in the doorless and windowless houses. We took the crowded road out of Wiju and came upon three oblong pine boxes on pushcarts. Alongside these pushcarts soldiers were digging three oblong holes in the ground. Unpleasantly expeditious, perhaps, but then the dead were dead and had no call to clutter the feet of war which trampled by on the crowded Wiju road infantry and cavalry, Red Cross and pioneers, ponies, bullocks and coolies, camp equipage and pack trains laden with fresh-sawed planks for the bridge-builders, no doubt again at work.

JAPS DRIVE RUSSIANS ACROSS YALU RIVER

ANTUNG (Manchuria), May 5, 1904.—That the Japanese are desperately brave and intelligent fighters and thorough masters of the machinery of modern warfare has been well demonstrated by the operations which culminated in their crossing of the Yalu on May 1st. Their disposition and handling of artillery far excelled the Russians. The latter may be said to have inflicted no damage with their guns. Beyond the loss of a man or two and several minor casualties, the Japanese were untouched. The powder burned in the Russian guns was just so much powder thrown away.

The Russian batteries were at all time ineffectual, while the Japanese batteries, especially on the last day of April and the first of May, did fearful execution. This was due to the precision of their fire, to their intelligence and shrewdness in the placing of their guns and to the absolute thoroughness with which they do everything.

A visit to the ridge and conical hill of the Russian position showed a surface plowed and pitted by the Japanese shells and carpeted with shrapnel bullets. In the center of the position, where the battery occupied the crown of the conical hill, one could literally step from shellhole to shellhole. Those who lived through that rain of fire must have taken away with them a first-hand knowledge of hell far beyond the imaginings of Dante and Milton.

But it was not alone the precision of fire that destroyed the Russians. Had they dug their trenches and protected their guns and themselves with half the thoroughness displayed by the Japanese they would not have suffered so terribly. On an unsheltered hilltop they only partially sheltered themselves. Even then their losses would have been much less during the artillery duels of April 29th and 30th had they not obstinately remained by their guns during the thick of the Japanese fire. There was no need for them to remain by their unsheltered guns when to remain meant heavy loss. They were not directly menaced. No infantry was advancing upon them under protection of the Japanese guns. Only were they being stormed at from the batteries across the river, and yet they remained.

In marked contrast was the behavior of the one Japanese battery I observed. This battery was situated near the Summer Pavilion of Wiju Castle, and when the Russian guns turned loose on it its gunners promptly sought refuge in the casemates.

After the artillery duel of April 30th, wherein the Russian position was swept by the Japanese fire, it is almost incomprehensible that the Russians should have retained it for their rear guard detachment next day. This rear guard detachment was composed of infantry. The guns had been withdrawn during the night. There was no protection for these riflemen from the Japanese fire which could be counted upon to concentrate on them, no guns of their own to reply and mitigate in the slightest the rain of shell and shrapnel.

The one glimmering explanation that arises is that the Russians did not intend to hold this position, but that they were caught before they could retire and choose a better by the Japanese swiftness of movement. Something like 8,000 Russians guarded the north bank of the Yalu. It was not their intention to make a determined stand, but merely to retard the Japanese advance. The lodgment of the East Division (Japanese) on the north bank and on the Russian left flank and the overpowering artillery brought to bear upon their whole position warned the Russians that it was time to retire. Accordingly, on the night of April 30th, they withdrew their guns, with their main force, leaving between 1,500 and 2,000 men as a detached rear guard.

And it was thus that this rear guard was cut to pieces. The Japanese army, strung out for a great distance along the Yalu, had shrewdly concentrated. The first light of next morning disclosed it on the sands of the Yalu and practically across the Yalu. The main channels were to the rear. Overwhelmed in an exposed position by the concentrated fire of the Japanese guns, having no guns with which to reply and at the same time charged by the concentrated Japanese army, nothing remained to the comparative handful of Russians but a losing fight.

Cut to pieces, destroyed, the rear guard failed in its task of protecting the retreat of the Russian guns, and the Japanese, taking up the pursuit, caught two batteries at Hamatan. Now Hamatan is only six miles back from the Yalu, and the question arises, Why, when the Russians withdrew their guns, the previous night, had they covered no more than six miles? Were they short of horses? Unwitting of the speed with which the Japanese move, had they dallied by the way? Undreaming of the concentration of the whole Japanese army, had they rested secure in the fancied protection of their rear guard? Or, laboring under all these misapprehensions, was it their intention to take up a new position with the two batteries, later to be strengthened by the arrival of the rear guard, and then renew their policy of worrying and retarding the Japanese advance?

These are questions which only the Russians can answer. Whatever were their intentions, the Japanese settled them out of hand, destroying the rear guard, capturing the guns and delivering a crushing blow to the Russians on the very soil they have elected to take for their own.

THE MONKEY CAGE[1]

ANTUNG (Manchuria), May 10. — The Japanese, following the German model, make every possible preparation, take every

[1] Also see *Jack London's Tales of Adventure*, edited by Irving Shepard. Hanover House, 1956.

possible precaution, and then proceed to act, confident in the belief that nothing short of a miracle can prevent success. Opposed to their three divisions on the Yalu was a greatly inferior Russian force, but the Japanese had to cross a river under fire and attack an enemy lying in wait for them.

By the manipulation of their three divisions, and what of their ruses, they must have sadly befuddled the Russians. At the mouth of the Yalu the Japanese had two small gunboats, two torpedo-boats and four small steamers armed with Hotchkiss guns. Also they had fifty sampans loaded with bridge materials. These were intended for a permanent bridge across the Yalu at Wiju; but they served another purpose—first, farther down the stream. The presence of the small navy and the loaded sampans led the Russians to believe that right there was where the bridge was to be built. So right there they stationed some three thousand men to prevent the building of the bridge. Thus, a handful of Japanese sailors kept 3,000 Russian soldiers occupied in doing nothing and reduced the effectiveness of the Russian strength by that much.

Another ruse was the building of a bridge in front of Wiju. This was in plain view of the Russians on the conical hill opposite and just east of Kieu-Liang-Cheng, and they consumed much time and powder in shelling it. This was precisely what the Japanese intended for the bridge. While it held the Russian attention, a little farther down the stream the Japanese were at work on another bridge, screened by small willow trees on the intervening island, and which, when completed, had never had a shot fired at it.

Have you ever stood in front of a cage wherein there was a monkey gazing innocently and peaceably into your eyes—so innocent and peaceable the hands grasping the bars and wholly unbelligerent, the eyes bent with friendly interest on yours, and all the while and unbeknown a foot sliding out to surprise your fancied security and set you shrieking with sudden fright? Beware the monkey cage! You have need of more than eyes; and beware the Japanese. When he sits down stupidly to build a bridge with his two hands before your eyes, have a thought to the quiet place behind the willow-screen where another bridge is being builded by his two feet. He works with hands and

feet, he works night and day, and he never does but one thing
expected of him, and that is the unexpected thing.

The night of April 29th and the day of the 30th was an
anxious time for the Japanese. Their army was cut in half, and it
was no less than the Yalu that divided it. One-third of its force,
the Z division, had crossed the river to the right and was in
Manchuria. They had no very accurate knowledge of the Russian
strength, and it was not beyond liability that the Russians might
make a counter attack on the Z division and destroy it. So
the X and Y divisions on the south bank were in momentary
readiness to prevent this by delivering an attack upon the
Russians straight across the river. But there was no need for
this. The Russians were not in sufficient force to attack a single
division, advancing as it was across mountainous country. This,
in turn, the Japanese did not know, but they prepared for the
possibility as they prepare for everything.

The Ai-ho river flows out of Manchuria and enters the Yalu
valley a mile or more above Kieu-Liang-Cheng. It also flows
down past that village, close to the Manchurian shore, thus
interposing an obstacle to the advance of the whole Japanese
army (even the Z division), after it had crossed the Yalu
proper. The crossing of the Ai-ho was seriously menaced by
the sixteen guns of the Russian right on the conical hill. The
day's work for April 30th was to put those sixteen guns out of
business. The Japanese bent themselves to the task. It was an
exposed position, and a concentrated fire lasting twenty-five minutes and in which time sixty common shells were thrown, did
the work. The Russian fire was silenced and the guns were
withdrawn that night. Incidentally the Japanese shelled the Russian camp, carelessly situated where it was exposed to view from
the Korean hills, and wrought great havoc.

On the night of April 30th the X and Y divisions crossed the
main Yalu and rested on the sands, with the Ai-ho between
them and the Russians. The X division, forming the Japanese
left, faced the Russian right on the conical hill. The Y division
was extended near the mouth of the Ai-ho; and up the Ai-ho,
extended for several miles, lay the Z division. Opposing these
three divisions was a Russian actual fighting force of about
4,000 men. The Russian line, extending some six or seven miles,

was not intact. In fact, because of the lay of the land, the Russians really occupied two positions—one on and about the conical hill at Kieu-Liang-Cheng, the other on the Ai-ho, from its mouth several miles up.

Against these two positions, each occupied by about 2,000 men, was hurled an army of three divisions (probably 25,000 men actually on the spot), backed by a powerful artillery of field guns and howitzers. Prevented by shell fire and shrapnel from doing their best to repel the general attack, in process of being flanked by the immensely superior force, the Russian left on the Ai-ho broke first and fled in the direction of Hamatan. The Russian right, on the conical hill, fought more tenaciously, the survivors in turn fleeing toward Hamatan.

The Japanese understand the utility of things. Reserves they consider should be used, not only to strengthen the line or to protect the repulsed line, but in the moment of victory to clinch victory hard and fast. The reserves, fresh and chafing from inaction, wild to take part in a glorious day, received the order for general pursuit. Right, left and center, they took after the Russians. The field guns, delayed by the Ai-ho, followed at a gallop.

The retreat became a rout. The Russian reserves, two regiments, had fled without firing a shot—at least the Japanese have no record of these two regiments. Hamatan is at the conjunction of three roads, six miles to the rear of the conical hill. Down these three roads the Russians ran, coming together and passing on to the main road—the Pekin or Mandarin road. And down these three roads, from right, left and center, came the fresh reserves, and after them the artillery.

In the meantime, however, far from the Japanese right and outstripping the rest of the pursuit, arrived one company of men in time to cut off fifteen Russian guns and eight maxims. The remnants of three battalions rallied around the guns. A hasty postion was taken. The rest of the pursuing Japanese did not arrive. But one company of men stood between the Russians and the Pekin road. And it stood. Its captain and three lieutenants were killed. One officer only remained alive. The last cartridge was fired. Those that survived fixed their bayonets ready to receive a charge. And in that moment, left, right and center, their pursuing comrades arrived.

The Russians were assailed from three sides. The tables were turned, but they fought with equal courage. The day was lost; they knew it; yet they fought on doggedly. Night was falling. As the Japanese drew closer the Russians turned loose their horses, destroyed or threw away the breechblocks of their guns, smashed the breeches of the maxims and then, as bayonet countered bayonet, drew white handkerchiefs from their pockets in token of surrender.

One other noteworthy thing occurred in the Japanese pursuit. Midway to Hamatan, flying on the heels of a rout, in the very heat and sweep of triumph, they dropped a line of reserves to receive and protect them should they be hurled back broken and crushed by Russian re-enforcements. Hand in hand with terrifying bravery goes this cold-blooded precaution. Verily, nothing short of the miracle can wreck a plan they have once started to put into execution. The men furnish the unfaltering braver, confident in the knowledge that their officers have furnished the precaution.

Of course, the officers are as brave as the men. On the night of the 30th, when the army took up its position of the Ai-ho, it was not known whether that stream was fordable. Officers from each of the three divisions stripped and swam or waded the river at many different points, practically under the rifles of the Russians.

"Men determined to die" is the way one Japanese officer characterized the volunteers who answer in large numbers to every call for dangerous work. Not knowing whether the Ai-ho was fordable, three plans were seriously considered. First, each soldier was to go into action on May 1st dressed in a cartridge belt and equipped with a rifle and a board, the latter to be used as a means for paddling across the Ai-ho. Second, same garb and equipment with a tub substituted for the board, and, third, the strongest swimmers to cross over with ropes, along which, when once fast on the other bank, the weaker swimmers and non-swimmers could make their way. In any case, had the river not proved fordable, Kipling's "Taking of Lung-Tong-Pen" would have been repeated on a most formidable scale. Surely the Russians would have broken and fled precipitately before so terrible a charge.

Every division, every battery was connected with headquarters by field telephone. When the divisions moved forward they dragged their wires after them like spiders drag the silk of their webs. Even the tiny navy at the mouth of the Yalu was in instant communication with headquarters. Thus, on a wide-stretching and largely invisible field, the commander-in-chief was in immediate control of everything. Inventions, weapons, methods, systems (the navy modeled after the English, the army after the German), everything utilized by the Japanese has been supplied by the Western world; but the Japanese have shown themselves the only Eastern people capable of utilizing them.

JAPANESE OFFICERS CONSIDER
EVERYTHING A MILITARY SECRET

ANTUNG (First Japanese Army), June 2. — It is all very well, this long-range fighting; but if the range continues to increase, and if other armies are as solicitous for the welfare of the correspondents as are the Japanese, war correspondence will become a lost art and there will be a lot of war correspondents entering new professions late in life.

In the first place, when the front of battle extends for miles and miles, no correspondent can see of his own eyes all that is taking place. What is happening to the right, miles away, behind the mountains where the Yalu curls into the east, and what is happening to the left, miles away, behind the mountains where the Yalu curls into the west, is beyond him. He cannot understand what is taking place before his eyes (or his field-glasses, rather, for his eyes show him nothing), without knowing what is taking place on right and left; and there is no one to tell him what is taking place on right and left. The officers may not tell him, because, in their parlance, it would be an exposure of a military secret.

This would not be so bad if they did not consider practically everything a military secret. Apropos of this, a correspondent, on his way up country, arrives at the village of Kasan. A skirmish had once taken place at Kasan. A month had passed. The front had moved up a hundred miles. The correspondent saw a few graves on the hillside. "How many Japanese were killed?" he asked an officer. The officer was a major. He replied, "I cannot tell you. It is a military secret."

The above may seem far-fetched, but it is not. It is merely typical. On every side is the military secret. The correspondent is hedged around by military secrets. He may not move about for fear he will pop on to a military secret, though what he may do with a military secret only the Japanese know. First, in order to get a military secret out of the country, he must show it to the censor and get permission. This obtained, he must dispatch it by Korean-runners to Ping Yang, a couple of hundred miles to the south, where it may be telegraphed by his agent to Seoul and from there be cabled, via Japan, to his paper. But granting that the military secret has survived all the vicissitudes of the journey to Ping Yang and not lost its time-value, it is not yet out of the country. Seven or eight days later a runner arrives with a note from his Ping Yang agent telling him that all cables are being held up. So the military secret, like the peasant who started for Carcassonne, dies unobtrusively of old age upon the way.

The position of the correspondent in the Japanese army is an anomalous one of interloper and honored guest. The restrictions which stultify all his efforts show the one, the solicitude of his hosts shows the second. If a skirmish or demonstration is to be made, word is sent to him to that effect—also, a further word to the effect that he is to assemble with his colleagues at a certain place and proceed and be directed under the management of an army officer told off for the purpose. He is further warned that neither he nor his colleagues may go individually. Still further, he has fresh in his mind the previous day's instructions from headquarters as, for instance, those of April 29th, from which I quote the following:

"There is no official news to communicate concerning military operations now proceeding or pending.

"Headquarters (unofficially) is aware that artillery has been engaged on both sides of the river.

"For the present and until further notice the transmission of any dispatches from the front where wireless telegraphy is employed is forbidden. The necessary steps are being taken to see that this order is obeyed.

"It may be found necessary to enforce a still stricter censorship than that already existing.

"From to-day and until further notice it is forbidden to take photographs or make sketches of any kind within the area now occupied by the Japanese troops. It is useless to apply for permission to do so, as applications of this kind will not be entertained.

"Correspondents may witness all military operations. They must keep well in the rear of the firing line. They are forbidden to approach certain (unspecified) works."

The peculiar force of this last order lies in that the correspondent who ventures out for a "look see" all by himself finds that just about everything in the landscape is unspecifiedly forbidden. The nearest I have succeeded in getting to a Japanese battery, and one not in action either, was when I crawled to the top of a hill half a mile to the rear and gazed upon it through field-glasses in fear and trembling.

Even before the taking of photographs was absolutely forbidden I once had the temerity to take a snap of an army farrier and his bellows. "Here at last was something that was not a military secret," I had thought in my innocence. Fifteen minutes' ride away I was stopped by a soldier who could not speak English. I showed my credentials and on my arm the official insignia of my position in the Japanese army. But it was no use. Something serious was pending. I was ordered to remain where I was, and while I waited I cudgeled my brains in an endeavor to find what military secret had crept in unawares.

I did not know of any, but I was confident that one was there somewhere. After much delay an officer was brought to me. He was a captain, and his English was excellent—a great deal purer and better than my own.

"You have taken a photograph of an army blacksmith," he said accusingly and reproachfully.

With a sinking heart I nodded my head to acknowledge my guilt.

"You must give it up," he said.

"It is ridiculous," I burst out.

"You must give it up," he repeated.

Then, after some discussion with the soldiers, he said I might keep it; but he added that the road was one of the unspecified forbidden places, and that I must go back. Back I went, but the field telephone must have beaten me, for they knew all my transgression at headquarters before I got there.

The functions of the war correspondent, so far as I can ascertain, is to sit up on the reverse slopes of hills where honored guests cannot be injured, and from there to listen to the crack of rifles and vainly search the dim distance for the men who are doing the shooting; to receive orders from headquarters as to what he may or may not do; to submit daily to the censor his conjectures and military secrets, and to observe article 4 of the printed First Army Regulations—to wit:

"Press correspondents should look and behave decently, and should never do anything disorderly, and should never enter the office rooms of the headquarters."

With one exception, the correspondents with the first army are what is called "cable" men. Theirs is the task to cable, telegraph, use runners and whatever means to hand to get news out of the country as quickly as possible. There is the censor to begin with. What little news they do manage to glean is pretty well emasculated by him before it is allowed to start. At the very earliest it will arrive in Japan five days later. From Japan it radiates to the rest of the world. But the headquarters is connected directly with Tokio by wire. That is to say, the headquarters news beats the correspondents' news to Tokio by five days. Not only that, for it has full details and is correct. In addition, the powers that be at Tokio are more liberal than the first army censor, so that Tokio makes public to the world a full account five days before the "cable" men's accounts begin to arrive. If other nations in future wars imitate the Japanese in this, the "cable" men would cease to exist. There would be no reason for them to exist. The regular news-gatherers in the capitals of the contending countries would serve the purpose just as well and a great deal better.

Remains the writing man. Long-range fighting, supervising officers who lead him about in the rear as Cook's tourists are led about Rome and Paris, military secrets, and censors do for him. When he has described two or three invisible battles and has had his conjectures trimmed down by the censor, he is done for. He can't go on describing the sound of rifles and guns, the bursting of shell and shrapnel, and the occasional moving specks for a whole campaign. Nor can he go on describing the transport trains in the rear, the only things he sees too much of and which, as yet, have not been placed under the taboo of military secret.

Personally, I entered upon this campaign with the most gorgeous conceptions of what a war correspondent's work in the world must be. I knew that the mortality of war correspondents was said to be greater, in proportion to numbers, than the mortality of soldiers. I remembered, during the siege of Khartoum and the attempted relief by Wolseley, the deaths in battle of a number of correspondents. I had read "The Light that Failed." I remembered Stephen Crane's descriptions of being under fire in Cuba. I had heard—God wot, was there aught I had not heard?—of all sorts and conditions of correspondents in all sorts of battles and skirmishes, right in the thick of it, where life was keen and immortal moments were being lived. In brief, I came to war expecting to get thrills. My only thrills have been those of indignation and irritation.

JAPAN PUTS END TO USEFULNESS OF CORRESPONDENTS

Examiner Editor's Note: Jack London, who has added to his literary fame new laurels gained as special commissioner of the *Examiner* to the war in the Orient, returned yesterday on the *Korean.* He dictated the following interview:

July 1, 1904.—When I landed at Yokohama I soon found that there were two ways of playing the game—either to sit down in Tokio as the Japs wanted me to and eat many dinners, or to go out on my own resources. I started out with the first brigade of the first army into Northern Korea and stayed with them about two months, seeing what I could see and taking pictures. They didn't seem to have orders concerning me and let me follow along. We got up into Northern Korea before I was ordered back to Seoul.

There we waited around for a while till some of us correspondents were assigned to go to the front. Fourteen of us were picked to go. I was one of the lucky fourteen that was graciously allowed to travel with the army. But this time it was different. It was like a party of Cook's tourists with supervising officers as guides. We saw what we were permitted to see, and the chief duty of the officers looking after us was to keep us from seeing anything.

We did see part of the battle of the Yalu from the outer walls of Wiju, where we had been led by the supervising officer. We saw the opening of part of the battle. The fight raged on and up to Hamatan, six miles' running fight, where the final desperate stand was made. One Japanese company was completely annihilated. All this time we were not permitted to follow the fight, or to get any of the details, but were ordered back to our camp, which lay behind the third range of hills from the Yalu. The details of this fight were not given us until May 9th; the fight took place May 1st and these details we were not permitted to send by the local censor.

From then on the Japanese treatment of the correspondents with the first army grew stricter and stricter. We crossed the Yalu and went to Feng-Wang-Cheng. There we settled down and had a beautiful ideal California camping trip. We lived in a grove beside a temple, where each of us had a magnificent little camp. There was nothing to do. We spent a couple of weeks there. Every day we went in swimming, played bridge, got up games and protested gaily against those who controlled our destinies to be allowed to see something. They in turn tightened the screws on us, so that our freedom of movement was limited to a circle drawn about the city of Feng-Wang-Cheng, the radius of which was a mile and a half. And there he stuck. And there we struck.

We got up a joint telegram, signed by every man at the front, and to be cabled to their respective papers in France, England, the United States, explaining the utter futility of the situation, and that further stay in the field was a useless expense. But the Japanese by their usual Asiatic indirection, which involved the subtlest dialectics and discussion of things metaphysical, and concerning all things under the sun except the point at issue, sidetracked the telegram. Then they made promises of giving us greater freedom of movement, which they did not fulfill. I, for one, in disgust started back. There was nothing to see, nothing to write about save the woes of correspondents, swimming pools and peaceful temple scenes.

The Japanese resembles a precocious child who talks philosophy one moment, and the next moment is making mud pies. One moment he is acting with the wisdom of the West and the next moment with the childishness of the East. For instance, they resolved at Wiju, before the crossing of the Yalu, that the correspondents could not date their telegrams from Wiju, for the reason that the Russians reading these dispatches in the English and American journals would conclude that the correspondents would be with the headquarters of the first army, and that therefore the headquarters of the first army were at Wiju. But the correspondents constantly evaded this restriction by stating in the body of the telegram that they were at Wiju. The Japanese did not wish the Russians to learn that they were attempting to build bridges across the Yalu. If the Russians did not read it in the newspapers they would never dream that the Japanese dreamed of crossing in that manner. One correspondent evaded this restriction in this way: "The Japanese are at work with the timbers in the river. I am not permitted to say what they are working upon. I can assure you, however, that they are not digging a well."

At Feng-Wang-Cheng the Japanese told us in their official information that at the beginning of the war they had thought their cavalry greatly inferior to the Russian cavalry, but that they had since learned, in numerous patrol affairs, that their cavalry was superior to the Russian cavalry and that they were compelled constantly to restrain their men. On top of this, for several days they told us officially of many patrol contacts in which there had been no casualties. One correspondent, from dearth of news compelled to telegraph something, innocently composed a wire which contained the following: "In numerous recent meetings of patrols discretion has been observed on both sides." When this was interpreted to Colonel Haginaw his face went red with wrath and he pounded the offending telegram with his fist and dashed out with it to the staff. Returning somewhat calmed, he said that the telegram could not be sent because it reflected upon the valor of the Japanese. To add to the correspondent's woe, on his return to camp he was nearly manhandled by his brethren because he had not revised the telegram to read: "In numerous recent meetings of patrols discretion has been observed by the Russians, indiscretion by the Japanese."

When I left Yokohama homeward bound, all the other correspondents, patiently playing the game according to Japanese etiquette, were still publicly dining and privily blaspheming in Tokio. The armies to which they were assigned had been for weeks at the front, and had fought many bloody battles. Nor did they have any definite assurance as to when they would be permitted to go to the front. I left Richard Harding Davis and John Fox Jr. at Yokohama, assuring me as they said good-by that as soon as they heard one shot fired they would hit the high places for the United States, but that they could not possibly return after the months of waiting until they had heard that one shot fired.

The Japanese does not in the least understand the correspondent or the mental processes of a correspondent, which are a white man's mental processes. The Japanese is of a military race. His old caste distinctions placed the fighting man at the top; next comes the peasant; after that the merchant, and beneath all the scribe. These caste distinctions are practically in force to-day. A correspondent from the West is a man who must be informed by printed instructions that he must dress and behave decently.

The Japanese cannot understand straight talk, white man's talk. This is one of the causes of so much endless delay. The correspondent talks straight to the Japanese, but he cannot realize that it is straight talk. He feels that there is something at the back of the correspondent's mind, and the Japanese must have a day or a week to meditate upon what is at the back of the correspondent's mind. Having done this, he has another talk; but again he must go away and meditate upon what is behind this new talk, and so nothing is accomplished from the correspondent's point of view.

Granting that no revolution arises in Russia and there is no interference of outside powers, I cannot see how Japan can possibly win. Not heroics on the battlefield, but economics at home, determines the outcome of modern wars. Japan, with all the prestige of their splendid land and naval victories, has floated a loan by pledging her customs at 6 per cent. What per cent will be demanded by the investor who takes a second mortgage on her customs? And what per cent will be demanded in case of a protracted war or in the event of disaster to her arms? This loan has been a colossal blunder on the part of her statesmen, and its retrievement a more difficult undertaking than that of the capture of Port Arthur.

THE MEXICAN CONFLICT
May to June 1914

In 1914, when the American Government sent our expeditionary force to Vera Cruz, Collier's Magazine asked London to go with General Frederick Funston's army as a correspondent. He accepted and with Charmian left the Beauty Ranch April 17 for Galveston, Texas. But he was destined for more frustrations. When he arrived, all of the other correspondents had received clearance for travel with General Funston on the transport Kilpatrick. He could not understand why he had not received clearance. Once more Richard Harding Davis came into the picture. He told London that it was because of the soldier's canard, a scurrilous pamphlet entitled "The Good Soldier" which had been circulated over London's name. Davis and others convinced the government officials that London was not the author and London got his orders to leave on the day the Kilpatrick sailed from Galveston.
"The Good Soldier" read:

Young Men: The lowest aim in your life is to become a soldier. The good soldier never tries to distinguish right from wrong. He never thinks; never reasons; he only obeys. If he is ordered to fire on his fellow citizens, on his friends, on his neighbors, on his relatives, he obeys without hesitation. If he is ordered to fire down a crowded street when the poor are clamoring for bread, he obeys, and sees the gray hairs of age stained with red and the life tide gushing from the breasts of women, feeling neither remorse nor sympathy. If he is ordered off as a firing squad to execute a hero or benefactor, he fires without hesitation, though he knows the bullets will pierce the noblest heart that ever beat in human breast.

"A Good Soldier" is a blind, heartless, soulless, murderous machine. He is not a man. He is not a brute, for brutes only kill in self defense. All that is human in him, all that is divine in him, all that constitutes the man has been sworn away when he took the enlistment roll. His mind, his conscience, aye, his very soul, are in the keeping of his officer.

No man can fall lower than a soldier—it is a depth beneath which we cannot go. Keep the boys out of the army. It is hell.

Down with the army and navy. We don't need killing institutions. We need life-giving institutions.

Both the Army and the Navy cleared London of the authorship of this pamphlet. In 1916, Lieutenant James D. Willson of the Navy issued and circulated a leaflet entitled "An Old Lie Nailed," in which was reprinted the following letter from London together with the canard, and stated "so-called Socialist publications" and "others whose practice it is to misrepresent the Army and Navy of the United States" were responsible.

In reply to your inquiry I will state that I never wrote a line of the "Good Soldier" canard. For years and years I have been denying the authorship of it, in England, in the United States, everywhere, by personal letter, by interview, by telegraph and by cable. There is scarcely a mail that comes to me which does not bring me a letter like yours, wanting to know whether or not I wrote the canard. As far as I can trace the history of this, it was originally published and circulated in Germany, and later on was brought over to the United States, translated and circulated with my name attached. And from there it has spread over the rest of the world. All you have to do is to read my books and newspaper work to find that for the newspapers I have done only war correspondence and prize-fighting, and that in my books I am hailed by the critics as the father of red blood fiction.

My opinion is that it behooves a country or nation like the United States to maintain a reasonable preparedness for defense against any country or nation that at any time may go out upon the way of war to carve earth space for itself out of weaker and unprepared nations.

Later, after London's death, Theodore Roosevelt, in a letter to Charmian, wrote that he was convinced of London's innocence in the matter.

A good friend of the Londons', Robert R. Burge, president of the Gulf Coast Steamship Co., presented Charmian with a ticket to Vera Cruz on one of his boats, with the admonition "but for good-

*ness sake don't go. The steamers are not suitable for ladies travel,
. . . but go if you really must." Charmian went.*

*She remained in Vera Cruz until London became ill (on May 30)
with acute bacillary dysentery. Nine days later they left Vera Cruz on
a cattle boat for Galveston and returned to the Beauty Ranch.*

*London made it a practice to give to Charmian a first edition of
each of his books with an inscription. The first book to come off the
press after his return from Vera Cruz was* The Strength of the Strong.
In it he inscribed, under the date of June 24, 1914:

> Dear My Mate-Woman:
>   Back again from Vera Cruz and all the world, you back with
> me from the war-game. I am almost driven to assert that our
> little war-game adventure was as sweet and fine as our first honey-
> moon.
>
>   Your mate,
>   Jack London.

May 16, 1914

THE RED GAME OF WAR

Wars and rumors of war. That, and naught else, was what was
to be heard flying across the country from west to east along its
southern border. Conductors, brakemen, porters, and the desert
dusty cattlemen who boarded the train at the last stop seemed
unaware of anything else under the dome of heaven but war.
And none so humble that he did not know how to conduct
that war impending to the south; and none so reticent but that,
on the slightest provocation, he would proceed to exposit just
how that war should be conducted.

Of course, the passengers, having nothing to do, talked war
all the time. It was difficult, speeding through the peaceful
country, to realize that these well-tailored, well-mannered, courteous men—some of them even with spectacles—could be so
easily divorced from their spectacles and clothes and become
raw savages, as ferocious as their talk.

The cool way in which they discussed battleships, submarines,
aerial bombs, torpedoes, and all the rest of the wonderful up-
to-date machine contrivances and devices for the abrupt and
violent introduction of foreign substances into the bodies of their

fellow mortals would have been peculiarly edifying to the contemplative mind of a philosopher. For, come to think of it, that is just what war is—the introduction of foreign substances into men's bodies with violent and disruptive intent.

The hunting animal so introduces claws and fangs. The savage so introduces arrowheads and spear points. We, in the clear white light of the full dawn of the twentieth century, so introduce pieces of iron which we propel enormous distances by virtue of our laboratory method of chemically mixing gunpowder. Also, we introduce pellets of lead, at high velocity, said pellets being cunningly jacketed with steel so that, while being still disruptive, they will not spread and be too disruptive.

So a concession must be made, after all, to the refining influence of civilization. Basically, the game is the same old red game of introducing the foreign substance. But to-day we at least introduce it according to certain set rules, agreements, and conventions. The intent, as of old, is to destroy the fellow creature who blocks our way of life or desire, but we do it with more technique and consideration.

The foregoing is not urged in the slightest spirit of sarcasm. What is, is beyond all peradventure. And the genus Homo is just precisely what he is—a highly intelligent animal with an amazing spiritual endowment that, on occasion, individually and collectively, functions in violent and destructive ways. War must be dreadfully human, else why did all those well-cultured, ethically trained men in the smoking room and observation car talk the way they did?

Far in the sands of western Texas our soldiers, who have been policing the border for the past two years, rode in to meet the train at every desert station in order to buy and eagerly read the newspapers for the latest war quotations. Where the heart is there the treasure is, and, to judge by the delight shown in their faces as they scanned the bull market in war stock, these soldier boys of ours certainly had their hearts in the game for which they were drilled and uniformed.

Yes, and it is a safe wager that in the heart of the last one of them, weary from long waiting, was the query "How long, O Lord, how long ere things break loose and we are started on our way?"

War and the rumors of war—there was no escaping: one breathed it, read it, heard it, dreamed it—yes, and ate it. For did not the primitive humor of the negro waiter in the dining car achieve the following sally: "Good morning, sah. Two nice scrambled Mexicans this morning, sah?"

Said the pullman conductor to me: "Lucky you're getting off at Houston. Big celebration to-day. Twelve thousand of our regulars are going to parade. San Jacinto Day, you know."

Verily it is so. We set aside holidays for the celebration of old wars and ancient battles. And we thrill, and get tickly sensations along the spine and moisten our eyes as we remember those old days and the deeds of our fathers. Not until we have evolved sufficiently to set aside days in honor of the inventions of industry and the discoveries of science will we cease going to war. In the meantime we are what we are, and it is most evident that we are still warriors.

But Houston was disappointed. The feet of war—or rather, the feet of twelve thousand of our young men—did not tramp along Houston's streets on San Jacinto Day. The feet of the young men were even then speeding south. The night before, Houston had seen them to bed in their wide-pitched camp. In the morning they were gone. Houston rubbed its eyes and stared at the great martial vacancy left on its landscape.

No finer need of praise can be given to the evacuation of Houston, when the word came over the wire from Washington, than to state that it was equal to the celerity and dispatch of our American circuses in their palmiest days.

From Houston to Galveston, flying fast as electricity could drive, across the green flat land one caught the first far glimpse of long lines of moving, canvas-topped commissary wagons and marching columns.

In the electric car were three girls who looked as if they had been weeping. For ever girls will love a soldier and ever girls will weep when the war medicine is made and the young men go forth.

While many of the men marched, those of the Fifth Brigade, having been selected to lead the way to Mexico, were hurried to Galveston by train. One such train, a long one, we overtook and slowly passed. The windows were crowded with the bright, expectant faces. Just boys they were—a long, moving picture of live, laughing faces. Young fellows, that was all, just young fellows —all trim, fine bodied huskies, smooth-shaven, boyish, bold, eager-eyed, efficient-looking, capable, adventurous, serving out their wanderlust of youth, as youth will do; for youth will be served, whether at Tampico or Vera Cruz, and youth is prone to like its service to be in foreign parts and oversea.

They were distinctively American faces, the great majority that laughed to us from the troop train. The percentage of blonds was high, and numbers of them were astonishingly blond. The brunets sparkled amid the blond types—ranged all the way from fairest yellow hair and palest blue eyes down through the richer tones to dark gray eyes and deep brown hair.

And as we passed that line of bright faces, first one girl, and then another, and, finally, the third, recognized her lover and was recognized. Greetings and love calls flew back and forth, until we drew ahead, whereupon the three girls dissolved in fresh tears. But I'll wager, just the same, no lucky young dog in that lucky Fifth Brigade, vanguard of the advance across the Gulf of Mexico, could have been persuaded by all the lovelorn lassies in the United States to stay behind, even though staying behind could be accomplished with honor. How was it that Laurence Hope voiced the plaint of the woman against the soldier lover? ". . . Desiring in my very arms the fiercer rapture of the fight."

And war rolled south on revolving wheels while the feet of the young men dangled and rested. Yes, and the iron-shod feet of war rested likewise, for car after car was loaded with army wagons and army mules.

Galveston was buzzing. Boys were crying extras, and fresher extras. The Hotel Galvez buzzed. Spurred officers came and went.

"Plenty of war talk in the village, eh?" queried the elevator boy.

Said the barber with impressive solemnity to the bootblack: "They's goin' to be somethin' doin' inside twenty-four hours— you listen to me."

Every porch in the city was a-clatter. Youth everywhere strained at home ties and duty in its desire to stampede to the nearest recruiting office. Old mothers who had lost sons and husbands in the Civil War days wept reminiscently in their rocking-chairs.

And while the youngsters were eager to volunteer, the oldsters were sitting back, saying:

"Let the youngsters go. When the pinch comes'll be time enough for us. Hell, ain't it, how a fellow gets patriotic when any other country gets gay with ourn?"

One soldier: "Well, what are they waitin' for? We're ready, ain't we?"

Other soldier: "Been ready two years an' over."

And both gaze yearningly out across the blue waters of the quiet Gulf and already see themselves upon it and steaming south for Tampico and Vera Cruz, or any other place so long as it is not this piping place of peace.

I remember the young men of Japan when they went out to war. Never did any generation of young men desire more madly to go out upon the red way. But they went almost holily to encounter the White Giant of the North, and they little expected and less desired to return.

Now our young men taking the sea path south are going out differently. Primarily, it is adventure. As a matter of course they are patriotic, but they have no sense of any seriousness before them. They feel they face no giant enemy in the south. They tell over again the tale of the Alamo, and recite with glee how Sam Houston lambasted Santa Anna at San Jacinto. Why, what they won't do to the Mexicans is . . . and they discover that speech is a most frail and inadequate means of expression of young blood and rollicking spirit.

Of course, if one were to pin them down to it—these bright blooded boys of ours whose feet itch to tread wider spaces and far places—they would admit that a few, a very few, are going to get hurt. But their next thought, which is scarce a thought but rather a blood count of emotion, would be: Aw, what's the use of youth and where's its wages if risks are not to be run in the high tide and heyday of life?

A sort of picnic, that's what, a sort of picnic . . . somewhat different, of course, from a Sunday-school picnic, and on a co-lossal scale, but still a picnic.

"A short campaign at the outside," say the youngsters.

But the oldsters shake their heads: "Look at the Civil War —called for three months' volunteers. You know how long that fracas lasted. You never can tell what you're goin' to do once you take hold. You can't leave go in a hurry."

A youngster: "Why, we could promenade through Mexico from end to end with twenty thousand men."

An oldster: "Yep, and take five hundred thousand men to police Mexico behind you while you promenaded on your way."

A young Texan of the Seventh Infantry: "Huh! Not if they was Texans. Why, I want to tell you we've threw the fear of —well, of Texas—into them so they ain't never forgot us. Say, d'ye know, I've heard more than one Mexican swear they could lick the whole United States if Texas was cut out of the scrap, an' d'ye know, I guess that's just about right."

"You mean . . . ?" I dared to query.

His words still ringing in his ears, he saw the trap his quick speech had led him into, and he laughed, disclaimed, and said: "I guess what I mean was cut out the whole United States and Texas could lick Mexico."

"Sure thing!" applauded the group, and the youngsters had the decision.

A minute later they were agreeing with the oldsters in one detail of managing the war, namely, that simultaneously with the movement on Tampico and Vera Cruz, the National Guards and Rangers should cross over and take possession of every Mexican Border town and water hole clear to the Pacific.

"The first line of defense is the enemy's territory," was the unanimous judgment.

Little they reck, these younglings of our nation, of what is before them. Their feet are a-tingle to be out on the old red way of man. Colts and calves play in the pastures. Our young men must also play, must romp, must be doing something, either sowing their wilderness of youth at home, or preferably, fighting abroad, vindicating themselves, and the fighting machine of an army which they compose—and, deeper, unreasoned, and unguessed, vindicating the institutions which have molded them and which are woven into the fibers of them.

But always, over it all, back of this glorious dance of youth, one visions the group of the old ones at Washington, the wise ones, the graybeards.

And, over it all and back of it all, most significant and sinister of all, looms the tragic figure of the man known among men as Huerta.[1] And a well-known man is he. This day they are chattering his name from London clubs and the war offices of world powers to the bazaars of India and the deep-matted, twilight rooms of the temples and tea houses of Nippon.

The current theory of Huerta's conduct in embroiling Mexico with the United States gives one pause to contemplate as amazing a situation as is conceivable in a particular man's affairs. Huerta, according to the classic Mexican custom established of very old, old time, has securely salted down in Europe 10,000,000 of pesos as a nest egg—or so runs the rumor on which is builded the theory. Huerta, it is said, was born a peon without a penny or a hope for two pennies all at one time to his heritage. Huerta, in the course of his dictatorship, by the devious ways long established of Mexican rulers, has accumulated and cached in Europe 10,000,000 of pesos extracted from the toil of his brother peons.

Madero[2] saved Villa's life when Huerta desired to execute Villa. Huerta, by custom established of old time, contrived to have Madero shot to death without witnesses, while Madero was in the act of attempting to escape in the darkness of night from a guard of Huerta's soldiers. This, by the way—this attempting to escape on foot by prisoners—is also a custom of old time invariably never practiced by Mexican captives of Mexicans. Yet statistics would tend to show conclusively that it is quite generally practiced. Only—well, sometimes statistics just must be doubted.

Villa,[3] still the theory runs, remembering the murder of his benefactor, red of beak and claw from many victories, is advancing south upon the failing Huerta with the sworn intent of avenging Madero's death. This means taking the life of Huerta.

[1] Victoriano Huerta (1854–1916), full-blooded Aztec Indian, came to power during the liberal regime of Francisco Madero (1911–1913). In February 1913 after an Army revolt in Mexico City he ordered the arrest of Madero and proclaimed himself Provisional President of Mexico. The United States refused to recognize his government.
[2] Francisco Indalecio Madero (1873–1913) was elected President of Mexico in 1911 after he forced Porfirio Díaz to resign.
[3] Francisco (Pancho) Villa (c.1877–1923), true name Dorotea Arango. Leader of the Rebel forces.

Perhaps not exactly that. There is the possibility that Villa will merely take Huerta prisoner and that Huerta, some dark night in an automobile, without witnesses, may inadvertently emulate Madero's feat with the same unfortunate and unforeseen end that Madero met. The how of Huerta's passing, if he falls into Villa's hand, is immaterial. The fact that he will pass is ordained.

So grows the picture and the theory of the tragedy of Huerta. Huerta, sometime peon, rules in Mexico. His ten millions reside in Europe. Death, in the form and visage of Villa, draws closer to him day by day from the north. Problem: how then may Huerta escape Villa and win to his treasure oversea? It is an interesting problem. To Huerta it is mighty interesting.

Might he not, the objection is sure to be raised, have escaped to the coast and away to Europe before ever the American flag was affronted at Tampico? Certainly not. Before he could have covered the distance between the palace and the railroad station he would have had a mob at his heels. The likelihood of getting away alive from the station would have been remote; and, even if successful in riding out his train from his capital a living man, the likelihood of his reaching Vera Cruz still alive, much less embarking alive from Vera Cruz, would have been too remote for consideration.

So Huerta remained in Mexico City with his problem. And, granting the theory, we get the picture of that desperate man in his high capital: ten millions of treasure awaiting him across the salt sea, ruler and prisoner in his great palace, playing the big game of life with death in the toss; Villa, who will kill him, sure as fate, drawing nearer day by day from the north.

And Huerta plays the game. The gringo is civilized and a humanitarian within limits of technique. There is only one way for Huerta to escape. The gringo must come and get him. The gringo would never turn him over to the tender mercies of Villa. The gringo would see him safe out of the country and turn him loose to connect with his ten millions.

Very well. Isn't the gringo doing it? Hasn't the gringo already started to come and get him? Huerta was no idiot over the technique of formal saluting of a flag.

It is a pretty situation. Primitive, 'tis true, but splendid pictorially and dramatically.

Incidentally, it will be rather an expensive rescue of one man on the part of the United States. The price will run to hundreds of millions of money, while no one dare forecast how many of the lives of our young men will be paid—all for the saving of the miserable life of a man who is himself already responsible for so many miserable deaths of other men.

But, correct or not, theory or fact, that mixed-blooded man is playing a big game of some sort there in his palace on the site of the ancient Aztec palace where Cortez long ago so magnificently played a freebooting game. Strange, also, is it to contemplate that in the veins of this mixed-blooded man run the strains of the blended races of Cortez and Montezuma.

Oh, well, not so long ago, and certainly a considerable time after Cortez and his captains were dead and dust, we, too, went a-freebooting, pilfered the owners of most of a continent of their land, and enunciated the working axiom that the only good Indian was a dead Indian. Yet there is a difference. We are reformed, and have developed quite a different and indisputably a better technique.

The last days at Galveston saw war glower red and redder. Extras appeared with increasing rapidity on the streets; and street boys, made giddy by such sudden wealth, took advantage of the excitement to sell any old paper as the very latest extra. The buzzards—for so are war correspondents named—began to gather. It is interesting to note that, within ten hours previous to the receipt from Washington of the order for the Fifth Brigade to embark, correspondents who had been on the way from New York and Chicago descended upon Galveston in a flock.

Scarcely had they arrived when the order came. The whisper invaded the dining room of the Hotel Galvez, but the news was received without excitement. Here and there an officer rose from the table and went out quietly to begin a night of unsleeping activity. That was about all.

In the ballroom the Fourth Infantry band continued to play and those officers danced who were not lucky enough to belong to the Fifth Brigade. Also, in the writing room every desk was occupied for a few minutes by young lieutenants getting off letters to the girls who just couldn't help loving a soldier at a distance.

In the misty gray of early morning the columns of marching soldiers in their dull olive drab had the seeming of long, lean torpedo-boat destroyers. They were not individuals to the eye, but war projectiles. Upon coming closer they showed a goodly, sturdy lot of trim, well-set fellows, clean and fit, marching as veterans march.

The twenty thousand spectators that flooded the transport docks did not seem to be at all in the way. There was no confusion, no shouting of orders. So quiet and orderly did the embarking of three thousand men with all their necessary fear proceed that one almost wondered if any orders were being issued.

Army wagons, buckboards, motor cars, and reluctant mules streamed steadily on board. It seemed that near the whole city was pouring into four transports without crowding them.

One pathetic note was the soldiers' dogs. Now it must be understood that soldiers' dogs are different from other dogs. They always accumulate about the fixed camps where the men remain for months. They are very wise. They know unerringly an officer from a soldier. They know enough never to presume or to intrude on an officer. Where officers walk they never walk.

They recognize that an officer's tent and the vicinity of an officer's tent are taboo, and never are they guilty of drinking from an officer's waterbucket. And they—soldiers' dogs of the Fifth Brigade—were bound for Mexico along with their masters. They crept demurely up the gangway in the thick of the lines of ascending soldiers, and when detected by a vigilant officer at head of the gangway, they obeyed, as soldiers' dogs should, and marched back down the gangway. And when so detected they betrayed no recognition of their master, for no soldier can recognize his dog—so heinous a circumstance is attempted stowaway. Nor did they whine or complain or voice a bark. They disappeared, these soldiers' dogs, and further deponent sayeth not, save that these same dogs ran down the gangway at Vera Cruz.

It may be nice to be an army woman in time of peace, but in war it is not so nice. Have our army women learned the control that plays so large a part in their husbands' business? Everything was quiet with them: there were no scenes, no violent sobbings, no hysteria. There were heavy eyes and moist eyes, last words, and yet again last words after, and that was all.

In short, in this act of saying farewell to their men folks the army women were splendid. Some I saw acceding to their husbands' wishes—saying a last good-by and departing before the whistles of the transports blew. One in particular I noted—a captain's wife. He led her down the gangway to the wharf and kissed her a long good-by, after which he returned on board. Then, her lips trembling, she turned and went straight down the dock to the shore. Not once did she turn her head and look back. A color sergeant, his wet-eyed wife beside him, held a very young baby in his arms. For a long time he gazed down on the tiny mite of life and said nothing. A young lieutenant hung about his mother, pressed the last lingering kiss on her lips, and, hand lingering in hand and loath to sever, he bowed his head in oldtime gallantry and kissed her hand.

High in the Gulf of Mexico, the lights of Galveston astern, the four transports, massed with lights from stem to stern, are being formed into a square, two abreast, under direction of destroyers that glide like a long row of shadows out of the gloom; that give orders through megaphones, and that glide away into the gloom, talking across the sea to one another in the medium of chimes of lights—red lights and white that flash and disappear in blinding lucidity on the short signal masts. Up above in the wireless room of the transport the words of the war men back at Galveston are being snatched out of the air.

Day on the Gulf of Mexico! All is peace under an azure sky. The sapphire sea is scarcely rippled by the trade wind gently blowing, and across this placid sea steam the white transports —soldier-loaded—with an ominous destroyer convoying on either flank, while a third destroyer scouts ahead.

A blur of smoke rises on the horizon and we know that the battleship *Louisiana* has come up from Vera Cruz to meet us. We know while all that is visible of her is the blur of smoke, for her name and errand have long since been snatched out of the air by wizards' apprentices at work in the wireless room.

May 23, 1914

WITH FUNSTON'S[1] MEN

Daybreak on a glassy sea and startled flying fish are struggling to fly in the absence of wind. Seaward the destroyers, like cardboard silhouettes, pass across the blood-red orb of the sun just clearing the horizon.

Ahead still steams our convoying battleship, the *Louisiana*. Astern, in line at half speed, steam our three sister transports. Coastward are the blinking light-house, a long blur of land that with growing day resolves itself into a breakwater, a low shore, a towered city, and a harbor of many battleships. So many battleships are there that they have spilled out of the crowded harbor until several times as many are in the open roadstead. And there are naval supply ships, hospital ships, a wireless ship, and colliers.

And overhead, to give the last touch of modern war to the scene, a naval hydroplane burrs like some gigantic June bug through the gray of day.

Here where Cortez burned his ships long centuries gone, and where Scott[2] bombarded and took the city two generations ago, lie Uncle Sam's warships with every man on his toes. Yes, and every soldier gazing eagerly ashore from crowded transports is on his toes.

All is peaceful, yet the feeling one gets of the many ships, the burring flying machines, and the thousands of men is that of being on tiptoe to begin.

Ashore all is as peaceful and as markedly on its toes as is the sea. Everywhere marines and blue jackets are cooking breakfast. From the roof of the Terminal Hotel sailors are wigwagging. Sailor aids of sailor officers gallop back and forth on commandeered Mexican horses, and commandeered automobiles dash by with officers on the seats and armed sailors standing on the running boards.

American women, quite like American women at home, with

[1] General Frederick Funston, Commander of the expedition to Vera Cruz.
[2] General Winfield Scott (1786–1866) led the campaign into Mexico in 1847, captured Vera Cruz March 26.

never an earmark of being refugees from the interior of Mexico, are breakfasting on the cool arcaded sidewalks of hotels bordering the Plaza. Overhead whirl huge electric fans along the lines of the tables where our women breakfast so composedly and sailor sentries pace back and forth. Sentries are everywhere. So are the newsboys with their eternal extras. Through the confusion of bootblacks, flower sellers, and picture post-card peddlers stride naval and marine officers in duck and khaki, and from the hips of all of them big revolvers and automatics swing in leather holsters. Down the street, in the thick of mule carts and mounted sailors, pass bare-headed Mexican women returning from market with big fish unwrapped and glistening in the sun.

In the Hotel Diligencia's bedroom where I write these lines under lofty, gold-edged beams, there is a spatter of fresh bullet holes on the blue wall. In the lace-patterned mosquito canopy over my bed is a line of irregular rents which, folded as they were originally, show the path of a single bullet. The glass of the French windows that open on the balcony is perforated by many bullets. The wrecked door shows how our sailors entered behind the butts of their rifles in the course of the street fighting and house cleaning. From the fretted balcony one can see the ruins of plate glass and mirrors in the shops and hotels fronting the street and Plaza.

Mexican officers seem to have notions different from ours in the matter of prosecuting war.

When the landing of our forces was imminent, General Maas, who was the Federal commander at Vera Cruz, released the criminal portion of the prisoners confined in the fortress of San Juan de Ulloa. These were the hard cases, the murderers and robbers and men guilty of violent and terrible crimes. The politicals General Maas was very careful not to release. And when our forces did land, General Maas fled for the hinterland before the fighting began, having first instructed his soldiers to shift for themselves. While the released prisoners did take some part in the street fighting and housetop sniping, in the main they devoted themselves to pillage. Hard cash was what they went after as for instance the smashed safes in Mr. Tansey's office at the Pierce Oil Refinery attest. Falling back before our men, these convicts terrorized the country people, looting everything of value and not refraining from attacking the women. So merciless were they that the outraged peons captured and summarily executed two of them who had lingered behind their fellows.

Yes, there is a decided evolution in technique of war as practiced by modern soldiers. Our fighting ships are ten and fifteen million-dollar electrical, chemical, and mechanical laboratories, and they are manned by scientists and mechanicians. They had the street cleaners out ere the bodies were picked up. In a matter of several hours they repaired and ran the two scrapped locomotives which the Federals had thought too worthless to run out. And while this was going on other sailors were rigging short wireless masts on top of a day coach and equipping the car with a complete wireless apparatus.

The ice plant of Vera Cruz had broken down, and Vera Cruz without ice was a condition not to be tolerated, so by afternoon the sailors had repaired the plant, and the sick and wounded as well as all the rest of the city had its ice again. When four knocked-down automobiles were discovered, volunteers were called for and in less than three hours the cars were assembled and were being driven about the city on military business by the jackies who had assembled them. As civilians remarked, our sailors are able to practice all trades and professions under the sun with the sole exception of wet-nursing. Even so, I have seen them carrying Mexican babies for tired mothers across the stretch of railroad which the Federals destroyed.

And the way our sailors drove and rode horses, mules, and burros was even more wonderful than their other achievements. They came off our ships sailors; they will return soldiers.

They tell of one young sailor who mounted a commandeered horse in a lull in the fighting. He had not minded the fighting, but it was with somewhat of the spirit one embarks on a forlorn hope that he got his legs astride the animal. "Well," he said as he settled himself in the saddle, "commence."

"What do I do now?" asked another jacky, mounting at the Plaza.

"Go ahead half speed," was the advice. "Keep your helm amidships to the corner, then starboard your helm and proceed under forced draft."

It is true that, when under forced draft, the jackies hold

on inelegantly by main strength of gripping legs; but the point is that they do hold on. I have looked in vain to see one of them separated from his mount. One misadventure only have I witnessed; and then the sailor, at a dead gallop, abruptly put his helm hard over at a sharp corner and capsized his four-legged craft. When the band struck up "The Star-Spangled Banner" at Admiral Fletcher's[3] flag raising, a marine, mounted on a Mexican horse, took its ear and turned it forward. "Listen to that, hombre," said the marine; "that's real music. It's American music."

On the *Arkansas* occurred an incident which serves to show to what extent our men were on their toes prior to landing. Lieutenant Commander Arthur B. Keating of the *Arkansas* battalion had selected the best and strongest of his men for shore work. The men who were not selected were sad and sore. At the last there remained but one man more to select, and two of the youngsters urged what was considered equal claims of health, strength, and record. How to decide between them was beyond the Lieutenant Commander. The boys themselves suggested the way. They put on boxing gloves and fought for it. Those who saw the battle aver that it was the hottest bout between amateurs they had ever witnessed. At the end of four rounds, it was a draw and Lieutenant Commander Keating was more perplexed than ever. His final solution of the problem was the only way it could be fairly solved. He took both lads. Later he reported that, as in everything else, they had played equally splendid parts in shore fighting and shore work.

Only very brave men or fools without any knowledge of modern shell fire could have fired upon our sailors and marines from the Naval School. Broadside on, at close range, lay the *Chester*. When the first shots were fired upon our men, the *Chester* went into action for a hot five minutes. Had the taxpayer at home witnessed the way those upper story windows were put out by the *Chester*'s shells, he would never again grudge the money spent of recent years in target practice. Onlookers say that it reminded them of Buffalo Bill's exhibitions of rifle shooting.

[3] Admiral Frank Friday Fletcher (1855–1928), commanded the divisions of the Atlantic fleet and naval forces which seized and occupied Vera Cruz.

The outside of the Naval School was little damaged. Inside it was a vast wreck. Practically every shell entered by way of the windows and exploded inside. When I visited the building, which is a huge affair, many buzzards were appropriately perched on the broken parapets. Inside, through burst floors, rent ceilings, and masses of fallen masonry, one could trace the flight of the shells through massive partitions to the spots where they had exploded.

There was all the evidence of the hot five minutes. In the big patio were great heaps of fallen cement balustrades from second-story balconies. Some of the shells went clear through the building, crossed the patio, and burst in the rear rooms. Many years had been consumed in the construction, equipping, and organizing of that building, and in five minutes it was to all intents and purposes destroyed. Such is the efficiency of twentieth century war machinery. Laboratories furnished with most delicate and expensive instruments were knocked into cocked hats by single shells.

One lecture room was filled with beautiful models of ships. One model, of a full-rigged ship, twenty-five feet in length, with skysail yards and all sails set, precise in every minutest detail aloft and alow, was undamaged save for a rent in her mainsail from a fragment of shell. Other and smaller models, shattered and dismasted, covered the floor with all the destruction of an armada. On a blackboard was scrawled "Captured by the U.S.S. New Hampshire, April 22, 1914."

In other lecture rooms, on blackboards alongside academic problems of war as demonstrated by Mexican cadets, were chalked records of boys from the Utah, the San Francisco, and the Arkansas.

Bloodstained cots and pillows showed that more than roof beams and masonry had been shattered. Through knee-deep riff-raff of discarded uniforms, sketches, maps, and examination papers, clucked and strutted one live thing left from the bombardment—a trim Mexican rooster that bore all the marks of a fighting cock.

But it was in the second story that the worst devastation was wrought. Roofs, floors, and walls were perforated and smashed to chaos. "Mind your foot," was the constant cry as one trod gingerly over debris and wove in and out among yawning holes.

The touch of the eternal feminine was not missing. My lady's boudoir seemed to have received the severest fire. Fourteen shell holes punctured the walls, the ceiling had partly fallen in, a great hole gaped in the floor, and one shell had burst directly on the brass bed. The floor was hillocked with masses of masonry and broken furniture, and all about were scattered pretties and fripperies of the lady—empty jewel cases, powder puffs, silver-mounted brushes. Most conspicuous of all was a pair of red, high-heeled Spanish slippers.

Down in the railroad station, where I boarded the rescue train that runs out each day to the Federal lines, our sailors and marines were cooking, washing clothes, and teaching the Mexican youth how to pitch baseball. All along the track, until the country was reached, our men were encamped and performing sentry duty.

A guard of bluejackets, under the command of Lieutenant Fletcher of the *Florida*, manned the train. The engine was run by our enlisted men, who had repaired it, as was also the wireless by the men who had installed it. Even the porter of the Pullman car was an unmistakable American Negro.

Two miles beyond our last outpost we came to the break where the Federals had torn up two miles of track, burning the ties and carrying the rails away with them. Here, also, was a block-house of advanced Federal outposts.

Under a white Turkish towel, carried by a sailor, Lieutenant Fletcher met and conferred with the Mexican Lieutenant in charge. The latter was small, stupid-tired, and a greatly embarrassed sort of man. The contrast between the two Lieutenants was striking. The Mexican Lieutenant strove to add inches to himself by standing on top of a steel rail. But in vain. The American still towered above him. The American was—well, American. Little of Mexican or of Spanish was in the other. It was patent that he was mostly Indian. Even more of Indian was in the ragged, leather-sandaled soldiers under him. They were short, squat, patient-eyed, long-enduring as the way of the peon has been even in the long centuries preceding Cortez, when Aztec and Toltec enslaved him to burden bearing.

One could not help being sorry for these sorry soldier Indians, who slouched awkwardly about while our Lieutenant scanned the far track across the break in the hope of some sign of our countrymen fleeing from the capital. Sorry soldier Indians they truly were. When I thought of our own fine boys of the fleet and the army back in Vera Cruz, it seemed to me that it would not be war, but murder. What chance could such lowly, oxlike creatures, untrained themselves and without properly trained officers, have against our highly equipped, capably led young men? These soldiers of the peon type are merely descendants of the millions of stupid ones who could not withstand the several hundred ragamuffins of Cortez and who passed stupidly from the harsh slavery of the Montezumas to the no less harsh slavery of the Spaniards and of the later Mexicans.

And yet one must not forget that each one of these sorry soldiers bore a modern rifle, the cartridges for which, loaded with smokeless powder, are capable of propelling a bullet to kill at a mile's distance and farther, and, at close range, to perforate the bodies of two or three men. Also, each of these sorry soldiers, at command, by the mere crooking of index fingers, could release far-flighted messengers of death. Also, the mark of the cross, rightly applied to the steel-jacketed nose of the bullet, can turn that bullet into a dum-dum that makes a small hole on entering a man's body and a hole the size of a soup plate on leaving. It requires no intelligence thus to notch a bullet. Even a peon can do it.

War is a silly thing for a rational, civilized man to contemplate. To settle matters of right and justice by means of introducing into human bodies foreign substances that tear them to pieces is no less silly than ducking elderly ladies of eccentric behavior to find out whether or not they are witches. But—and there you are—what is the rational man to do when those about him persist in settling matters at issue by violent means?

I am a rational man. I firmly believe in arbitrament by police magistrates and civil courts. Nevertheless, on occasion, I find myself in contact with men who are prone, say, to rob me of my purse, and who elect to do it by violent and disruptive means. So, on such occasions, I am compelled to carry an automatic in order to dispute with such men my path in life which they are blocking and ambuscading. Personally, and for a lazy man, carrying a big automatic is a confounded nuisance. I hope for the day to come when it will not be necessary for any man to carry an automatic. But in the meantime, preferring to be a live dog rather than a dead lion, I keep thin oil on my pistol and try it out once in a while to make sure that it is working.

As it is with rational men to-day, so it is with nations. The dream of a world police force and of a world court of arbitration will some day be realized. But that day is not to-day. What is is. And to cope with what is, it behooves nations to keep thin oil on their war machinery and know how to handle it.

Texas was long notorious as a gun-fighting State. To-day it is against the law for a man to carry a revolver in Texas. Times do change. But there is always the time between times. As one regarded the Mexican Lieutenant with this peon soldiers, it was patent that the old order still obtained, and that each peon was equipped with sufficient cartridges to destroy the rationality of a hundred men like me.

And we stood there under our white Turkish towel, surrounded by armed men, and quested across a stretch of ruined railroad for the sight of some of our own men, women, and children making their way down to the coast from mobs that looted, plundered, and cried death to them.

"I've found him at last," said a friend, a Texas civilian and ex-roughrider.

All the way out of the train he had been lining himself up against one and another of the husky, broad-shouldered sailor boys and lamented that he could not find a man he could lick. Now he gazed with satisfaction at the little Mexican Lieutenant and muttered in my ear: "I just wish it was up to him and me to settle this whole war. Take him on on any terms—bite, gouge, or anything up to locking us, stripped, in a dark room."

A train appeared in the distance between green walls of jungle. Through our glasses we could make out parasols and sunshades that advertised women of our race who had escaped the perils of the mob-ridden interior.

Permission was reluctantly accorded us, and we advanced a mile along the destroyed track to meet our countrymen. Glad as we were to see them, their gladness at seeing white men from the coast was almost pathetic. For three days and nights they had not had their clothes off nor lain in a bed, nor had they ever been certain of their lives during that time.

It seems the Mexican officers have a very simple and very clever technique of waging war on civilians of the United States. The officers themselves rob civilians of revolvers. This enables the next mob of death-shouting Mexicans to put words into deeds without the slightest risk of being hurt. Of course the Mexican army cannot be held responsible for all the actions and the murders committed by such mobs. Also, officers are richer by the number of weapons they accumulate from fleeing Americans.

By the time our refugees reached the train and saw the American uniform they were stating that it was the finest thing they had ever seen in their lives. As the train backed into Vera Cruz the landscape continued to grow more beautiful, for it was covered everywhere with sailors and marines on sentry duty or in camp. But the sight of the inner and outer harbors filled with our warships was the finishing stroke.

Said one of the refugees, a doctor: "I just wish the fellows at Washington who are running things could have had our experience. It would change their views on diplomacy and on army and navy appropriation bills. I tell you, if they had been robbed and mobbed and thrown into jail along with their wives and children, and heard the roar going up all about them of 'Muerto los gringos!' and then, finally, got down the country as we have, with their tongues hanging out, and seen these warships and bluejackets—I tell you they couldn't get back to the States quick enough to start working for a larger army and navy."

The views of American residents of Mexico should be of value at the present time, and I shall repeat them without comment to show how blows the wind with those whose personal interests are vitally involved.

"Somehow," said one of them, "we don't enjoy seeing the United States call on the ABC class in Spanish and Portuguese to help her out of this mess."

Another declared: "This waiting and watching, our Fabian

offensiveness, is a whole lot easier at Washington than at Vera Cruz. Besides, I can't help worrying over what the Mexicans have done or are doing to my wolfhound. That dog—why, sir, just standing on her four legs, she could reach her head over and take anything from the center of this breakfast table."

"How are the people at home feeling now?" inquired a refugee. "They got us into this mess. Are they going to get us out of it?"

The thorough agreement of all American residents is that the present crisis was brought on by the policy of our Government, and that the only way out is to go on through. The taking of Vera Cruz by the naval forces of the United States precipitated the bad feeling against Americans that has been fermenting during the past several years, and if the United States should recede from its present position, it will forever be impossible for Americans again to live in Mexico.

As one man, a twenty-year resident, said: "I've lived here ever since I was man-grown. I know what I am talking about. Humpty Dumpty has had a great fall. Chile, Brazil, and Argentina can never put him together again. Only our army and our navy can put us Americans back again and insure us a fair deal. And when I speak of ourselves I mean the people who have made Mexico what it is to-day, or, rather, what it was the other day before the Tampico flag incident. More than any other country —than all other countries added together—have we put in the capital, the brains, and the technical skill; we've supplied the mechanical engineers, the mining engineers, the agricultural chemists, and the scientific farmers. By virtue of what we have done in Mexico we have a right here, and we should be protected in that right, especially since our Government by its own action has endangered that right."

Said a man of action, his State obvious by his remark: "Never mind the rest of the United States. Just turn Texas loose and we'll lick them to a frazzled finish."

"Huh!" from another man of action. "Send a single man up-country with a big bag of money and the whole thing could be settled out of hand."

Another long dweller in the land: "I've lived on Oaxaca fifteen years, and I make the statement, founded on personal knowledge, that 80 percent of the middle class and educated Mexicans throughout Oaxaca would hail intervention by the United States. They are tired of this era of continual revolution."

A mining engineer: "My people represent millions invested in development. We are not afraid of the next step the United States may take. What we are afraid of is that she may not take any step."

A locomotive engineer: "Well, our country has got us in bad. It's up to her to get us out good."

A marine guarding a sand hill: "This is a hell of a war."

A business man from the City of Mexico: "They have insulted me, broken windows of my home, and looted my store. Also, they have robbed me of my automobile; on the way down to Vera Cruz a Mexican officer took my revolver away from me. At the present moment I have two hundred pesos and the clothes I stand up in, and my country is talking compromise."

Another business man: "For years the United States has been watching and waiting. Now it has made one step into Mexico, imperiled all our lives, caused us incalculable losses of property and personal possessions, and is hesitating whether to withdraw from that one step or not."

A university man: "I thought I understood the English language. I find now that I don't. My brain is fuzzy with trying to get ordinary sense out of our diplomatic utterances."

An officer of marines: "We've lost many times as many sailors as were lost in the Spanish-American War, and yet this is not war. We have merely occupied a customhouse and courteously taken the government of Vera Cruz out of the hands of Mexican officials."

A staff officer of the Second Division: "It is not a question with me of the merits or demerits of the affair. I am the servant of my country. It spent a whole lot of money training me. When it says advance I advance; when it says retreat, I retreat. Nevertheless, I remember that my old father was always fond of quoting Davy Crockett's 'Be sure you are right and then go ahead.' Well, we've come ahead from Galveston to Vera Cruz. And here we stop. What's the matter? Did the United States go ahead and then find out that it was not right?"

Another officer: "It wasn't the flag incident at Tampico; it was the sum of many incidents preceding the flag incident."

A lawyer: "But, as a jury decided long ago in England, two hundred blackbirds do not make a black horse."

"And twenty thousand looted refugee Americans plus a thousand insults to our nation make a sum no larger than the smallest of the parts, and therefore no *casus belli*," was the retort of a fellow lawyer.

"Whisper!" says an American farmer from Cordova. "Within a week look to see Huerta in Vera Cruz, safely on board a foreign warship, and headed for Europe."

Again is limned the lurid picture of that Indian dictator in his high city—with Villa threatening death from the North, with Zapata[4] unpacified in the South, with a great treasure cached in Europe—trying to solve the desperate problem of how to get from his high city to the sea coast and to Europe.

Speaks up a refugee: "I came out of Mexico City two days ago. Huerta was then sandbagging the palace."

"Against American shells?" queries the latest newspaper man from the United States.

"No," answers the refugee. "Nor against Villa. He is sandbagging the palace to withstand attacks from the populace!"

May 30, 1914

MEXICO'S ARMY AND OURS

Many officers and men have I shaken hands with in the brief days since this wave of war rolled south and broke on the shore of Mexico, and no officer nor man have I found who was immune to a certain infection. The infection, however, might be described in surgical jargon as "beneficent." On the face of it every mother's son of them has told me something that cannot possibly be true. Only one out of all of them could have told the truth, and it is beyond my powers of discernment to pick out this man. But I have yet to meet an officer of soldiers or marines who has not only solemnly assured me but with glistening eyes of enthusiasm has averred that his regiment or battalion, officers and men, for discipline and efficiency, is the finest

4 Emiliano Zapata (1883–1919) first joined Madero against Díaz, later joined forces with Villa and entered Mexico City triumphantly in 1914 forcing Carranza to flee.

in the entire army of the United States. Furthermore, each one disclaims any personal prejudice in the matter and usually concludes with the statement that it is generally conceded in army circles that his regiment or battalion is the finest. I wonder if such esprit de corps exists in the Mexican army. What our army and navy is was splendidly demonstrated when our bluejackets marched aboard their ships before our drawnup soldiers while Admiral Fletcher transferred the command of Vera Cruz to General Funston. Boys they were, all boys, the flower of the young men of our land, and they marched with the clacking rhythm of "boots, boots," on the pavement along the broad lane formed by the regulars on one side presenting arms and on the other side cheering American civilians. It was a joy to see the faces that tried not to smile with pleasure over the applause for work well done, and to catch the involuntary sideward glances of boyish eyes not yet quite disciplined to the level impassive look of war.

These thousands of sailors marched straight down the dock end and disappeared. The effect was uncanny. What was becoming of them? The smokestacks of a couple of tugs showed at the dock end, and that was all. And yet the river of men flowed on and on, sailors and marines, officers, bands, hospital squads, and moving banners, sun-tanned men of the *Arkansas*, the *Florida*, the *Utah*, the *San Francisco*, the *New Hampshire*, the *South Carolina*, the *Vermont*, the *Chester*, and the *New Jersey*, all without hitch or halt, and disappeared. It reminded one of the tank of the New York Hippodrome, when the long lines of stage soldiers march down into the water, knee-high, hip-high, shoulder-high, then heads under and are gone.

But out at the dock end, besides the tugs, was a flotilla of launches and cutters that received those thousands as fast as they arrived and carried them at a single trip to the battleships lying in the inner and outer harbors.

Our soldiers and sailors are markedly different in type. It must be curious how this happens to be so. Do land life and sea life make the difference? Or does one common type of man elect the sea and another common type elect the land? The sailors are shorter, broader shouldered, thicker set. The soldiers are taller, leaner, longer legged. Their faces are leaner, their lips thinner. They seem to the eye tougher, stringier, sterner. The sailors' faces seem broader across the cheek bones. Their lips seem fuller, their bodies more rounded.

Most notable is the difference when they are grouped into marching masses. The sailors have a swinging, springing, elastic stride. The soldiers' legs move more mechanically, more like clockwork legs, with a very tiny minimum of waste motion. It is prettier to watch the sailors marching with all the swaying elasticity of their bodies, and yet one receives the impression that, when it comes to the long killing hiking, the soldiers would easily outwalk their comrades of the sea. A great throng of Mexicans, numbers of them without doubt having sniped our sailors during the first days, looked on this display of what manner of men we send to war. The haste and advertisement with which they doffed their hats to the Stars and Stripes were absurd and laughable.

One cannot but imagine what the situation would be like were it reversed—were Vera Cruz populated by Americans and in the possession of a Mexican army. First of all, our jefe politico, or mayor, would have been taken out and shot against a wall. Against walls all over the city our soldiers and civilians would have been lined up and shot. Our jails would have been emptied of criminals, who would be made soldiers and looters. No American's life would be safe, especially if he were known to possess any money. Law, save for harshest military law, such as has been meted out by conquerors since the human world began, would have ceased. So would all business have ceased. He who possessed food would hide it, and there would be hungry women and children.

Quite the contrary has been our occupation of Vera Cruz. To the amazement of the Mexicans, there was no general slaughter against walls. Instead of turning the prisoners loose, their numbers were added to. Every riotous and disorderly citizen, every sneak thief and petty offender, was marched to the city prison the moment he displayed activity. The American conquerors bid for the old order that had obtained in the city, and began the bidding by putting the petty offenders to sweeping the streets.

No property was confiscated. Anything commandeered for the use of the army was paid for, and well paid for. Men who owned horses, mules, carts, and automobiles competed with one another to have their property commandeered. The graft which all business men suffered at the hands of their own officials immediately ceased. Never in their lives had their property been so safe and so profitable. Incidentally, the diseases that stalk at the heels of war did not stalk. On the contrary, Vera Cruz was cleaned and disinfected as it had never been in all its history.

In short, American occupation gave Vera Cruz a bull market in health, order, and business. Mexican paper money appreciated. Prices rose. Profits soared. Verily, the Vera Cruzans will long remember this being conquered by the Americans, and yearn for the blissful day when the Americans will conquer them again. They would not mind thus being conquered to the end of time.

An exciting sight was the cleaning up of the Naval School, which has been so disorganized the first day by the five minutes of shell fire from the *Chester*. Immediately the city had been turned over to the army by the navy, the first battalion of the Fourth Infantry and Fourth Field Artillery descended upon the Naval School. In a trice every window was vomiting forth the debris that clogged the interior. And then was fought the second battle of the Naval School. Thousands of poor Mexicans—men, women, and children—surrounded the building and battled over the old shoes, shattered furniture, and discarded clothes. It was the women who fought fiercest and most vociferously, and, to the accompaniment of much hair pulling, many a pair of linen trousers had its legs irrevocably separated. They struggled and squabbled and ran hither and thither like ants about a honey-pot. For once war was kind to them, and, instead of being looted, they were themselves tasting the joys of looting. And alas! I saw the ruined pretties rain down amid the mortar dust from my lady's boudoir and the two red, high-heeled Spanish slippers borne off in opposite directions by gleeful Indian women.

As I write this, beneath my window, with a great clattering of hoofs on the asphalt, is passing a long column of mountain batteries, all carried on the backs of our big Government mules. And as I look down at our sun-bronzed troopers in their olive drab, my mind reverts to the review the other day of our soldiers and sailors. Surely, if the peon soldiers of Mexico could all have been brought down to witness what manner of soldiers and equipment was ours, there would have been such a rush for the brush that ten years would not have seen the last of them dug out of their hiding places.

And yet this is not fair. The peon soldier is not a coward. Stupid he well is, just as he is illy trained and sillily officered but he is too much of a fatalist as well as a savage to be grossly afraid of death. The peon bends to the mailed fist of power, but never breaks. Like the fellah of Egypt, he patiently endures through the centuries and watches his rulers come and go.

Changes of government mean to the peon merely changes of the everlasting master. His harsh treatment and poorly rewarded toil are ever the same, unchanging as the sun and seasons. He has little to lose and less to gain. He is born to an unlovely place in life. It is the will of God, the law of existence.

With rare exceptions he does not dream that there may be a social order wherein can be no masters of the sort he knows. He has always been a slave. He was a slave to the Toltecs and Aztecs, to the Spaniards, and to the Mexicans descended from the Aztecs and the Spaniards. It must not be concluded that there is no hope for him in the future. He is what he is to-day, and what he has been for so long, because he has been made so by a cruel and ruthless selection.

If a breeder should stock his farm with the swiftest race horses obtainable, and employ a method of selection whereby only the slowest and clumsiest horses were bred, it would not be many generations before he would have a breed of very slow and very clumsy horses. Life is plastic and varies in all directions. Occasionally this breeder would find a beautiful, swift colt born on his farm. Since kind begets kind, he would eliminate such a colt and perpetuate only the slow and clumsy.

Now this is just the sort of selection that has been applied to the peon for many centuries. Whenever a peon of dream and passion and vision and spirit was born he was eliminated. His masters wanted lowly, docile, stupid slaves, and resented such a variation. Soon or late the spirit of such a peon manifested itself and the peon was shot or flogged to death. He did not beget. His kind perished with him whenever he appeared.

But life is plastic and can be molded by selection into diverse forms. The horse breeder can reverse his method of selection, and from slow and clumsy sires and dams breed up a strain of horses beautiful and swift. And so with the peon. For the present generation of him there is little hope. But for the future generations a social selection that will put a premium of living on dream and passion and vision and spirit will develop an entirely different type of peon.

But we must not make the mistake of straying after far goals. The time is now. We live now. Our problem, the world problem, the peon problem, is now. The peon we must consider is the peon as he is now—the selected burden bearer of the centuries. He has never heard of economic principles, nor a square deal. Nor has he thrilled, save vaguely, to the call of freedom—in which event freedom has meant license, and, as robber and bandit, he has treated the weak and defenseless in precisely the same way he has been accustomed to being treated.

I was through a Mexican barracks. It was like a jail. All the windows were barred. They had to be barred so that the conscript peon soldiers might not escape. Most of them do not like to be soldiers. They are compelled to be. All over Mexico they gather the peons into the jails and force them to become soldiers. Sometimes they are arrested for petty infractions of the law. A peon seeks to gladden his sad existence by drinking a few cents' worth of half-spoiled pulque. The maggots of intoxication begin to crawl in his brain, and he is happy in that for a space he has forgotten himself in God knows what dim drunken imaginings. Then the long arm of his ruler reaches out through the medium of many minions, and the peon, sober with an aching head, finds himself in jail waiting the next draft to the army. Often enough he does not have to commit any petty infraction. He is railroaded to the front just the same.

He does not know whom he fights for, for what, or why. He accepts it as the system of life. It is a very sad world, but it is the only world he knows. This is why he is not altogether a coward in battle. Also it is why, in the midst of battle or afterward, he so frequently changes sides. He is not fighting for any principle, for any reward. It is a sad world in which witless, humble men are just forced to fight, to kill, and to be killed. The merits of either banner are equal, or, rather, so far as he is concerned, there are no merits to either banner.

He prays to God in some dim, dumb way, and vaguely imagines when he has been expedited from this sad world by a machete slash or bayonet thrust or high-velocity steel-jacketed bullet that all will be made square in that other world where God rules and where task-masters are not.

Yet, deep down in the true ribs of him, there is a vein of raw savagery in the peon. Of old he delighted in human sacrifice. To-day he delights in the not always skilled butchery of bulls in the game introduced by his late Spanish masters. He likes cock-fighting with curved steel spurs that slash to the heart of life and cast a crimson splash upon the dull gray of living.

And still the peon is not exposited. There is another side to him. He is a born gambler, as well as fatalist, and he is not averse to taking a chance; though his own life be the stake, he plays against another's life. How else can be explained his nervy conduct, deserted by his officers, in defending Vera Cruz against our landing forces?

Now I am not altogether a coward. I have even been guilty on occasion of taking a chance. And yet I am frank to say that I would not dream of taking a chance on the flat roofs of Vera Cruz against thousands of American soldiers and a fleet of battleships with an effective range of five thousand yards.

But this was the very chance many a peon soldier took. He sniped our men from the roofs in the fond hope that he could kill a man and escape being killed himself. Also, he was stupid in that he did not realize how little chance he had. Nevertheless, and on top of it all, he was not afraid.

They say that he and his fellows even dared to crawl unwounded, amid the wounded, into the hospital cots under the Red Cross, and to draw blankets over themselves and their Mausers, and to crawl out occasionally to the roofs for another shot at our sailors. When it became too hot for them they hid among the wounded again. Now this is a deed too risky for my nerve or for the nerve of any intelligent man. But I insist that these Mexican soldiers were stupid enough voluntarily to take the chance. From this another conclusion may be drawn, namely, that the sorry soldier of Mexico is not altogether amiable and is prone to be nasty and dangerous to the American boys who have crossed the sea to take "peaceable" possession of a customhouse.

I saw the leg of a peon soldier amputated. It was a perfectly good leg, all except for a few inches of bone near the thigh which had been shattered to countless fragments by a wobbling, high-velocity American bullet. And as I gazed at that leg, limp yet with life, being carried out of the operating room, and realized that this was what men did to men in the twentieth century after Christ, I found myself in accord of sentiment with the peon: it is a sad world, a sad world!

It is a sad world wherein the millions of the stupid lowly are compelled to toil and moil at the making of all manner of commodities that can be and are on occasion destroyed in an instant by the hot breath of war. I have just come back from the vast Cuartel, or Barracks, of Vera Cruz. Such a destruction of the labor of men! Bales upon bales and mountains of bales of cloth-ing, or uniforms of wool, of linen, of cotton, disrupted, torn to pieces, scattered about, infected by possible diseases that compel a final cleansing by fire. Huge squad rooms, knee-deep in the litter of things the toil of men has made—hats, caps, shirts, modern leather shoes and rude sandals of the sort worn on the north Mediterranean half a thousand years before the days of Julius Caesar; saddles and saddle bags, spurs, bridles, and bits; entrenching tools, scattered contents of soldiers' ditty boxes, can-teens and mess kits of tin, serapes from the north, mats from the hot countries, meals partly eaten, half-cooked messes of food in the kitchen pots, smashed Mausers, cymbals and tubes, drums and cornets of a brass band that had departed abruptly and bandless.

In the matter of a few minutes the feet of war had trod under foot and passed on. Those who fled had fled hastily, leaving their last-issued rations behind. Those who pursued had paused but long enough to fire a myriad shots and race on. The empty bandoleers marked the trail of the American sailors and marines. In the stables were the officers' automobiles and carromatas with seats for grooms behind. But there were no horses, and the auto-mobiles had been smashed. Thousands of hours' toil of men's hands had been annihilated.

The streets of Vera Cruz teem with beggars. Our soldiers are pestered by the starving, ragged poor. A thousand meals cluttered the Cuartel, already mildewed and being eaten by cockroaches

and stray cats; woven cloth and manufactured footgear sufficient
for ten thousand poor were destined for the flames. I agree with
the peon: It is a sad world. It is also a funny world.

The query inevitably rises: How is the peon to get a square
deal? And who will give a square deal? By square deal is not
meant the Utopian ideal dreamed of a far future, but the measure of fair treatment that is possible here and now in civilized
nations. The men of the civilized nations are only frail, fallible,
human men, with all the weaknesses common to human men
just in the process of emerging from barbarism. Nevertheless, with
such men a squarer deal obtains than does obtain in savagery.
The much-mixed descendants of the Spaniards and Aztecs can
scarcely be called civilized. They have had over four centuries of
rule in Mexico, and they have done anything but build a civilization. What measure of civilization they do possess is exotic. It
has been introduced by north Europeans and Americans, and by
north Europeans and Americans has it been maintained. The
peon of to-day, under Mexican rule, is no better off than he was
under Aztec rule. It is to be doubted that he is as well off. On the
face of it, his much-mixed breed of rulers cannot give him the
square deal that is possible to be given by more intelligent and
humane rulers—that is given to-day by such rulers in other countries of the world.

This is the problem to-day for the big brother to the nations
of the New World. Oh, make no mistake! The big brother's
hands are not clean, nor is his history immaculate. But his hands
are as clean and his history is as immaculate as are the hands
and histories of the other nations in the thick of transition from
barbarism and savagery. He even has societies for the prevention
of cruelty to animals, the members of which very frequently interfere between a horse and its owner, and hail the owner to court
for punishment.

The mixed-breed rulers of Mexico seem incapable of treating
the peon with the measure of fairness that is possible in the
world to-day and that is practiced in the world to-day. The Mexican peon residing in the United States at the present time—and
there are many thousands of him—is far better treated than are
his brothers south of the border.

Never mind what his legal status may be or is alleged to be.

The fact is, the peon of Mexico, so far as liberty and a share in the happiness produced by his toil is concerned, is as much a slave as he ever was. He is so much property to his rulers, who work him, not with treatment equal to that accorded a horse, but with harsher and far less considerate treatment.

Of course the owner of a horse, when arrested by an agent of a humane society, indignantly protests that the horse is his property. But a wider social vision is growing in the foremost nations that property rights are a social responsibility, and that society can and must interfere between the owner and his mismanaged property. But somehow the old order is hard to change. There is a narcotic magic in phrases and precedents. It is an established right for society to step in between a man and his horse, but it is still abhorrent for a nation to step in between a handful of rulers and their millions of mismanaged and ill-treated subjects. Yet such interference is logically the duty of the United States as the big brother of the countries of the New World. Nevertheless, the United States did so step in when it went to war with Spain over the ill treatment of the Cubans. But it required the blowing up of the *Maine* to precipitate its action.

And here in Mexico the United States has stepped in, still dominated by narcotic precedent, on the immediate pretext of a failure in formal courtesy about a flag. But why not have done with fooling? Why not toss the old drugs overboard and consider the matter clear-eyed? The exotic civilization introduced by America and Europe is being destroyed by the madness of a handful of rulers who do not know how to rule, who have never successfully ruled, and whose orgies at ruling have been and are similar to those indulged in by drunken miners sowing the floors of barrooms with their fortunate gold dust.

The big brother can police, organize, and manage Mexico. The so-called leaders of Mexico cannot. And the lives and happiness of a few million peons, as well as of many millions yet to be born, are at stake.

The policeman stops a man from beating his wife. The humane officer stops a man from beating his horse. May not a powerful and self-alleged enlightened nation stop a handful of inefficient and incapable rulers from making a shambles and a desert of a fair land wherein are all the natural resources for a high and happy civilization?

June 6, 1914

STALKING THE PESTILENCE

In all the long red history of war, disease has stalked at the heels of armies. In the present generation it bids fair to cease stalking, at least at the heels of armies that are scientifically and modernly handled. I have just been studying the mortality statistics of Vera Cruz for the last sixteen months. There is a peculiar blank space at the head of the column marked "Cerebrospinal Meningitis." For the first six months of 1913 there were no deaths from meningitis. In July there were three deaths. By December, in that month alone, there were twenty deaths. The abrupt appearance of this disease led me to inquire of Major F. M. Hartsock for an explanation.

The appearance of meningitis in Vera Cruz seems to have been due to Mexico's customary way of doing business. From far up to the north a drove of Constitutionalist prisoners, infected with meningitis, was sent south. They were moved right along. No one in authority cared to segregate them and stamp out the disease. This wretched drove became a perambulating plague. It was a case, in poker parlance, of "passing the buck."

At last they arrived in Mexico City, where they promptly infected their prison. Again the buck was passed, and they were shipped on to Vera Cruz. I do not possess the date of their arrival in the latter city, but it is patent that it must have been some time in July, 1913, at which date the death figures suddenly appear in the meningitis column.

There seems to have been no further place to which to pass them along, so they were finally segregated in prison. From the first to the twentieth of April, 1914, there were six deaths from meningitis. It was about this time that the American forces landed and took possession of Vera Cruz while General Maas, his soldiers, and released prisoners took to the brush. And they took their meningitis with them, for there has not been a case of it since in Vera Cruz.

What the adventures of this meningitis will be now that it has again gone wandering may be imagined. The very clothing of these men, as well as themselves, is saturated with meningitis, and that they will spread the infection cannot be doubted. At any rate, the times have changed, for the disease left town with old-fashioned war when modern war marched in.

Smallpox appears to be endemic, rather than epidemic, in Vera Cruz, while tuberculosis, strange to say, collects a greater toll of death than all the more serious diseases added together. Here, in the tierras calientes, or hot lands, where it is so continuously warm that in a room flung wide to the outer air and every vagrant breeze even a sheet over one at night is suffocating, the natives crowd into small, unventilated rooms, weaken their lungs, and fall victims to the White Plague. Malaria, also, is a never-absent disease, the death line of it rising rhythmically in the rainy season and falling in the dry season. It, too, by its weakening effect on its victims, is the cause of their contracting other diseases from which they perish, chiefest of which, of course, is tuberculosis.

But our army surgeons, wise in tropical diseases from their service in Cuba, Puerto Rico, Panama, and the Philippines, are not apprehensive of any grave epidemics in Mexico. They have learned much and rapidly in the last decade and a half and what they have learned is demonstrable by statistics.

Typhoid has ever been a grisly monster to north European and American armies. The Latins and the Asiatics are more immune, this being doubtless due to a rigid selection, operating through many centuries, by which typhoid killed off all that were predisposed to typhoid. Thus, whenever men are gathered together in armies, there will be found a far greater proportion of nonimmunes among the north Europeans and Americans than among the Latins and Asiatics.

In 1898, in Florida, the United States mobilized 12,000 men for a period of four months. During this time there were 2,600 cases of typhoid and 480 deaths from typhoid. Nor is this the whole story. The soldiers carried the disease with them into Cuba, where many another death resulted from the four months spent in Florida.

In 1911, in San Antonio, Tex., 12,000 soldiers were mobilized for four months. During this period there were two cases of typhoid and no deaths.

In 1913 and 1914, at Texas City and Galveston, 12,000 soldiers were in camp for many months, during which there was not a single death from typhoid nor a single case of typhoid. In this last long mobilization all other infectious diseases were practically negligible. In the year 1913, in the entire army of the United States, whether stationed at home, in Panama, Hawaii, or the Philippines, there were only six cases of typhoid. This remarkable record, covering so brief a period of time, has been made possible by two things: first, the education of the soldiers in camp sanitation and personal hygiene; and, second, the inoculation, or vaccination, of the soldiers against typhoid.

The United States was the first country to inoculate its soldiers and sailors against typhoid, and it is safe to assume, no matter in what other ways its soldiers may lose their lives in Mexico, that none will die from typhoid. This inoculation is a fairly simple matter. The serum is hypodermically injected into the arm in a series of three injections, the intervals between injections being ten days. In a way, the injectee becomes a sort of peripatetic graveyard. The first injection puts into his blood the nicely dead carcasses of some 500,000,000 micro-organisms along with all their virtues of deadness which bring about a change in the constitution of the blood that makes it resistant to future invasions of full-powered, malignant typhoid micro-organisms. With this first injection, theoretically, the man has had reduced the 100 per cent of his nonimmunity to typhoid to 32 per cent.

The second injection, ten days later, consists of a thousand million nicely dead carcasses of the disease. Also, it reduces his nonimmunity to 8 per cent. The third injection introduces another billion of the same ably efficient carcasses, and reduces his nonimmunity to zero. In short, when his body has become the living cemetery of half a billion more dead bodies than there are live humans in all the world, he has become so noxious to the particularly noxious and infective typhoid that he may be classed a positive immune.

It is very easy, the actual process of inoculation. I have had the pleasure of reducing my nonimmunity of 100 per cent to zero per cent. The first inoculation was perpetrated in a transport hospital, the second in a captured academy turned into an army hospital, the third in a field hospital. The stab of the hypodermic syringe, different from the manner of administering morphine just under the skin, goes straight down and squarely down into the meat of the arm for half an inch; but the pang of the stab is no severer. The hurt of the stab is over the instant the skin is punctured. It is only the nerves of the skin that protest in either case.

After an inoculation there is no indisposition. The arm is a trifle sore for several days, and that is all. Some inoculatees aver that they awaken from the first night's sleep with a dark brown taste in their mouths. In rare cases a mild increase of temperature is noted, reaching its height some six hours after the inoculation and fading quickly away. I have talked with a daring one who took the total quantity at one time, and who stated that the impact was equivalent to a man's fist between the eyes and that he was not quite himself again for all of twenty-four hours.

But the big thing about the whole affair is the statistics. Individuals do not count. What counts is the results achieved by the inoculation of thousands of men. What counts is the reduction to nothing of typhoid cases in the army hospitals. What counts is the reduction to nothing of the army funerals due to typhoid. Modern war of men against men on the field of battle is now preceded by micro-organic war on the part of our surgeons before ever our men depart for the front. And, Heavens, what tremendous wars are waged by the surgeons! The mortality stuns one when endeavoring to contemplate its totality. When two billion five hundred million micro-organisms are slain merely to make one soldier immune against one disease, the sum total of slain micro-organisms for a whole army is as much beyond mere human conception as is the entire visible sidereal system along with what is invisible outside of it. Yet there can be no discussion of the efficacy of inoculation against typhoid. The morbidity and mortality tables of our large-scale army experiments tell the incontrovertible tale.

No healthy recruit, having successfully passed the rigid physical examination, is any longer permitted immediately to join the organization to which he is allotted. Healthy recruits have a way of coming down with all sorts of diseases as soon as they change their environment, particularly with measles, mumps, diphtheria, whooping cough, and scarlet fever. In the old days so recent, before it was understood, the recruits spread these diseases among the regiments they joined.

But to-day, ere they are received into the ranks of their company and regiment, no matter how healthy they may be at the time, they are forced first to undergo twelve days of isolation. In this phase the clean record of the Texas City and Galveston mobilization in such simple diseases exceeded the record of the previous mobilization at San Antonio. While all this is a very recent practice, it is a practice wider spread than the army. No scientific hog breeder to-day, whether importing a prize boar from another State, another country, or another farm, is rash enough immediately to turn it in with his herd. It must first undergo its quarantine in a segregated part of the farm.

The army surgeons to-day are our foreloopers and pioneers. Not only do they stay at home with the army and make it fit, but they scout ahead of the army so that its fitness may continue in strange lands and places. They gather the data on the diseases prevalent in all countries, and their battles and campaigns are planned and mapped and ready to be fought on an instant's notice, no matter to what intersection of latitude and longitude the army may be summoned.

So it is, first, that every soldier up to the present moment landed in Mexico is free of all disease and immune to such diseases as smallpox and typhoid; and, second, that a completer and better body of data has been gathered by our surgeons on diseases in Mexico than has been gathered by the Mexican Government. Our men start uninfected with a fair promise of escaping infection when they tread Mexican soil.

Thanks to our discoveries in Cuba some years ago regarding yellow fever, Vera Cruz was cleaned up. Hitherto, along with Panama (since cleaned up by us), it ranked with Guayaquil as one of the three plague ports of the New World. Remains Guayaquil—still revolutionizing—as great a yellow fever pesthole as ever. We have cleared yellow fever out of Panama, and it is to be doubted if a single case of yellow fever shows itself among our troops in Vera Cruz.

Yellow fever is so simple a thing to manage. Yet we paid a terrible death penalty for our ignorance through all the centuries down to just the other day. We know now that a certain breed

of mosquito is the only carrier of the disease. We know that the
way such a mosquito becomes infected is by biting a human
being who is stricken with yellow fever. We know that only in the
first three days that a human being is so stricken is it possible
for the uninfected mosquito to become infected.

The remedy, or rather the preventive, is equally simple. First,
wire screen the yellow fever patient so that no mosquitoes may
be infected by him. Second, fumigate the house in which he lies
so that no possibly infected mosquitoes therein may infect other
humans. Third, and purely a prevision, destroy all mosquitoes in
the neighborhood.

In the days of the Paris Commune the petroleur flourished.
To-day, in the American armies on service in the tropics, the
petrolero flourishes. He is the man who spreads oil on all stagnant
waters. The larva of the mosquito cannot hatch in running water,
nor in fish-inhabited water. But it can hatch in a sardine can or
in the depression made by a cow's hoof in soft soil when such
receptacles are filled with rain water.

Not content with their own tropical experience, our army
surgeons in Vera Cruz are reinforced by such experts from the
Marine Hospital Service as G. M. Guiteras and Rudolph von
Ezdorf, who have taken charge of the public health of this onetime death hole of Vera Cruz.

Killing two birds with one stone, or performing two actions
with one movement, is a joy forever and cuts down the overhead.
It so happens that the same preventive measures for yellow fever
are preventive of malaria. Every wire screen about a patient, every
drop of oil on the surface of standing water, performs the double
duty. Further, purely as a prophylactic measure, each soldier will
receive a determined number of grains of quinine daily until
such time that Vera Cruz has been metamorphosed into a health
resort.

The authorities of Vera Cruz did not know as much about
their own water supply as did our army surgeons before our expedition started. They knew that the source of the water supply,
the Jamapa River, was a fast-flowing stream and uncontaminated.
Also, to make doubly sure, they were in possession of analyses of
the water.

Amebic dysentery is of rare occurrence in Vera Cruz. Smallpox is no longer a thing of which to be afraid. And, further, most of it seems to have deserted Vera Cruz along with General Maas and his soldiers.

The United States is large. The United States army is small. It is scattered here and there in army posts. The average citizen knows less of his own army than he knows of north and south polar exploration. As regards the duties and activities of the army surgeons he does not dream of anything beyond the fact that they keep the soldiers well in time of peace, and in war, dress wounds and amputate limbs. It would make him sit up and take notice if he could see how complex and multifarious are their activities here in Vera Cruz.

To commence with, the army is not their only problem. To keep the army well, they must keep the city well. Not only must they attend to their own sick and wounded, but they must attend to the sick and wounded of the Mexican populace and army hospitals, public hospitals, charity hospitals, women's hospitals, and orphan asylums. Now Uncle Sam is somewhat meager in such matters. The people of Vera Cruz supported these institutions before, says Uncle Sam. Therefore make Vera Cruz support them again. Do you think I am spending my money like a drunken sailor? Uncle Sam concludes indignantly.

And our surgeons go and do it, though it takes all the rest of the army to help. Vera Cruz must pay for these institutions. But these institutions are two months behind in their bills and salaries, and there is no money in the city treasury. The last was clean looted by the officials who had charge of it. Army officers are told off to handle the collection of taxes. So far as the Vera Cruzan taxpayer is concerned, the taxes are as they always were. But for the first time in the history of Vera Cruz the taxes are expended without graft for public service. The back bills and salaries are paid, and the future bills and salaries are guaranteed.

The hotels and cantinas are crowded with thirsty refugees, soldiers, sailors, and foreign guests, all with a penchant for long, cool drinks. More ice than ordinarily is consumed. The ice plant is a private enterprise. Its output is limited. There is not enough to go around. Hotels and cantinas are cash buyers and they pay a premium for ice. Result: (a) the hospitals are skimped in ice; (b) the surgeons make the suggestion and the army takes charge of the ice plant, supplying the hospitals first and letting the hotels and cantinas have what is left.

The naval authorities have already taken possession of the island and lazaretto of Sacrificios, just outside the port of Vera Cruz. There is no yellow fever at present, but if a sporadic case should appear, Sacrificios is just the place to segregate it.

I was in the field hospital just after an operation for appendicitis had been performed on one of our officers. In old San Sebastian Hospital lie many of the sick of the city and many of the soldiers that General Maas left behind to fight from the housetops. Many amputations had been performed, and more were being performed.

Also, I watched the dressing of the wounds of these poor Federals, and I want to register my protest right now that modern war, for the man who gets bullet wounded, is not at all as romantic as old-time war. Furthermore, a modern bullet, despite its steel jacket which keeps it from spreading, is a terrifically disruptive thing to have introduced into one's body. I would far prefer being struck with an old-time bullet than with a modern one.

It seems that the flight of our long, sharp-nosed, lean, cylindrical, modern bullet is divided into three flights much as the spinning of a top is divided into three spins. When first a top is spun, it jumps and bounces, and bounds about in an erratic way. After a time it attains equilibrium. This is its mid-spin. It makes no perceptible movement, and to the eye seems stationary and dead. It is this stage that the small boy calls "sleeping." Then comes its last spin. It bounds and wobbles about as it loses the last of its momentum, and it finally lies down on its side and is dead.

Almost precisely the same thing occurs with the modern bullet. Its first flight is something like seven hundred yards. During this period, like the top, it is erratic. It wobbles. If it hits anything while it is wobbling, a bad smash-up is inevitable.

In its mid flight between seven hundred and twelve hundred yards, it "sleeps." If it hits anything while it is sleeping, it drills a clean hole. From twelve hundred yards on, losing momentum and equilibrium, it again wobbles, and this is no time to be struck by it.

In the hospital of San Sebastian I examined the wound of a finely formed and muscular young man. Midway between knee and thigh a wobbling bullet had ploughed a path two inches wide and three inches deep. It was a clean path. Not an atom remained of the flesh that had filled that groove. You who read this, just draw with a lead pencil a groove two inches wide and three inches deep, and you will more fully comprehend what happens to human flesh when a high-powered, wobbling bullet goes tearing through it.

The effect of such bullets on human bone can be readily imagined. There is no reason, with modern antiseptic surgery, why a clean-drilled hole through flesh and bone cannot be healed nicely. Unfortunately, such being the terrific impact and wobble of our high-velocity bullets of to-day, the bone is shattered for too great a distance into too many minute fragments. The only thing to do is to take off the limb.

When leaving the amputated in the wards of San Sebastian, I chanced to wander into the hospital chapel. The Chapel of Bethlehem it had been called once upon a time. It was very old, some two centuries or so, and was a fine example of the architectural feats achieved by the Spaniards in brick and stucco in a day when reinforced concrete was unheard of. Wide arches of incredible flatness and supporting enormous weights were revealed to be of brick by the spots where the plastering had come off. High arches spanned deep-embrasured windows, in which some of the ancient, hand-hewn sashes still remained. The high walls, rising to rafters far above, had caught the dust of years on the uneven plaster, which gave a fathomless velvet depth to the surface. The floor was of great, square marble flags.

The statues of Christ, the Virgin, and the Saints that had graced the altar were long since gone. Gone, too, was the altar. Nothing remained save the lofty walls and cool depth of shadow to suggest that it had been a chapel. And as I stood in this place whence the worship of the gentle Nazarene had departed, strong on my vision were the amputated limbs, gaping wounds, and ruined bodies caused by our wobbling bullets.

Came another picture: I seemed to glimpse a massed background of machinery and electrical apparatus, of weary-eyed astronomers searching the heavens, and chemists and physicists dissecting the atom, of teachers and preachers and great libraries of books. And against this background, well to the fore, were two groups of men whose brows were the brows of thinkers, and whose hands worked unceasingly at the making of devices. One group toiled at the mixing of chemicals and the making of mechanisms for the purpose of blasting human flesh and bone at longer distance and more efficiently. The other group toiled likewise with chemicals and instruments, seeking out new methods and greater knowledge of the constitution of man in order that they might repair the blasted flesh and bone caused by the devices of the first group.

Some day in the far future pictures will be painted like that, and our descendants will gaze at them, shake their heads, and laugh at their silly ancestors, just as we to-day gaze at pictures of witch burning, and shake our heads and laugh at the silliness of our very immediate ancestors. Man has climbed far. It would seem that his climb has only begun.

Out across the inner and outer harbors, in the midst of a fleet of similar monsters, the grim monster, the *Arkansas* was a striking sample of the mechanisms produced by the war makers. Twelve million dollars she cost. Her great guns, turned upon Vera Cruz for an hour or so, could level the city to the ground as a stream of water would level a house of sand. Magnificent universities have been founded on less than it cost to build and equip her. The money expended on her would save from the White Plague a hundred thousand times more lives than she will ever destroy.

Over a thousand skilled men are required to man her—skilled men such as built the Panama Canal and whose skill might well be devoted to making the Mississippi flood proof. Why, down in the bowels of the *Arkansas*, imbedded in the thickest of armor plate, in the battle control station, an enlisted sailor in the course of describing the new gyrocompass, gave me a lecture that no college professor could have bettered and that no tyro in such matters could have understood. Could Columbus or Captain Cook have stood beside me, listened to the lecture, and tried to master the details of the intricate compass, I swear their brains would have flown apart and they would have bitten their veins and howled.

Quite in contrast, and lying not far away, was the solitary

hospital ship, the *Solace*. Spick-and-span, and sweet and peaceful, and very antiseptic she was. I was followed up the gangway
by two young men just brought off from shore. I walked up the
incline on my good two legs. They came up on their backs
in wire-basket stretchers. A long roll of body-blasted young
men had preceded them in the previous few days. Seventeen
of these young men lay embalmed in caskets covered by the
Stars and Stripes, waiting transshipment to their homes in the
States. Two more young men lay dying. Threescore and more
in various stages of recovery from body blasting lay in the bright
and airy 'tween-decks wards. A number of amputations had been
performed on them. The careful doctors, waiting, knew there
were yet other amputations to be performed to save the lives
of some of the young men.

Passing through the wards, one was again struck by the pre-
ponderance of youth. Lord, Lord! they were boys, healthy-bodied
and lusty so short a time before, now lying, lax-muscled, with
drawn faces that told all the story of the body blasting they
had endured. One, alive and so lively just the other day, now
with one leg, searched my eyes as if for understanding and
sympathy for the terrible stump that screamed advertisement
of the cropper he had received—smashed down, from the back
of life, to be a cripple to the end of his days. Another, a very
boy, red-lipped and bright-eyed with fever, smiled wistfully.
There was little hope for him. He was conscious, and, perhaps
as men sometimes will be in such grievous circumstances, he was
aware that time would soon cease for him.

Oh, there was no whining among those lads! They tell of one,
shot in two places, who was fetched aboard crying bitterly and
indignantly. His plaint was that the Mexicans had got him unexpectedly before he had had a chance to get even one of them.
As he said, he wouldn't have minded his own catastrophe if he
had got one of them—only one of them.

The beautiful operating room was well appointed. There
were convalescent wards, segregated wards for infectious diseases,
and, here and there, offices and workrooms presided over by
experts, such as ear and throat specialists, eye specialists, stomach
specialists. Also there was a dentist and a completely equipped
dental parlor.

On deck, under the awnings, we drank long, cool drinks and

gazed across the creamy-crested, pea-green waves to the big looming battleships, and on to the tiny, half-submerged atolls with lagoons of chrysoprase, and to the low-stretching break-water, the lighthouses slim and white as votive candles, and the old fortresses of Santiago and San Juan de Ulloa. Suddenly all the panorama narrowed to a sleek gray dove that perched on the rail a dozen feet away, settled its wings, and preened its feathers.

Somehow, that little gray dove reminded me that, while a fleet of battleships lay about us, the *Solace* was the only hospital ship in the entire United States navy. More than that—I remembered that she had not been originally designed for the purpose, being merely a merchant vessel purchased by the Government and made over. Also, I remembered having traveled, years before, in tropic steamers, mere merchant vessels built for money making, that were far better fitted for the tropics than was the *Solace*.

Surely the United States, that pays twelve to fifteen million dollars for ships like the *Arkansas*, the *Texas*, and the *New York*, should be able to afford the modest cost of a real hospital ship, designed, not for the making of dollars, but for the alleviation of the ills and injuries that afflict its sailors and marines.

But there is justification for the existence of that array of war monsters among which we lay. As long as individuals in a wild country—say the head hunters and cannibals of the Solomon Islands—carry killing weapons, even a philosopher, traveling among them, would be wise to go armed. Neither algebraic equations nor high ethical arguments are efficacious dissuadements to a kinky headed man-eater with an appetite. In those Solomon Islands more than one scientist, for lack of a rifle, has had his head decorate the grass huts and his body served up succulently from the hot ovens.

On a coral beach on the windward coast of Guadalcanar [sic] stands a monument to the memory of the "Austrian Expedition." This was a party of professors. They were equipped to pursue the vocations that obtain in a high civilization. They carried sextants, barometers, thermometers, artificial horizons, cameras, and fountain pens. They carried naturalists' shotguns of the tiniest caliber, butterfly nets, geologists' hammers, and note-books for all sorts of records, also certain instruments with which to make skull measurements of the natives they might meet. But what they did not carry was Mauser rifles and long-barreled revolvers. They were not equipped for the anthropophagi they encountered. One man came back from that expedition to tell the tale, and he was merely a man in the employ of the professors. The column stands on the beach to mark that once they had been. Their heads remain to this day up in the bush of Guadalcanar.

As with individuals, so with nations. As long as certain nations go armed in a wild and savage world, just so long must the enlightened nations go armed. The wild and savage world, with its silly man-killing devices, is doomed to pass. But until it passes, it would be silliness on the part of the enlightened nations to put aside their weapons.

An international police force and an international police court will mark the beginning of the end of war. But as yet these two institutions have not been founded. So the United States will be compelled to go on building $15,000,000 battleships and training its young men to the old red profession.

The point is: when wild and savage conditions make it imperative for a man or nation to go armed, it is equally imperative for the man or nation to go well armed. Ever has the sword, in the hands of the strong breeds, made for wider areas and longer periods of peace. In the end it is the sword that will make lasting and universal peace. When the last savage nation is compelled to lay down its weapons, war will have ceased. War itself, superior war if you please, will destroy itself.

But in the meantime—and there you are—what would have been the present situation if the United States had long since been disarmed? Somehow, I, for one, cannot see the picture of Huerta listening to and accepting the high ethical advice of the United States.

June 13, 1914

THE TROUBLE MAKERS OF MEXICO

The commonest, as well as the gravest, mistake in human intercourse is that very human weakness of creating all other individuals in one's own image. What "I like" I can see no reason but what everybody else should like. What is good for me is good for you. If I am fascinated by a certain book, I am astounded to learn that you do not like that book. If I find vegetarianism provocative of good health in me, ergo, it will be provocative of good health in you. If black coffee produces sleeplessness in me, I am appalled when you drink two cups of black coffee in the evening.

When my wife and I fall out, it is because I ignore the fact that she feels, reasons, and acts in ways different from my ways. She, likewise, makes the same mistake about me. Her entire family and mine may fail to patch the matter up, and, in the end, a judge, equipped with the wisdom of the race embodied in our law, may divorce us because we are different from each other—incompatible, in short. I once knew the dearest, sweetest, and most sympathetic of women, who was unable, when she lacked in appetite, to comprehend that anybody else could be hungry.

In the same way different groups of people, of the same race and country, fail to understand one another. The cowboys of the open range never understood the settler with his barbed-wire fences. The East does not understand California to-day in her attitude on the Japanese question. The East thinks California is like the East and that Californians are like Easterners. In brief, the East recreates California in her own image.

Since such mistakes of understanding are common among groups of peoples of the same breed and country, it is patent that deeper and more disastrous mistakes may be made among people of different races dwelling in different countries.

The chief cause of our misunderstanding to-day of the Mexicans is that we have created them in our own American image. With a comfortable sense of fairness we have put ourselves inside the Mexicans, along with our morality, our democracy, and all the rest of our points of view, and accepting therefore that the Mexicans should think, feel, and act just as we would under similar circumstances, we are shocked to find out that they won't do anything of the sort. Instead of having our eyes opened by this cardinal error, we proceed to reason that their conduct should be made to become like our conduct, and that we should treat them and deal with them as if they were still just like us, with a history behind them similar to ours, with institutions similar to ours, and with an ethic similar to ours.

Here, in the portals of Vera Cruz, the talk about Mexico and Mexicans buzzes high all day long and far into the night. Never was there a more animated and indefatigable debating society. One listens to the talk and wonders what it is all about, what bearing it has on the situation. I, for one, cannot comprehend how it is germane whether Madero was a patriot or a grafter; whether Huerta is a heroic figure of an Indian or a lunatic black Nero; whether Huerta murdered Madero or Madero committed suicide; whether the Huerta government should have been recognized by the United States long ago or that United States intervention should have taken place long ago.

What I see, with all this talk of little things filling my ears, is a torn and devastated Mexico, in which twelve million peons and all native and foreign business men are being injured and destroyed by the silly and selfish conduct of a few mixed breeds. I see a great, rich country, capable of supporting in happiness a hundred million souls, being smashed to chaos by a handful of child-minded men playing with the tragic tools of death made possible by modern mechanics and chemistry.

These child-minded men are playing with the tools of giants. It is like a family of small children playing with sticks of dynamite on the front porch, in the basement, and up in the attic of their dwelling. One can see a hurry call sent into the nearest police station by the good citizens of the neighborhood for a squad of police to take the dynamite away from the children.

From garret to basement the dwelling of Mexico is being torn to pieces by the dynamite in the hands of the contending factions. The stay-at-home American listens to the slogans uttered by the various leaders of this anarchy, makes the mistake of conceiving the leaders in his own image and of thinking that "Liberty," "Justice," and a "Square Deal" mean the same to them that they mean to him.

Nothing of the sort. In the four centuries of Spanish and Mexican rule, liberty, justice, and the square deal have never existed. Mexico is a republic in which nobody votes. Its liberty has ever been construed as license. Its justice has consisted of an effort at equitable division of the spoils of an exploited people. That even thieves' honor did not obtain among these thieves is shown by the numerous revolutions and dictatorships. In a country where a man is legally considered guilty of a crime until he proves himself innocent, justice must mean an entirely different thing from what it means to an American. And so it is with all the rest of the bombastic and valorous phrases in the vocabulary of the Mexican.

Now the foregoing must not be taken as a denial of any right or good in the people of Mexico. On the contrary, the great mass of the Mexicans have nothing to do with the matter at all; but, being different from the American, being unversed and uninterested in the affairs of government, they sit supinely back and let the petty handful of leaders despoil them and the country.

Also, there have even been isolated cases of leaders, such as Juarez, to go no further, who were animated by ideals somewhat resembling our own. In the Madero revolution there were similar men. The test of the matter is the whole matter, and the whole matter is that no measure of liberty, justice, and the square deal has been achieved in all Mexico in the last four hundred years.

There is all the difference in the world between fighting and government. Anybody and anything can fight. Dogs and cats, centipedes and scorpions fight. Fighting is a very primitive sort of exercise. Governing is a high achievement, especially governing with peace and honesty and fair dealing, and this is something which the Mexicans have never succeeded in doing from the day they broke away from Spain's palsied grasp.

After the fall of Iturbide, in 1824, a republican constitution was adopted and promulgated. In the forty-seven years between 1821 and 1868 the form of government was changed ten times, federal republics, central republics, and dictatorships alternating one with another. In those forty-seven years over fifty persons succeeded one another as presidents, dictators, and emperors. One authority states that in the same period there were three hundred attempts, more or less important, at revolution. Clearly, the Mexicans have demonstrated a penchant for fighting, but what they have not demonstrated is the high ability requisite for governing.

Even the deeper read and widely traveled American, able somewhat to refrain from seeing Mexico in his own image and in his image of his own country, is guilty of the error of seeing Mexico in the image of a Latin country. It should be understood at the outset that Mexico is not a Latin country. Mexico is an Indian country. The people of Mexico are not Latins. They are Indians. And they are Indians, only somewhat resembling the Indians of the United States. They are not merely a different tribe. They are a different race of Indians.

Sixty-five per cent of the inhabitants are pure Indians; 15 per cent are pure Spanish, Americans, English, and other foreigners. The remaining 20 per cent are mixed Indian and Spanish. It is this mixed 20 per cent that, according to the stay-at-home American notion, constitutes the Mexican, and practically the totality of the Mexican population.

And it is just precisely this 20 per cent half-breed class that foments all the trouble, plays childishly with the tools of giants, and makes a shambles and a chaos of the land. These "breeds" represent neither the great working class, nor the property-owning class, nor the picked men of the United States and Europe who have given Mexico what measure of exotic civilization it possesses. There "breeds" are the predatory class. They produce nothing. They create nothing. They aim to possess a shirt, ride on a horse, and "shake down" the people who work and the people who develop.

These "breeds" do politics, issue pronunciamentos, raise revolutions or are revolutionized against by others of them, write bombastic unveracity that is accepted as journalism in this sad, rich land, steal pay rolls of companies, and eat out hacienda after hacienda as they picnic along on what they are pleased to call wars for liberty, justice, and the square deal.

They claim the government of Mexico is theirs, these gentlemen with shirts, on the backs of stolen horses. And government, to them, means just precisely the license to batten upon the labor and industry of the country. The trouble is, so lacking are they in the ability for government, that they cannot maintain for any length of time the battening government of their dreams.

They continually quarrel over the division of the spoils, and fight among themselves for a monopoly of the governmental battening privilege.

As I have said before, they are devoid even of thieves' honor. They cannot trust one another. They cannot believe one another. For once, each correctly conceives the next one in his own image. Aware, in his heart of hearts, that he wants nothing less than 100 per cent of the swag, that only by accident could he ever be guilty of telling the truth to a fellow robber, that he is continually bent upon over-reaching and double-crossing his fellow comrades of looters, he cannot expect anything else from his fellows.

To paraphrase Kipling, the consistency of these half-breeds is to know no shred of consistency. Because of this they are not even successful robbers. Tammany could give them cards and spades in the game they play and win out against them hands down.

They are brave on occasion. But they are not courageous. Their honor and valor reside in their tongues. They are turn-coats from moment to moment. They will dine in the homes of their gringo friends one evening, and, before daylight, go gunning for their gringo friends and for the pay rolls and gold watches of their gringo friends.

They are what the mixed breed always is—neither fish, flesh, nor fowl. They are neither white men nor Indians. Like the Eurasians, they possess all the vices of their various commingled bloods and none of the virtues.

It is impossible for the average American to understand them. Honor is one thing to them, another thing to an American; so likewise with truth, probity, and sincerity. There is no comprehending them by the rules of conduct and forms of reasoning habitual to the American. As a sample of this, I relate the following Federal explanation of the killing of six Americans at San Pedro, in the State of Chiapas.

This is the way the Mexican authorities explain the mishap: When the Americans took possession of Vera Cruz, the authorities in Chiapas, fearful for the safety of the handful of American small farmers because of the inflamed condition of the populace, sent a detachment of rurales to rescue them. When the Americans saw the armed body of rurales approaching, fearing they were about to be attacked, they barricaded themselves in one of their houses. So intent was the rescue party on saving them that a hot fire was opened on the house. For three hours the rurales toiled heroically at the task of rescue, pouring a heavy fire into the house from every side. At the end of this time, the six American men being dead, the rurales stormed the house and saved the lives of an American girl of eighteen and an American boy of fourteen, whom they bore away to be mobbed through the streets of Tuxtla Gutierrez ere they were safely put in jail.

Now it is not the killing that is the point of the illustration. It is the explanation made by the Mexicans of the horrible mistake made by the Americans in not understanding that the rurales were rescuing them. Surely no American brain nor north European brain could conceive such an explanation. Our reasoning processes are different. We could no more imagine that such an explanation would hold water than would we commit a three hours' attack on persons we were trying to save.

I should be inclined to doubt my harsh generalization on this half-breed class in Mexico were I alone in my opinion. It is because of this that I give the following extract from the "Encyclopaedia Britannica," which epitomizes the condition of affairs obtaining in Mexico from the time of Mexico's independence to the beginning of Díaz's rational despotism:

"On both sides in Mexico there was an element consisting of honest doctrinaires; but rival military leaders exploited the struggles in their own interest, sometimes taking each side successively; and the instability was intensified by the extreme poverty of the peasantry, which made the soldiery reluctant to return to civil life, by the absence of a regular middle class, and by the concentration of wealth in a few hands, so that a revolutionary chief was generally sure both of money and men."

Not only is this half-caste class but one-fifth of the total population of Mexico, but only a very small portion of this half-caste class is actively engaged in fomenting the anarchy that is destroying the country and merits the harsh strictures applied to it. Educated Mexicans assert that Huerta, Carranza,[1] Villa, and Zapata do not represent more than one hundred thousand people. There is no such thing as a national movement or a popular movement.

Here is a spectacle of fifteen millions of people, without equipment or ability for government, being harried and destroyed by a group of one hundred thousand who likewise have neither equipment nor ability for government. Surely, there can be no discussion of this. What is is. What is, is incontrovertible. And the unhappy situation of misgovernment in Mexico to-day is a fact and is incontrovertible.

There are three millions of the half-castes. When they permit, as they do, by their passivity, the pernicious and anarchic activity of the small group of one hundred thousand of them, they are themselves negatively responsible for the present state of affairs. The point is that they likewise have no aptitude for government.

Heavens, when it comes to the mere matter of ability to make organized trouble, the very half-breeds themselves are dependent on the peons! The two strongest men to-day in Mexico are the ex-bandit peon and Indian, Villa, in the north, and Huerta, the Tlaxcalan Indian, in the south.

The attitude of the hundred thousand active half-breeds is that the government belongs to them and not to the fifteen millions. It is their government, and, by the Eternal, they are going to do what they please with it. Civilization? They are not interested in civilization. Civilization can go smash, and in faith, they will smash it themselves if they have a mind to.

These men have talked republic since the year 1824, yet Mexico has never been a republic. Certainly it was not a republic under the capitalistic dictatorship of Porfirio Díaz. Elections here are either slates put through by dictators and their cliques, or straight-out revolutions, in either case the one object being unadulterated loot. Now they do not say this, these child-minded men. They spout patriotism and valor, liberty, justice, and the square

[1] Venustiano Carranza (1859–1920) in 1910 joined the revolutionary forces of Madero. Elected President of Mexico in 1917, Alvaro Obregón led a successful revolt against him. Carranza was ambushed and killed in 1920.

deal—all of which glorious phrases mean nothing of the sort, but are synonymous with loot.

They are not men in a world of men, these half-breed trouble makers. They are child-minded and ignoble-purposed. The stern stuff of manhood, as we understand manhood, is not in them. This stern stuff is in the pure-blooded Indians, however; but it manifests itself all too rarely, else it would be impossible for the many millions of Indians to have endured slavery for four hundred years at the hands of their tiny group of masters.

Huerta is the flower of the Mexican Indian. Such Indians have appeared, on occasion, in the United States. Huerta is brave. Huerta is masterful. But even Huerta has never betrayed possession of high ideals nor wide social vision.

And Huerta has made mistakes. Two of these mistakes, to be mentioned in passing but which are not apposite to the contention of this article, are: (1) his not killing Zapata when he had the chance; (2) his very grievous error in not killing Villa the time he had him backed up against a wall facing a firing squad. It was on this latter occasion that he compelled Villa, on his knees, arms clasped about Huerta's legs, to beg Huerta for his life. Villa has not forgotten that little episode. And it is fair to assume that sometimes the memory of these two mistakes flits regretfully through Huerta's mind as he sips a drink at the Country Club and contemplates Villa moving irresistibly down on him from the north; both his coasts blockaded by American warships and all arms and war munitions embargoed; Zapata at his back to the south and west like a hungry tiger; his credit exhausted, but a small portion of his own country left in his hands, and his own people in his capital city ripe to turn on him the instant he totters. I should not like to be Villa or Zapata if only for five minutes Huerta should get hold of me. Nor should I like to be Huerta if only for five minutes Zapata or Villa should get hold of me.

Egyptian and Mayan hieroglyphics cannot obfuscate the mind of the stay-at-home American as do the phrases and slogans of the Mexican "breeds." A hieroglyphic means nothing. The phrases and slogans of the Mexicans do not mean what they seem to mean. Countless Americans think the present revolution is an expression of the peon's land hunger. Madero raised that cry.

Zapata still raises the same cry. Orozco[2] promised the peons free farms in his plan of Tacubaya, when he was already the bought tool of the great hacienda owners who had employed him to cause confusion of Madero. Carranza, in veiled words and vague promises, shied at the division of the great haciendas. Villa still shouts "free land."

But how about the peon? There are twelve million peons. They have had four centuries to get interested in the subject. Considering the paucity of the numbers of their masters, they have evidently not considered the matter to any purpose. I doubt by a count of noses, if one-fourth of one per cent of the peons of Mexico are bearing arms for the purpose of gaining free land or of gaining anything else their leaders desire.

Villa confiscated the great estates of Chihuahua. To each adult male in the State of Chihuahua he gave sixty acres of land. But there was a string on the gift. For ten years the land was to be inalienable. His explanation of this string is that the peon has lost his ancient land hunger, and that, if given the land outright, he would immediately sell or gamble away his holding.

Of course the peon should have the land. Some day he will have it. But when no more than one-fourth of one per cent of the peons have risen to take the land, the feebleness of the peon land hunger is fully told. So another magic phrase means one thing to the American mind and quite another thing to the Mexican mind. It is impossible to conceive of twelve million Americans gnawed by the land hunger, arming and sending into the field one-fourth of one per cent of their number to fight for the land. Either the peon is different from the American, or land hunger is one thing to the one and another thing to the other. Apparently both contentions are true. The American is an Anglo-Saxon. The peon is an Indian, and a Mexican Indian at that. Furthermore, the Mexican Indian, before the Spaniard came, did not hold land individually; he held it communally.

Further to discredit this one-fourth of one per cent of peons bearing arms, two things must be taken into account. Numbers

[2] Pasqual Orozco rebelled against Madero in March 1912. He was driven out of Mexico by Huerta.

of them are restless and rough-natured only, rather than sustained by a belief in the rightness of the war they wage. Numbers of them are criminal and disorderly individuals. Numbers of them fight on either side according to the fortunes of battle. Numbers of them are happy-go-lucky, preferring the fun and adventure of guerrilla war-fare to the stay-at-home, plodding life of the farmer.

The second thing is no less important. They like the job. They have got the habit of revolution. What peon, with any spunk in him, would elect to slave on a hacienda for a slave's reward when, in the ranks of Zapata, Carranza, or Villa, he can travel, see the country, ride a horse, carry a rifle, get a peso or so a day, loot when fortune favors, and, if lucky, on occasion kill a fellow creature—this last a particularly delightful event to a people who delight in the bloody spectacles of the bull ring.

The totality of the Mexicans being so incapable of government that a handful of disorderly and incapable "breeds" can play ducks and drakes with the whole land, poor Mexico is in such a situation to-day that, unaided from without, the game can be played interminably. There is no other Porfirio Díaz in sight. There is no strong "breed" capable of whipping the rest of the disorderly "breeds" and the country into shape. There is no popular movement on which such a strong man might depend for support. Nor is there a national cause. The educated Mexicans, the wealthy Mexicans, the business and shopkeeping Mexicans, hail American intervention with delight. The vast majority of the peons ask merely to be let alone, and not to be drafted into the fighting ranks of this leader and that leader and of the many leaders continually arising. Victories, presidencies, and dictatorships can be only temporary. The handful of anarchs cannot pacify Mexico, because Mexico does not need pacifying. They cannot pacify themselves, which is the actual need of Mexico, because they are too weak, too inefficient, too turbulent, too disorderly.

Spain, despite her world empire, which she picked up at a lucky stroke, much as a Hottentot might pick up a Koh-i-noor, never possessed any genius for government. The descendants of the Spaniards in Mexico, interbred with the native Indians, have likewise displayed no genius for government. Facts are facts.

What the Spaniards and their descendants have not succeeded in doing in Mexico during the last four hundred years is an eloquent story.

Mexico must be saved from herself. What Mexico really needs is to be saved from the insignificant portion of her half-breeds who are causing all the trouble. They should not form the government at all. And yet they are the very ones who insist on forming it, and they cannot be eliminated by those who should form it, namely, the twelve million peons and the nearly three million peaceably inclined half-breeds.

June 20, 1914

LAWGIVERS

The bronze clangor of the cathedral bells marks the hours. Out of the night day bursts with an abruptness of light and of birdcalls. Newsboys' voices announce the first editions of the Mexican morning papers and the fall of Tampico. There are dog yelps, the rattle and grind of big-wheeled mule carts, a clatter of cavalry hoofs on the asphalt, bugle calls, and Vera Cruz has begun another day.

Bareheaded women, betraying little of Spanish and much of Indian in their faces, pass on their way to market. Cargadores slither by on leather sandals, and peddlers carrying their stocks in trade on their heads. Spigotty police, in wrinkled linen uniforms, swing their clubs valiantly, and, in contrast with our husky sentries of the regular army, appear pathetically small of stature, pinched of chest, and narrow of shoulder. And in the cathedral Indians and mixed breeds pray to the gods and saints of their believing, perplexed by the incomprehensible situation of their beloved city in the possession of armed white-skinned men from over the sea.

These natives of Mexico have never possessed more than a skeleton of law. They were two entire ethnic periods behind the Spanish when Cortes landed his mail-clad adventurers on their shore. And Cortes and the generations of acquisitive adventurers that followed him, themselves with no genius for government, intermarried with the Indian population and made no improvements in government.

Primitive government is simple, religious, and rigid. When the Indian governmental machinery was thrown out of gear, with here and there a smashed cog, lacking in plasticity, the millions of Indians fell an easy prey to the Spanish conquistadores. The compromise, resulting from the blending of a people backward in governmental development with a people unpossessed of the genius for government, brought about the weak and inefficient government that has been Mexico's for the last four centuries.

Come now, in the year 1914, from the United States, the white-skinned armed men with an inherited genius for government. Here is Vera Cruz with a population of 30,000; here, in addition, there are thousands of American soldiers and thousands of American and Mexican refugees from the interior. Problem: how to get these many thousands up out of bed in the morning and to work or play; how to get them home and to bed at night, all in decent and orderly fashion.

There must be safety for all. They must not quarrel with one another. They must keep themselves clean and the city clean. They must pursue the multifarious activities by which only can a city exist. They must not hurt one another, either by theft or violence, or by squalidly cultivating infection. And they must not even hurt, by excess of cruelty, the scrubby four-legged creatures that are their draft animals.

And the thing is done, decency and order made to reign, and all by the white-skinned fighting men who know how to rule as well as fight. Never, in the long history of Vera Cruz, has the city been so decent, so orderly, so safe, so clean. And it is accomplished, not by civilians from the United States, but by soldiers from the United States, and it is done without graft.

Captain Turner of the Seventh Infantry makes the following interesting announcement in the Mexican newspapers:

"As I have taken charge of the administration of the State taxes for this canton, by order of the Provost Marshal General, I beg to advise the public that from the seventh day of this month this office will proceed with its usual business under my orders.

"The public is hereby advised that persons who have not paid up taxes on city property which were due on the thirtieth day of April, 1914, will be allowed until the twenty-fifth day of the present month in which to pay them; but if any or all of them are not paid by the date mentioned above the property will be subject to the usual legal processes."

Comes Major Miller, his sword for the time being laid aside while he serves as chief of the Department of Education, with this advertisement:

"Professors and teachers formerly employed in the public schools of Vera Cruz, and who have not already signified their intention to resume work, but who desire to do so, and others who are qualified to teach and desire such employment, are requested to make application to this department. The latter class of applicants should present proper credentials and proofs of qualification."

Also, Major Miller announces that the Biblioteca del Publico will reopen on May 20.

Colonel Plummer of the Twenty-eighth Infantry advertises that the sale of cocaine and marihuana is prohibited except on a doctor's prescription, and that violation of this order will be severely punished. Since Colonel Plummer is Provost Marshal General, his advertisements include all sorts of prohibitions, from spitting on the sidewalks and in public places to warning shopkeepers not to extend credit to soldiers, and pawnbrokers not to receive pledges of Government property.

General Funston serves notice that every inhabitant of Vera Cruz must forthwith be vaccinated.

The work of war is not forgotten. The lines of outposts and trenches circle the city; the waterworks are protected; the hydroplanes scout overhead; and night and day, on lookout and in the trenches, men and officers stand their regular shifts. But, inside the lines, colonels and majors, captains and first lieutenants turn their hands to governing and operating the Departments of Law, Public Work, Public Safety, Finance, and Education. Then there is the Military Commission, with powers of life and death, grimly sitting on the cases of persons charged with infractions of the Laws of Hostile Occupation and the Laws of War. Further, there are four Inferior Provost Courts and one Superior Provost Court sitting regularly every day. The jurisdiction of the Provost Court is limited to criminal cases, and these courts are far from idle.

The ordinary citizen in any city at home may pursue his routine of life for days, weeks, and months, and see nothing out of the way or disorderly. And yet, day and night, and all days and nights, disorderly acts will have taken place and the many offenders will have been combed by the police from the riffraff of the city and brought before the courts.

Vera Cruz, at the present time, despite its military occupation, has all the seeming of such a city. All is quiet and seemly on the streets, where just the other day men were killing one another on the sidewalks and housetops. The very spigotty police, known, some of them, to have engaged in sniping our men, have been put back to work under our army administration. And yet, for a city of this size, more than the usual combing of the riffraff is necessary. It is the desire of the military government, among other things, to rid the city of all able-bodied loafers, whether Mexican or foreign. If Mexican, they are sent out through the lines; if foreign, they are deported to their respective countries. On the other hand, there is nothing hasty in this cavalier treatment. Petty offenders continually receive dismissals or suspended sentences for first offenses. Nor is the right to be represented by counsel denied anyone.

A visit to the Inferior Provost Court in the Municipal Palace proved most illuminating. Here, at a desk across which flowed a steady stream of documents, in olive-drab shirt and riding trousers, with a .45 automatic at his hip, sat a blond lawgiver, taken from the command of his company in the Nineteenth Infantry to administer the law of Mexico and the orders, above Mexican law, which have been issued by the Provost Marshal General.

At the desk beside the Captain-Judge, an enlisted man, in uniform, pounded a typewriter, kept a record of decisions, fines, imprisonments, and probations, and performed the rest of the tasks of a police-court clerk. Soldiers clacked across the square marble flags of the court-room floor, and came and went, carrying messages, appearing and disappearing through high doorways and under broad arches. In one corner a soldier telegrapher operated an army telegraph.

Strapping soldiers, with bayonets fixed, guarded the doorway that led both to freedom and to the cells. Between these guards, small people, furtive or sullen, came and went—if witnesses, summoned from without by an alert little spigotty bailiff; if prisoners, escorted by armed soldiers.

As is usual with our police courts at home, not one but many cases are going on simultaneously. A fresh witness in a case of theft, sent for half an hour before, arrives and gives evidence between the payment of a fine and the fuddled protestations of an Indian woman that she was not drunk the preceding evening. While the court interpreter has halted the testimony of a suspected fence in order to look up in the dictionary the English equivalent for a Spanish phrase the Captain-Judge admonishes a hotel keeper in the conduct of his house, dispatches a policeman to bring into court two pairs of stolen trousers evidently germane to some other case that is somehow in process of being tried, and listens to the remarks of a Spanish lawyer appearing for some man not yet brought from the cells.

The stream of many cases thins for a moment, and the Captain-Judge, who has the bluest of blue eyes and the fairest of fair hair, calls the name, "Francisco Ibáñez de Peralta."

A peon, covered with rags for the price of which six cents would be an extortion, shambles up and bows humbly.

"Tell him that he was drunk and disorderly on the street last night," the Captain-Judge says to the interpreter.

This being duly communicated, the culprit makes brief reply which is translated by the interpreter as: "That's right. He says he was drunk all right and is sorry."

"Has he steady work?" asked the Captain-Judge.

"No. He says he is a cargador and works when he can."

"Tell him if he is brought here again he will be given sixteen days—turn him loose" is the verdict.

Next appears Serafina Cruz. She is blear-eyed and semi-comatose.

"Tell the lady she was drunk again yesterday," says the Court to the interpreter.

Serafina acknowledges the soft impeachment with a "Si," a nod, and a yawn.

"Second offense, sixteen days in which to sober up—she needs it," is the Court's judgment, and Serafina is trailed away to the cells by a big American soldier.

María de la Concepción de Henriquez, a gentle-faced, soft-voiced woman whose ancestors, by the tokens of race in her face, pronounced their names by means of many Aztec "z's" and "x's" denies flatly that she was drunk the preceding morning. The arresting spigotty officer, being duly sworn, deposes that she was so drunk that he was compelled to transport her to the lockup in a handcart. María de la Concepción assures the Court that the arresting officer is a dog and worse than a dog; that he is the broken mustaches of a gutter cat, a grubless buzzard, a wingless pelican; that the truth is not in him; and, furthermore, that she was not drunk.

Captain Callahan, a blond Celt in American uniform, taking oath, affirms that he did see the lady arrive, dead drunk, in a handcart propelled by the aforesaid spigotty policeman.

María de la Concepción rolls her eyes in an expression of grieved shock at such unveracity on the part of such a gentlemanly appearing American gentleman, and assures the Court that she was far from drunk—so far from drunk, in fact, that she had not taken even a drop.

The patient Captain-Judge settles the matter out of hand.

"Tell her," he commands the interpreter, "that it happens I saw her myself when she was brought in on the handcart. Ask her where is her home."

Back, via the interpreter, comes the information that she has no home.

"First offense—five days—what is the matter with that man?" says the Captain-Judge all in one breath.

"That man," from his bright, keen, elderly face, evidently is not a drunk. Also, in his face there are no signs of evil, so one wonders what he has done.

His name is José de Garro, the interpreter says for him. During the days of street fighting, while he lay hid, the United States sailors made use of his handcart, which happens to be his sole means of livelihood. He has now discovered his handcart. It is being used by the servants of the proprietor of the Hotel Diligencia, and said proprietor has declined to return it to him.

The Court does not ponder the matter. Like the crack of a whiplash, his orders are issued:

"Send a policeman to the Hotel Diligencia and bring the handcart and the proprietor here. Find from the complainant two men who will swear to his identity and to his ownership of the handcart, and send a policeman to bring the two men he names. Mercedes de Villagran!"

While Mercedes de Villagran is being brought from the cells, two thieves, Messrs. Bravo de Saravio and Pedro Sorez de Ulloa, already sent for and just brought from the cells, are considered. Captain Callahan is interrogated by the Court from without through an open window, and Captain Callahan's information causes the Court to command that the two thieves be remanded, the case being grave, and be kept incommunicado waiting the evidence in process of being gathered.

Mercedes de Villagran proves to be a wizened little old woman, very worn, very miserable, very frightened, who is charged with having in her possession munitions of war. Worst of all, a double handful of Mauser cartridges is exhibited in evidence. In a thin, quavering falsetto she explains that after the street fighting, pursuing her regular vocation of garbage picking, she did find and retain possession of the munitions of war, deeming them of value and unaware that possession of them constituted a grave offense or any offense at all.

"Case dismissed—turn her loose," and the Captain-Judge has forgotten her on the instant and forever in the thick rush of his crowded life, but him she will ever remember, to her last breath, in her chatter of gossip with her garbage-picking sisters of Vera Cruz.

A prisoner is called, whose entry on the docket causes the Court's brows to corrugate: for the man has no name, and is entered as "P," with a note to the effect that Captain Callahan will explain.

Captain Callahan, not for the moment findable, possibly engaged in receiving another lady in a handcart, the Court tries two more cases of drunk, one, a second offense, receiving sixteen days and a warning that on a third offense he will be sent out through the lines.

Captain Callahan arrives, rolls up the sleeve of the man "P," shows a letter "P" inked on the man's arm, and explains that the defendant, arriving at jail so hopelessly drunk as to be speechless, could be entered in no other safely identifiable way, wherefore he had inked the man's arm, and there was the proof of it. Mr.

"P," somewhat recovered after a night's sleep, is able to state that his name is Alonzo de Córdova y Figueroa. The soldier clerk, remembering the face and searching the record, announces that Alonzo de Córdova y Figueroa is a second-timer, and Alonzo de Córdova y Figueroa, in debt to the United States with his time to the extent of sixteen days, is taken away.

The handcart, the proprietor of the Hotel Diligencia, and the policeman arrive in high garrulity. The proprietor is a squat, stoop-shouldered, pock-marked, white-haired Cuban, whose state of mind is one of amazement in that the handcart, on which he never laid eyes before, should have been found on his premises.

The handcart man looks on his property with joy, and cannot understand why the Captain-Judge does not immediately permit him to take it away, while the Captain-Judge receives particulars of a house raid the previous night in which four Mausers and a thousand rounds of ammunition had been unearthed.

Appears Tomás Martín de Poveda, charged with the ghastly crime of maintaining unclean premises. After a brief lecture on hygiene and sanitation, the Court gives the culprit twenty-four hours in which to clean up, and Tomás Martín de Proveda departs, shaking his head at such administration of justice by the thrice lunatic gringos.

A shopkeeper and a cigar maker arrive, take oath, and testify that José de Garro is truly José de Garro and that the handcart is truly his property, and José de Garro goes on his way rejoicing that God's still in heaven and justice in Vera Cruz.

The cases of three thieves, charged with stealing from the customhouse, and of a fence who bought the stolen property, are inquired into and continued. Follows a Jamaica negro cook and a cockney steward from an English steamer jointly charged with stealing a gold watch from a Spanish refugee.

The Court interrogates all three, discharges the negro, holds the cockney for trial, and dispatches a summons for the master of the ship to appear in court next morning, accompanied by a polite request first to search the cockney's belongings on board ship.

More men are warned for maintaining unclean premises; and one man, for having struck his wife, a dark-skinned, bovine-eyed Indian Madonna who testifies reluctantly, receives ten days, and is thunderstruck that such maladministration of justice can be.

A thin-faced widow, in a blight of black, pays the fine of her roistering eldest born, who while crazed with several centavos' worth of ninety-proof aguardiente, demolished a window and portions of the anatomy of a spigotty policeman. The Captain-Judge has seen service in Cuba, Puerto Rico, and the Philippines, and his "Carabao English," so learned, stands him in good stead. Not merely on occasion, but on many occasions, he corrects and checks the interpreter when that worthy fails properly to interpret shades of meaning or engages in animated discussions with prisoners and witnesses on irrelevant topics. Another thing that characterizes the efficiency of this blond lawgiver of a regular army captain, whose ancestors must have been more than closely related to Hengist and Horsa, is his combined patience, swiftness, and certitude. Rough and ready his justice is, but legal always, and unswayed by the seriousness or lightness of any case. He opposes directness and simplicity to the garrulity and immateriality of the Vera Cruzans. His patient questions go to the point, he achieves his conclusion in the midst of some longwinded explanation of things concerning other things and not the things at issue, and suddenly, like a shot, he enunciates his decision: "I find you guilty—forty days"; or: "Not guilty—next case."

He finds Martín Oñez de Loyola, a full-blooded Spaniard, guilty of a particularly mean crime and sentences him to six months—this merely to hold him until he can be deported to his native country, which is Spain. But the Captain-Judge is thorough. He gives instructions that when the convicted man is deported the Chief of Police of Havana be warned to keep him on his steamer and the Chief of Police of Barcelona be warned to nab him when he disembarks on his native soil.

This case of Martín Oñez de Loyola merits the harshness of the sentence. A well-to-do but ignorant Mexican woman of the capital had married her deceased husband's brother, equally well-to-do and ignorant. Loyola, becoming aware of the matter, had assured them that it was a terrible crime, and had bled them, at different times, of over ten thousand pesos. In order to escape him they had started to flee the country; but Loyola, true leech that he was, followed them through the lines of two hostile armies to Vera Cruz. And so, thanks to the Captain-Judge, they were able to return to Mexico, while their persecutor, willy-nilly, made the voyage to Spain.

Francisco Hernández, trouble-eyed and stupid, charged with stealing a barrel of wine, positively declares himself not guilty, and the patient Court unravels the tangle. Pedro de Valvidia, owner of a cantina, and his barkeeper, García de Mendoza, testify to catching the thief in the act and to apprehending him with the barrel already rolled out on the sidewalk and merrily rolling onward.

Two peon witnesses testify to having seen Francisco Hernández captured while rolling the barrel, and the case begins to look dark for Francisco Hernández, who had pleaded not guilty. But he receives inspiration. He acknowledges all the facts testified to. He was not the owner of the barrel. He did go into the cantina and roll out the barrel. He was caught by the owner and the barkeeper in the manner described, but—and he makes the explanation that is as ancient as the first theft of portable property—it happened that as he came along the street looking for a job, his profession being that of cargador, two strange men approached him and hired him to convey the barrel of wine, which they had just purchased, to their residence. That was all. He was as innocent as a new-born babe. What did he want with a whole barrel of wine? What could he do with a whole barrel of wine, being a temperate as well as an honest man?

"Where were you going to deliver the barrel?" the Court demands.

Francisco Hernández somehow cannot remember the address.

"Who were the men?"

Francisco Hernández says they were strangers.

"Describe them."

And one can actually see Francisco Hernández's imagination working at high pressure as he paints the portraits of the two mythical strangers.

The Court asks several other questions not very important, merely concerning his whereabouts earlier in the day and how often he succeeded in getting work, and Francisco Hernández, believing that his tale is believed, grows confident.

"Describe the two men," the Court suddenly commands.

Poor Hernández is taken by surprise. He stumbles and halts,

tries to remember his extempore description of the two non-existent individuals, diverges, slips up, falls down, and, in the midst of his gropings and stutterings, is astounded to hear the Captain-Judge decisively utter just three words: "Guilty—six months." And while the interpreter is transposing this misfortune into understandable Spanish terms, the Captain-Judge is already into the thick of the next case.

And this is a case destined to make the entire native population of Vera Cruz sit up and take notice that never was similar justice dispensed before, albeit 4,000 soldiers and 20,000 marines and bluejackets, to say nothing of $100,000,000 worth of warships, were required to install the Captain-Judge in the Municipal Palace.

It is a sordid squalid case. Rosalia de Xara Quemada and Cristóvel de la Cerda are the culprits. Alonzo de Xara Quemada is the husband of Rosalia, and is also the complainant. He is a bulgy-eyed, cadaverous-cheeked, vulpine-faced individual, and he grins vindictively and triumphantly as he makes his charge.

Rosalia is frightened and dumbly defiant. She has a full, oval face, wavy brown hair parted in the middle and neatly bound with a light blue ribbon, and dangling earrings. There is just sufficient Spanish in the Indian of her to give her temperament and to account for the inimitable draping of the brown shawl about her shoulders and hips. Cristóvel, the lover, is a depressed and gloomy young man who keeps books for a living.

Rosalia and Cristóvel plead guilty, and are prepared for merciless judgment at the hands of the Captain-Judge who transacts justice with a big automatic at his hip and with armed soldiers for his attendants. But the Captain-Judge is not satisfied. He asks Rosalia and her husband, Alonzo, many penetrating questions. They have five children. For four years Alonzo has not contributed a centavo toward their support. Rosalia, by scrubbing, by peddling, by cooking, and by various other ways has given the entire support to her brood of five.

As all this comes out, Rosalia seems to take heart of courage and grows voluble, while Alonzo glowers at her in a way that would bode a beating were there none present to interfere. The reason her husband had had her arrested, Rosalia volunteers, was that just previous to the arrest she had refused to lend him five pesos. At other times in the past she had loaned him money. No, he had never returned a single loan.

The Captain-Judge orders the culprits to step forward to receive sentence, knits his brows for a moment in thought, and proceeds:

"Cristóvel de la Cerda. You have pleaded guilty of the grave offense of adultery. By the Mexican law of this State I could sentence you to two years. But I shall not be harsh. I shall sentence you to six months. The sentence, however, will be suspended and I release you here and now on probation. You will report to this court every Saturday morning at nine o'clock with a letter from your employer attesting your good behavior."

As the interpreter turns this into Spanish, the husband's face is a rich study. At the mention of two years, it is hilarious. The six months' sentence leaves it still hilarious, but not so hilarious. The suspension of the sentence positively floors Alonzo, and the angry blood surges darkly under his skin.

Rosalia is similarly sentenced, released on probation, told to report every Saturday morning, and admonished to be good. But the case is not over. Alonzo de Xara Quemada, distraught with this frightful miscarriage of justice, is ordered to stand forth.

"Alonzo de Xara Quemada, your conduct has been most reprehensible."

While the interpreter struggles with the dictionary for the Spanish equivalent of the introductory sentence, Alonzo looks as if he expects to be backed up against a wall the next moment and shot.

"These five children are yours just as much as they are Rosalia's. From now on you shall do your share toward supporting them. Each week you shall pay to Rosalia the sum of five pesos. Each Saturday morning at nine o'clock you shall appear before me with the receipt for the five pesos. If you don't, we will see what six months in jail will do for you."

The whole thing is too unthinkably hideous for Alonzo. He blows up, and in impassioned language forswears and disowns Rosalia, the five children, and all memory of them and responsibility for them; forever and forever. Furthermore, he will not pay the weekly five pesos. Who ever heard of such a thing? He denies the Captain-Judge's right in the matter, and all in wild harangue announces that he will appeal to the Mexican courts against such injustice.

Whereupon the Captain-Judge's fist comes down on the desk, and the Captain-Judge thunders:

"There is no Mexican law here. I am the law. You will pay the five pesos. Today is Thursday. Next Saturday you will appear before me with the receipt for the first five pesos. Vamos."

Alonzo de Xara Quemada starts to screech protest, but two soldiers, with wicked-looking bayonets on the ends of their rifles, step forward, and Alonzo subsides.

I departed on his heels, greedily enjoying the maledictions he muttered down the street. And on Saturday morning I made it a point to be present at the Provost Court at nine o'clock. Sure enough, Alonzo de Xara Quemada was there, sullenly exhibiting a receipt for five pesos signed by one Rosalia de Xara Quemada.

And all the affairs and transactions I have described in this article constitute but a portion of one morning's work in one Provost Court of the five Provost Courts sitting in Vera Cruz.

Before I cease, I cannot forbear describing a little scene I witnessed right after Alonzo's plaint had died away down the street. Captain Callahan was engaged in receiving a lady who was more difficult to receive than if she had come in a handcart. A sweaty and disheveled spigotty policeman had brought her, and she had fought him all the way to such effect that he stood near the entrance to the cells too exhausted to move her a step further. In vain Captain Callahan ordered him to proceed with her. She was the stronger, and she had caught her second wind. Just as she flung herself on the policeman in savage onslaught, a big American soldier strode to her and tapped her authoritatively on the arm. She turned and stared up at him. He spoke no word, but with a curt thrust of his thumb over his shoulder indicated the way to the cells. She wilted into all meekness and obedience, and meekly and obediently, without a hand being laid on her, walked into the cell room.

June 27, 1914

OUR ADVENTURERS IN TAMPICO

One must go and see in order to know. My advance impression of Tampico, for one, was of a typical Mexican port infested with smallpox, yellow fever, and a few American ad-

venturers of pernicious activities and doubtful antecedents. There
were also oil wells, I understood in and about Tampico, operated
by the aforesaid adventurers. And that was about all I knew of
the place until I went and saw.

Aboard my steamer were oilmen returning after being driven
out to our warships by the Mexicans the day our forces landed
in Vera Cruz, and after being shanghaied by our State Department to the United States. A big steel barge, swept by every
breaker, was pounding to destruction on the end of the break-
water that projected into the Gulf.

"That's our barge," one of the oilmen told me. "When the
Federals fired our wharf, her mooring lines burned away and she
drifted down the river."

He looked at me grimly when I remarked that they had got
off lightly.

"Wait and see," was all he said.

Once in the mouth of the Pánuco River, the landscape on
either side sprouted into the enormous, mushroom growths of the
tank farms. I was quite impressed, not having dreamed that our
adventurers had done so much work. It was a creditable showing,
a very creditable showing. But as we continued up the river,
more and more terminals and tank farms lined both banks of it.
This was the Corona terminal, and that was the Aguila on both
sides, and adjoining were the huge solid buildings of Standard Oil.
And still the names of companies were rolled off to me. There
was the National Petroleum, there the Waters-Pierce, the Gulf
Coast, the Huasteca, the Mexican Fuel, the Magnolia Petroleum,
the Texas, the International Oil, the East Coast Oil—and thereat
I ceased taking account of the companies and realized that there
was quite something more to Tampico than I had anticipated.

"Ah," I remarked, "there's the city at last," indicating great
masses of buildings on the north bank. But I was informed that the
city was yet miles away, and that what I had mistaken for it was
the boiler stacks, still stacks, warehouses, paraffin plants, and
agitators of the refineries.

The ruined walls of a huge building were pointed out. "Six
hundred thousand dollars went up there," I was told. "Two hundred and fifty box cars went up with it. The shells from the
Federal gunboats did it."

We hoisted the doctor's flag and dropped anchor off a quarter of a mile of burned wharf.

"You see," it was explained, "the rebels were working two machine guns here and a bunch of sharpshooters, and the Federals from the *Zaragoza* let us have it good and plenty. That was all brand-new wharf. In fact, we hadn't quite finished it. Three of our barges were sunk by the shells. Right there at the bottom lies the *Topila* and the *Spindletop*, and, just beyond, the *Santa Fe*. See what the fire left of that tank on top of the hill. It gave us a hot time. While it was burning we fought to keep it inside the fire wall, and all the time the *Zaragoza* was shelling us. Don't talk to me about the peon. I was right there with a gang of them. They were working for a day's wages, but no trained soldiers could have behaved better. As soon as we'd jump up to fight the fire the *Zaragoza*'d loosen up on us. Inside ten minutes we'd have to lie down until the shells and machine guns slackened, and then we'd up and go at it again. And not a peon showed the white feather, and we held that burning oil where it was until it burned out. Some peons, hombre, some peons."

And while we waited for the port doctor, big ocean tanker after big ocean tanker in long procession came in from sea, flew the doctor's flag and dropped anchor.

"They come in, load, and go out all in the same day," I was told. "The *Huasteca* can load 9,000 barrels an hour. Why, there are tankers that have been coming in here for a year whose crews have never set foot on land."

I began to gather statistics of the pernicious activities of our American adventurers. One company alone had two roofed concrete tanks holding 1,250,000 barrels along with 120 steel tanks holding 55,000 barrels each. Since a steel tank costs 30,000 pesos, the cost of 120 steel tanks will total 3,600,000 pesos. At the rate of exchange prior to Mexico's present troubles, this investment in mere steel-tank equipment means 1,800,000 American gold dollars. When it is considered that this is but part of the one item of oil-storage equipment of one company, and that there are many other equally expensive items of equipment, the grand total of the equipment of the many companies is vaguely adumbrated.

The port doctor finally boarded and passed us and we continued up the river to Tampico. The Pánuco is a noble stream, deep of channel, swift of current, and wide; and as we rounded a grand bend between the interminable tank farms a whole fleet of anchored merchant steamers appeared, as well as warships, flying the flags of various nations. The *Des Moines* flew the only American flag.

Passing the customhouse and emerging through the Fiscal Dock, a long line of mounted Constitutionalists made me for a while forget oil and oil tanks. Before I knew what was happening, I found myself in the company of 500 of the Constitutionalists, dispatched to aid in the pursuit of General Zaragoza and his 4,000 Federals.

Never on the warpath have I encountered a bunch of warriors so harum-scarum, so happy-go-lucky, so brimming over with good food and high spirits. Every one was mounted. Every horse was stolen. On the horses were the brands of every ranch and hacienda from the Rio Grande to the Pánuco. Occasionally there was a grizzled oldster. But the big percentage was youthful. There were boys of ten, eleven, and twelve, magnificently and monstrously spurred, astride lifted broncos, with pictures of saints in their sombreros and looted daggers and bowie knives in their leggings, with automatics and revolvers at their hips, bewaisted and beshouldered with belts and bandoleers of cartridges, and with the inevitable rifle across their saddle pommels. And there were women, young women all, mere soldaderas as well as amazons, the former skirted and on sidesaddles, the latter trousered and cross saddled, and all of them wickedly armed like their male comrades, and none of them married. When a soldadera comes along I should not like to be a stray chicken on the line of march nor a wounded enemy on the field of battle.

Crossing the Pánuco to the south bank on a barge, I tried to take the picture of a coy and skirted soldadera. But all was vain until I won the good services of the Lieutenant Colonel by snapping him and his fellow officers. They were so delighted that all that they possessed was mine, and the soldadera was commanded to face the camera. The proud Colonel even interrupted proceedings in order to decorate the soldadera with his own cartridge belt, knife, and revolver. She was young, strong, uncorseted, cotton-frocked, all Indian, and she had ridden, as I learned, for two years with the revolutionists. She came from far in the North, and her near goal was Mexico City.

Ashore on the south bank, endeavoring to catch two or three of the rebels with my camera, I suffered from an embarrassment of riches. All the soldiers crowded into the immediate foreground —there were half a thousand of them—and my lens was not wide-angled. In twos and threes they struck the most bloodthirsty attitudes, and I could only escape them by patiently faking a pressure of the bulb and a rolling on of the film. They were as proud as peacocks, as excitable and naïve as children. Just as I pressed the bulb on a long row of them on horseback, one of them, beside himself with too much valor, accidently discharged his rifle. His fellows laughed at him. His officers did not even frown. It was too common an occurrence. They were merely sky-larking boys on the rampage, these rebels who had exchanged the tedium of the day's work for a year-long picnic. Picnic was what it was with a horse to ride, a peso and a half a day, good grub, a chance to loot, and, best of all, a chance to shoot their fellow men, which last is the biggest big-game hunting that ever falls to the lot of man. Through the fires of sunset—men, women, and small boys—they rode up the winding trail in single file and disappeared south on the road to Mexico City, their hearts high with the hope that they might overtake and terminate the lives of some of the unfortunate, limping, poor devils of Federals lagging behind the beaten army of Zaragoza.

Returning by launch, I found that Tampico was mostly sur-rounded by water and was half a Venice. The backyards, or patios, rather, of the water-front dwellers overhung the canal, which teemed with dugout canoes and chalans (the open, native boat), on which lived many families. But in addition to all this was the evidence of the activity of our American adventurers. Everywhere boat building and repairing was going on. There were paint shops, machine shops, and shipways; and there were river steamers, barges, and launches, not by the score, but by the many hundred.

A carriage, drawn by the thinnest, boniest, mangiest, pair of horses I had ever seen, took me to the hotel. The reason for the condition of the horses was obvious. Only such animals could have escaped for half a year the horse-stealing Federals and rebels.

The hotel was modern, five-storied, had elevators, and was in every detail—from the cafe tables copied after Sherry's to the Tom Collins glasses that were duplicates of Martin's—a New York hotel. Mine host even had cold beer, having added to his stock by purchase from the Constitutional officers of a carload which they had confiscated at Monterey, and which they had run into Tampico over the Mexican Central Railway, also confiscated.

But the hotel was not the interesting thing. It was the men in it—Americans all, who were already gathering back after their enforced journey to the United States. The atmosphere was of the West, of the frontier, of the mining camp. I was more nearly reminded of the men of Klondike than of anywhere else. In truth, within an hour I encountered a dozen sourdoughs. Two of them I had known in the old days in Alaska. Said one from whom I had parted seventeen years before in Dawson City:

"Jack, this ain't no Klondike. It's got Klondike faded to a fare you well and any other gold camp the world has ever seen. You know my old claim on Eldorado, from rim rock to rim rock and 500 feet up and down stream—well, that was a humdinger and it cleaned up half a million. But shucks, that ain't anything alongside of these diggings. Why, there's the old well at Ebano, the first in the country, a gusher when they struck it twelve years ago, and still a-gushing. They ain't had to pump it yet. It just naturally gushes.

"And the Dutch, up above Pánuco, have got an ornery eight-inch hole, nothing to look at, but it can throw 185,000 barrels a day when it ain't pinched down. Figure it up. Say oil at 50 cents a barrel, that makes $90,000 gold a day; in ten days $900,000; in a hundred days $9,000,000; in a year, allowing sixty-five days for delays and accidents, $27,000,000—and that's gold, United States gold coin with the eagle and the Indian. Eldorado and Bonanza together, mouth to source, bench claims and all, didn't turn that much out in the first two years of skimming the cream."

I learned that the Pánuco field alone was estimated by conservative expert oilmen to contain at least $2,000,000,000 worth of oil. One really conservative expert put it at $2,500,000,000, but after a moment, without prompting, amended his figures to $2,000,000,000. And the Pánuco was only one of three big fields, the other two being Ebano and Huasteca, while there were two lesser fields, the Chila and the Topila, each with its noteworthy producing wells, and all five fields as yet scarcely scratched.

And from oil and oilmen I drifted into war and soldier men in the shape of a couple of rebel officers. One, a colonel, with no English, presented me with a handful of Federal money confiscated at Monterey and declared worthless by the Constitutionalists. That was why he gave it to me, and, promptly and absent-mindedly, I bought cold beer with it for all of us and received good Constitutional money in change from the large bills. The other officer, a major, was soft voiced and gentle faced as a woman, and at the same time as sanguinary as any hero of the bull ring. He had been in the field four years. He had fought under Madero. He was now fighting under Villa and Carranza. Two of his brothers had been killed in battle. All his property was destroyed. He had but recently recovered from a bullet which had perforated him just under the heart, right side to left, in and out again. "We shoot our men who loot," he said softly, with no more emphasis than if he had announced that they slapped looters on the wrists. "We shot four of our men here in Tampico. It is true we are civilized. At Monterey we shot one colonel and one captain for looting. No, it is not permitted. We are not savages."

Yes, he was a four years' veteran. It had been a long fight, with many a day and week of hunger when the very thought of a tortilla made one sick with longing. And straight beef after a month, cooked hot from the hoof, did sometimes make one tired. Had I heard how Huerta shaved? Well, Huerta stood erect while the barber shaved him, one hand in his pocket on a revolver with which to get the barber if the barber cut his throat.

It was all lies about the Constitutional atrocities. All such things were committed by the Federals. They dragged their wounded enemies to death with lariats, while the Constitutionalists took their wounded enemies to hospital and nursed them. It was true they did sometimes execute captured Federal officers, but only when such officers were known assassins and traitors.

"Zaragoza?" he repeated, after my question at parting. There was a white flash of small, even teeth, and the soft voice enunciated ever so softly: "He is in the trap. He cannot escape."

"And when you catch him?" I queried.

"He is an assassin," came the answer, indirect it was true, but a complete, straight-out answer.

In the morning, in a speed boat, accompanying the general superintendent of an oil company, I went up the Pánuco River. Except where there were wharves for loading oil, or where the cut banks were too steep, the rich alluvial soil was farmed by the Indians to the water's edge. And here, amid coconut palms, banana trees, and trees of the mango and the avocado, I saw demonstrated the statement that soil and climate were such as to permit the raising of three crops of corn a year. Side by side there were patches of corn just sprouting, of corn that was in the tassel, and of corn that was being harvested.

It was amazing to see the cattle drinking knee-deep in the river, and horses and mules along the bank. Not all the stock had been run off by the soldiers. From time to time our swift craft swerved in nearer to the bank in order that the superintendent might try to identify familiar-looking animals. In this he was occasionally successful, the animals having escaped from the fleeing Federals and drifted back to their own pastures.

Where the Tamesí River flowed in we passed the drawbridge wrecked by the Federals, and the sunken gunboat, the *Vera Cruz*, abandoned with open sea cocks when the Constitutionalists took the town.

We continued up the Pánuco, past the tiled roofs of Americans who farmed the land, past the grass huts of the natives, and past many brown-skinned September Morns bathing in the shallows. The American farms were deserted, the owners not yet having come back from their forced trip to the United States. One such holding consisted of 1,300 acres, 1,000 of which were in bananas. Other Americans had gone in for grapefruit, and all ran stock in the rich pastures. No hay is cured in this land, nor do the natives feed grain even to their work animals. The horses and mules are grass-fed and leaf-browsed, and grass and leaves are green the year around. Rain falls every month in the year, the "rainy season" merely connoting the period of excessive rain.

The Pánuco River was alive with traffic. The first returning adventurers were already moving oil. River steamers and ocean tugs moved up and down with long tows of tank barges, and here and there, against the banks, barges were loading oil from the pipe lines of near-by wells. Also, we passed the sites of ancient towns, whose totality of inhabitants, in numbers of from twenty-five to fifty thousand, had been massacred by the Aztecs or taken up for the great sacrificial festivals in the lake city of the Montezumas.

There were, on the river, many hundreds of the chalans, or long poling boats of the Indians, going upstream with purchases from town, coming down on the current loaded with chickens, vegetables, charcoal, corn, raw sugar, bananas, pineapples, sugar cane, and all manner of things from the soil that fetch a price in Tampico. The honesty of these Indians is proverbial. From the headreaches of the Pánuco they are sometimes months in making the round trip, and they are often trusted with thousands of pesos with which to make purchases in Tampico.

From every foreigner in Mexico comes the same testimony of the rock-ribbed integrity of the Indian. It is always the mixed breed who is unveracious, dishonest, and treacherous. It was the mixed breeds who composed the mobs in Tampico that cried death to the gringos. And many of these half-breeds, so crying, were the very employees of the gringos they wanted to kill and whose property they wanted to destroy. And it was the peon, the Indian, who remained faithful to his salt.

As an example of this, part way on our journey in the Topila field, the superintendent ran the boat in to a small wharf where an Indian was loading two barges with oil. When the Americans were driven out, this Indian, without instructions, threatened by the soldiers, had stuck to his post and moved the flowing oil from wells to tanks and to the emergency reservoirs. Nor had a barrel of oil been lost. Yet three times the Federals had strung him up by the neck in an effort to persuade him to volunteer in the army. As he told them, and he is legion:

"I don't want to fight. I have trouble with nobody. I don't want trouble. When I first came to work here for the gringos I had nothing. I went barefooted. Now I wear shoes. When I worked I got sixty centavos a day. Now I get four pesos a day. I have a nice house. There are chairs in my house. I have a talking machine. Before I lived like a dog. No, I won't be a soldier and fight. All I want is to be left alone."

Forty-seven miles above Tampico we came to the superintendent's wells in the Pánuco field. Two days before, his handful of American employees had returned to the looted camp and begun moving oil and building new emergency reservoirs against the time when they might again be driven out. The foreman in charge, a lean, low-spoken Texan, in reply to the superintendent's query for news, said:

"Oh, everything's moving along slowly. The trouble is that our peons have taken to the brush and there'll be some time getting confidence into them to come back. You know so-and-so—well, the cuss was out here this morning, with a few drinks in him, and throwing the fear of God into the few peons I have gathered in, telling them that we'd soon be gone and that every one of them that had worked for us would be shot. Oh, and he cussed us out good and plenty to our faces, telling us that what would happen to the peons wasn't a circumstance to what was coming to us."

The superintendent turned to me with a weary smile.

"That man," he explained, "is the Mexican, the same old half-breed type, with no virtues and all vices. He runs one of the biggest stores in Tampico. Our books will show that we have spent in his store in the last twelve months over $100,000 gold. And he has been invariably courteous and friendly to us. And now he selects our particular camp in which to voice his threats."

That a blunder was made in not landing our troops at Tampico the same time we landed them at Vera Cruz cannot be doubted by anyone who has gone over the ground and studied the ground and studied the situation. To make matters worse, our American warships were withdrawn from the river and anchored in the open Gulf, ten miles away. The Mexicans, inflamed by the invasion of their country at Vera Cruz, took this withdrawal of our naval forces from Tampico as a sign of timidity. Mobs formed in the streets, and the Americans—men, women, and children—took refuge in the hotels, while the mobs tore down and spat upon American flags and cried death to all Americans.

It is a curious sort of reasoning that brings about a conclusion that the only way to save the lives of our countrymen and countrywomen is to run away and leave them in such a city under such circumstances.

To make matters worse, the United States, by virtue of the old Monroe Doctrine, had warned the other powers off and announced her ability to deal with the situation. The captains of the Dutch and English war vessels declined to interfere for the deserted Americans even when the captain of the German warship approached them to join with him in a shore party to rescue the besieged Americans. This was on the night that succeeded the day of the landing at Vera Cruz.

That night, for an instance, over a hundred Americans, including their women, were sheltered in the Southern Hotel. Those who did not have guns had armed themselves with machetes and clubs for what looked like the last stand. The mob roared in the street and repeatedly attacked the doors with battering rams. And at one in the morning two German officers arrived from the battleship. The English and the Dutch captains had declined to cooperate, and the German commander was acting on his own responsibility. And so, thanks to the Germans, the Americans in Tampico were rescued.

But there were several hundred men, women, and children far up in the oil fields. From Tampico to the Pánuco field was forty-seven miles by the winding river, and ten miles away, in the opposite direction from Tampico, lay the American warships. A superintendent, accompanied by a young Texan, braved the streets in the early morning of the second day. They were spat upon and reviled, and were only saved by an armed guard. But they managed to win across the river and to get the crew of a sternwheel steamer to volunteer to go up to Pánuco. Fired at by soldiers and looters, followed by troops of Federal cavalry along the banks, they nevertheless cleaned up every camp and brought back with them some three hundred adventurers of their kind. Yes, somebody blundered in this Tampico affair.

When General Zaragoza, with his 4,000 Federals, evacuated Tampico, he retreated on a number of long railroad trains. But beyond Ebano the tracks were blocked by the rebels. Abandoning the trains, General Zaragoza retreated across country to the Pánuco oil fields. On this march he shot fifteen of his lagging men as a spur to the rest to keep up. In the oil town of Pánuco he rested while getting horses and provisions for his men. He was a beaten man, and, but for one thing, he would have been destroyed. He sent a message to General Pablo Gonzáles, commanding the rebels that had driven him out of Tampico.

"I am a beaten man," was the tenor of Zaragoza's message. "My men are exhausted. I am short of ammunition. If you attack me, I am lost. But the moment you attack I shall fire the oil wells."

And the rebels did not attack. It was a pretty situation. The rebels planned to add to their treasure by shaking down the oilmen. If the oil wells were ruined, the oilmen would have nothing for which to be shaken down. Zaragoza took his time ere he drifted away south across the hot lands in his effort to find a way up the mountains to the great tableland.

Child-minded men, incapable of government, playing with the weapons of giants! A $2,000,000,000 oil body, a world asset, if you please, at the pleasure of stupid anarchs! And all that saved it, the desire of a portion of the anarchs to loot, by forced contribution, the gringos who had found and developed the oil fields!

Two thousand feet under the surface lies the Pánuco oil body. The formation overlying the oil sands is so broken and creviced by ancient upheavals that the casings are not tight. To seal a well under such conditions would force the oil to rise to the surface outside the casing. At the best, with the wells "pinched down" to the limit of safety, the flow of all the wells could not be reduced below a daily run of 100,000 barrels. From the time when the oilmen were driven out and shanghaied to the United States this great volume of oil accumulated in the tanks and in the open emergency reservoirs. A wad of cotton waste, saturated with kerosene and ignited and tossed into the oil, could have started the $2,000,000,000 bonfire. General Zaragoza could so have started it. So could any drunken peon.

Perhaps no oil region has been tapped that will compare with the Tampico region. The wells on all the five fields are gushers, and, unlike most gushers, are slow in gushing themselves out. The well at Ebano, previously mentioned, has been flowing for twelve years. In the Huasteca field is a well that has gushed

23,000 barrels a day for four years. To-day it is still gushing its 23,000 barrels, the oil has the same twenty-two gravity, has yet to show a trace of moisture, and carries less than two-tenths of 1 per cent of sediment.

In passing, it may be remarked of the last-mentioned well that, when the Americans were forced out and the half-breed employees had gone to rioting, an old Indian employee took charge of his fellow Indians, and in twenty-two days handled the 500,000 barrels of oil and pumped it over the pipe line to the tank farm and terminal, 105 kilometers away. Not a barrel of oil was lost, and when the Americans returned they found it ready to load into the ocean tankers.

But, while the Tampico oil region is unthinkably big and rich, so much time and money have been required in development that, out of eighty-nine oil-producing companies operating during the last fourteen years, only three have so far paid dividends. One particular company has invested $38,000,000 and has paid but a dividend and a half. There are other companies that have invested more than this one. A single company, which has so far paid one dividend, has 4,000 men on the pay roll, a monthly wage list of $100,000 and a monthly grocery bill of $10,000.

I spent a quiet Sunday with the chiefs of one of these companies. The superintendent and I had last parted at the tail of a glacier on the slope of Chilcoot Pass. He was a mere adventurer, of course, but just the same I desire to describe just a little of this, his Mexican adventure.

We sat in a hot room. The afternoon breeze had not yet sprung up. The house stood on a hill. All about were the visible evidences of pernicious activity. The low hills were crowned with steel tanks and reservoirs. The slopes down to the river were covered with machine shops, carpenter shops, warehouses, an ice plant, an electric-light plant, a foundry, and parks of wagons, auto-trucks, road scrapers, graders, and rollers. The river was wharf-lined and the wharf was lined with tankers loading oil. There were dredgers, pile drivers, launches, barges, river steamers, harbor tugs, huge ocean going tugs, and a fast steam yacht (bought a year before for the purpose of rushing the American employees away to the safety of the sea in case of need).

And there was more than could be seen. This particular company ran truck farms, chicken farms, and orchards of avocados, oranges, lemons, grapefruit, and figs—all for feeding its employees. I knew that to the west, in the Ebano field, were this company's hospitals, clubhouses, and railroad shops. Oh, yes, it possessed two railroads which it had built as well as run. Also, at Ebano, was its asphaltum refinery, reckoned the largest in the world, and a mere stock farm where imported Hereford bulls, Percheron stallions, and Missouri jacks graded up the inferior stock of Mexico, and where 10,000 head of animals had run prior to the raids by Federals and Constitutionalists.

From this house on the hill ran a graded wagon road through the jungle, built by the company, into the far Huasteca country, connecting with the terminal of the company's railroad at Dos Bocas. All this distance, and more, to a hundred miles away, ran the company's telephone lines. Two pipe lines for oil, one for water, and one for gas paralleled the wagon road.

In that hot room of the house on the hill the telephone was never idle. Now the superintendent, now one chief, and now another answered it. A call would come from some distant station. Two horses had been run off by Constitutionalists. Another call: the Federals had just killed five cows and a bull for food, and the superintendent, in return, desired to know if his pony was still safe.

An employee arrives on the porch with the news that four of the auto-trucks lifted by the rebels have been recovered in Tampico and are being brought across the river on a barge. Another employee brings the word that the launch *Doodle-bug* has just been commandeered by the rebels.

Over the telephone comes word that General Zaragoza, with 3,400 of his men, has burned a village and is lifting every horse and mule in sight. The Federals are drifting toward Amatlán the voice over the wire goes on.

"Getting close to our mules," remarks one of the chiefs, and then to me: "We've got 600 mules down there—200 of them from the States."

A tidy item that—sixty to seventy thousand dollars' worth of mule flesh; and the superintendent, over the phone, orders the moving of the mule herd to another potrero away from the line of Federal driftage.

The water station at Tamcochin sent in word that the Federals were reported drifting down on Tamcochin.

"All right," advises the superintendent. "Keep the tanks full to the last moment, and be prepared to run for it. Have a horse saddled for each one of you, and run the rest off now."

In a lull one of the chiefs begins inquiring over the line for the pursuing rebels, and locates a station through which 500 of them had passed two hours earlier.

A call announces that the 600 mules are on their way to potreros green and hidden.

The chiefs try to reason the drift of the Federals. It is concluded that so far they have failed to gain the tableland, but that they are bound to try again because, to the south, they are blocked by the rebels, who have captured the port of Tuxpan.

"It does hurt to be called an adventurer," one of the chiefs begins, but is interrupted by a clatter of hoofs and the eruption of a splendid specimen of an Indian who dismounts and reports that after recovering thirty of the company's horses he has just had them taken away by a bunch of rebels.

Another station telephones a rumor that the 500 rebels have run into the 3,400 Federals and are having a hot time of it.

One of the chiefs telephones a subordinate to hire a launch to take the place of the commandeered *Doodle-bug*. Scarcely is this done when a slender half-breed presents himself with a fresh commission to be a colonel and to raise a regiment of 500 men for the rebels. The superintendent shows the new Colonel every consideration. He is compelled to, or else the Colonel will enlist the men from the company's laborers. Also, the Colonel wants to borrow a launch for a couple of days. It is blackmail, but the superintendent smilingly lends it, and as soon as the Colonel is gone sends orders to hire another launch for the company in Tampico. Following that, at his suggestion, a chief telephones a lone man in a lone station in the path of the Federal drift to be ready to disconnect the wires and cut and run for it.

Between telephone calls a broken conference is held on the

problem of moving the Ebano oil. A chief states that the company's shop at Ebano is occupied by seven engines which the rebels have captured from the Mexican Central and are repairing. Another chief, whose activities are patently diplomatic, is instructed to attempt to persuade the rebel leaders to use the repair shops at Tampico. It is decided, since the Ebano oil must be moved because of lack of further storage, to get the rebels to move it over the captured Mexican Central.

"If they won't or can't," the superintendent concludes, "then propose that they let us move it over their lines. We can furnish our own trains, crews, and everything."

And the foregoing is just a sample of what went on for all that blessed day and half the night in that hot room of the house on the hill. One last thing I must give. Over the telephone came the verification of the earlier report of fighting. The 3,400 Federals had pretty well cut to pieces the 500 rebels, who were dropping back. Also, the Federals had ceased drifting and were making fast time for the mountains. And in the evening I fell asleep in my chair while the telephone rang on and on, and while the superintendent and his chiefs conferred and planned and considered immediate problems vastly profounder than any I have mentioned here.

PART TWO

Sports Articles

After London returned from the Yukon in the summer of 1898, he determined to become a writer. On September 17 he wrote the editor of the Bulletin (San Francisco) asking him if he would be interested in a four-thousand-word article describing a trip from Dawson to St. Michaels in a rowboat. The answer was negative.

London had passed the civil service examination for a post office job at which he would earn forty dollars a month. His family and his friends tried to convince him that he should take the work and have a regular income, but London had a firm belief that he could write and a grim resolve to write. In a letter to Mabel Applegarth dated November 30, he wrote:

> Nor has anybody ever understood. The whole thing has been by itself. Duty said "do not go on; go to work." So said my sister, though she would not say it to my face. Everybody looked askance; though they did not speak, I knew what they thought. Not a word of approval, but much of disapproval. If only someone had said, "I understand." From the hunger of my childhood, cold eyes have looked upon me, or questioned, or snickered and sneered. What hurt above all was that some were my friends—not professed but real friends. I have calloused my exterior and received the strokes as though they were not; as to how they hurt, no one knows but my own soul and me.
>
> So be it. The end is not yet. If I die I shall die hard, fighting to the last, and hell shall receive no fitter inmate than myself. But for good or ill, it shall be as it has been—alone.
>
> Mabel, remember this: the time is past when any John Halifax Gentleman ethics can go down with me. I don't care if the whole present, all I possess, were swept away from me—I will build a new present; if I am left naked and hungry; if I were a woman I would prostitute myself to all men but that I would succeed—[by writing] in short, I will.

A month later The Overland Monthly published his first story ("To the Man on Trail"), for which they paid five dollars. A month later (February 1899) The Black Cat offered forty dollars for a short story entitled "A Thousand Deaths."

Now he devoted full time to writing and wrote a variety of items including short stories, triolets, essays, and jokes. On June 24, 1900, the San Francisco Examiner published "Uri Bram's God" (or "Which Make Men Remember") and paid him forty dollars for the story which he later included in his collection The God of His Fathers. It was a break for London. He became known to the Examiner staff and during the next year contributed seventeen articles, includ-

ing the "Schützenfest" series and the Ruhlin-Jeffries fight. The San
Francisco Examiner *Saturday morning, July 13, 1901, printed:*

Jack London Will Describe Opening of Schützenfest For The *Examiner*

Jack London, the story writer, the young man who has made fame for
himself and for California in the world of letters, will write a description of the opening of the third great national Bundes shooting festival.
He will watch the Sunday morning parade in this city and will then go to
Shalmound to witness the lining up at the butts of the men of steady
nerve, iron hand, and keen sight. Then he will write in his own graphic
style what he has seen.

He received two hundred dollars for the ten "Schützenfest" articles.

His second sports assignment was the Jeffries-Ruhlin fight of No-
vember 16, 1901. James J. Jeffries had won the heavyweight world's
championship from Bob Fitzsimmons in an eleven-round bout at
Coney Island, New York, June 9, 1899. Jeffries defended his title un-
til 1903. In 1905 he retired from boxing and induced Marvin Hart,
whom he had once defeated, and Jack Root to fight for his vacated
title, which they did and which Jeffries refereed. Hart won the fight
and Jeffries proclaimed him champion.

Tommy Burns, whose real name was Noah Brusso, challenged Hart
and fought with him on February 23, 1906. Burns won by a decision
and claimed the heavyweight championship.

As London became known, his compensation increased. The San
Francisco Examiner *paid him one hundred dollars to cover the Britt-*
Nelson lightweight fight September 10, 1905.

James Britt had won it by defeating Joe Gans, 1904. The chal-
lenger, Oscar (Battling) Nelson, won the fight by a knockout in the
eighteenth round.

During the Cruise of the Snark *(1907–9) both of the Londons de-*
veloped health problems and went to Sydney, Australia. It was the
end of the Snark *voyage, and the boat was left in Sydney for dis-*
posal. However, while in Sydney, London reported the Burns-Johnson
world heavyweight championship fight for the New York Herald &
Syndicate and an Australian paper, The Star. *For this report he re-*
ceived twenty-five cents a word or a total of $275.

After his return from Australia, London recovered his health and
continued his intensive output of stories, essays, and novels. During
the year of 1910 he published thirty-six stories or essays (including
eleven on the Johnson-Jeffries fight) and two novels, Burning Daylight *and* Adventure. *When the Johnson-Jeffries fight was scheduled*
for Reno, Nevada, July 4, 1910, the New York Herald & Syndicate

asked London to cover the training period and the fight. Under the date of February 15, 1910, the Herald *editor wrote him:*

> . . . Mr. Bennett has cabled me that you are to represent *The Herald* at the Jeffries-Johnson fight and *The Herald* will appreciate any services performed for you as its special correspondent on that occasion. If you can use the Postal Telegraph Company's wires when filing your story, kindly do so.

The New York Herald & Syndicate *also offered London one hundred dollars a day and expenses to cover the eleven-day period in the Johnson and Jeffries training camps in Reno, Nevada, and the fight.*

James Barr in a book review entitled "Is the Prize-Ring Doomed?" wrote:

> *The Abysmal Brute* is by Jack London, than whom no man on earth is more entitled to write of prize-fighting. He has seen the biggest big fights that have been waged these last two decades, he has the penetrating brain, the knowledge of the world, and the tense, vivid vocabulary best suited to write a true picture of the ring. And a truly tremendous tale he has made of it. In his own picturesque Western style Jack London bustles the reader through the whole process of preparing for the winning, a world's heavy-weight championship. And when you have finished reading through *The Abysmal Brute*, you will realize that the soul of the prize-fighting, with all its gallantry and sordidness, its heroic points and drab grossness, has been laid bare."[1]

London *also wrote a second novel of prize fighting called* The Game *and two excellent short stories, "A Piece of Steak" and "The Mexican."*

SCHÜTZENFEST NO. 1

July 15, 1901.—The Goths have entered Rome! Aye, it is so. But there was no cry in the night, no clamor of hasty flight, no skurrying with household gods to the citadel. Rather, did San Francisco throw wide her gates and fraternize with her Teutonic invaders. On the other hand, these descendants of the Germanic tribesmen who swept down out of the forests of middle Europe some two thousand years ago, are quite unlike their savage forebears. They are not clad in the skins of wild beasts, and though they bear weapons in their hands, we do not

[1] *Red Magazine.* London, England. January 1, 1912.

fear; for they come not in war, but in love; not as foes, but as blood-brothers. And though their ancestors of old time looted many a fair city, we need keep no anxious eye upon our possessions. We have but one thing which they might appropriate, and which they surely would appropriate if they were able—and that is our climate.

It was a unique parade, that which passes through San Francisco's peaceful streets Sunday forenoon. Beneath fluttering banners and between packed rows of spectators, to the martial music of band and fife and drum, marched two thousand men, and picked men all. Not since our own "Californias" has so splendid a body of men been in our midst. And picked men they certainly are, picked from all the States, these men of the shooting clubs, these sharpshooters, these Schützenbrüder.

Men from the cities and men from the fields and forests; riflemen and sharpshooters from the Eastern centers, and hunters and fighters from the plains and mountains of the West. From Montana, Idaho, Arizona and Colorado, from Chicago, New York and Boston, and even from Europe they have come to take part in the Third National Bundes Shooting Festival. They are skillful men, eagle-eyed and steady of nerve, who have won trophies everywhere—gun experts and crowned kings of the target, to say nothing of princes and knights galore, who have demonstrated their fitness in rifle ranges the world over, and who have come together here, by the shores of the Pacific, in friendly contest.

Promptly at the target *The Examiner*'s siren the parade swung into motion from the corner of Market and New Montgomery streets; and right here, in passing, it is meet to state that promptness pre-eminently characterizes these riflemen. No delays; no lagging. They achieve the impossible feat of doing everything on schedule time.

Grand Marshal Robert Weineke led the long column of many divisions, and with the assistance of innumerable aides on gaily caparisoned horses, went over the line of march in splendid order. The route was up Market to City Hall avenue, around the Lick monument, countermarch on Market to Kearny, to California, to Montgomery and down Market to the Oakland ferry.

The banners were many and beautiful, but it was the uni-

forms that especially caught the eye. Gray and green predomi-
nated. And it is indeed a pretty sight, a body of stalwart men
clad in the traditionary hunting green, with black drooping plumes
of ostrich in their dark slouch hats. But with the recent develop-
ments of the machinery of warfare in one's mind, one would not
forbear looking a second time at the unobtrusive, inconspicuous
grays. They would surely conceal more easily a sharpshooter's
movements at a time when discovery would mean to invite
a whirlwind of death-dealing missiles. And the grays were pretty,
too—in fact, all the uniforms were neat and tasty.

From the ferry a special boat, and from the Oakland mole a
special train, carried the sharpshooters to Shell Mound Park. And
there, at 12 noon, to the stroke, Captain F. A. Kuhls, President
of the Shooting Bund, made the opening address. This part of
the programme took place in the big pavilion, with the furled
standards swaying beneath golden eagles of victory and the marksmen leaning picturesquely on their rifles.

Grand Marshal Robert Weineke, for all that he had done, was
honored by the addition of another badge to the many on his
coat. But he was not alone, for the breasts of the President and
the group about him on the platform were bespangled and blazing
with innumerable medals. It was a martial scene, and it dissolved
in true martial manner to the rattle of drums, the unisoned tramp
of feet and ringing German cheers.

Then the great crowd scattered and spread over the grounds
in quest of restaurants or quiet places where hampers and lunch
baskets might be opened, and also in quest of that national beverage that made Milwaukee famous.

At 1 o'clock sharp President F. A. Kuhls opened the great
shooting contest by firing three shots into the air. The first
was "for our adopted country," the second "for the old Fatherland," and the third "for the commonweal of the National
Shooting Bund."

At once followed a wild scramble for the honor of making the
first bull's-eye, and the hasty firing only eased down when loud
cheers proclaimed the lucky individual.

Then what seemed like an indiscriminate fusilade set in. There
were so many targets and so many shooting boxes that the
whole thing seemed confused and disorderly. That there was any

sanity about it, an adjacent lady could not be convinced. "How does anybody know anything?" she demanded excitedly, her voice pitched high in order to get above the roar of the guns. "Who is shooting? What are they scoring? Who is judging? Who is keeping track? And where are the targets?"

Nay, she could not see them. There were no targets. Preposterous! But a young fellow in the uniform of the United States artillery calmed her apprehensions after a quarter of an hour of endeavor, whereupon she undertook the hopeless task of re-explaining everything to her grandfather.

And well might she be forgiven her minutes of anxiety lest the whole shooting contest had gone to smash. At first glance it was indeed hard to locate the targets amid the maze of timbers and uprights that studded the range. Besides, two hundred yards is not to [be] sneezed at, and a black bull's-eye at that distance does not appear over large.

What really gave the impression of disorder, however, was the smoothness with which the machinery was running. The whole trouble was subjective. There was no evidence of the mind of some man behind and directing it all; no creaking of the wheels, as it were; but gradually, as one grew accustomed, order began to appear out of chaos. Each man was firing in turn. The shooting secretaries were at their posts; and down at the far end of the range the targets were constantly being replaced, and the long-handled spotters and vari-colored flags of the markers were indicating the scores as fast as they were made.

And in this manner did the ten days' contest commence; and not only is it the greatest shooting festival California has ever had, but it is the greatest ever held in the United States. It might well put the tournaments of the Middle Ages to scorn; for in those same Middle Ages it is to be doubted if knights ever jousted for as princely prizes or for honors more highly esteemed and verily, in those days it was a rare knight who fared three thousand miles or more to a tilting match.

The glittering array of prizes in the Temple of Gifts cost not a cent less than $100,000, while the honor that accompanies them is something that cannot be measured by worldly and commercial standards. Yes; the standards are quite different from those of old time. Here at the Bundesfest they will crown a man king. He

will be a common-man king, crowned not because of what his
father or grandfather chanced to do, but crowned because of the
things he himself has done; and to be king of American riflemen;
to possess the steadiest nerve, the keenest eye, the finest and
subtlest judgment, and to be so adjudged by one's own fellows
—surely this is finer and bigger than to sit vacuously in a high
place because, forsooth, some greater and stronger robber-ancestor
ground a people under the iron heel.

And while the sires and sons and husbands and brothers line
up at the firing butts their womenkind and children are not a whit
behind in enjoying themselves. All over the big grounds is frol-
icking and merrymaking of young and old; children in the
swings and on the hobby-horses; lusty young fellows doing the
giant swing on the bars or striking with the heavy mallet till they
ring the bell three clips out of four; and then, since there are
many men to shoot and only so many targets, there is dancing
going on at both pavilions, and it must be confessed the floors are
crowded with whirling couples. Everywhere is the clink of glasses
to genial laughter, while over all, ringing and reverberating
throughout the place, are the rifles. And for ten days without intermission, with balls, receptions and concerts in the evenings,
this will continue.

This is the Schützenfest.

SCHÜTZENFEST NO. 2

July 16, 1901.— Promptly at eight o'clock, ere the sun had
dissipated the morning mist, the contestants at the Bundes Fest
let loose with their rifles. They were canny marksmen, these,
who left their snug beds at such a chill hour; for they knew when
the light was good, and wished to try their skill when the air
was quiet, before the sea-breeze came romping in from the Pacific.

And they were ambitious, too; for a cash prize was the reward of him who made the first bull's-eye of the day. This early
and successful bird was B. Jones, a local man of ability and
reputation. After this first little flurry the marksmen settled down
to business, and thereafter until noon, when they knocked off
for an hour to go to lunch, there was no cessation from the
continuous firing.

It was a rare treat to watch a sharpshooter settling down
to work. With shooting-case and gun slung over his shoulder he
would tread his way to a vacant place at a table, shaking hands,
nodding greetings, and bandying persiflage right and left. Once
at a table, off with coat, collar and cuffs, up with the sleeves
and on with a short and very business-like apron.

Then comes the unpacking, for quite a bit must be done ere
he burns his first powder. The gun must be set up and every
part explained and wiped with painstaking care. The oil, which
he so solicitously put into the barrel the evening before, must
as solicitously be taken out again on cotton rag—if he wishes
the weapon to do its very best possible by him. And one by one
he examines the cotton rags carefully as they emerge, until at
last one comes forth immaculate and innocent of grease.

Then there is the loading outfit. The caps and cartridges and
bullets must be taken out and arranged, ready for use. By the
way, all the sharpshooters load their own shells, and load them
on the spot. They are very finicky, these knights of the target,
and very wise. They will not trust the most reputable firearms
company to do their loading for them, and they know just what
is what when they do it for themselves. Each has a particular
number of grains that constitutes his favorite charge of powder,
and he sees to it that that particular number of grains, neither
more nor less, goes into place behind his bullet. However, so
fine have they got it down, there is little variation in the weights
of their charges. The great majority shoot from 41 to 44 grains
of semi-smokeless powder. Besides greater evenness, another advantage accrues from loading one's own shells—one always knows
the exact condition of his powder.

The tables in the shooting hall are pitted curiously with countless holes. One wonders; but when the sharpshooter screws his
powder measure into the surface of the table the phenomenon is
explained.

Screwing the palm-rest on and adjusting and blackening the
sights with a burning match, he gives his gun a final look-over
and turns to the loading. Most of the guns are muzzle-loaders—
that is to say, the bullet is loaded via the muzzle, the shell
and powder by way of the breech. The bullet has a slightly
wider base, and as it is shoved down cleans the gun as it goes,

gathering and sweeping before it whatever dirt happens to be in its path. Thus, the marksman shoots with a uniformly clean barrel, and uniformity is what he strives after, especially when he has scored two bull's-eyes on the "honor" target and has only one more shot coming.

Deftly capping the shell, the sharpshooter slips it beneath the aperture in the powder-measure. A couple of twists of a thumb-screw and it is filled with the precise charge of powder desired. A thin wad completes the process, and with the rifle in one hand and the shell in the other, he goes to his shooting-box and takes his first whang at the target. Then he must return and go over the whole performance again.

In the hey-day of a machine age, when we are accustomed to the finest mechanisms, these target rifles are, nevertheless, marvelous creations. And creations they may be rightly called, for to the exquisite article turned out by the gun maker we must add the personal equation of the owner. Each marksman makes his gun over to suit himself, recreates it, so to say. Out of all the guns it is to be doubted if any two would be found that are even roughly alike. The most cursory glance suffices to indicate that there is just as much individuality about them as there is about the men who fire them. With proper training one could doubtless study human temperament from these things of wood and steel.

In sights alone there are innumerable devices—in fact, as many kinds as there are kinds of eyes. And out of butt-plates, longhorned and short, curling and straight, "Schützen" and "Swiss" and "Hunting," rubber and nickel and brass, could be epitomized a complete course in comparative anatomy.

While as for palm rests—there is no end of them. Among the throwing-sticks of the Alaskan Indians one may look in vain for two alike, and so with the palm rests of the Schützenbrüder. Just as each man possesses a hand quite his own and quite dissimilar to all other hands, just so does each palm rest resemble no other palm rest under the sun.

And they are expensive affairs, these rifles, the average cost of each being somewhere around $100. Nor are they toys, either. To be under fire from one at half a mile would be more edifying than comfortable, while at even a mile or more a man would be struck with an irresistible desire to head for tall timber.

The Pope rifles seem to be the favorite, and though calibers up to 45 are permitted the 32-40 is the standard. And here in a way is illustrated the infinite care and study which must be taken by a man if he would be a sharpshooter. The bullet of a 38-55 is larger than that of a 32-40. Being larger, the chances are, with precisely the same aim and landing in precisely the same spot, that it would cut the ring a little bit closer, get in a little bit farther—in short, make a little bit bigger score. But, on the other hand, the recoil is heavier, as it naturally is in proportion to caliber. So the sharpshooters, after delicate and prolonged experiment, have concluded that better results can be obtained with a minimum recoil than with a maximum cutting bullet; and the 32-40, for all-round target purposes, seems to give the greatest satisfaction.

It is not all in the mere aiming and firing, in the loading and cleaning and handling. Important though they be, there are other things which must be taken into consideration. A man must bring into play the finest and subtlest judgment. He must be able to estimate on the instant the true values of virtually intangible things. And the ability or non-ability to do this constitutes the chief difference between a crack shot and a bungler. The study of the light is a science in itself, while the wind drift is probably harder to calculate than all other things put together.

No cause is without an effect, and no force can be without result when acting upon a flying object cut free from everything save gravitation. And so with the wind upon a bullet. In the two hundred yards which the bullet must traverse between the muzzle and the target there is ample time for the wind to deflect it from its course. And the least deflection will prove fatal to the score, while the wind, acting with never twice the same velocity and veering very often in its direction, must be mastered or the marksman fails. And since there are men who make good scores, it is obvious that the wind is often mastered.

Again, a good sharpshooter must know himself—must know his own physical condition to a nicety. The dictum of the physician that a healthy stomach is the correlative of a sound mind is something more than a mouthful of words. And all public speakers have learned at severe cost that their best efforts have been made when their stomachs were in best trim. And it is so with the sharpshooter, who, if any man ever does, must call upon the finest and most delicate resources of his mind. If a man be not at his best and if he knows his business, he will not attempt any of the big shooting.

King Hayes, who has hit a ten-inch bull's-eye 198 times out of a possible 200, at 600 feet, and who has worn the crown of the Schützenfest for three years, thoroughly understands this. "No, I shall not shoot," he said to-day; "not until I feel better. A heavy cold on the stomach, you know; so I dare not dream of entering the lists."

Frank Dettling of the Sacramento Helvetia Club, the man who shot the first center bull's-eye of the fest, was the only one in the morning who ventured his skill against the Honor Target Germania. Each member of the National Bund is entitled to only three shots all told, so they are not in a hurry to try conclusions with it. But Dettling, unafraid, made a score of 55 out of a possible 75, and since so many prizes have been offered he is not anxious to sell his score card.

A. H. Pape, king of the California Schützen Club, scored 46, 47 and 49 out of a possible 150 on the standard target, 8 on the ring target made 71 and 72 out of a possible 75.

The most splendid shooting, however, fell to the credit of C. M. Henderson of the Golden Gate Rifle and Pistol Club. At the man target he made three flags and a 19 in succession—that is to say in four shots he made 79 out of a possible 80, beating Harry M. Pope by three points.

That this may be appreciated by the non-elect it were well to explain this man target. It represents the head and upper part of a man's body, the whole figure being black. It is divided in perpendicular lines half an inch apart, the center line counting 20 and the numbers running down on each side to 1. Now at 600 feet this target simply appears black to the eye, yet Mr. Henderson put three shots dead into the center and the fourth but half an inch off.

"Pretty close to $200 for the ten days!" his friends cried jubilantly as they crowded around to congratulate him. It is highly improbable that any competitor during the remainder of the fest will make the 80, while the possibilities for even a tie-score are not many. Anyway, M. Henderson does not see his way to accept $190 for his chance of getting the $200.

It will not come amiss, in conclusion, to speak of the precautions taken against accidents. No smoking is allowed in the shooting hall. In the same place, under all circumstances, the rifle must be carried perpendicularly, the muzzle toward the ceiling. And all manipulations with the rifle, all alterations and aiming for the purpose of regulating the sights, must be done on the stand, the muzzle pointing toward the targets.

But all this is in the very nature of the men of the Bundes Schützenfest. What else could be expected of men who are so definite and coherent in all they do and who take such fastidious care of their guns? No horseman ever tended his pet racer more tenderly than do they their rifles, and many a lover loves his loved one not half so well.

SCHÜTZENFEST NO. 3

July 17, 1901. — Tuesday was California Pioneers' and Native Sons' day, and many of the men who shot swiftly and sure in the "days of gold" were in evidence at the firing boxes where they watched how the young idea had learned to shoot. As for the young idea—the native sons—why many of them were doing the shooting, being members of the National Bund as well as sons of California.

The native sons of the California Schützen Club, appropriately celebrated the day by capturing the first bull's-eye.

The knights of the target turned out in stronger force than on Monday morning. They have learned the best time for shooting when the light is most equal and the air calmest. But yesterday was a good all-around shooting day, for even in the afternoon the wind was nothing to speak of. As fast as they arrived the marksmen fell to in a business-like way, working steadily and seriously at the task of gathering in their fair share of the trophies arrayed in the Temple of Gifts.

C. M. Henderson's remarkable score of Monday on the man target, by which he tied the world's record, did not seem to deter the bold-hearted men of the Schützen clubs. The shooting at that difficult target was fast and furious, and early in the day Mr. Ross made 73 and Mr. N. L. Vogel made 70. But this is out of a possible 80, and Mr. Henderson hugs his score card of 79 closely and laughs. But then there are other prizes to be won on the man target, valuable ones, too, and plenty of them.

The men are beginning to warm up as the Schützenfest wears old, and there was shooting all along the line. The glass shooting-boxes of the Honor Germania and Eureka targets were in use all day, though no record-breaking scores were made. M. F. Blasse of the Golden Gate Rifle and Pistol Club had his card punched to 64, followed by Ben Jones of the San Francisco Turner Schützen Club with another 64, which was good but not quite so good. In case of a tie it will be found that the bullets in his targets will not have cut quite so closely as those in the targets of Mr. Blasse.

On the Standard American target D. M. McLaughlin, at an early hour, ran up 48 out of a possible 50. Mr. McLaughlin is one of San Francisco's best shots and a jolly good fellow to boot. W. W. Yaeger, the Colorado expert, followed with 46, being tied by H. M. Pope and J. Utschig.

Jacob Meyer of the Sacramento Helvetia Schützen made the best 71 out of a possible 80 on the ring target, being tied both by T. R. Geisel of Massachusetts and H. M. Pope, a member of the New York Club.

And now that the ice is broken the "king shooting" has likewise begun, though none of the contestants has yet completed the requisite 200 shots.

S. C. Ross, first king of the National Bundes, hammered steadily away at the butts all day, getting into trim. William Hayes, the reigning king, was also present throughout the day, though he did not touch hand to rifle. It is to be hoped he recovers soon from his severe cold, else, as he said yesterday morning, he will not be able to compete.

Jolly Louis Ritzau, with his American flag mascot, was pretty much to the fore in pinging away at the targets; and it is whispered on the side that Mr. Faktor has an abiding faith in that same mascot.

The outlook is bright that the next Bundesfest will be held

at Denver. Sentiment seems to favor some point midway between
New York and San Francisco, and upon the map Denver locates
near that very point.

At first thought it appears strange that the best marksmen hail
from the cities. Both the present and past kings of the Schützenfest are city men, Mr. Ross Hailing from Brooklyn and Mr.
Hayes from Newark, N.J.; but on second thought it is not so
strange. There are specialists in shooting as well as in anything
else. What more natural than that the city man does his work at
the target, the country man his at big game? The methods are so
different; different faculties, different powers are called into play.
Not that the target man would make a poor hunter; far from
it; but, rather, being a crack at the target does not indicate that
he would be equally good at big game. And vice versa, of course.

Out of the twenty men from Colorado some five or six use the
palm rest, while the remainder hold their guns in the old-
fashioned, ordinary way. They are hunters, these men—hunters
primarily. They are used to drawing beads on big game at times
when seconds and fractions of seconds count, and they have
become expert without the aid of some of the intricate contrivances favored by their city brothers. None the less, they have
well demonstrated their skill at the targets, these cool-eyed men
from the mountains, and some dark horse may crop up among
them to bear away the crown.

SCHÜTZENFEST NO. 4

July 18, 1901.—Most notable was the entrance upon the scene
of Mr. Julius Becker, who, when it comes to Schützenfests, is
one of the old war horses. On his breast he proudly wore a
silver medal cast in the figure of a war-harnessed knight and
won at a fest of the Danzig Schützenguild of West Prussia in
1854.

Among other medals, and some imperial, he had with him,
won in competition from the early fifties to the late seventies.
Very young it makes us Americans feel to sit at the knees of
such a man, who calmly relates that he became first knight of
the 525th annual fest of the Marienwerder Schützenguild, and
that that happened a quarter of a century ago!

Nearly six centuries gone, Winrich von Knieprode, first knight of the name, made his stronghold in a castle perched on a rock near Marienburg. This same castle it was that the Maltese knights built when they gave over crusading and fell to conquering the pagan Prussians; and from this same castle Winrich von Knieprode waged successful war against the Robber Knights and gave law and order to the devastated land.

And this was the knight who founded the first Schützenguild 550 years ago. And that guild, of which Mr. Becker is a member, still flourishes to-day and treasures the great medal chains of silver presented to the first Schützen König by its founder. These chains weigh twenty-one pounds and each year the target determines which member of the club is to receive the great honor of holding them in charge.

When Napoleon Bonaparte brought Prussia to her knees, he entered Danzig with the express intention of looting these chains. But in vain were the royal servants browbeaten and threatened, and in vain were the gardens and cellars of the King dug up. The unconquered Corsican went on his way empty-handed; and as the only thing, but the greatest thing saved, the King produced the chains and caused the glad tidings to be sent to all the people.

Mr. Becker's shooting days are over, but as he sits and watches us younger men and measures us by the traditions of centuries, we feel very young indeed. Many a long cycle and strange event must come to pass ere our children's children and their children's children shoot for kingship at the 550th fest of an American Schützen.

Wednesday was All People's Day, and all people's day it turned out to be, with the smoke thick on the firing line and the men lining up for a chance at the targets. It was an ideal day, with just enough wind to cool the air and not enough to discommode the marksmen.

That is, it was cool except in the glass shooting-box of the honor targets. Here strange and startling temperatures ranged, and, to judge from the sweat dripping from some of the men as they emerged, even a government thermometer could not have withstood the pressure.

"Hot?" one of the unfortunates remarked, sweeping the moisture from his fevered brow; "just let me tell you that the steam-room of the Olympics is out of the running." And thereat he turned away, weak and tottery, to meditate upon the mystery of things in general and of honor targets in particular.

All the sharpshooters have balked at these targets for three days now, and not a few of them are still balking. And small wonder. During all the fest a member is entitled to but three shots on them, while the prizes to be gained thereby are the most valuable and the honors overwhelming.

The fun has begun, however, though it is anything but fun to the nerve-tried men who go into the glass box. Finally, when they have steeled themselves to the ordeal, they walk up very quickly, with determined faces, and duck in without a glance to right or left.

Here is where A. H. Pape fell down yesterday. Pape is reigning king of the Californian Schützen Club, and from the opening of the Festival has backed his reputation with skill and credit. Yesterday morning, having just made 23, 25, and 24, on the ring target, and feeling rather good because of it, he decided that then was the time to tackle the Honor Target Eureka. Well each shot is a possible 25, and his first shot netted him 9.

His next shots brought him 21 and 22, but too late to avert the Waterloo. Then he grew reckless, went up against the Honor Germania, dropped the red flag the first shot, missed the second, and declined to fire the third.

What causes merriment among the sharpshooters is the fact that his father F. Pape, who is 63 and who was never reckoned a crack, stands third high on the same target, with a score of 67. It is rumored that Pape the younger made the failure out of filial respect; that he could not bear to beat his father. But Papa Pape says nothing, though his eyes wink significantly.

SCHÜTZENFEST NO. 5

July 19, 1901. — Things are warming up at the firing butts. The Fest opened Thursday morning with a rush, and swept onward and upward, from climax to climax, throughout the day. Rifles blazed at the stroke of eight and kept the secretaries and markers on the jump till night-bell, when the Temple of Gifts opened its gates to the victors.

Records were broken and smashed, and scores deemed impossible were made. Ringing cheers heralded these performances, and rushes to where the Rhine wine flowed free followed them. Hands closed on hands in the grip of fellowship, and men, ordinarily decorous, clasped arms about one another's necks and shouted congratulations.

It was a great day, with King—shooting and honor—shooting furiously hot all along the line. But greatest of all was the breaking of all the records of the previous kings of the Schützenfest. The dark horse has been sprung, and midway in the game, and lo, he belongs to us of the Golden West, and nothing less than a San Francisco man is Adolph Strecker, who, when the Fest is ended, will doubtless be crowned king of American riflemen.

It is an education to watch these target princes at work, and the more one watches the more marvelous does their work appear. In the mere facing the firing butts, individuality is most manifest. All of them, except the left-handed ones, of which there are several present, present the left side of the body to the target; but at that point similarity ceases. Nevertheless, somehow, in one way or another, they manage to approximate results—that is, bull's-eyes.

First of all, they lean the muzzle of the rifle on the board before them and snuggle the butt in against the arm just outside the shoulder. Then the muzzle is elevated with a quick movement and there is more snuggling of the butt-plate. No child's play, this Bund shooting! It is noticeable that many of the men draw two or three long breaths before aiming, completely exhausting and expanding the lungs each time and doing the work on a full breath.

After the gun is up, and before they go any farther into the matter, they shake their legs a bit, as though to settle down any shifted ballast, or, perhaps, to polarize the fleshly molecules for greater firmness. And this, notwithstanding the fact that their feet rest on solid cement. Then comes the sighting, about which they are very deliberate, often dropping the muzzle to the board and beginning all over again, and it is not unusual for them to leave the firing stand without having fired a shot. Slowly, back and forth and around, the rifle wavers, and then, suddenly, it freezes, and the man freezes too.

There is no better way of describing it, unless to say that they petrify before one's eyes—man, gun, everything turns to stone. Think it is hard? Try it. Never mind the gun or position; just stand upright, with arms by the side, and discover how unstable you are; feel one muscle after another slacking up and giving way, and your weight shifting, and your body swaying this way and that. Further, and just to enter into the psychology of it a bit, suppose that you have two bull's-eyes on the Honor Germania target, and this is your last shot, and you know that you'll have to wait three years before you are entitled to three more shots— just suppose all this and take just into account the reputation you have to sustain and the critical eyes of your comrades focused upon you, and you will understand something of what the target princes have to endure, and you will gain somewhat of a knowledge of the tremendous self-control they must exercise.

A 32-40 range rifle, charged with forty to forty-four grains of semi-smokeless powder, makes a report heavy enough to jar the atmosphere and shock the nerves of the bystander. And yet the marksman, when he has petrified with whole body, brain and gun, and even every faculty and thought finely poised, shows not the slightest apparent disturbance when a gun goes off in an adjoining box a yard away.

But to return, when the rifle has stopped its wavering and the man has petrified sufficiently he presses the trigger, the gun goes off and the score card is made or marred. But that trigger! It may respond to the slightest pressure and the man may be able to hold the gun motionless for ten seconds, and for all of that his shots may yet go wide. He is so constituted that he fails when it comes to pressing the trigger. Just at the moment when everything is in line and he knows that everything is in line, at the moment when from the brain a message flies to the finger "to pull," at that moment of moments there is an involuntary preparation, an unpreventable stiffening of the muscles and the aim is spoiled and the bullet sped.

If by mere thought a gun could be discharged without the transmitting of a nerve message or the consequent movement of a muscle, far higher records would be made. The man who best overcomes this, other things being equal, runs up the biggest scores. But right here at the pulling of the trigger is where many men fall down, and they fall down all along the way, so that the skilled sharpshooter is a creature of the keenest selection. He has passed scores of successive tests at which his fellows have been weeded out.

The prize shooters discover a variety of ways in holding their guns. The majority use the palm rest, but among them some bring the rifle up to a nearly erect head and others lower the head to the rifle. Other men shoot with right elbow up and left arm straight and supporting the gun far out near the muzzle. Others balance the gun just under the chamber with extended thumb and fingers of left hand. And still others rest the trigger hand in hollow of left arm and clasp left hand about right elbow. Then some elect to stand with both legs firm and stiff, the weight of the body divided evenly between them; some with feet together; some with feet wide apart, and some with one leg stiff and carrying the whole weight and the other slack and idle.

Most of the shots use the pinhead and aperture sight interchangeably, though a few stick to one or the other. These sights are a revelation to the ordinary non-shooting man, whose only knowledge of such things comprises the beads on revolvers and shotguns, and they explain, to some extent, how the sharpshooters are able to do such marvelous work.

Take the pinhead sight for instance, which is used by some when the light is dim or flickering. With it the aim is not ordinarily taken at the center of the twelve-inch blank spot 600 feet away. At that distance the center would only be conjectural. So, with a pinhead sight the aim is directed at the lowest point in the circumference of the black circle. And if the aim be directed precisely at this lowest point in the circumference, the bullet will strike just six inches above in the dead center of the bull's-eye.

The aperture sight operates quite differently. It is, as its name indicates, a small circular opening, and it is used as a front sight. When the gun is in proper position and the marksman looks through the aperture, it is seen to encircle the twelve-inch black bull's-eye with just a little bit to spare. This bit to spare rings the black with a circle of white. And when this ring of white is uniform in width all around the black, it is time to pull the trigger. Thus the shooter is not concerned with the center of the bull's-eye at all. It does not in the slightest enter into his calculations. As with the pinhead, his business is with the bottom edge of the black spot, so in this case it is with the circumference of the black spot—a big improvement, it must be granted, on the old-time method of sighting.

Sighting is an intricate matter, and requires a wide knowledge of many things. In the morning, when the light is gray, there is a tendency to shoot low. This is countered by elevating the sights, and all is well until the sun comes out full and strong, when the tendency is to shoot high, until the sights are readjusted.

All good game shots shoot with both eyes wide open, the right eye making the sight, the left following the game. In target work this is not to be expected, but nevertheless many of the men so shoot. In such cases the left eye does not work, its line of vision being intercepted by the black card surrounding the back sight. But the advantage sought and gained is the placing of nothing more than a normal working strain on the right eye. The man who squints his left eye tightly is looking in an unnatural manner with his right. At the end of a heavy day his right eye will be unduly fatigued; and not only that, for if he persist through a long period of time the chances are large that his eyesight will be ruined.

So it is not all beer and skittles and Rhine wine for these men who go up to the firing butts and with definiteness and coherency split the air with little pellets of lead. In the days of old the mightiest muscle drew the longest bow; but to-day it is the finest and most delicate nerve that touches off the trigger. Brain has conquered brawn in the struggle for human mastery, and it is well that it is so.

SCHÜTZENFEST NO. 6

July 20, 1901.—But, while the rifles are cracking, and little fortunes in powder are going up in smoke and little fortunes in lead are hurtling through the air, the complicated machinery of this huge shooting gallery is running so smoothly that it seems automatic.

Every bullet has its billet and of the countless shots fired not one goes unrecorded. Yet the targets duck up and down, vari-colored flags flash messages through the air, wires move back-ward and forward, wheels speak in cipher, and all the time not a human being is in evidence. The casual observer, without thought, is prone to accept it as part of the cosmos; on first thought it seems uncanny; and on second thought he is seized with an itching desire to go and see how it is done.

But there are obstacles to be overcome. The casual observer will learn that the target-pit is a holy of holies, and that not even the National President of the Bund can enter it unless accompanied by two of the shooting masters. For the markers have it in their power to make or break the scores of the sharp-shooters, and the sharpshooters are only human men, and am-bition is oftentimes an overpowering passion.

Surely, I thought, it must be great to go down there into the pit and listen to the swift-winged bullets singing their song of death not a yard above my head—all the effects of a modern battle, where the bullets are thickest and swiftest in the hottest part of the zone of fire! So I made it an object in my life to get there.

The shooting masters swung off down the path in a long stride as though they had a journey in prospect, and ere that journey's end was reached, I, trotting at their heels, realized fully the distance traversed by the bullets from gun-muzzle to target.

"Shooting master" was an open sesame; and given in response to the gruff "Who's there?" the barred door swung open and the pit yawned at our feet. It was dug between two great bulk-heads of sand, one of which received the bullets fired at the targets, and the other protected the men at their work.

It was very cool and quiet in the pit, with the waters of the bay dashing softly beneath and catspaws of the sea breeze drifting by now and again. There was no sound of voices and the put-put of the rifles came to the ear faint and far off.

But where was the battle? Where the impact of the bullets and the zip of their flight? True, the long line of men with scarlet-banded markers' caps produced a military effect, heightened by the lancelike spotters held in their hands and by the colored pennants; but that was all.

All traditions on the subject are violated at Shell Mound. These bullets do not fly shrieking through the air. They sing no song of death or score. I know that a yard above me, invisible to the eye, a steady stream of lead is flying, hundreds upon hundreds of bullets as the minutes tick off; and yet there is absolutely no sound. Bullets may sing at one hundred yards and they may sing at three hundred yards, but I, here and now, make affirmation that they do not sing at two hundred yards, soldiers and war correspondents to the contrary.

It was fascinating—the contemplation of that silent, invisible stream, replete with the potentialities of death and defying objective realization. One knew that it flowed up there above, steady and unceasing, but the knowledge was based largely on faith. There was no direct evidence, for the evidence furnished by the double line of markers and targets was what the courts of the land constitute "hearsay."

Put! put! put-a-put! put! went the rifles, and the markers' flags and wheels, in constant motion, signaled the result of each shot. I looked at the target before me—a twelve-inch circular black spot in the midst of a white paper square. On its unchanging surface I saw nothing occur, yet the markers waved a blue flag in token that it had been pierced somewhere within six inches of the center.

A fresh target takes its place and I resolve to watch more intently. Put! put! put! go the rifles, but they do not guide me. There are twenty and odd other targets and the men of the Fest are shooting at all of them. So I put my soul into my eyes and strain at the paper object. The marker suddenly thrusts up a white flag and indicates the tiniest of holes, low down and to the right. Yet the paper had not even quivered as the bullet passed through it.

I watched more intently. Time and the world and the Schützenfest swing on unheeded. My whole consciousness, life and being are summed up in that paper target. And there, even as I look, a little hole has taken shape. But I did not see it take shape. The instant before it was not. The instant after it was. But so swiftly had it come that it escaped the eye.

Behind the target line the sand flies up to sprays of diamond dust. A snug fortune of lead must lie in that heap of sand and I should like to grubstake a couple of men into it with pick and shovel and I would, too, were it not for the fact that Captain Siebe located the mine years ago.

Friday was Ladies' Day, and the jolliest day of the week. The traditional hospitality and sociability of the Teuton were ably vindicated by the wives and daughters of the local sharpshooters. These ladies of the Schützenfest received the ladies of the visiting members.

There was a concert by Ritzau's American Ladies' Orchestra, dancing in the pavilion, and singing and merrymaking everywhere; and last, but not least, there was the charming Schützen Liesel, her picturesque costume giving the quaint old-time touch necessary to complete the picture and make the color true.

When night drew down, the festivities increased, and after the laurels of the day had been distributed from the Temple of Gifts, the park was illuminated, and amid the spluttering of fireworks and blazing rockets a grand ball and general jollification wound up the day. Nor were the marksmen idle. The smell of powder was strong in the shooting hall, and O. J. Barnes, of the Colorado contingent, probably made the record of the Fest in successive bull's-eyes, dropping the red flag eight times. In the king-shooting the members of the Bund, undaunted, hammered steadily away at the targets on the heels of Adolph Strecker, and their cards are running big. That they will overtake him is not probable. If they do so, it will mean that they have broken the record of a phenomenal recordbreaker.

SCHÜTZENFEST NO. 7

July 21, 1901. — Never before in the United States, nor probably in the world, has there assembled a finer aggregation of marksmen than that now breaking records at Shell Mound. And as one watches them at their work, keen-eyed and iron-nerved, displaying the most delicate adjustments and subtlest judgments, one cannot avoid speculating on the part these men would play in modern warfare.

And right here let it be stated that these target knights are not knights of the carpet merely. In every war the United States has undertaken, the sharpshooter companies have been among the first to gird on their harness and go forth. And the work they have done has not been of the kind which may be classed as spectacular. A thousand men, molded into a huge projectile and sweeping irresistibly across the field of carnage, is something which catches the war correspondent's eye and which later blazons the pages of history. But the lonely sharpshooter, perched precariously in a tree or groveling in a scratch in the earth, fights his fight by himself. He must be General and army and observation corps all in one. He must do his own scouting, map out his own campaign and advance or retreat as he sees fit. And to do all this requires the highest individual efficiency, and to do it well is to make the extreme demand upon a man's courage. Men are bravest in bunches, and the man who could storm the ramparts of hell with a thousand fellows may falter at facing one foe in a lonely wood.

But to return. The sharpshooter has always played an important role in war, but never so important as now. The conditions of war have changed. Armies can no longer come into close contact. The bayonet and cavalry charge are obsolete. Cold steel is no longer possible. Where the squadrons once thundered to victory are now the barbed-wire fence, the electric mine field and the inexorable zone of fire.

Rapidity of fire, greater range, greater precision and smokeless powder have revolutionized warfare. The substitution of chemical for practically mechanical mixtures of powder and the reduction of calibers have given greater range, and by flattening the trajectory of the bullet, greater penetration. At half a mile a bullet will go as easily through a pile of men as through the body of one, and for a mile and a half it is deadly. And because of all this, the function performed by the sharpshooter in battle has become a hundred-fold more important.

Julian Ralph, writing from South Africa, said: "Place Germany in a trench, and all the world could not drive her out until her ammunition or her supplies were exhausted." And bearing this in mind, we realize the value to the community of the men of the Schützen clubs now in our midst. Several hundred of them, anywhere in our mountains, would block the passage of Europe's proudest army.

Nor is this an empty boast. From the facts of the case let us speculate. The development of the machinery of warfare has invested frontal attack with an overwhelming fatality. The British at the battle of Omdurman opened fire on the advancing dervishes at 2,000 yards, and with deadly effect; and the nearest any dervish approached was 200 yards. The whole dervish army was slaughtered beyond that distance.

Our men of the Bund are disposed in the mountains, no one knows how. The enemy, not knowing how many men oppose it, would devote itself to skirmishing, scouting and tentative flank movements, all the while exposed to the withering, exasperating fire of the sharpshooters. The air would be filled with little invisible messengers of death, and, remember, at more than a mile smokeless powder makes no sound.

Watch a scouting party, a "feeler," detach itself from the great army and fare forth to locate the mountain enemy. A half-dozen mounted men it is, and they push forward quietly and unobtrusively. There is nothing to be seen; so they must "feel"—that is, expose themselves to the enemy's fire in order to discover the enemy, and, if possible, find out its force.

The horsemen ride out on an open place. The mountains and ravines, patched with clumps of trees and bare spaces, stretch out before their eyes. All is silent. Not a foe is in sight. They alone seem to draw breath in that wide expanse. They rise slightly in their saddles to search more closely the peaceful scene.

Suddenly one of the men grunts, whirls in the saddle with throat a-gurgle, and pitches to the ground. His comrades are shaken. Not a sound has been heard. There was no warning. They search carefully. No smokewreath floats slowly up to indicate the position of the hidden sharpshooter. There are a thousand spots in the field of vision where he may lie hidden, and with him may lie a thousand others. But where? Ay, that's the agonizing question, for even as they ask it, for aught they know, the bullet that brings them death is on its way.

Another falls; a horse goes down; and they turn tail and fly madly. This is not war. There is nobody to fight. What else can they do but flee before the silent and invisible enemy? And their report to the waiting army—How many men? They do not know. Where? Up there, somewhere, they know not where.

In such a region, under such circumstances, several hundred sharpshooters could multiply themselves into many thousands. Always, between them and the enemy, would intervene a mile of death which the enemy would be chary of venturing into.

And if the exasperated General should send heavy "feelers" forward, with orders to go on and on; and if they did come in touch with the sharpshooters and charge, be it remembered, still, that with the new, self-charging, six-millimeter Mauser, a man can fire seventy-eight unaimed, or sixty aimed shots per minute. Thus, 100 men of the Bund, securely ensconced, could pour into the advancing force 6,000 aimed shots a minute!

But suppose things get too hot. All the sharpshooters have to do is to retreat a bit. There are many mountains, and for each of those mountains the enemy would have to sacrifice many men, as witness Buller on the Tugela. And each mountain would mean that the thing would have to be done over again. But time is precious, and large armies are expensive, and never was the economic problem of warfare so important as it is to-day.

But suppose the great army gives over and tries elsewhere. Large bodies move slowly, and the men of the Bund, in small detachments, could speedily outstrip the army and confront it again. And this is not theoretical. It is costing England a million dollars a day in South Africa. And the British are anything but cowards. A lesson is being taught down there, and the world is looking on and learning while Great Britain does the work and foots the bills.

In the evolution of the weapon from the first hand-flung stone to the modern rifle, the conditions of warfare have changed many times. What the next change may be we do not know. But just now, for to-day and to-morrow, the sharpshooter is one of the most important factors; and in the battles to come, the nation with the largest number of sharpshooters and the best equipped, will be the nation, other things being equal, that lives. So all hail to the men of the Schützen clubs! Every record they break adds to our strength and fits us better to face whatever dark hours may betide.

SCHÜTZENFEST NO. 8

July 22, 1901. — There are times when sensation is more potent than thought; when intuition exceeds reason and obedience to subconscious promptings produces bigger results than can the finest skill of the world. And the men of the Schützen clubs who make and break records out at Shell Mound are aware of this. And when they listen to the still small voice whispering admonition or encouragement and obey, they very often avoid spoiling their records or succeed in placing them a notch or so higher than ever before.

Between himself and his audience the public man knows when he has established a perfect correspondence. The demagogue knows when his listeners are with him; so the actor and the preacher. Mark Antony knew that the Romans were hanging upon his every word when he made his historic speech, knew that they were responding perfectly to each secret suggestion, were being swept unwittingly along with him to the end designed.

Likewise the sharpshooter. There come times when he feels that everything is with him, his eyes, his hands, his muscles, nerves, the gun, the target, the shooting range, and all the natural forces. He does not know why; he cannot tell why; he simply "feels." He feels that then is the accepted time, that then he can perform prodigies of marksmanship.

And if he be in normal condition, this feeling is true. He can go ahead and shoot far more ably than is his wont. But if he be in an abnormal, nervous condition, the chances are large that this feeling or intuition is false. Ay, and there's the rub—how to tell? Is the "feeling" a result of over-excitation? Or is it produced in some sub-conscious way by the thorough co-ordination of all his parts?

This thorough co-ordination comes but seldom, yet it is when it does come that the greatest shooting is done. Every part of his complex organism must be fitted and running smoothly. The digestive juices must be doing their work. The heart must be pounding away the same as it would if the man were asleep. There must be no inflammation or fatigue of the eye. There must be neither too much nor too little blood pulsing through the brain.

In short, the most delicate balance must exist between all his parts. If the equilibrium of one be disturbed, all must work to re-establish that equilibrium. No one part may act without the instant communication of that act to all the other parts, and all the other parts must then and at once act in correspondence.

But the marksman, when he is in this perfect condition, does not know it. It must be impressed upon him somehow. His shooting, if it has been commonplace before, begins to pick up. The red flags are dropping in quick succession. He is doing well. Then, like a flash, and without thinking, there comes to him the feeling that now is the time!

He warms up to the work, loading and firing rapidly. His blood is bounding, fresh and vigorous. His vision becomes clarified. He is aware of an exhilaration, of an elevation of the spirit, and he is no longer aware that he has a body, so perfectly does that body correspond.

All sluggishness has departed from him. His brain is lucid and working without effort. Every fact recorded there throughout his life, and related to shooting, stands out clear and sharp. He may utilize them as it is not given often to him to utilize them; for they are all there before him and he may select from them all. When he estimates the wind-drift, or the flickering light, or the changing atmosphere, he does so without exertion, so easily and quickly that he does not know he is doing it. He knows where each bullet strikes before the marker can give the signal. He has become as a god and knows all things without thinking. In reality he is thinking, but so perfect is the whole correspondence that he is unaware.

This is exaltation, inspiration. He is keyed up to concert pitch. He is oblivious to everything save the work he is doing. His brain, clear on shooting only, is dim to everything else about him. He hardly knows himself. Faces of bystanders appear vague and indistinct. He moves as in a dream, aware of nothing but shooting, shooting, shooting.

In such exquisite poise is he, such delicate balance that he has become like a somnambulist. The slightest thing may upset him. The least intrusion of the world he has withdrawn from may snap the tension. At a man's speaking to him he may collapse. Then is the time for his friends to keep away from him and to keep everybody else away from him. And it is not too much to say that he would consider himself justified in killing on the spot a man who harshly aroused him.

Many call this condition luck, but the wise marksmen, King Hayes among them, will shake their heads when questioned about it.

"It is perfect trim," they will say, and they are right. It is when in such condition that the artist, the man who creates with head and hand, produces his greatest, most enduring works. It is, to sum up, the condition when no part of the organism is unduly excited or unduly lethargic, but when an equable excitement has been communicated to all the parts, has elevated their pitch and given them unity.

This was the condition of Strecker on that memorable Wednesday afternoon when he fired the 160 shots that put him on the high road to the kingship. He was dreaming, and dreaming greatly. He waved congratulating friends from him in an absent-minded way, for he knew his inspiration was upon him and did not wish to waken. Nor did he waken until the targets closed down at 7 o'clock, when he came back to the world and his friends.

On the other hand, this is a condition marksmen try to induce. Before venturing their fate, for instance, upon the Honor Eureka, they devote themselves to the ring target, and shoot, and shoot, and strive to bring about a perfect co-ordination of parts. This conscious effort to produce an exalted condition which will sweep them on to victory tends to bring about overexcitation. After three or four good successive shots they are prone to believe that the time has come. They feel it, but they feel falsely. They then tempt the honor target and are undone. A lying spirit has whispered them to destruction.

A. H. Pape had an experience of this kind. He was shooting exceptionally well on the ring target, which is twin to the Eureka. He was striving, after the manner of marksmen, for that exalted condition, and he thought it had come to him. And when he made in succession 23, 25, 24 out of a possible 25, he was sure of it. So he presented his honor card to the secretary and trained his rifle on the Eureka and, lo! his first shot, which should have brought him 25, brought him 9. He had not run upon his luck, or, in other words, had not established the fine poise to delight equilibrium of mind and body.

There is another interesting phase of range psychology, quite different from that of exaltation. It is the itching to know one's fate, the excitation produced by a good score and the knowledge that the next and last shot will make or mar everything, and the inability to overcome this excitation or to wait until it has passed away of itself. On Tuesday McLaughlin, the crack San Francisco shot, made four 10s in succession on the standard American target. All he had to do was to repeat what he had already done four times, make one more 10, and the record of the Fest was his. This very knowledge was sufficient to produce a strong nervous excitement, while the desire to know the best or worst was irresistible. So he fired his fifth shot and made an 8.

Wednesday morning, on the same target, Strecker made four 10s. But he had the will requisite to prevent him going up at once to know his fate. He restrained himself for two days before he fired the fifth shot; but even then he only made a 9. However, had he taken his chance at once the probabilities are large that he would not have made even an 8. As it was, his waiting enabled him to beat McLaughlin and to tie the high man.

And finally there is F. E. Mason, who is displaying perhaps the most splendid self-resistraint of all. On Friday he got in 150 shots on the king-shooting, making an average of 1.9½ per shot. Strecker's average for his 200 is a fraction under 2. This makes Mason the only rival for kingship in sight, and his next fifty shots will decide. Yet for two whole days he has restrained himself and attempted nothing. "Waiting until conditions are favorable," he says; which means waiting until he feels the right serenity of soul and body that accompanies perfect co-ordination, and until he hears the still small voice whispering to go in and win. Upon his ability to feel and hear correctly trembles the kingship of American riflemen.

SCHÜTZENFEST NO. 9

July 23, 1901. — Whenever men do things with head or with hand, a pardonable curiosity is aroused, and thus it is with the big men of the Bundesfest. Who are they? What are they like? How and why do they do these things? Are there not facts to generalize from? Can we not learn some of the qualities which enable a man to shoot his way to pre-eminence at the butts?

This is the tenor of the questions asked by other men who do not line up at the butts or expect to line up, but who nevertheless would like to know. In answer one can only say that the facts are many and oftentimes contradictory. The nationality of the crack sharpshooters varies; likewise experience with rifles and targets. Some are old and some are young, while some seem to be all nerves, and others to have no nerves at all.

S. C. Ross for instance, the first king of the National Bund, is a slender brunette of medium height. He is native born and his clean-cut features are not distinctive of any particular race, but portray rather the cosmopolitan admixture of diverse races which is common of the American.

He has an eye, black, with clear whites, and quick of movement. When it comes to rest, which it rarely does, it betrays that peculiar piercing quality as though he gazed right through one. In repose his face sometimes takes on a sad expression, which is quickly put to flight by the least human occurrence around him. He has a bright smile, quick to come and quick to vanish; nor is he slow to acknowledge a greeting or pass the good word along. His mind, as his eye, travels everywhere and is alert, eager, quick to see the point and cap it with another.

Quickness characterizes him. He seems to be a bundle of nerves, to have more than his share of the American kind of nerves—the kind that makes men get up and dare things to the ends of the earth—the high-tension, finely strung, concert pitch kind—the kind that cannot brook defeat and fight to the death on a stricken field.

But for all that, Ross possesses restraint, control. When it comes to holding a sight on the target no man petrifies more solidly than he. His powers of concentration are likewise large, and necessity seems to have developed them. When he is shooting he is shooting, and that's all there is about it. He'll see you later; but just then, no. And it is an emphatic "no."

William Hayes, the reigning king, is a medium sized blond, and not withstanding his fifty-four years he has not put on flesh. He is slow of gesture and occasionally his speech lapses into a just perceptible drawl. Looking him full in the face and listening to him talk reminds one in a vague sort of way of Mark Twain. There must be something temperamentally akin in the two men. His full blue eyes move slowly and steadily, without haste, but with certainty, and dwell upon whomever he is talking with or upon whatever his hands are doing. Severe in repose his face and eyes break into the most winning of smiles. These smiles have a habit of lingering, and in this respect are quite unlike those of Ross, whose smiles come and go in a flash.

Steadiness seems to best characterize King Hayes. Not that he is slow, though. He conveys an impression of potency, of powers to do, and while there is less nervous waste one feels in that wiry figure all the quickness of a cat.

Like Ross, he is no big-game shot and has had little field experience, though a veteran at the target. He is native born and first began to shoot in 1869. He has been at it ever since, having attended most of the important contests of the intervening years.

W. W. Yaeger, the crack Colorado shot, is also native-born and a blond. But he is a big-game shot as well, and wind and sun have bronzed his fair skin and put upon it the weatherbeat common to men who live in the open. Further, and worthy of comment, he is the only one of the big marksmen who really shoots offhand. He is remarkably slight of figure and weighs but 114 pounds. His cheek bones are prominent, with large hollows underneath, and altogether he has a wan and cadaverous look. After a cursory glance one would deem Yaeger to be the most nervous of men. But, on the contrary, if ever a man was devoid of nerves, he is. He has all the steadiness and solidity of poise and carriage one would expect to accompany 250 pounds.

His movements are very slow and very deliberate. Nothing shakes him. There is never a quiver or tremor, and it is a joy to see him handle a gun. There is no flash to the eye or haste

in his actions. It simply appears that he has something to do
and is doing it. He may be characterized as deliberate, or, rather,
as the nerveless incarnation of deft deliberateness.

But what ever generalizations may have been arrived at so far
are knocked in the head by Adolph Strecker, the heir apparent
to the Schützenfest crown. He is the last man in the world one
would pick out as a sharpshooter, much less as king of sharpshooters—that is, until he faces the target. His record extends
over a quarter of a century. Crowned king of American riflemen
in 1874 at Baltimore, his star has shone brightly ever since, but
never so brightly as today. And still he does not look like a
marksman.

Long and lean of limb and tall, narrow-shouldered and narrow-
chested, with grizzled iron-gray beard and hollow cheeks, his
forty-nine years have weighed far more heavily than have the
fifty-four of King Hayes. The latter looks much the younger
man. Strecker is also blue-eyed, but a native of Germany. His
face is sad in repose, even melancholy, and when he smiles he
looks boyish to a degree. He appears far from strong, and one
wonders that he was capable of the prolonged strain of firing
160 of his king shots in a few consecutive hours.

His eyes are unlike those of the other fine marksmen. They
are not keen and sharp and piercing, but seem filmed over
with a dreamy softness of the kind one would expect in the
eyes of a maid. Yet those are the eyes that out of 200 bullets
guided 197 into the bull's-eye.

But when he faces the target he undergoes a transformation.
He becomes cold, absolutely cold, as though cast in chilled
steel. His whole nervous organization seems to stiffen and harden.
And there lies his power. Nothing feazes him, startles him.
He has that peculiar ability to utterly forget the world and he
can call upon the last least shred of his strength and knowledge
and concentrate it all upon the work at hand. On the day he
did his remarkable shooting the rest of the sharpshooters ceased
firing and joined the spectators at his back. The excitement
grew intense. Every time he raised his rifle hundreds of eyes
were focused upon him, boring into him, and he knew it, but
did not permit it to affect him. In fact, the more he fired the

better he scored, and he was grieved when the lists closed for the day.

By the way, Strecker is extremely conservative, and never goes in for improvements until he is forced. He was the last crack shot to give up the old-style muzzle-loading weapon, and he only gave up then and purcheased a Winchester because the progressive men were overtaking him.

Then came the Pope sharp-shooting rifle, with the Pope system of loading, and the progressive younger element invested and began to catch up with him. But Strecker fought shy until his record was in peril, and until the thirty-two caliber bullets were rattling in the worn barrel. Then he sent the old Winchester back to the Pope Firearms Company, had it bored out to a thirty-three caliber, and built over to accommodate the Pope loading system. This is the gun with which he did the work at the present Bundesfest, the same old Winchester he first used, all battered and worn from over ten years' service. It reminds one of the small boy with the bent pin and piece of twine catching the biggest trout in the stream.

Ittel, the Pennsylvania expert who cropped up late in the fest and came within three of beating Strecker, is native born, but of remote German ancestry. Strecker is the only one of the very big experts who is foreign born. While the majority are of German descent, in from two to half a dozen generations, Hayes traces back to the little green isle and Ross' name speaks for itself.

In looking over these men one striking thing is manifest. None of them is unusually tall or stout. The men big in stature or girth, while they have done good work, have not done the very best. On the other hand, the men who have done the very best are of medium height or under, and are prone to leanness. This is hardly a coincidence. There must be some reason for it, biological or psychological, or otherwise.

SCHÜTZENFEST NO. 10

July 24, 1901. — The king is dead—long live the king! Ay, and the Schützenfest is dead—long live the Schützenfest! Amid a grand furor of enthusiasm King Strecker received his crown from his comrades-in-arms, and the last hours of the festival waned away in wassail and revelry that required special trains and boats to see the heroes home.

And the Schützenfest died hard. All of Tuesday morning the rifles barked and the bullets thudded home. The smell of powder was strong, and to the last the men lined up at the honor targets. And at the stroke of twelve, when the twenty and odd targets went down on the run, there were rifles steadied and eyes straining along the sights for a last bull's-eye.

At once the Temple of Gifts was rifled of its precious hoard, and on the long tables of the shooting hall was displayed the glittering array of prizes. Gold there was galore—gold yellow and mellow, rippling down the tables in shining streams, spreading out into miniature lakelets and dazzling the eye with its shimmering witchery. And there were tall mugs, huge bowls and loving cups of precious metal; nor was the flash of diamonds or glint of gems wanting to complete the splendid picture. It was the loot of a province spread fittingly there where the rifles had fought out the battle, and the beribboned and bemedaled Prize Committee apportioned the plunder among the men who had done the work.

The rafters rang and rang again with cheers of greeting to the prize winners, and it was noted that the high-score men smiled broadly, and continued to smile broadly. May the affliction become chronic. Next in honor to King Strecker was Dr. Schumacher, who made the record on the Honor Eureka and received the magnificent Hearst trophy. On the shoulders of his brother marksmen, to the strains of "America" from the band, he made his exit from the Shooting Hall, madly waving in either hand his hat and a silver laurel wreath.

Well, it is over. Never in the history of the Bund has there been anything like it, and many a day will come to pass ere the like is done again. Nor has it alone been a spectacular affair with success achieved through lavish expenditure and magnificence. There has been shooting done besides, and the greatest of its kind. Every record of the previous test has been broken, and many records have been broken many times. From every standpoint it has been an unqualified success.

And now that it is over, let us make confession. There are

things our German-American brother can teach us. We can, among other things, sit at his knee and learn how to be sociable. We understand democracy, but our democracy is Anglo-Saxon in its traditions and there is an aloofness and an aggressiveness about it. We are not prone to come together in large numbers and forget our individual sovereignty. One man is as good as another, therefore let one man get out of another man's way. No crowding. Toes are liable to be stepped upon, and then there will be trouble.

But while we understand democracy in its political sense, the German understands it better in its social sense. We have much to learn from him in democratic good-fellowship, for in that he excels. In his past history he has not had so much to say as others concerning liberty, equality, fraternity; he has been too busy doing them. In the Fatherland, straining against feudal forms and harsh lines of caste, he has been handicapped; but in the United States there was opportunity, and right well has he advantaged by it.

He takes life less seriously than we, and more slowly. He puts a rhythm into it, as it were, and works and plays; while we race along, keyed up to the highest tension, at break-neck pace, always a jump ahead of the second-hand. We haven't time to laugh. Faith, life is too short and too strenuous. We sweat over our pleasure as well as our work, and take a vacation when the doctor forbids us our desk or shop. The Epworth Leaguers came in a flurry of special trains, jammed into our city, and departed in a tangle of baggage—they haven't caught their breaths yet; while the men of the Schützen clubs were here first and in leisurely full swing, and are still here, and though the shooting is over have an unfinished itinerary of feasts, picnics, and excursions.

And though the German takes time to laugh, it is a jolly laugh, and in it is none of our haste-induced hysterias and none of the cynic levity of the French, which is the antithesis of laughter. There is room in life for a healthy, wholesome, good time, and if life over here seems crowded the German none the less makes room. Let the world and its cares wag on; he knows all about it and shoulders his fair share; but when he packs his lunch basket for a good time he sees to it that the world and its cares are left out. Sufficient unto the day, he holds, is the pleasure thereof.

Last Sunday, out at Shell Mound, there came together a huge family party of ten thousand heterogeneous men, women and children. But the Teutonic influence was over them and they danced, played and made merry, and went home in glee. There was no wrangling or fighting or harsh word spoken. Good nature ruled the day and each did as his fancy dictated—so long as it did not infringe on the happy fancies of others, in which case he didn't. Some elected to dance, others to shoot. Hundreds stripped their lean, lithe bodies and pitched the shot, did gymnastics and flashed through the air in running, in high jump; hundreds preferred to dance; hundreds sang in chorus on the elevated platform, and for variety carried their leaders around on their shoulders; and hundreds more chose to sit around the tables, drink beer and look on. And it was well. Each followed his particular bent, extracted his maximum of joy out of the day, and contributed his share to the general hilarity.

Innate in the Teuton is the spirit of democracy. He believes in equality of opportunity and that a man should stand on his own legs. The history of the Bund, taking its rise as it does out of the old Schützen-guilds of Germany, corroborates this. There the man who does the finest shooting receives the highest honors, and no matter who his father was, class distinctions fall away. A cobbler, if he be crowned Schützen König, takes precedence over the Emperor during the festival. The Emperor may sit beside the cobbler on his throne, but the cobbler's commands are flat and the Emperor's are not. As Julius Becker said the other day, "Not even the field marshal or the highest general would dare so much as brush the soot from his sights."

And so to-day, transplanted to the fruitful soil of America, the same spirit obtains and it is the spirit of democratic goodfellowship. It is said that in one party from the East there are nineteen millionaires. Well, I looked for those millionaires, and I failed to find them. From appearances there were no millionaires, or else they were all millionaires.

A good illustration, and to the point, concerning fellowship is a little Teutonic trick in the giving of medals. In the average American contest the medal-winner, if he be not overprosperous in this world's goods, is usually forced to the verge of insolvency in standing for the crowd. But the Germans line their medal cases with gold pieces, so that the winner may hold up his end of good-fellowship and not have his good luck metamorphose into calamity.

During the fest the Germans, among many things, manifested that they were good trenchermen. But, unlike the Latin, who eats for the eating's sake and takes a pride in the cookery, the German eats for sociability's sake. Dinner is a god-given hour, wherein he may meet his brothers in closer contact than a mere rubbing of shoulders in the course of carrying on the work of the world.

Nor did he neglect this hour out at Shell Mound, even when the firing was hottest and the excitement most intense. Promptly at the dinner hour the rifle was laid aside, and though there were records broken and records yet to break, he lingered for an hour or so at the table, where jovial company held forth and song and toast passed up and down. Surely the American tendency would have been to snatch a sandwich on the fly and go on with the shooting.

A spade is a spade, and when the men of the National Bund said they were going to have a festival they meant festival. And, looking back, a festival it was. California outdid herself in her open-armed welcome; the fest committee outdid itself in its arrangements; and it is not hazarding too much to say that the visitors did likewise in the good time they have not only had but given. So here's to you, and standing, men of the Schützen clubs, jolly good fellows all, as good in comradeship as in jollity and as good in citizenship as in both!

JEFFRIES-RUHLIN FIGHT

SAN FRANCISCO, California, Nov. 16, 1901.—A big, dark male [James J. Jeffries], hairy of chest and body, in one corner; in the other corner a big, light male [Gus Ruhlin], smooth of skin and serious of face; overhead an artificial sun, and all around ten myriads and more of spectators; problem—which male, dark or light, and for a king's ransom, can beat the other into insensibility or helplessness?

So the fight summed itself up ere it had begun. But the big, light male was serious of face, too serious, and he seemed too little the animal to go up against the big, dark male. There was no hair on his body, no hair and an obvious lack of sheer animality and grit.

And when these two young giants, both in the fairest prime, came together, the light man it was who first cried protest to the referee. Now, it is not good to cry protest. It does not seem in keeping with the game. It is hard to imagine the animal in the wild spending strength and breath in crying protest to the jungle powers, and it is hard to reconcile oneself to the human crying protest when that human had been elected to play the animal in the wild.

But the light male cried aloud and looked still more serious, and ran away backward till a fear and a panic dawned in his eyes. And the dark male smiled—not viciously, not insolently, not vaingloriously, just simply smiled and smiled, and fought. He was dark of skin, and he remained dark. It seemed natural the thing he was doing. But the fair skin of the light male flushed and blushed to a crimson tide which seemed to mark his conduct as unnatural. It was patent that one was a fighter, that the other was not; and it was patent that one must win, that the other could not.

So they came together, these big-thewed men, with great muscles swelling and bunching under satiny skins, quite in contrast to the clever little men who had preceded them. And when they missed, and chest met chest, the sound of the impact was like that of young bulls in rutting combat.

The dark man spat blood from his mouth and smiled, and the blood ran down his chin. And the blood, conveyed by the gloves, marked lightly the bodies of both men with crimson splashes. And the skin of the light man flushed and flushed and beaded with perspiration. The strength went out of his blows, and he fell to the floor before a blow which could not warrant such a performance. The time-keeper shouted off the seconds, and the crowd yelled in exultation at the sight of the dying gladiator. But the gladiator did not die. It was disappointing. He would not play the game out as animals are accustomed to play it out. He came to his feet and struggled feebly about, to later retire to his corner and calmly sit down while his seconds tossed up the barbaric emblem of defeat—the sponge.

But it was good to see, the crowd, the spectacle, the artificial sun, and the second of the preliminaries. And under this veneer of a thousand years of culture, I, for one, found that the endless savage centuries still lived. I, who had come to note the blood cry of the crowd, came to myself with sickening consciousness to find that my voice, too, was issuing forth with lusty joy and thrilling abandon. One does not break lightly from his heritage. When man smote man and the body blows smacked loud, and smiter and smitten sighed, the one with the vehement outgoing breath and the other from the checked intake—why, then I would find myself lifting up from my seat, breath suspended, myself and the world forgotten, utterly merged in the struggle before me.

In one lucid interval I chanced to note that the crowd wanted blood more thirstily than did the two men in the ring. The crowd was clamorous for blood; but the fighters had more the end of the king's ransom in mind. Another thing I noted. In the clinches the dark man hung his weight upon the other's neck and shoulders, and calmly and without even protest in his muscles, waited the referee to separate them. On the contrary, the light man supported the unwelcome weight, and both his body and mind were in constant protest and anxiety. And when they broke away he edged backward, while his opponent held ground like a rock. Also, the opponent, the dark man, freely and frankly spat out the blood from his cut mouth, instead of striving to hide and swallow it as other fighters have been known to do.

It was a picturesque scene, this twentieth century arena, this machine-age gladiatorial contest. The house in darkness and the ring a white blaze of light; the tick-tick of the telegraph keys, the monotonous dictation to the stenographers of each blow and parry and maneuver, and the excited voices of glad men sure of their winnings; and under the clustered arc lamps, in the blinding glare, the two battling elemental males, and around all the sea of faces stretching away and fading into the darkness— a vast crowd, eager to see two men beat and batter each other into pulp, or, rather, a vast crowd divided in its interest as to which man should beat and batter the other into pulp.

"To be a fair stand-up boxing match"—so begins the Marquis of Queensberry rules. To stand up is the point of the game, to stay on one's feet, to not lie down, to not run away, to hold a twenty-foot ring of earth against the world. This is the point of it and the spirit; and when all is said and done, the prize fighter, big-muscled and brutish and barbarous is a finer thing than a decadent. There is a promise in the one; it is excessive, elemental masculinity, but from it noble strength can be refined. But in the other there is no hope; nothing but disease and insanity and death can proceed from the weak-kneed and emasculated. It is vastly better to be elemental than decadent. And for those who to-day are healthy and strong and yet recoil from a prize fight, it would be well for them to recollect that they have come down from the loins of elemental men; that the decadent has no issue.

We know the brutality of the battlefield. Pink teas are preferable to many. But it were likewise well to remember that battlefields make pink teas possible; that for the poet that sings there is a soldier that fights, and were there no soldier fighting there would be a poet wailing.

Well, I was not decadent, and I saw the fight, and I must confess to one disappointment, a grievous disappointment. Why, O why, did this man who elected to play the animal, why did he not play it out? It was inconsistent. It is unforgivable.

BRITT-NELSON FIGHT

COLMA, California, Sept. 10, 1905.—In the first round [Jimmy] Britt hit [Battling] Nelson half a dozen blows. At each blow Nelson was coming on. The blows did not stop him. He kept coming on.

Then Nelson hit Britt, and Britt was staggered by the blow. The whole story of the fight was told right there. Blows did not stop Nelson from coming on. Blows did stop Britt; also they staggered him.

Nelson is a fighting animal. Britt is an intelligent animal with fighting proclivities. This is another way of telling the story.

It was the abysmal brute against a more highly organized, intelligent nature. Now, do not misunderstand me. I do not wish to call Nelson a brute; but what I wish to say is that Nelson possesses to an unusual degree the brute that you and I and all of us possess in varying degrees.

Let me explain. By abysmal brute I mean the basic life that resides deeper than the brain and the intellect in living things. It is itself the very stuff of life—movement; and it is saturated with a blind and illimitable desire to exist. This desire it expresses by movement.

No matter what comes it will move. It came into the world first. It is lower down on the ladder of evolution than is intelligence. It comes first, before the intellect. The intellect rests upon it; and when the intellect goes it still remains—the abysmal brute.

Let me explain a step farther, if you are to understand this fight between Britt and Nelson as I saw it.

Here are you and I, average creatures, fairly normal and fairly rational. Our minds are clear. We reason. We conduct ourselves with the intelligent poise of mind. But a sharp word is spoken, a sneer is made, an insult is given. At once our poise of mind is gone. We are angry. The mind no longer dominates us. The abysmal brute rushes up in us, muddies our clear brain, takes charge of us.

This is a moment of anger. We are temporarily insane. Reason is gone. The brute has charge of us. The difference between us and the man in the insane asylum is that the brute always has charge of him.

It is this abysmal brute that we see in a man in a Berserker rage or in a jealous spell of anger. We see it in a horse, tied by too short a rope, frantic, dragging backward and hanging itself. We see it in the bull, bellowing and blindly charging a red shirtwaist; in the strange cat, restrained in our hands, curving its hindquarters in and with its hind legs scratching long, ripping slashes.

And now to return. Nelson is the lower type. Britt is the higher type. Nelson is more callous to pain and shock, has less sensibility. At the same time the abysmal brute in him gives him a tremendous capacity to move and to keep on moving. Britt is more delicately organized. He is more easily put out of gear. At the same time he possesses less capacity to move and to keep

on ceaselessly moving. Had he Nelson's capacity to move, plus
his own intelligence, he would have whipped Nelson. But Britt
did not have this power of movement; was too far removed from
the brute, and was himself whipped. The best man won—according to the rules of the game.

All the preliminary fuss of the battle showed that bullheaded
stubbornness and balkiness were on the Nelson side, and that
intelligence was on the Britt side. "No Jeffries!" was the stubborn
Nelson cry.

The Nelson side had balked like any fool horse, and was hurting
itself all the time. The Britt side, being intelligent, gave in. It
gave in intelligently, at the eleventh hour, spectacularly, throwing
all the odium upon the Nelson side, winning all the sympathy
for itself. Nelson was hooted; Britt was cheered. Intelligence won
hands down, but it was only in the preliminary.

Britt stripped and showed himself deep chested and shouldered.
His lines were soft and rounded. He was beautiful as a man goes
and his condition was perfect, while his eyes were clear and
bright.

When Nelson stripped he looked like a proletarian that had
known lean and hungry years of childhood. His face was weazened,
his eyes were small, his hair was colorless, his neck was thin, his
naked body was not beautiful as Britt's was beautiful.

As they faced each other, one or the other seemed to belie his
weight, for Britt looked much the larger. The contrast was
striking. If Nelson looked the lean and hungry proletarian, Britt
looked the well-fed and prosperous bourgeoise. It was like a scrub
and underfed creature facing a thoroughbred. Nelson's eyes and
face were vicious. Britt's face was inexpressive. His mind was in
control. Whatever feelings stirred within him, they were well
hidden.

The first round has been told. Nelson forced the fighting.
He moved. He moved always. And he always moved forward.
When Britt backed away, Nelson moved forward. When Britt hit
him, he moved forward more swiftly. That was all.

It was the whole fight. From start to finish, for eighteen savage
rounds. Nelson kept boring in. Britt could not keep him back.
No matter how often and how hard Britt punched him, he
bored in just the same. Always Britt backed away from him,

smashing him cruel blows from a distance; and always he kept advancing after Britt.

And when Nelson got inside Britt's arms he went to work. Punch, punch, punch, right and left on stomach and kidney, and uppercuts to the face. It was here that the force of Nelson's blows was demonstrated. When he shot in an uppercut Britt was appreciably lifted by it.

In the clinches Nelson did practically all the punching, while Britt strove to protect himself. Nelson had little success in reaching Britt from a distance. It was at close quarters that he got in his work. He punched at the beginning of a clinch. He punched through the clinch. He punched in the breakaway. And the next moment he was moving forward again upon Britt in order to get at close quarters and deliver himself of some more punches.

On the other hand, Britt was not idle. He landed six blows to the Dane's one. Had Britt received the blows he gave Nelson Britt would have been out long before the eighteenth round. But Nelson scarcely seemed bothered by the punishment. One thing was strikingly noticable. His blows, when they did land, jarred and often staggered Britt, while Britt's blows did not seem to jar nor stagger Nelson. He met these blows as he came on, and he kept on coming on just the same.

In the sixth round came the test of the two men. Nelson punched Britt groggy. This is another way of saying that Britt was dazed and weak.

His clear reason was reeling because his body was going back on him. It could not move, and move, and continue to move. He was too highly developed, too finely organized. There was not enough of the brute in him to save him. But the gong saved him. Another minute and he would have been out.

Britt recuperated wonderfully, but in the next round could do nothing with the Dane. A blow, two blows, a dozen—the Dane received them all, but they did not deter him from keeping right on and boring in. From the standpoint of blows landed, it was Britt's round. But from the standpoint of winning the fight by a knockout, it was no more Britt's round than was any other round of the fight. Victory was hopeless for him from the first round.

And so the battle went until the fourteenth. In this round

Britt went groggy and for a while was all but out. Then it was that he made a terrific rally. He did not fight with his head. It was his own share of the abysmal brute that rose up and fought. He fought like a madman. Blows were exchanged frankly without attempts to protect. Boxing ceased. It was punch, punch, slug, exhausting all his [Britt's] reserve of strength.

In the fifteenth round Britt's mind resumed its sway. A minute of rest had brought it back. He was intent on resting his tired body. But the Dane never ceased from pursuing, from boring in and fighting at close quarters. The life that was in him moved, moved, ceaselessly moved.

When Nelson was hit on the nose or chin or jaw his head came forward in advance of his advancing body. No blow of Britt's seemed capable of sending that head back. But Nelson's blows when they landed sent Britt's head back with a snap.

The 15th, 16th and 17th rounds might be all called Britt's rounds. By appearance they seemed so. In reality they were the Dane's, for Nelson never ceased from boring in and forcing the fighting. He was wearing Britt out, punching him out; while Britt, even if he did give many more blows than he received, was not wearing the Dane out, nor was he punching the Dane out.

Nelson did not knock Britt out with a blow, nor with a series of blows, in the 18th round. Britt was knocked out by the whole fight he had fought from the beginning of the first round. His multitude of punches on the Dane had not counted. The far smaller number of blows landed by the Dane had counted. It was the sum of the blows struck by the Dane, plus the exertions of Britt, that put Britt out. He had consumed all his strength, all his vitality.

Fighting with his intellect, and with his body as well, Britt was knocked out because his body was not strong enough to keep his mind poised in control and directing his body. When the body was weakened the mind was overthrown, and his cleverness and his intelligence counted for nothing.

Not so with the Dane. The abysmal brute in him fought on. It was the will of life itself, the fleshly life as a thing apart from the mind and the spirit, that moved on in him and that out-moved the same kind of life that was in Britt. Britt is the finer human. Nelson is the finer fighting animal.

Nevertheless all hail to both of them! They play the clean game of life. And I, for one, would rather be either of them this day at Colma than a man who took no exercise with his body to-day but instead waxed physically gross in the course of gathering to himself a few dollars in the commercial game.

BURNS-JOHNSON FIGHT

SYDNEY, Australia, Dec. 27, 1908. — Full credit for the big fight must be given H. D. McIntosh, who has done the unprecedented. Equal credit, however, must be given to Australia, for without her splendid sport-loving men not a hundred McIntoshes would have pulled off the great contest on Saturday.

The Stadium is a magnificent arena, and so was the crowd magnificent, which was managed by that happy aptitude which the English have for handling big crowds. The spirit of the Stadium crowd inside and out, with its fair-mindedness and sporting squareness, was a joy to behold. It was hard to realise that those fifty or sixty thousand men were descended from generations that attended old bare-knuckle fights in England, where partisan crowds jammed the ringside, slugging each other, smashing the top hats of gentlemen, promoters, and backers, and swatting away with clubs at the heads of the poor devils of fighters whenever they came near to the ropes.

Never in my life have I seen a finer, fairer, more orderly ringside crowd, and in this connection it must be remembered that the majority were in favour of the man who was losing. That many thousand men could sit quietly for forty minutes and watch their chosen champion hopelessly and remorselessly beaten down, and not make the slightest demonstration, is a remarkable display of inhibition.

There is no use minimizing Johnson's victory in order to soothe Burns's feelings. It is part of the game to take punishment in the ring, and it is just as much part of the game to take unbiased criticism afterwards in the columns of the Press. Personally I was with Burns all the way. He is a white man, and so am I. Naturally I wanted to see the white man win. Put the case to

Johnson and ask him if he were the spectator at a fight between a white man and a black man which he would like to see win. Johnson's black skin will dictate a desire parallel to the one dictated by my white skin.

Now, to come back to the point. There is no foolish sentimental need to gloss over Burns's defeat. Because a white man wishes a white man to win, this should not prevent him from giving absolute credit to the best man who did win, even when that best man was black. All hail to Johnson. His victory was unqualified. It was his fight all the way through, in spite of published accounts to the contrary, one of which out of the first six rounds gives two rounds to Burns, two to Johnson, and two with the honours evenly divided. In spite of much mistaken partisanship, it must be acknowledged by every man at the ringside that there was never a round that was Burns's and never a round with even honours.

Burns was a little man against a big man, a clever man against a cleverer man, a quick man against a quicker man, and a gritty, gamey man all the way through. But, alas! men are not born equal, and neither are pugilists. If grit and gameness should win by decree or natural law then Burns, I dare to say, would have won on Saturday, and in a thousand additional fights with Johnson he would win, but, unfortunately for Burns, what did win on Saturday was bigness, coolness, quickness, cleverness, and vast physical superiority.

From any standpoint the fight between Cripps and Griffin last Wednesday night was a far better contest. The men were evenly matched, and the result was in doubt from round to round and moment to moment, and this delicate balance was due to their being equally matched. Each man had opportunity to show the best that was in him. That opportunity was denied Burns.

Bear with me for a moment. I often put on gloves myself, and take my word for it I am really delightfully clever when my opponent is a couple of stone lighter than I am, half a foot or so shorter, and about half as strong. On such occasion I can show what I've got in me, and I can smile all the time, scintillate brilliant repartee and dazzling persiflage, and, in the clinches, talk over the political situation and the Broken Hill trouble with the audience. But, heavens! suppose I were to don gloves with

Burns. I could no more show what I had in me than Burns showed
against Johnson. That is the whole fight in a nutshell. The men
were so unevenly matched that Burns was barred from showing
anything he had in him, with the exception of pluck. Johnson
was too big, too strong, too clever. Burns never had a show, he
was hopelessly outclassed, and I am confident that had a man
from Mars been present at the ringside witnessing his first fight, he
would have demanded to know why Burns was ever in the ring
at all.

It's hard to talk, Tommy, but it is no harder than those
wallops you received on Saturday, and it is just as true that it is
no dishonour to be beaten in fair fight. You did your topmost
best, and there's my hand on it, and on all your pluck, grit, and
endurance.

Jack Johnson, here's my hand, too. I wanted to see the other
fellow win, but you were the best man. Shake.

"Stop the fight?" The word is a misnomer; there was no fight.
No Armenian massacre would compare with the hopeless slaughter that took place in the Stadium. It was not a case of "too much
Johnson," but of "all Johnson." A golden smile tells the story,
and that golden smile was Johnson's. The fight—if fight it can
be called—was like unto that between a Colossus and a toy
automaton. It had all the seeming of a playful Ethiopian at
loggerheads with a small and futile white man, of a grown man
cuffing a naughty child, of a monologue by one Johnson, who
made noise with his fist like a lullaby, tucking one Burns into his
little crib in Sleepy Hollow; of a funeral with Burns for the late
deceased and Johnson for undertaker, grave-digger, and sexton.

Twenty thousand men were at the ringside, and twice twenty
thousand lingered outside. Johnson, first at the ring, showed
in magnificent condition. When he smiled a dazzling flash of gold
filled the wide aperture between his open lips, and he smiled
all the time. He had not a trouble in the world. When asked what
he was going to do after the fight, he said he was going to the
races. It was a happy prophecy.

He was immediately followed into the ring by Burns, who had
no smile whatever. He looked pale and sallow, as if he had not
slept all night, or as if he had just pulled through a bout with

fever. He received a heartier greeting than Johnson, and was favourite with the crowd.

It promised to be a bitter fight. There was no chivalry nor good will in it, and Johnson, despite his care-free pose, had an eye to instant need of things. He sent his seconds insistently into Burns's corner to watch the putting on of the gloves, for fear a casual horseshoe might stray in. He examined personally Burns's belt, and announced flatly that he would not fight if Burns did not remove the tape from his skinned elbows.

"Nothing doing till he takes 'em off," quoth Johnson. The crowd hooted but Johnson smiled his happy, golden smile and dreamed with Ethiopian stolidness in his corner. Burns took off the offending tapes and was applauded uproariously. Johnson stood up and was hooted. He merely smiled. That is the fight epitomised—Johnson's smile.

The gong sounded and the fight and monologue began. "All right, Tommy," said Johnson, with exaggerated English accent, and thereafter he talked throughout the fight when he was not smiling.

Scarcely had they mixed when he caught his antagonist with a fierce upper-cut, turning him completely over in the air and landing him on his back. There is no use giving details. There was no doubt, from the moment of the opening of the first round, the affair was too one-sided. There was never so one-sided a world's championship in the history of the ring. It was not a case of a man being put out by a clever or lucky punch in the first or second round; it was a case of a plucky, determined fighter who had no chance for a look in at any single instant of the fight. There was no fraction of a second in all fourteen rounds that could be called Burns's. So far as damage is concerned Burns never landed a blow, he never grazed the black man.

It was not Burns's fault, however. He tried every moment throughout the fight, except when he was groggy. It was hopeless, preposterous, heroic. He was a glutton for punishment, and he bored in all the time, but a dewdrop in Sheol had more chance than did he with the giant Ethiopian. In all justice it must be urged that Burns had no opportunity to show what he had in him. Johnson was too big, too able, too clever, too superb. He was impregnable. His long arms, his height, his cool-seeing eyes, his timing and distancing, his footwork, his blocking and locking, and his splendid out-sparring and equally splendid in-fighting, kept Burns in trouble all the time. At no stage of the fight was either man extended. Johnson was just as inaccessible as Mont Blanc, and against such a mountain what possible chance had Burns to extend himself? He was smothered all the time.

As for Johnson, he did not have to extend. He cuffed and smiled and smiled and cuffed, and in clinches whirled his opponent around so as to be able to assume a beatific and angelic facial expression for the benefit of the cinematograph machines. Burns never struck a body blow that would compare with Johnson's, nor a cross nor straight nor upper cut; while as for kidney blows, Johnson's most frivolous and pensive taps were like thunderbolts as measured against Burns's butterfly flutterings in that painful locality.

Johnson frivolled with Burns throughout the fight. He refused to take Burns seriously, and with creditable histrionic ability played the part of a gentle schoolmaster administering benevolent chastisement to a rude and fractious urchin.

The "mouth fighting" on the part of both men must have seemed bizarre to the Australian audience; nevertheless, mouth fighting as a ring tactic has won more than one battle, but on Saturday it neither won nor lost anything. Burns's remarks failed to ruffle his opponent's complacency in the slightest, while there was no need for Johnson's airy verbal irritations, for Burns was as angry as could be from the stroke of the gong, and though Johnson proved a past master in the art of mouth fighting, even his pre-eminent ability in that direction failed to make Burns angrier by one jot or tittle.

There was, however, one result from word sparring, an unfortunate result to Burns. He was fighting desperately and his last hope lay in making the big negro lose his head; instead he nearly lost his own by having it punched off. Not that he irritated Johnson in the least by what he said. Far from it. Johnson never ceased smiling when the uncomplimentary remarks were addressed to him, nor did he cease smiling as he proceeded to wallop the naughty boy for his impertinence, but wallop him he did, in so smiling and summary a fashion as to take the steam out of Burns's verbal punches. In fact, after two distinct adventures of this sort Burns concluded that that tactic was too disastrous and abandoned it.

Not Burns, but Johnson did the in-fighting; in fact, the major portion of the punishment he delivered was in clinches. At times he would hold up his arms to show he was no party to the clinch. Again, he would deliberately and by apparently no exertion of strength, thrust Burns away and clear of him, and yet again he would thrust Burns partially clear with one hand, and upper-cut him to the face with the other; and when Burns instantly fell forward into another clinch, thrust him partially clear and repeat the upper-cut. Once he did this five times in succession, as fast as a man could count, each upper-cut connecting and connecting savagely. But principally in clinches Johnson rested, smiled, dreamed. This dreaming expression was fascinating, it seemed almost a trance. It was certainly deceptive, for suddenly the lines of the face would harden, the eyes glint viciously, and Burns would be frightfully hooked, swung, and upper-cut for a bad half minute; then the smile and dreamy trance would return as Burns effected another clinch.

At times, too, when both men were set, Johnson would deliberately assume the fierce, vicious, intent expression, only apparently for the purpose of suddenly relaxing and letting his teeth flash forth like the rise of a harvest moon, while his face beamed with all the happy, care-free innocence of a little child. Johnson play-acted all the time. His part was the clown, and he played with Burns from the gong of the opening round to the finish of the fight. Burns was a toy in his hands. For Johnson it was a kindergarten romp. "Hit here, Tahmy," he would say, exposing the right side of his unprotected stomach, and when Burns struck Johnson would neither wince nor cover up. Instead, he would receive the blow with a happy, careless smile directed at the audience, turn the left side of his unprotected stomach, and say, "Now here, Tahmy," and while Burns hit as directed, Johnson would continue to grin and chuckle and smile his golden smile.

One criticism, and only one, can be passed upon Johnson. In the thirteenth round he made the mistake of his life. He should have put Burns out. He could have put him out; it would have been child's play. Instead of which he smiled and deliberately let Burns live until the gong sounded, and in the opening of the fourteenth round the police stopped the fight and Johnson lost the credit of a knock-out.

But one thing remains. Jeffries must emerge from his alfalfa farm and remove that smile from Johnson's face. "Jeff, it's up to you, and, McIntosh, it's up to you to get the fight for Australia. Both you and Australia certainly deserve it."

JEFFRIES-JOHNSON FIGHT

London went to Reno for the New York Herald *to write a story a day for the ten days preceding the fight and to cover the fight.*

RENO, Nev., June 23.—Reno has always been a live town, but just now it is quickening to a greater and growing liveliness than any it has ever known. Every train, east or west, brings in the sporting men, fight followers and the inevitable correspondent. It is to wonder. On the other hand, there is no wonder about it. There must be a large remnant left of the large-bloodedness of the English-speaking race to evince such a tremendous interest in the particular sport of sports which it originated and developed until it became stamped today into the crystallization of many generations, the Marquis of Queensberry rules.

Everybody is arriving in Reno. All the men whom one has met in all the earth he meets again here, in Nevada's metropolis. From all the lions of the old days down to the latest cubs, they are here, fight fans, grizzled and time-worn, who remembered far beyond the aching thirty-nine rounds at Chantilly, France, between Sullivan and Mitchell, down to the youngsters of yesterday, who were not dry behind the ears when Corbett and Fitzsimmons fought their historic fight in Carson, Nev.

Never in a war, at any one place, was congregated so large a number of writers and illustrators. When the Japanese threw 50,000 men across the Yalu into the teeth of the Russians on the Manchurian shore, on the walls of Wiju, but eleven correspondents looked on. Many men were killed, and the fate of great empires and ancient dynasties hung in the balance, yet only eleven men were there to tell what they saw to the world. But here in Reno today were ten times that number of correspondents.

Nor are they here to witness a bloody battle and the deaths of thousands. They are here to witness two strong men, hearty and husky, who will not kill each other but who will attempt, by skill and wit and gameness and endurance, to outdo each other in a sport that calls to the uttermost for the exercise of all these faculties.

For the man who would know life as it is, in all its naked facts, and not life as he surmises or dreams it ought to be, there is something of big and basic importance in the contemplation of the world-wide interest manifested in this fight. Why do men fight? Because of the money in it. An apt answer, but it will not apply to the following question: Why do men go to witness fights? Certainly not to spend money. There are easier ways of spending money than by traveling all the way to Nevada. They want to see fights because of the old red blood of Adam in them that will not down. It is a bit of profoundly significant human phenomena. No sociologist nor ethicist who leaves this fact out can cast a true horoscope of humanity.

There is another way of looking at it. The newspaper editors are skilled purveyors to the public of information the public wants. Did a few men only desire this particular information, the editors would be guilty of gross stupidity in sending to the front so large and expensive an aggregation of star sporting writers. But the editors are making no mistake. The point is that the public wants this information. The conclusion is that the public, despite countless asseverations to the contrary, is interested in prize-fighting.

Certainly Reno is interested. Reno is also proud. She considers herself fortunate. Once again, as in no other modern way, will she put herself and the State of Nevada on the map. No masterpiece of prose, poetry, painting or sculpture could achieve this distinction for Reno. Well, it is a fact of life, and as a fact of life it is worthy of contemplation.

But Reno got the fight and is putting forth a great effort to make good in the matter of the housing and feeding and entertaining the army of guests that is descending upon her.

Jack Johnson has not yet arrived, but it seems as if all the rest of the world were already here. Jeffries is comfortably installed at beautiful Moana Springs. Today, in an old-fashioned game of two in and nine out, he swatted and batted and pitched and ran bases like a juvenile Cyclops. He was good to look upon. To such degree did the massive bulk of him loom up that other old-time heavies in the game with him, such as Corbett and Choynski, looked like middle-weights. Of entirely different build and texture is Jeffries from them. He is a big bear, heavy and rugged, and he is physically a man that one may well say occurs no oftener than once in a generation.

Jeffries was examined today by Mike Murphy, than whom there is no other who can better judge to the finest hair of a man's condition. Murphy's report was unequivocally favorable. More than that, it was enthusiastic. And yet a year ago Jeffries was reckoned a has-been. He has certainly devoted himself seriously and faithfully to the preparation for this fight.

To demonstrate that human nature is human nature the world over, whether in ships' forecastles, sewing circles or training camps, Sullivan and Corbett celebrated their meeting to-day by indulging in a tiff of neither mean nor dire proportions. Nobody was hurt and the militia was not called out.

JEFFRIES-JOHNSON NO. 2

RENO, Nev., June 24. — Bag and baggage, bull pups, bass viols and phonographs, Jack Johnson stepped off the train at Reno today to be greeted by fully as large a crowd as met Jeff when he arrived. Whirled away in an automobile to Rick's resort, he appeared unperturbed and happy, despite the fact that his train was three hours late and that it was a Friday.

His voice was just as jovial, his handshake as hearty, his smile as dazzling as when I last saw him in Australia. Commenting on the fact, he announced that he was feeling much better and stronger than a year and a half ago in the Antipodes. In shirt sleeves, his shoulder muscles and biceps bulge knottily. Like Jeffries, he, too, is every inch a big man. But they are vastly different types of men. Under all his large garniture of fighting strength, Johnson is happy-go-lucky in temperament, as light and carefree as a child. He is easily amused. He lives more in the moment, and joy and sorrow are swift passing moods with him. He is not capable of seriously adjusting his actions to remote ends.

Though fresh arrived from an irritating railroad journey, fraught by vexatious delays, his face was placid and lineless. Nor was there the hint of a sign of care and worry, such as would be expected from his disagreements with his manager, from the abrupt shift of training quarters at the eleventh hour, and from joy rides interrupted by rude police.

This quality, differing so widely in the two men, cannot be over emphasized if one is to get an adequate comprehension of the fight when it takes place. They say that Johnson cannot hold a grudge. The man who does him a real or fancied injury to-day is received heartily by him a week hence, and this is so because a moment of life at a time is good enough for him. He cannot hold on to more than the moment, be it a moment of fierce hate or joyful friendship.

Possibly a good conception of this difference between the two may be gained from my own feelings about them. If Johnson should rush upon me in anger and with full intent to do me bodily injury, I feel that all I would have to do would be to smile and hold out my hand, whereupon his hand would grip mine, and he, too, would smile. On the contrary, I am certain, if Jeff rushed at me in wrath, that if I did not die of fright there and then, I should bite my veins and howl in maniacal terror.

The illustration may seem far fetched, but it is just the way I feel, and it serves to show the essential difference in the characters of the men. Jeff is a fighter, Johnson is a boxer. Jeff has the temperament of the fighter. Old mother nature in him is still red of fang and claw. He is more a Germanic tribesman and warrior of two thousand years ago than a civilized man of the twentieth century, with the civilized trade of boilermaker, and he has bridged the gap by turning pugilist and becoming the mightiest walloper of men in all the earth.

Another thing, despite Jeff's primitiveness, he is more disciplined than the other man, vastly more disciplined, as instance the rigid adjustment of action to a remote end when he began a year and a half ago and faithfully carried through the heroic course of training that put him in the superb condition he is in today. Johnson, mastered by the moment, could make no such an adjustment. He would forget all about that remote end a year and a half away. The passing moments would tantalize him into pursuit of immediate and momentary ends.

And by the same token, down in the heart of him, this fight does not mean to Johnson what it does to Jeff. If Johnson loses the fight, he won't be worried much. If Jeff loses, it will almost break his heart. Under that dark and somber seriousness that characterizes him, there is a race pride of which he is intensely self-conscious. Then, too, there is the pride in himself as a man and as a subduer of men. Leaving out the world, he has pledged himself, to himself, to win this fight, and that pledge he voiced to the world, when, after stating that he was refraining from agreeing to fight Johnson until he could make certain that he was able to defeat him, he announced his certitude and signed the articles. Of one thing I am certain, the loss of any half dozen of his other fights would be less of a blow to Jeff than the loss of this coming fight with Johnson.

Jeffries' erratic selection of times for training and sparring is the despair of the fight fans and newspaper scribes. The whisper passes around that he is going to do things about 4 in the afternoon. Long ere the time, the electric cars running to his quarters are packed and jammed, and nothing happens. The rumor spreads that Jeff will be out and hard at it at peep of day.

The first cars out to Moana Springs are crowded, and even before the first car runs a string of automobiles has sneaked in the same direction. The hours pass. Nothing happens. Everybody waits, until at last, weary and hungry, the return is made to town for something to eat, and lo, it turns out that that particular portion of the day was selected by Jeff for work.

But no one can blame him. It is his fight and his training, not theirs; and he knows what he wants and when he wants it a whole lot better than they do. And right here the difference between the white champion and the black is manifested again. Johnson is more willing to please the public. Jeff does not care a red cent for the public. The fight is a week away, and Jeff remembers that and that only. Johnson cannot remember it, because the public is pressing at his doors for an exhibition there and then of his prowess and development. It is the moment, the everlasting, tantalizing, immediate moment, and Johnson succumbs.

JEFFRIES-JOHNSON NO. 3

RENO, Nev., June 25.—Despite the scribes and sports who fell to the rumor that Jeff was to box at three this morning and who journeyed vainly out to Moana Springs at that unearthly time, Jeff himself selected the perfectly respectable hour of 10 A.M. He skipped rope and shadow-boxed to the time of many tunes which he whistled himself instead of panting for air in the high altitude, and the punching bag rat-tatted to the left of Mendelssohn's "Spring Song."

For another thing, he evidenced a remarkably good temper and cheerfulness. He has passed through the strain and drag of his long and terrific training, and, with that far behind him, perforce yields to the good spirits that are the emanation of perfect well-being. All through his couple of hours of hard work to-day he was kittenish and frisky in a huge way, full of joshes and bubbling over with grim laughter. One does not imagine him laughing heartily ever. It is his nature and his makeup to hint of grimness, even when he is jovial to the top of his bent.

For, after the rope-skipping, he stripped and showed the wonderfully built man he is from the ground up. His legs were like columns—not gnarled and knotty columns, but clean-swelling columns, soft-lined and in keeping with the soft-lined strength of the rest of him. There is little doubt that in the history of the ring there was never a heavy-weight so well and symmetrically proportioned.

His thighs are so mighty that they remind one inevitably of the legendary Teutonic warrior who, by the grip of his thighs, made his war horse groan beneath him. It would have to be an armor-plated, steel-crossed horse that Jeffries could not make groan.

Lean-bellied as a Greek athlete, the muscles of his torso begin their long, deep swell outward and upward from the waist. His back muscles play in matted masses, while those of the shoulders and biceps leap into a twisted roll at the slightest uplift of the arms. And they are all the right kind of muscle. They are not hard and knotted like those of the professional strong men and weight lifters. They do not bind and hold him by their inflexibility and weight.

And this is something that the uninitiated do not understand. While those that knew looked on and gloried in Jeff's condition, someone remarked naïvely that they were surprised at his softness and at the sheath of fat that encased him. Fat; there is not any fat on him. Those soft mounds and ridges and rolls are the finest grade and quality of muscle a man can possess. One might as well call a cat fat because, when it is relaxed, its muscles become all velvety softness. That may best describe Jeff's muscular condition at the present moment—a velvety softness, splendid and superb.

Take one of those soft pads of Jeff and watch it. Suddenly it leaps and quivers, takes form and bulk, is alive with swift and excessive energy, then relaxes and sinks back and down into the soft pad that it was. Now that is a muscle. It is the real thing.

And let it be said that Jeff right now is fit and ready to go into the ring. The best thing for him to do from now till the Fourth is to go fishing and to take only moderate exercise. He is at concert pitch and ready for the summons, "let her go."

The floor on which he skipped rope was very slippery, and once he went down. But the quick play of those supple, powerful muscles saved him. He is a heavy man, and to fall on his kneecap meant serious injury. You and I and most all the rest of us under the same circumstances would have received the injury. Not so with Jeffries. Like lightning the foot and leg muscles of the leg that slipped flexed into action, taking the weight of the falling body and saving the knee.

That Jeffries is no mean judge of distance was shown when, in the shadow boxing, he made occasional passes at the noses and jaws of his training staff. They were stiff and snappy punches and hooks, yet they passed or whistled by the mark with no more than half an inch or an inch to spare.

Out at Rick's it was the same old Arthur Johnson who sparred fast and furious with three of his sparring partners in rapid succession. I should not like to be a sparring partner in Johnson's camp. Kaufman was glad when his four rounds were ended, and Cotton showed no signs of regret when his turn was finished.

Both had been cuffed and pummeled to the queen's taste, both were short of wind and complaining of the altitude, and both were bleeding profusely from mouth and nose. And Johnson, unconcerned, was taking on a third man and making him look serious as he went after him.

One thing is certain, barring a lucky punch, which is an extremely unlikely happening, the fight on July 4th is not going to be a short one. Johnson is so clever on the defensive that it would take a long time for Jeff to get him, while, on the other hand, Jeff is no slouch at defense himself, and he is such a behemoth that it would not be in two punches, nor forty, that Johnson could get him. Whoever gets it will have to work for it and work hard.

It was the same old Jack Johnson of a year and a half ago, looking, if anything, stronger and better than in his Sydney fight. He had his full bag of familiar tricks with him—the old cleverness of defense, the old letting his opponent hit him repeatedly on his unguarded stomach; the old dreaming and sudden awakening to fierce onslaught for three or four seconds; the old placing of his hand on his opponent's biceps to stop a blow; the old smiling into the camera while in a clinch and the old rubbering trance-like at the audience or passing of facetious remarks while at the same time duffing his opponent or blocking and withstanding a violent assault.

Johnson seemed to take to the altitude well. Beyond profuse sweating under the hot sun there was no evidence of exertion. When Kaufman sparred with him the former devoted himself almost wholly to ripping at Johnson's stomach. It may be that this is in anticipation of the terrible rips to be expected from Jeff.

Make no mistake, the fight on the Fourth is going to be a great one. There are only two heavy weights that are at the top notch, and they are Jeff and Johnson.

JEFFRIES-JOHNSON NO. 4

RENO, Nev., June 26. — In considering the relative merits of the two big men who are to try conclusions a week from to-day, it must be remembered that neither man has ever been compelled to endure to the uttermost. Barring a lucky punch in the opening rounds, endurance will play a large part in determining which man is the better. And by endurance is meant the capacity not only to assimilate punishment, but the capacity to administer punishment and to keep on administering more and more punishment.

This question of endurance is worthy of analysis. Men are made differently. Some have but a slight life-grip in their bodies and muscles. Others are apparently impossible to kill. One man can walk seventy-five miles in a day, and walk a second seventy-five the next day. Another man will collapse at the end of a twenty-mile jaunt and be a lame and groaning wreck for a week to come. Yet both these men will be organically sound, of the same size and weight, and their chance of passing a life insurance examination would be equal. Then what makes the difference? In the fibers of the one resides a primitive vigor and capacity for exertion that the other lacks. Their muscles may look alike, may be of the same size and density, yet the protoplasmic, energy-generating quality is different.

Take a professional weight lifter. He may tip the scales at 160 pounds. He can elevate a 200-pound dumbbell with one hand. Another man, tipping the scales at the same mark, cannot elevate 100 pounds. He is as sound and healthy as the other man, yet he cannot do it. He can faithfully train and exercise for five years, or ten, and yet he will be unable to elevate 200 pounds with one hand. Nor has will anything to do with it. He may have ten times more will power than the other, but will power can't lift the 200 pounds for him. He lacks in the quality of his muscle; that is all.

This protoplasmic vigor may be our brute heritage, but whatever it is it is a good thing to have whether one is a prize fighter or not. It was in describing the fight at Colma with Jimmy Britt that I pointed out the possession of this muscular quality by Battling Nelson. I called him an abysmal brute, and he never forgave me. Yet I meant it as a compliment.

Of two boxers, equal to look upon in every way, equally well trained, with equal organs, equal gameness and equal will power, one will reach his limit in five or ten rounds; the other, fighting just as severely, will be able to last thirty or forty rounds, or even fifty. It was this peculiar quality that Battling Nelson possessed to such an extreme degree. Jimmy Britt did not possess it. He could outspar and outpunch Nelson, but he could not keep on sparring and punching as long as Nelson could. At the Colma fight he was not knocked out by Nelson. He was merely exhausted. He had reached his limit. He could not move any more. He lost the fight because he knocked himself out by his own exertions.

Corbett lacked this abysmal brutishness to any considerable degree. Choynski had far more of it. So did Sharkey and Fitzsimmons. But when it comes to Jeffries and Johnson there is no line on them at all. They have never been called upon to demonstrate it. Neither knows that he possesses it. Neither has ever engaged in a long, hard, grueling fight, round after round, striking and being struck, consuming energy at an enormous rate and still going on fighting furiously, on and on, endlessly.

Of the two men Jeffries has thought more about himself, studied himself more, and he has hinted that he believes he possesses it. He has called it reserve power, a sort of second wind that does not depend on the lungs, but resides in the muscles themselves. But seeing and believing are different, and he has yet to show it to the world. Nevertheless, I venture a shrewd guess that he has it. Also, he may be called upon to show it on the Fourth of July.

Nor does the world know that Johnson possesses this abysmal brutishness or lacks it. Johnson does not know himself. He has never had a chance to find out. And in this connection it is not a question of yellow streak or will power. No matter to what superlative degree Johnson possesses this prothoplasmic vigor, it will go for naught if he proves yellow. On the other hand, he has never shown any hints of yellowness, and, it must be added, he has never been in a fight that forced a test of this particular quality.

There is one quality in which Johnson has the advantage over Jeffries, and that is in relaxation. Jeffries, while cool and keen, is always more tense. The tensing of a muscle consumes energy. Boxing calls upon the use of all the muscles in the body and five minutes of unnecessary tension out of thirty minutes of fighting of all these muscles means a serious consumption of energy.

This is one of Johnson's great assets. He has the art of relaxing perfectly. His fiercest rallies are always followed by intervals of repose. In a clinch, except when he is punishing, he invariably rests. It is because of this relaxing so continually that he is notorious with the sporting public as a loafing fighter. And he seems to relax in mind as well as in body. He seems to stop thinking and perceiving even, and in a clinch he goes into a sort of resting trance. His very flat-footed way of fighting takes off from the tension of the legs. It is far less tiring to shuffle about flat-footedly than to spring and poise with the muscles tensed from the hips down.

One thing is certain. A week from to-day Johnson will be compelled to put up the fight of his life. He has never in his career faced so formidable an antagonist. With Jeffries it remains to be seen whether Johnson can make him put up the fight of his life.

JEFFRIES-JOHNSON NO. 5

RENO, Nev., June 27. — A lot of moot points will be threshed out in the Reno arena a week from now, or may be threshed out if the fight is not a quick one. Three things only can make it a quick fight. First, a lucky punch; secondly, the blowing up of one or the other of the fighters; and thirdly, a display of the hypothetical yellow streak on the part of Johnson.

One is justified in forecasting that there will be little liability of a lucky punch being landed in the opening rounds. Both men, in their fighting history, have managed to avoid receiving lucky punches, while neither has made a record of delivering lucky punches. Also, as the fight progresses and the men lose their velvet vigor there is less and less chance of a lucky punch.

Again, viewed in the light of their fighting history, neither man has ever blown up. They have always displayed a condition that enabled them to last. It is argued that the high altitude will have a strong tendency to make them blow up. It certainly would if it were 14,000 feet, or even 7000 or 8000 feet, but 4000 feet will have little effect, especially when it is taken into consideration that both contestants will have had quite a number of days to accustom themselves to the lighter air. It must also be remembered that some pretty long fights have occurred in Nevada between sea-level dwellers, as for instance, the forty-two rounds between Nelson and Gans under the blistering Goldfield sun.

Now, concerning that yellow streak. Bob Armstrong has put himself on record as being certain that his brother in color will very speedily flaunt that pennon when he faces Jeff in the ring. Perhaps this is a case of projected psychology on Bob's part. At any rate, he has no fact in Johnson's career on which to base such a notion. The one thing to bear in mind is that this yellow streak is purely hypothetical. It may be that Johnson may lack in physical stamina and succumb to punishment. But this would be a very different thing from being yellow, from lying down in abject cowardice without receiving any punishment to speak of. A cat can have both barrels of a shotgun emptied into it and still struggle on, while a single sharp rap with a lead pencil can kill a rabbit; yet the rabbit cannot be called yellow because it so easily succumbs, and so with Johnson. It remains to be seen whether he is yellow and whether he possesses as extraordinary power for assimilating punches as he has for delivering them.

And so, by all the tokens, one is led to believe that the Reno fight will not be settled in short order. The chance is large that it will be a long fight, with ten or twelve rounds as the very minimum. The chance is even large that it may go to twenty rounds, and there are many expert fight dopers who would not be surprised to see it run to thirty rounds and even beyond.

It is contended when Jeff begins landing his awful rips that Johnson will speedily and genuinely, after very few rounds, go down for the count. In reply to this let it be pointed out that Jeff has first of all to land those awful rips, and that he will have to land them on one of the cleverest defensive fighters the ring has ever known. Johnson is not going to rush the fight, and, no matter how much Jeff may want to rush it, Johnson will be able for a goodly time to rob those rushes of their effectiveness. It is contrary to Johnson's famous loafing tactics, which, I do believe, are very little deliberate and largely temperamental. It is his way. He has always done it, and there is not one chance in a million that in this forthcoming fight he will revolutionize his whole method.

An opposite contention is that Jeff will be speedily undone

because of the mental effect produced by the negro's cleverness. It is urged that Jeff, after vainly trying to land a few of his rips, and after being rapped soundly in return, may lose his temper and rush wildly. This would certainly be peaches and cream for Johnson. The only thing against it is that Jeff has never shown real temper in the ring. In his own way he has always been a cool-headed fighter. One has only to remember how, in his battles with Corbett and Fitzsimmons, those men put it all over him round after round. Yet he kept cool and fought on and on, with but one thing in his mind, namely, the putting out of the man opposite him who temporarily was making a dub of him.

Another thing is that Johnson is a past master at mouth fighting when in the ring. In his battle with Tommy Burns, Johnson engaged in mouth fighting with Tommy, with Tommy's seconds and with the whole Australian audience, and the honors of every exchange belonged to him. It must be added as well that not one vile word or harsh epithet fell from his lips. Everything he uttered was pure fun, genuine wit, keen-cutting and laughter-provoking. Because of this ability of Johnson's it is argued that he may say things that will cause Jeff to lose his head and deliver the peaches and cream. In this connection all that has to be pointed out is that Jeff is a silent fighter. He has never indulged in verbal tilts in the ring, and, no matter how hard Johnson wanted to, he would find it impossible to engage in witty repartee with a man who won't open his head.

Nevertheless, there will be seconds in Jeff's corner and ring-side outlookers who will venture remarks and who will have it put over them by the colored wit. Unless Johnson is quickly in a bad way at the hands of Jeff there will be more than one good sally and general laugh at the ringside.

JEFFRIES-JOHNSON NO. 6

RENO, Nev., June 28.—Here is the problem. At 1:30 o'clock on the afternoon of July 4 two men, a white and a black, are going to face each other in a squared ring, elevated in the centre of a large arena. They are not going to try to kill each other. They are to fight each other, true, but the fighting will be done with natural weapons, and according to very rigid and restricted rules. They are to strike each other with their hands, and their hands only. No other blow will be permitted. They cannot wrestle with each other or throw each other down. The very area on which they are allowed to land their blows is limited. It is the upper portion of the body. From the waist down all striking is tabooed. Nor may a blow be struck when a man is off his feet. The fists, which are their only fighting weapons, will be encased in padded gloves that weigh one-third of a pound. A naked knuckle can cut and injure, and it is a thing to be avoided. A third man will be in the ring with them to see that all the rules are observed. He is the referee. His word is law. Whatever he says must be obeyed. If a man strikes a foul blow, the referee will immediately disqualify him and award the victory to the other man. The referee will watch closely, circling about the two men, sometimes speaking to them in a low voice, sometimes touching one on the shoulder and sometimes the other.

And what are these two men, with the padded gloves, the rigid rules and the referee, in the ring for? What is their desire to achieve? Simply this: By means of blows with their gloved hands to see who can put the other down on the ground, and put him down so hard that he will stay down for 10 consecutive seconds. And why do they want to do this? For honor and fame and a prize for $100,000.

It sounds silly on the face of it, doesn't it? But when it is considered that from 15,000 to 20,000 men, paying each from $10 to $50 for a seat, will be in the arena to watch the two men, that millions of dollars will be spent on this contest, that men will journey from the uttermost ends of the earth to witness it, that the ablest journalists and cartoonists of the country will be present, and that it has been and will be for a week to come the one overshadowing issue of the whole United States, all to see which of the two men can put the other down for 10 consecutive seconds, why, it would seem to become a colossal silliness.

But is it such a silliness? Is it a silliness at all, when the pages of all the newspapers are daily filled with it, the only concession that a very large portion of the people of the country are interested in it? There is a reason for their interest, just as there is a reason for my interest, and why am I interested? In the next paragraph let me show you. But here let me stand up and announce that I am so keenly interested, so overwhelmingly desirous of witnessing this contest, that there are moments when sudden fears assail me, such as that the fight will not come off, that it may be prevented by some great earthquake or terrific cataclysm of Nature. Why, I want to see that fight so bad that it hurts.

This contest of men with padded gloves on their hands is a sport that belongs unequivocally to the English-speaking race, and that has taken centuries for the race to develop. It is no superficial thing, a fad of a moment or a generation. No genius or philosopher devised it and persuaded the race to adopt it as their radical sport of sports. It is as deep as our consciousness, and is woven into the fibers of our being. It grew as our very language grew. It is an instructive passion of race. And as men to-day thrill to short Saxon words, just so do they thrill to the thud of blows of a prize fight, to the onslaught and the repulse and to the exhibition of gameness and courage. This is the ape and tiger in us, granted. But like the man in jail, it is in us, isn't it? We can't get away from it. It is the fact, the irrefragable fact. We like fighting—it's our nature. We are realities in a real world, and we must accept the reality of our nature and all its thrillableness if we are to live in accord with the real world, and those who try to get away from these realities, who by ukase will deny their existence, succeed only in living in a world of illusion and misunderstanding. These are the people who compose theatre panics, fire panics and wreck panics. They are so far out of accord with the real world that they can make no adjustment with it when the supreme moment comes.

It goes without discussion, so patent is it, that an audience composed wholly of prize fighters would never engage in a theatre panic. They would be too close to the real, too wide-seeing and clear-seeing and cool to stampede like a herd of brute cattle. The chance is that they would stay and put out the fire.

Another thing which merits pointing out is that our sport of prize fighting is a fair sport. It gives play to our ethical natures. No one can disbelieve this who has ever heard a fighter, guilty of a foul blow, hooted by an indignant and outraged audience.

Our sport of prize fighting is hedged with ethical restrictions. It is synonymous with fair play. It is different from the fighting of the jungle, of which it is a development. There is absolutely no fair play in the jungle fighting. So has man improved. By that much is he less rid of fang and claw. By that much has he climbed up the ladder of life. Don't rush his development too hard. He will climb higher.

JEFFRIES-JOHNSON NO. 7

RENO, Nev., June 29. — Certainly no hero ever cared less for adulation than does big Jim Jeffries, who of a surety bulks heroically right now in the public eye. Not only does he not care for adulation, but it seems positively to hurt him. Instead of putting up with it, he runs away from it. The presence of an admiring crowd at his training quarters usually signifies the fact that he will not make an appearance. He does not want any admiring crowd, and his delight is to trick such crowds, and put in his best licks when no one is around, and as for compliments, I know, for one, that if the spirit moved me to address a compliment to his face, it would be only after I had got my life insured and armed myself with an ax.

His brusqueness is astounding, and he is just as brusque to the Governor of a State as to the latest cub reporter away from home for the first time. I shall never forget the first time I met him. Our hands went out and clasped, and I smiled my pleasantest. "How do you do," Jeff grumbled, as if he were mad at all the world and at me especially for daring the impertinence of seeking his acquaintance. At the moment our hands gripped, he gave me a deep, solid, searching look straight in the eyes. There was no geniality in his eyes, no kindliness. Instead, they seemed to smolder in a somber, resentful sort of way.

At any rate, so forbidding was his expression that speech froze on my lips. It was an awkward half minute. So taken aback was I that I could not think of a blessed thing to say, while all the time I was praying fervently for him to say something. He didn't. At the end of half a minute he abruptly turned his back on me and the conference ended. It was not until I had seen these scenes enacted with others that I came to understand, and now I take great joy in watching beaming innocent personages go up to the slaughter of an introduction with the big fellow.

Now, under the ordinary circumstances, when so received by an ordinary man one would be likely to say, "You little, insignificant snipe, who are you to treat me in this fashion?" But you don't say it to Jeff. I don't know why, unless it is that he is not little and insignificant. Also, possibly, deep down in one's subliminal self is a sudden remembrance that life is sweet and the sun good to look upon.

Now if all the foregoing were a pose on the big fighter's part, if it were a change of manner noted in recent years, the public would have some cause of complaint against his brusqueness and his fooling of audiences at the training camp. But this is no pose on his part. It has always been his way, since the first time he came into the public eye, a raw youngster of 20, down in Los Angeles. Nor does this peculiar attitude of his proceed from shyness or embarrassment.

Modest he is, and unassuming, with no touch of the braggart about him, but he is not shy. He is merely himself, with the strength of character to be himself. A peculiar character, self-granted, but still himself. In his way he is an iron man, simple and quiet and reposeful and not gregarious in a wide way. He feels no impulse to be a hale fellow well met with Tom, Dick and Harry, and he is honest enough not to simulate a feeling he does not possess. All the same, it is darned hard on the public.

It is because Jeffries is misunderstood that some of the near-thinking fight dopesters have raised a question which they fire at one unexpectedly with all the confidence that it is an unanswerable conundrum. "If he is so afraid of a crow," they say, "that he doesn't dare train before a couple of hundred spectators —well, what under the sun is he going to do when he faces 20,000 spectators the day of the fight?"

Yet the answer is simple. He has fought before some very sizable crowds ere now and he has never shown any evidences of stage fright. Another thing is that he is a thinker. A silent man is usually a thinker, and because Jeffries does not blurt out all he knows to the first chance comer is no sign that he does not know a great deal back behind those searching black eyes.

Quite in contrast is care-free, happy Jack Johnson. Nobody was ever more gregarious than he, ever happier to greet old friends and make new ones. He likes crowds, thrives upon them, and in turn does his best to give them a good time. Let him decide on a certain day that he is not going to spar, and then inform him that 200 persons have journeyed all the way out to his camp to see him work, depend upon it, Johnson simply couldn't let them go away disappointed. Out would go the word to his sparring partners, and a few minutes later he would be in the thick of a ten or twelve round exhibition.

Out at his training camp Johnson is always in the thick of things. Usually he is chief entertainer, whether in making music, playing games, presiding at mock trials or spinning yarns. And always his voice is raised to others, inviting them to kick in and have a good time.

On the Fourth these two strangely different men come together for the first time, the silent fighter and the garrulous fighter. Two things I look for from Johnson. As the fight progresses he will talk less and less, and his famous smile will fade from his lips, unless it be frozen there, for there is no doubt that this is the fight of Johnson's career, and if he is ever deadly grim and serious in his life it will be in the ring that day after the opening rounds have brought him down to brass tacks. Of Jeffries it is safe to forecast that he will be no more voluble in any round than he is in the first, and that in the first he will not utter a sound.

JEFFRIES-JOHNSON NO. 8

RENO, Nev., June 30. — Of course, every fight fan believes he knows just how the fight is going to go. I find myself no exception to this, and I am filled with quite definite ideas, in a general way, as to how the big fight will open and move on toward its finish.

For, in the first place, barring accidents, lucky punches and yellow streaks, it will not be a short fight. There is practically no chance at all that it will be over within ten rounds. Twenty would be nearer the mark, though it may go thirty. Thirty-five rounds is the maximum I dare suggest, beyond which it is unthinkable that the contest can continue.

Neither man is a knocker out in the sense that Fitzsimmons was or that Sullivan was. Neither carries the sedative kick in his biceps and shoulder muscles that can put a man abruptly to sleep at any stage of the fight. Both men depend upon the cumulative effect of their blows, Jeffries with his rips and Johnson with his right smashes. Their method has usually been to reduce an antagonist a blow at a time, piling up an account of weakness and distress. Thus, when the end comes, if come it must, one of three things will happen. The referee may stop the fight and award the decision because one or the other man is in a bad way. One or the other man, or his seconds, may throw up the sponge because his is in a bad way, or, one or the other, being in a bad way, from the cumulative effect of punches received will go down for the count before a blow not necessarily severe, but sufficient enough to do the work on his weakened condition.

Thus, so weakened was Britt at Colma that almost any sort of a punch from Battling Nelson was sufficient to finish him. Corbett did not really knock out Sullivan at New Orleans. While it is true that in the latter part of the fight Corbett administered a lot of sharp punishment, nevertheless Sullivan was ready, and had been long ready, to take the count, having exhausted himself by vainly trying to reach the wily dodger. The blow that put Sullivan down for keeps would not have shaken him in the opening rounds of the fight. Quite different was the blow Fitzsimmons used to finish Corbett in the Carson fight. That blow was a genuine knocker out. Whether delivered in the first round or the last, or in any intervening round, Corbett would have gone down for the count just the same.

Neither Jeffries nor Johnson carries such a kick in his arms. As a result, always barring accidents, of course, the fight will be of fairly long duration, each man striving to pile up the score of cumulative punishment, and how will they go at it? It is fair to assume, from the history of the two men, that the first several rounds will be easy. It is scarcely plausible that Jeffries will start to rush the fight at the sound of the gong, and Johnson certainly will not rush it. There won't be much tearing-in in those first several rounds. The men have never met before; they will take it easy, feel each other out, learn slowly and safely what to expect, what to avoid and how to get in their own licks best.

It is in this opening part of the fight, as sure as "pigs is pigs," that Jeffries will receive the greater portion of the punishment. The man never lived who could prevent Johnson landing on him. That Jeffries will receive during the opening period three blows to every one he gives is not too wild a thing to believe. Jeffries himself has said that he is prepared for this and that he is quite willing to exchange blows at the ratio of one to three. He bases this willingness upon two things—his belief in his greater stamina for assimilating punishment, and his belief that his own punches have far more punishing power than Johnson's.

One thing noticeable in this fight will be Jeffries' quickness. He will be quicker than ever before. This can be depended upon, though his quickness may not be so evident because he will have to employ it against a phenomenally quick and clever adversary. Jeffries' own cleverness will be a surprise to many who have never seen him in action, or who have not seen him in action since his early fighting days. Nevertheless, more than once as he comes in, crouched, with his shoulder, into a clinch, will his head be lifted by Johnson's right. Another thing that will be manifest is that Johnson will better measure time and distance. Jeffries will pay the penalty for this, but will continue doggedly to bore in at the ratio of one for three back. He has done it before. He will do it on the Fourth.

As the fight progresses, it can be depended upon that Jeffries will land more frequently and that he will reduce the ratio of exchange; and right here arises one of those little problems that only the fight itself can solve. Johnson's great dangerous blow is his smashing right uppercut. He has always used it with signal success on right-handed men. Now Jeffries is left-handed. Suppose he should elect to fight leading with his right hand instead of his left. What will happen? Suppose he adds his ancient crouch to the combination. Will he baffle that right of Johnson's? Who can forecast? It remains to be seen.

Many things remain that can be known only by being seen. For instance, who will loaf in the clinches and rest his weight on the other? Johnson is notorious for this. Yet Jeffries is the taller and heavier. Will he burden and tire the negro with his weight, or will he come in on the crouch, using his shoulder, and find the negro's weight on him?

One thing most certain is that Jeffries will force the fight and persistently hunt his man from gong to gong. Johnson, too, likes to make the other man lead so as to time him. But, suppose that Jeffries hunts and hunts, and leads and leads, and that Johnson backs and shuffles and runs away from him? Will Jeffries follow up the chase that may or may not be vain? Or will he take his stand in the centre of the ring and demand of the referee that Johnson fight him?

The thing I am most curious to see is what will happen when these two strong-shouldered men come together in the clinches.

Johnson has always been noted for his strength and skill at such times, in blocking, locking arms, stalling and so entangling an opponent's arms as to make him helpless. Can he do this with Jeffries? It must be remembered that for the first time in his life Johnson encounters an opponent who is just as strong as he in the shoulders and arms, if not stronger. In fact, Jeffries may be far stronger. No one knows just how strong he is in that particular. Will Johnson entangle Jeff's arms and make a toy of him, or will Jeff teach him, at such moments, what strength is? I am curious to know. I am curious to know.

JEFFRIES-JOHNSON NO. 9

RENO, Nev., July 1.—I am glad I'm here. There was never anything like this Reno at the present moment, with the great impending event only three days away. I should hate like poison if some Croesus should offer to pay me to stay away from the fight, telling me to fix my own price. Surely, there is a money price that would keep me away from the fight, but the attempt to calculate the amount would be very fatiguing. In lieu of the Croesus, all that I am afraid of now is that I'll be run over by a Reno electric car and miss the fight. However, when I consider the Reno street car I take heart of courage and think I shall have a fair chance.

Seriously, no man who loves the fighting game, has the price and is within striking distance of Reno should miss the fight.

Viewed from every possible angle, there has never been anything like it in the history of the ring, and there is no chance for anything like it to occur in the future—at least within the lifetime of those alive today. Even if no more stringent legislation is passed against the game, even if every state threw itself wide open to prize-fighting, still there can be nothing like this fight for a generation to come.

In the first place, never have two men like these ever faced each other in the ring. In all the contests of its long history, no two comparable giants have ever locked in combat. And in their own generation there is no third man who approaches them. It has taken not only a generation, but two races to produce them.

Johnson is a dusky wonder. For his size there has never been so clever a defensive boxer. Nor has there ever been a cooler-headed boxer. This coolness of his is one of his most remarkable attributes. So cool is he that his fighting at times seems lackadaisical, while at the same time it never has the seeming of brutality. In action there is very little hint of the fighting beast about him. There are hints of it, true, when sudden fierce moments come upon him and his face and force become tigerish. But it is not genuine. He simulates it. He is a play-actor deliberately playing a part. He is not mastered by this tigerishness. He is manufacturing it. Back in that cool brain of his he decides he needs this display of tigerishness in his business, and so he displays it.

Another of his remarkable attributes is an instinct for a blow that is positive genius. Locked in a clinch, body relaxed, his mind elsewhere, his gaze fixed on some one off to the side and outside the ring, himself talking to that outsider, say, about the disposition of the contents of a certain suit case—at such a moment his opponent starts a blow for his jaw, and he, without seeing or gauging or thinking, by some automatic divination, knows all about that blow, its force, sweep and direction. He merely rolls his head or pulls it back just far enough and not a fraction of an inch farther, and all the while, without a break, keeps up his conversation about the contents of that suit case. A wonderful fighter, indeed, is Johnson, utterly unlike any other fighter, a type by himself.

And against this man will stand Jeffries, an even more remarkable man, a grizzly giant, huge and rugged, of a type we are prone to believe was more common in other days when the world was young. And, despite his hugeness and ruggedness, he is so well proportioned from heel to head that the combination is startling. His is a perfection of symmetry that is the fruit of the highest organic development. And, if science tells aright, we are justified in believing that no such symmetry obtained among those giants of the younger world. The human in those days was in the process of becoming. It was muscular efficiency minus beauty of form and line. This big modern Jim Jeffries has both.

So far as the boxing game is concerned the contest next Monday is well named "the fight of the century." These two men, in a class by themselves so far as other fighters go, yet so radically different from each other as to have practically no salient characteristics in common, will fight a battle in a setting like unto nothing the ring has ever displayed. For the first time, two undefeated heavy-weight champions battle, and each goes up against the most dangerous and formidable man he has ever tackled. And they will fight in the presence of four other and earlier heavyweight champions. Again are all the records broken, for next Monday, in the ring and the arena, will be six men who have held the honor of being world champion heavy-weights. Think of it—Sullivan, Corbett, Fitzsimmons, Burns, Jeffries and Johnson.

From the standpoint of the sporting world, there has never been so amazing a gathering. Almost every champion and exchampion of every class will be at the ringside. There will be the famous trainers and conditioners of athletes, men like Muldoon and Murphy. There will be the athletes themselves, victors and leaders in all the games. And as for the noted and notorious sport followers, they will all be here. Every figure of sportdom, from Billy Jordan, the well beloved veteran announcer, down to the latest and youngest fight promoter, they will all be on the ground.

And they will watch these two strangely diverse heavy-weights battle, beside whom all other heavies look like middle-weights. Johnson, the fighting boxer, will go up against Jeffries, the boxing fighter. Both are cool, both are experienced, both are terrible. It will not be a short fight. It will be a great fight.

And so I say again to all you men who love the game, have the price, and are within striking distance of Reno—come. It is the fight of fights, the crowning fight of the whole ring, and perhaps the last great fight that will ever be held. Also, to you lovers of the game, who desire to see in flesh and blood the celebrities of the game, I say come. It would take years of traveling and fight following to see all the figures of sportdom that can be seen here in Reno in one day, and no admission charged. I, for one, hope for a toothless old age, when nothing is left but to mumble reminiscences, and in that time one of my greatest joys will be to maunder over all the wonderful details of the great fight at Reno—"yes, sir; in 1910, at Reno. I was there and sat by the ringside."

JEFFRIES-JOHNSON NO. 10

RENO, Nev., July 2.— It seems to me that in this discussion about Jeffries coming back, several little points have been ignored. For instance, there is a little science called histology, which has a whole lot of bearing on Jeff's case. Men are intricate and complicated fabrics woven and builded out of cells. All the tissues, nerves, muscles and organs are composed of enormously interrelated colonies of cells. The muscle cells store up energy and release it into action. This is at work, and this work breaks down the cells, burns them up, destroys them, and new cells take their place.

These cells have a way of reproducing themselves, and according to the number of times they can reproduce themselves is the life of the individual or the average life of a species. Thus, parrots possess such cell reproductiveness that their tissues go on renewing for 100 years. There are certain flies whose cell reproductiveness is so small that they live for an hour or two.

Each creature, be it bug, beast or bird, is born with so many potential cell generations. When these generations are used up the creature dies. Its organism disintegrates, because of the simple fact that it can no longer renew itself. There are no more new cells out of which to manufacture new tissue. The tissue breaks down and there is a funeral. It is the same with men. Each man, at birth, comes into the world with so many potential cell generations. Barring accidents and excesses, one man will break down and die of senile old age at 65. Another man will live to 90 before the same thing happens. The difference between the two is the difference in their cell potentialities when they were born.

Each man has only so many cell generations, which means that each man has only so much work in him. Now, a man can use up quickly or slowly these cell generations that are the life of him. The more quickly he uses them the shorter the time he lives. A hard manual worker wears out quicker than an easy office worker. The manual worker will look stronger, healthier, ruddier, but he won't live as long. This is no place to consider exceptions. We must deal with averages. The life insurance companies, who are past masters in handling averages, will tell you that the average life of a laborer is shorter than the average life of an office worker. And now the argument leads up to the fighting game and gets near the old Jeffries. Every man is born with just so much work in him, which he may expend quickly or slowly. Each fighter is born with so many fights in him. When he has made these fights he is finished. He may try to fight more, to come back, but he is doomed to defeat. His spirit is willing, but his flesh is weak. His flesh is weak because it can no longer reproduce itself with the old vim. The cell generations come more slowly and in dwindling numbers. The man is fading, passing, moving toward the final cessation.

Prize-fighting is a terrific destroyer of cells. A man in a hard fight will lose pounds and pounds of weight and he will shorten his life correspondingly—both his entire life and his fighting life. Let us consider two prize-fighters. Each is born with a potential cell reproductiveness that will permit him twenty fights. In short, he is born with twenty fights in him. When they are fought, he is finished. There is no come back. There can be no come back. Now one of these two men is lucky. He goes against opponents whom he puts away easily. He has no hard, long, gruelling fights wherein he burns himself up to the uttermost pitch of human endurance. The second man is unfortunate. His opponents are more formidable. Fight after fight is long, hard and gruelling.

As a result he uses up his cell generations at a terrific rate, and he is a has been, out of the ring, for a long time before the first man follows him.

What has happened to this man? The fight fans say he has lost his stamina. This is an abstraction and a confusion. For there is a stamina that is residual to the brain and that is called gameness. This particular man can be as game as ever, and yet be unable to come back. Then what has happened? He has lost the stamina of his flesh. He has consumed the vitality of his tissues. When he exercises and breaks down cells, they break down more quickly. Also new cells are built up more slowly, and they come in decreasing numbers. He can't go the twenty fast rounds, or the ten fast rounds, he used so easily to go.

And now we come to Jeff. He was born with so many cell generations in him, with so many fights in him—how many only time can tell. What has he done with those cell generations? What have his fights been, and how many are they? Right here the investigation shows its straight aim at the problem whether or not Jeff can come back.

How has Jeff dealt with those cell generations of his? How often has he fought? How long has he fought? How hard has he fought? His record is a short and easy one. In 1896 he knocked out Dan Long in San Francisco. In 1904 he knocked out Jack Munroe in San Francisco. Both were two-round fights. His fight career has thus been only eight years. But when it is considered that Jack Munroe was a joke, and that the fight of 1903 with Corbett was an easy one of only ten rounds, his fighting career may be said to have ended in 1902, when he knocked out Fitzsimmons for a second time. This means, to all practical purposes, that he was fighting for only six years.

All told, he has fought twenty battles. In the light of cell consumption, all analyses of these twenty battles are worth while. Then we may know better how many of the fights he was born with have been used up. One of the fights was a single round. Four were two-round affairs. Two went to three rounds. There were two fights of four rounds, one of five rounds, one of eight rounds and one of nine rounds. Already twelve of the twenty fights have been disposed of, and they cannot be called long, hard and gruelling fights. They never strained Jeff, never unduly consumed his cells. There remain eight fights. Two of these were of ten rounds and one of eleven rounds. Nothing exciting there in the way of wearing out his tissues. And finally, he fought three twenty-round battles, one of twenty-three rounds and one of twenty-five rounds. None of these fights was long and hard and gruelling. None of his opponents ever compelled him to fight at topmost pitch. Never was he in a bad way, fighting for time, and life, and the gong. Never once has he even been knocked off his feet. He has never been seriously hurt. He has never been really jarred. His endurance can scarcely be said to have been tested. He has never burned up tissue at the prodigious rate that practically all other pugilists, at one time or other, have been compelled to burn theirs up. What he is capable of no one knows. He has never been put to the test. He has never had the chance to put up a soul-breaking, heart-breaking, body-breaking, cell-destroying battle.

The point of all which is that of the fights Jeff was born with, very few at all have been used. He still has them. They are there, alive in his muscles, now, along with the goodly cell generations which he never consumed. Can Jeff come back? It would be remarkable if he could not. He brings back with him what he took away with him, and that is pretty near everything he was born with. And don't forget that he has not tried to come back in a hurry. Beginning lightly, and steadily increasing his training, he has been coming back for a heroic year and a half. Can Jeff come back? Pardon me. He is here. Can he whip Johnson? This is another story.

JEFFRIES-JOHNSON NO. 11

RENO, Nev., July 3.—It is the lull before the storm. The fighters are resting, the fight fans are resting, and, it being Sunday, the very gambling hazards of Reno are resting. The last argument has been given, the last theory expounded, yet everything remains in the air, unproved, and the partisans have paused, open-mouthed, waiting for to-morrow when Billy Jordan says, "Let 'er go," the gong sounds, and the black giant and the white proceed to let go at each other and to prove or disprove the ten thousand

and ten thousand pros and cons that have been advanced the last week—or for the last whole year.

The one thing Jeffries hates is applause. Out at his training quarters "Farmer" Burns pleads with the spectators, with tears in his voice, not to clap their hands. Applause always gives Jeffries the grouch, and so one is led to believe if Jeffries wins the fight and 20,000 men tear themselves loose in the wildest outburst of applause that the Sagebrush State has ever heard that Jeff will have the most profound, confounded and enormous grouch that ever a man possessed.

A trifle of prophecy: If the fight goes any decent distance, bent and dented ribs for Johnson, if not broken ones.

There are no illusions among all these fighters, fight followers, and trainers as to conditions of men. They know the sport for what it is and they know it intelligently. Any person who believes that prize-fighting is nothing but pure brutality and barbarism would learn much by a day's contact with this army of fighters and fight fans that has poured into Reno, and such a person would be surprised that there is more in the game than two men pummeling each other. The game is a myriad times finer and greater than that.

In the eleven days I have been in Reno, during which time I have rubbed shoulders with all these men who know the game, not once have I heard the whisper passed of "fake." There is not one man on the ground who entertains the slightest suspicion that the fight is fixed in any way. This old cry of fake was raised several months ago, but it died from lack of sustenance. Not one thing was found on which to feed it. Depend upon it, the big fight is absolutely on the square.

One of the most touching things I have seen here has been the devotion and loyalty of every fellow in the training camp to Jeff. Especially, will I never forget an exhibition of this by Sam Berger. Sam was one of the group that believed the big fellow should do more sparring, and Sam argued for it passionately, late and early, and all the time. The last day of his active training Jeff boxed some fast rounds with Choynski and "Brother Jack." Finishing with the latter, Jeff proceeded to take off his gloves.

"Hold on!" Berger cried: "I'm here," and to those near him Berger said in a low voice: "I'm going to give it to him as long

as I last," and he did, too. He surged in like a hurricane, walloping
the big fellow as hard as he was able, crying aloud from the
very effort of the blows he delivered, taking his punishment in
return, and keeping it up until toward the end, all but out from
a heavy rip to the stomach, he was held up by Jeff to prevent him
from falling to the mat.

Sam wasn't yearning for this punishment, but out of his heart-
felt anxiety and loyalty for his leader he did his little best, better
to fit him for the big fight.

Especially, do I remember how Sam received Jeff's shoulder.
It was a blow of such crushing impact that it would have finished
there and then any man of Berger's weight who did not make a
practice of boxing.

Prize-fighting may be brutal, but, in my humble opinion, there
are many things worse. Prize-fighting has rigid fair play rules.
Foul blows are not permitted nor are big men allowed to fight
with the little men. Heavy-weight fight with heavy-weights, middles with middles, and light-weights with light-weights. But out
in the world this fair play does not obtain. If a rebate is a foul
blow in the business world, what can be said of food adulteration,
the packing of life preservers with scrap iron, and the bribery of
the people's legislators and representatives? Can the worst that
ever happened in any prize-ring compare with short weighing the
Government, which is the people? How about a big man who
pounces on 1000 little children, puts them to work in a factory,
and destroys them, bodies and souls? Or what of the big merchant, who, by the club of hunger, compels his women employees
to labor long hours on a semi-starvation wage?

As for me, I prefer something that may be, in its way, brutal,
but that at the same time is eminently fair. There is not a little
learned from prize-fighting. If some of the fairness of the prize-
ring were carried into business life it would be a much more
beneficial world in which to live.

Jeff is going to extend himself in this fight. Will he make
Johnson extend himself and, if so, how long will it take him to
do it?

Jeff is not so slow. Ask Fitzsimmons, who has fought twice
with him, and who ought to know. Fitzsimmons vouches for Jeff's
quickness.

Johnson has a remarkable arm and shoulder development, so has Jeff. Question: Will Jeff be able to put it over the negro in the roughing of the clinches? This will be worth watching for.

Another trifle of prophecy. Neither of the big fellows is going to spring anything new. Each is going to fight in the same old way he has always fought. It is the combination of these two men that is new.

Query: Suppose Jeff wins and retires again? Won't that leave Johnson in the ring as the heavy-weight champion of the world? and won't the championship situation be just where it was before Jeff decided to re-enter the ring? Of a certainty, outside of Jeff, there is no other heavy-weight who can best Johnson.

JEFFRIES-JOHNSON FIGHT

RENO, Nev., July 4. — Once again has Johnson sent down to defeat the chosen representative of the white race, and this time the greatest of them all. And, as of old, it was play for Johnson. From the opening to the closing round he never ceased his witty sallies, his exchanges of repartee with his opponent's seconds and with the spectators. And, for that matter, Johnson had a funny thing or two to say to Jeffries in every round. The golden smile was as much in evidence as ever, and neither did it freeze on his face nor did it vanish. It came and went throughout the fight spontaneously, naturally.

It was not a great battle, after all, save in its setting and its significance. Little Tommy Burns down in far-off Australia put up a faster, quicker, livelier battle than did Jeff. The fight today, and again I repeat, was great only in its significance. In itself it was not great. The issue, after the fiddling of the opening rounds, was never in doubt. In the fiddling of those first rounds the honors lay with Johnson, and for the rounds after the seventh or eighth it was more Johnson, while for the closing rounds it was all Johnson.

Johnson played, as usual. With his opponent not strong in the attack, Johnson, blocking and defending in masterly fashion, could afford to play. And he played and fought a white man in a white man's country, before a white man's crowd. And the crowd was a Jeffries crowd. When Jeffries sent in that awful rip of his the crowd would madly applaud, believing it had gone home to Johnson's stomach, and Johnson, deftly interposing his elbow, would smile in irony at the spectators, play-acting, making believe he thought the applause was for him—and never believing it at all.

The greatest battle of the century was a monologue delivered to twenty thousand spectators by a smiling negro who was never in doubt and who was never serious for more than a moment at a time.

As a fighter Johnson did not show himself a wonder. He did not have to. Never once was he extended. There was no need Jeff could not make him extend. Jeff never had him in trouble once. No blow Jeff ever landed hurt his dusky opponent. Johnson came out of the great fight practically undamaged. The blood on his lip was from a recent cut received in training which Jeff managed to reopen.

Jeff failed to lead and land. The quickness he brought into the fight quickly evaporated, and while Jeff was dead game to the end, he was not so badly punished. What he failed to bring into the ring with him was his stamina, which he lost somewhere in the last seven years. Jeff failed to come back. That is the whole story. His old-time vim and endurance were not there. Something has happened to him. He lost in retirement, outside of the ring, the stamina that the ring itself never robbed him of. As I have said, Jeff was not badly damaged. Every day boys take worse lacings in boxing bouts than Jeff took today.

Jeff today disposed of one question. He could not come back. Johnson in turn answered another question. He has not the yellow streak. But he only answered that question for to-day. The ferocity of the hairy-chested caveman and grizzly giant combined did not intimidate the cool-headed negro. Many thousands in the audience expected this intimidation and were correspondingly disappointed. Johnson was not scared, let it be said here and beyond the shadow of a doubt. Not for an instant did he show the flicker of fear that the Goliath against him might eat up.

But the question of the yellow streak is not answered for all time. Just as Johnson has never been extended, so has he never shown the yellow streak. Just as a man may rise up, heaven alone

knows where, who will extend Johnson, just so may that man
bring out the yellow streak, and then again, he may not. So far
the burden of proof all rests on the conclusion that Johnson
has no yellow streak.

And now to the battle and how it began. All praise to Tex
Rickard, the gamest of sports, who pulled off the fight after countless difficulties, and who, cool, calm and quick with nervous
aliveness, handled the vast crowd splendidly at the arena, and
and wound up by refereeing the fight.

Twenty thousand filled the great arena and waited patiently
under the cloud-flecked wide Nevada sky. Of the many women
present, some elected to sit in the screened boxed far back from
the ring, for all the world like olden Spanish ladies at the theatre.
But more, many more women, sat close to the ringside beside their
husbands or brothers. They were the wiser far.

Merely to enumerate the celebrities at the ringside would be
to write a sporting directory of America—at least a directory of
the 400 of sportdom and of many more hundreds of near four
hundreds. At 1:56, Billy Jordan cleared the ring amid cheers,
and stood alone, the focal point of 20,000 pairs of eyes, until
the great Muldoon climbed through the ropes to call tumultuous
applause and ringing cheers from the 20,000 throats, for the
State of Nevada, the people of Nevada and the Governor of
Nevada.

Beginning with Tex Rickard, ovation after ovation was given
to all the great ones, not forgetting Fitzsimmons, whom Billy
Jordan introduced as "the greatest warrior of them all." And so
they came, great one after great one, ceaselessly, endlessly, until
they were swept away before the greatest of them all—the two
men who were about to do battle.

It was 2:30 when Johnson entered. He came first, airy, happy
and smiling, greeting friends and acquaintances here, there and
everywhere in the audience, cool as ice, waving his hand in salute,
smiling, smiling ever smiling, with eyes as well as lips, never
missing a name nor a face, placid, plastic, nerveless, with never a
signal flown of hesitancy nor timidity. Yet was he keyed up,
keenly observant of all that was going on, even hearing much
of the confused babble of tongues about him—hearing, ay, and
understanding, too. There is nothing heavy nor primitive about

this man Johnson. He is alive and quivering, every nerve fiber in his body and brain, withal that it is hidden, so artfully, or naturally, under that poise of facetious calm of his. He is a marvel of sensitiveness, sensibility and perceptibility. He has a perfect mechanism of mind and body. His mind works like chain lightning and his body obeys with equal swiftness.

But the great madness of applause went up when Jeffries entered the ring two minutes later. A quick superficial comparison between him and the negro would lead to a feeling of pity for the latter. For Jeff was all that has been said of him. When he stripped and his mighty body could be seen covered with mats of hair, all the primordial adjectives ever applied to him received their vindication. Nor did his face belie them. No facile emotion played on that face, no whims of the moment, no flutterings of a light-hearted temperament. Dark and somber and ominous was that face, solid and stolid and expressionless, with eyes that smouldered and looked savage.

The man of iron, grim with determination, sat down in his corner. And the care-free negro smiled and smiled. And that is the story of the fight. The man of iron, the grizzly giant was grim and serious. The man of summer temperament smiled and smiled. That is the story of the whole fight. It is the story of the fight by rounds.

At the opening of the first round they did not shake hands. Knowing the two men for what they are, it can be safely postulated that this neglect was due to Jeff or to the prompting of Jeff's corner. But it is not good that two boxers should not shake hands before a bout. I would suggest to these protagonists of a perishing game, if they wish to preserve the game, that they make the most of these little amenities that by custom grace their sport, and give it the veneer of civilization.

Both men went to work in that first round very easily, Johnson smiling, of course, and Jeff grim and determined. Johnson landed the first blow, a light one, and Jeff, in the clinches, gave a faint indication of his forthcoming tactics by roughing it, by crowding the negro around and by slightly bearing his weight upon him. It was a very easy round, with nothing of moment. Each was merely feeling the other out and both were exceedingly careful. At the conclusion of the round Johnson tapped Jeffries playfully on the shoulder, smiled good-naturedly and went to his corner. Jeff, in the first, showed flashes of cat-like quickness.

Second round, Jeff advanced with a momentary assumption of his famous crouch, to meet the broadly smiling. Jeff is really human and good-natured. He proved it right here. So friendly was that smile of Johnson, so irresistibly catching that Jeff, despite himself, smiled back. But Jeff's smiles were doomed to be very few in this fight.

And right here began a repetition of what took place down in Australia when Burns fought Johnson. Each time Burns said something harsh to Johnson, in the hope of making him lose his temper, Johnson responded by giving the white man a lacing. And so to-day, of course, Jeff did not talk to Johnson to amount to anything, but Corbett, in the corner, did it for Jeff. And each time Corbett cried out something particularly harsh, Johnson promptly administered a lacing to Jeff. It began in the second round. Corbett, in line with his plan of irritating the negro, called out loudly: "He wants to fight a little, Jim."

"You bet, I do," Johnson retorted, and with that he landed Jeff a stinging right uppercut.

Both men were tensely careful, Jeff trying to crowd and put his weight on in the clinches, Johnson striving more than the other to break out of the clinches. And at the end of the round, in his corner, Johnson was laughing gleefully. Certainly Jeff showed no signs of boring in, as had been promised by his enthusiastic supporters.

It was the same story in the third round, at the conclusion of which the irrepressible negro was guilty of waving his hands to friends in the audience.

In the fourth round Jeff showed up better, rushing and crowding and striking with more vim than hitherto shown. This seemed to have been caused by a sally of Johnson's and Jeff went at him in an angry sort of way. Promptly Jeff rushed, and even ere they came together, Johnson cried out:

"Don't rush me, Jim. You hear what I'm telling you?"

No sign there of being intimidated by Jeffries' first dynamic display of ferocity. All he managed to do was to reopen the training cut in Johnson's lip and to make Johnson playful. It was most anybody's round, and it was certainly more Jeff's than any preceding one.

Round five brought Jeff advancing with his crouch and showed that the blood from Johnson's lip had turned his smile to a gory one. But still he smiled and, to balance things off, he opened Jeff's lip until it bled more profusely than his own. From then until the end of the fight Jeff's face was never free from blood, a steady stream later flowing from his right nostril, added to by the opened cut on his left cheek. Corbett's running fire of irritation served but to make Johnson smile the merrier and to wink at him across Jeff's shoulder in the clinches.

So far no problems had been solved, no questions answered. The yellow streak had not appeared. Neither had Jeff bored in, ripped awfully, nor put it over Johnson in the clinches. Yet one thing had been shown. Jeff was not so fast as he had been. There was a shade of diminution in his speed.

Johnson signalized the opening of the sixth round by landing stinging blows to the face in one, two, three order. Johnson's quickness was startling. In response to an irritating remark from Corbett, Johnson replied suavely, "Too much on hand right now," and at the same instant he tore into Jeff. It was Johnson's first real, aggressive rush. It lasted but a second or two, but it was fierce and dandy, and at its conclusion it was manifest that Jeff's right eye was closing fast. The round ended with Johnson fighting and smiling strong, and with Jeff's nose, lip and cheek bleeding and his eye closed. Johnson's round by a smile all the way through.

The seventh round was a mild one, opening with Jeff grim and silent, and with Johnson leading and forcing. Both were careful, and nothing happened, save that once they exchanged blows right niftily. So far, Jeff's roughing, and crowding and bearing on of weight had amounted to nothing. Also, he was doing less and less of it.

"It only takes one or two, Jim," Corbett encouraged his principal in the eighth round. Promptly Johnson landed two stingers. After a pause he landed another. "See that?" he chirped sweetly to Corbett in the corner. Jeff showed signs perceptibly of slowing down in this round, rushing and crowding less and less. Johnson was working harder and his speed was as flash light as ever.

Jeff's slowing down was not due to the punishment he had received, but to poorness of condition. He was flying the first signals of fatigue. He was advertising, faintly, it is true, that he had not come back.

The ninth round was introduced by a suggestion from Corbett, heroically carrying out the policy that was bringing his principle to destruction. "Make that big stiff fight," was Corbett's suggestion. "That's right; that's what they all say," was Johnson's answer, delivered with true Chesterfieldian grace across his adversary's shoulder. In the previous rounds Johnson had not wreaked much damage with the forecasted punch, the right uppercut. In this round he demonstrated indisputably that he could drive the left hand in a way that was surprising. Be it remembered that it had been long denied that he had any sort of a punch in that left of his. Incidentally, in this round he landed a blow near to Jeff's heart that must have been discouraging.

The tenth round showed Johnson, with his deft, unexpected left, as quick as ever, and Jeff's going slower and slower.

The conclusion of the first ten rounds may be summed up as follows: The fight was all in the favor of Johnson, who had shown no yellow, who had shown condition, who had shown undiminished speed, who had not used his right uppercut much, who had developed a savage left, who held his own in the clinches, who had not the best of the infighting and the outfighting, who was unhurt and who was smiling all the way. Jeff was in bad shape; he was tired, slower than ever, his few rushes had been futile, and the sports who had placed their money against him were jubilant. There were men who proclaimed they saw the end.

I refused to see this end, for I had picked Jeff to win, and I was hoping hugely—for what, I did not know; but for something to happen, for anything, that would turn the tide of battle. And yet I could not hide from myself the truth that Jeff had slowed down.

The eleventh round looked better for Jeff. Stung by a remark of Corbett's, Johnson rushed and provoked one grand rally from Jeff. It was faster fighting, and more continuous than at any time in the preceding ten rounds, culminating in a fierce rally, in which Jeff landed hard.

Round twelve found Johnson, if anything, quicker and more aggressive than ever.

"Thought you were going to have me wild?" Johnson queried sweetly of Corbett.

As usual, every remark of Corbett's brought more punishment to Jeffries. And by the end of this round the second of two great questions was definitely answered. Jeff had not come back.

The thirteenth round was the beginning of the end. Beginning slowly enough, but stung by Corbett, Johnson put it all over him in the mouth fighting, and all over Jeff in the outfighting and infighting. From defense to attack, and back again, and back and forth, Johnson flashed like the amazing fighting mechanism he is. Jeff was silent and sick, while, as the round progressed, Corbett was noticeably silent.

A few entertained the fond hope that Jeff would recuperate. But it was futile. There was no come back to him. He was a fading, failing, heartsick, heartbroken man.

"Talk to him, Corbett," Jeff's friends appealed, in the fourteenth round. But Corbett could not talk. He had long since seen the end.

Yet through this round Johnson went in for one of his characteristic loafing spells. He took it easy, and played with the big gladiator, cool as a cucumber, smiling broadly as ever, yet as careful as ever.

"Right on the hip," he grinned once, as Jeff, in a desperate, dying flurry, managed to land a wild punch in that vicinity.

Corbett, likewise desperate, ventured a last sally. "Why don't you do something?" he cried to the loafing, laughing Johnson. "Too clever, too clever, like you," was the response.

Round fifteen, and the end. It was pitiful. There happened to Jeff the bitterness that he had so often made others taste, but which for the first time, perforce, he was made to taste himself. He who had never been knocked down was knocked down repeatedly. He who had never been knocked out was knocked out. Never mind the technical decision. Jeff was knocked out. That is all there is to it. An ignominy of ignominies, he was knocked out and through the ropes by the punch he never believed Johnson possessed—by the left, and not by the right.

As he lay across the lower rope while the seconds were told

off, a cry that had in it tears and abject broken plea went up from many of the spectators.

"Don't let the negro knock him out, don't let the negro knock him out," was the oft-repeated cry.

There is little more to be said. Jeff did not come back. Johnson did not show the yellow streak, and it was Johnson's fight all the way through. Jeff was not old Jeff at all. Even so, it is to be doubted if the old Jeff could have put away this amazing negro from Texas, this black man with the unfailing smile, this king of fighters and monologists.

Corbett and Berger and the others were right. They wanted Jeff to do more boxing and fighting in his training. Nevertheless lacking the come back as he so potently did, this preliminary boxing and fighting would have profited him nothing. On the other hand, it would have saved his camp much of the money with which it backed him.

It was a slow fight. Faster, better fights may be seen every day of the year in any of the small clubs in the land. It is true these men were heavy-weights, yet for heavy-weights it was a slow fight. It must be granted that plucky Tommy Burns put up a much faster fight with Johnson a year and a half ago. Yet the American fight follower had to see this fight to-day in order to appreciate just what Burns did against this colored wonder.

Johnson is a wonder. No one understands him, this man who smiles. Well, the story of the fight is the story of a smile. If ever a man won by nothing more fatiguing than a smile, Johnson won to-day.

And where now is the champion who will make Johnson extend himself, who will glaze those bright eyes, remove that smile and silence that golden repartee?

PART THREE

Miscellaneous Articles

THE HOME-COMING OF THE *Oregon*[1]

Jack London is usually known today only as a writer of fiction—the novel and the short story—but during his life he contributed many articles to newspapers and magazines that reveal his dynamic style, his wide range of interests, and his insights into the many problems and facets of man's existence.

That he was recognized early in his career as a reporter is evidenced by the following statement in the Examiner *of June 14, 1901, which preceded "The Home-Coming of the Oregon":*

> It's one thing to get news, it's quite another thing to know what to do with it after you get it. On a given day three newspapers may tell of the same facts. But in one of the papers it will be written in good, sprightly English, and displayed in a manner to attract and please the eye of the reader; while in the others it appears as dull, heavy, uninteresting accounts of things happened. The difference is like that between light, sweet, wholesome bread, and the sour, heavy, doughy lump that comes from the hands of the ignorant and unskillful cook. It is the aim of *The Examiner* not only to get the news, but to dress it in attractive shape—to give its readers the best of writing as well as the best of the news. That is why it got Jack London to write up the home-coming of the *Oregon* yesterday, and that is why in the course of the year most of the prominent writers in the world are found as contributors to its columns. As an instance of the way that *The Examiner* treats its readers, we ask them to compare the fresh, lively and picturesque account of the home-coming of the *Oregon*, from the pen of Jack London, with the accounts furnished by our contemporaries. The vivid and virile English in which the event is described by the author of *The Son of the Wolf* [London's first collection of short stories] doubles the intrinsic interest of the home-coming of our famous battleship. "The best news and the best writing" is *The Examiner*'s motto.

The wharf ends were blackened with people and men ceased from their work to watch the pride of San Francisco go by. The cabins of the ferry-boats disgorged their passengers upon the decks, and the *Oregon* was on everybody's lips. Craft after craft flung out their colored banners, and whistle after whistle added to the volume of joy.

Up, up she swept grandly on the breast of the flood tide, this huge gun platform, this floating fort, this colossus, this mighty 10,000-ton projectile, capable of driving a blow at a velocity of

[1] The San Francisco *Examiner*, June 14, 1901.

thirty feet per second! At her stern rippled the Stars and Stripes;
and from the peak of her one lone fighting mast streamed the
homeward-bound pennant—a prodigious, sinuous thing of red,
white and blue, greater by far than her own length and in fact
and fitness the greatest pennant in the world. Four hundred and
twenty feet, if twisted, out from the masthead, while the ship
whose home-coming it symbolized measured less by nearly a
hundred feet.

With the huge thirteen-inch muzzles projecting from the for'ar
[sic] turret like the uncovered fangs of a vicious bulldog, she
barked the requisite thirteen times to the Admiral's flag on the
Iowa, received the return, and passed on. At her heels, like petty
terriers, scrambled launches and tugs galore and from the shore,
gayly decorated from stem to stern, hurried the *Governor Markham* with General Warfield and party aboard, and best of all,
the wives and daughters of a number of the officers whose task
it is to direct this mighty projectile across the face of the as-
tonished sea.

Well past the *Iowa* and *Philadelphia*, with sea room in plenty
for her bulk, she swung to the right, and her long white side,
flung full in the face of the westering sun, burst suddenly into
dazzling brightness. But the grimness still remaining. Fang after
fang was exposed till she fairly bristled with teeth which have
tasted.

In truth, one tingled at the sight, and the hot blood rushed
backward through all the generations of culture and civilization
to things primordial and naked. And in truth, those who rise by
the sword, perish by the sword. And still in truth, be it remembered, those who have risen by the sword, and foresworn the
sword, none the less have perished by the sword. It was a
righteous tingle, a righteous back, and the knowledge that such
a splendid fighting machine was ours, made by us, and fought
by us, was us—was a good knowledge. To-morrow?—Ah, yes,
to-morrow, when the lion shall lie down with the lamb, we shall
beat our *Oregons* into automobiles and electric railways; but to-
day it were well that we look to our *Oregons* and see that they
be many and efficient.

Swung full around, with nose to sea and tide and sun and
wind, the great anchor leaped into the bay and clenched its stout

grip on the muddy bottom. The *Oregon* was home! Home, and here at rest on the very spot which saw her formed and launched and christened. Home, after 55,000 miles of faring and fighting across the zones, from California to the Horn and from the Antilles to the East Indies.

Who has forgotten that record-breaking trip of hers down by Callao and Magellan, up the Atlantic past Rio Janeiro [sic] and the Barbadoes, up, up, and in time enough to intimidate the *Cristóbal Colón* at Santiago with her thirteen-inch guns? Such a distance, at such a pace, for a battleship, was a thing unheard of, and the world watched and wondered, while the naval experts of all the Powers shook their heads gloomily. Well may Swinburne sing, "Praise unto man in the highest, for he is the maker of things," and well may we sing, we who made this thing, this *Oregon!*

Once aboard, and well lost in her immensity, I looked me about for heroes, specimens rightly and highly prized of the genus homo. And I found them. I chanced upon them in all manner of places, in strange subterranean passages, on open windy places, between the muzzles of frowning guns and precipitous walls of armor, and in the bellies of steel turrets where one felt walled in from all the world.

And right here I wish to revise my conception of heroes. Forwardness, braggadocio, strut and puff? Not a bit of it. And hard it was to realize that these quiet, soft-spoken men had seen life and done deeds and lived romances. Modest they were, and backward; generous of praise to others but hesitating at self-mention, as though it were self-accusation of some monstrous villainy.

I chanced upon one, Murphy—J. E. Murphy—boatswain's mate. Strong, well-built, with cool-looking eyes and the smile of a maid, the flush of health was on his cheeks and the bronze of sunbeat and weather tan. He was limping cruelly from an accident received at his post of duty at Honolulu and his head was badly gashed. While superintending the letting go of one of the *Oregon's* anchors, the cable parted and as he leaped for his life to clear it the flying links struck him on the foot, spun him heels over in the air and hurled him to the deck, nearly fracturing his skull. A crippled home-coming for the wedding he looks forward to.

But bravely he takes it—as bravely as when a like thing happened him on the collier *Merrimac* one dark night in Santiago channel.

"I was on the *Iowa*," he said, "when the call came for volunteers for Hobson's expedition." On pressing, he reluctantly admitted that he was the only one chosen out of the 250 men in the crew of the *Iowa*.

go the bow-anchor and of setting off the for'ard [sic] mine. I went on, in a low, pleasant voice, "where I had charge of letting go the bow-anchor and of setting off the for'ard [sic] mine. I could never quite make out what did it," he mused, "whether it was the mine or a Spanish shell."

"What? Did what?"

"Oh, when I got the signal—"

Then I threw up my hands in despair and he saw that he would have to come down to sordid details.

"Well," he began again, this time somewhat defiantly, as though it were a nasty job, and he might as well go through with it— "Well, when we were a quarter of a mile away from the entrance, each mother's son of us as naked and silent as sin, the Spaniards opened fire. And they kept it up, too. As we neared, the *Merrimac* began to give off and Hobson called to the man at the helm 'to port.'

"'Port! Hard a-port!' he cried, the second time. 'Hard a-port she is, sir,' the man answered. And the *Merrimac* still refused to answer. You see, the Spaniards had shot the rudder clean away.

"Then Hobson, from the bridge, pulled the signal rope fast to my arm three times—the signal to let go, and he meant it to swing the *Merrimac* around and into place by a last desperate effort. When I felt the jerks I let go with the anchor and brought together the two wires which made the contact for the mine."

"And?" I asked.

"Well, I don't know what it was, but just then I was lifted into the air and came down across the chains."

"It may have been the mine, but I think it was the explosion of a shell. Then I went aft and reported to Lieutenant Hobson."

"What did he say when he learned you were hurt?"

"O, he didn't know. I didn't think it worth while to report a little thing like that when the whole fleet and all the forts were blazing out at us at close range and our own boilers pierced and blowing up besides.

"There was nothing to do then but wait, so we all laid down under the superstructure. Hobson and Ganner Sherritt called the roll and we were all there except Kelly. We worried about him, but when he did come, in the dark, we drew our revolvers on him. With everything going to smash about us, he looked at us coolly and said, 'Bedad, an' how long is this going on? I thought the New York was firing blanks.'

"This raised a laugh and the next thing we know the *Merrimac* was standing on end, bow in the air. Then down it came and it kept on going down and I kept floating up on the hatch cover. Most of the men were drawn under by the suction, but they all came up and collected around the catamaran, which had turned bottom up.

"When Admiral Cervera came out on the launch and picked us up, he congratulated us upon our marksmanship. You see," Boatswain Murphy explained with a twinkle in his eye, "the Dons had been firing into each other and thinking it was us. That is all, I believe"—he paused a moment to consider—"except that the Spanish papers published full accounts of a United States battleship and 250 men destroyed."

Then I fell in with a lot of gay young cubs who, while not "heroes," had all the making of heroes, given only the chance; and certainly to look at them they ached for the chance. And gay they were, with health-flushed faces and full of vitality, the free roll and large airs of the sea in their carriage. But little satisfaction did they give, and little could be expected of time-expired men in a home port and gazing at San Francisco on her many hills. Life was fresh and joyous; there was a pay day at hand, and they were drunk with sheer delight.

"What speed did the *Oregon* make when she chased the *Colón?*"

"Sixteen and one-half knots."

"Ah, gwan! Seventeen!"

"Don't I know?—17:2'!"

"Seventeen? Seventy-five by the log."

General laugh, after which a merry-eyed fellow pipes up, "That will be all right when Scott fixes it."

Another huge open-air laugh.

"That's what Murphy said when he broke his leg!"

"And Captain Dickens when we went on the rocks in Pechili!"

So, I gave them up and departed into a turret, where I found a pearl beyond price—J. R. Rose, a native son and a captain of a six-inch gun at the battle of Santiago. And if ever a man were cursed with two attractions which prevented him telling a good story, why that man was J. R. Rose, gunner's mate. The first was that he was home. At Newark, just over the bay, were his people and all his children's scenes. This was God's country and the fleshpots of old times did not compare.

And the second was the *Oregon*. Never was there such a ship! For soundness, durability and efficiency she had no equal. Nothing ever broke, nothing ever went wrong with her. She was a marvel of perfection! Even the rocks of Pechili only temporarily embarrassed her.

And that was not her fault. And just look how she had stood it! "Scott will fix it?" he demanded, ironically. "There's nothing for Scott to fix." And as for speed, just look at her record.

However, he was in the battle of Santiago. *Oregon* fired the first shot. Gunner O'Shea did it. Yes, everybody was glad when they knew the battle was on. There was some cheering, and every gun was ready for action before the Spaniards were fully out of the harbor. They came out with their big No. 1 Flags flying—a beautiful sight. A calm, bright day, the water like a mill pond. And then—why, then the Americans proceeded to batter them to pieces, to sink them and to pile them up on the rocks. That was the way it was. Yes, he felt somewhat exhilarated when he went into action, then he settled down to the work, and it was for all the world like target practice. Ah! but the *Oregon!* Of the whole American fleet she displayed the fastest speed, and three shots from her big thirteen-inch guns were sufficient to frighten the *Colón* onto the rocks.

"'Bully boy,' is what Commodore Schley said, when he passed the *Oregon* in his gig," were the last words of J. R. Rose, native son and gunner's mate, as I crawled out of the turret; and I doubt not he is sitting there yet, full of the delight of being home and descanting upon the virtues of the *Oregon*.

THE ROAD

According to London's Magazine Sales No. 1, this article was first submitted to the San Francisco Examiner in 1897 before London went to the Yukon. It is probably one of his earliest attempts in journalistic writing.

The Magazine Sales entry continues to read:

> sent to
> San Francisco Chronicle   Mar. 19/99
> The American Press Association   Mar. 24/99
> New York World   April 12/99
> Arena   April 25/99
> Arena offered $10 in subscriptions and $10 cash in publication and one dozen copies of number in which published.
> returned ms.   Mar. 1900
>   with note "unavailable under amended policies of new owners"

The article was never printed. The version printed here was taken from London's original manuscript.

However, London did publish, under the title of The Road,[1] a number of articles which he referred to as "tramping experiences." He published an article called "The Tramp" in the Wilshire Magazine, February–March 1904. All the articles in The Road were serialized by Cosmopolitan between May 1907 and March 1908.

Among the letters written to London is a vitriolic attack upon him for publishing such articles for the American boy to read which the writer said destroyed the image of the boys' ideal of Jack London.

The "Road," the hog-train, or for brevity's sake, the hog: It is a realm almost as unexplored as fairyland, yet hardly as impregnable. Nay, in fact, destiny not only entices but forces world-weary mortals into its embrace. It entices romantic and unruly boys, who venture along its dangerous ways in search of fortune or in rash attempt to escape parental discipline. It seizes with relentless grip the unfortunate who drifts with, or struggles against the tide of human affairs. Those who cannot go whither must come thither, all hope behind. It is the river of oblivion, of which the soul-wanderer, shuddering with coward's

[1] Jack London, *The Road*, The Macmillan Company, New York: 1907, 224 pages.

heart (or religious scruple) at self destruction, must drink. Henceforth all identity is lost. Though with many aliases, not even the semi-respectable number of the convict is his. He has but one designation; they all have it:—Tramp. But the law aids him, however, if reputation grows with syllables, for under it he is known as vagrant. Yet herein is a double injustice done. While all tramps are vagrant, all vagrants are not tramps: Many are worse, a thousand times worse than the tramp. And again, the small bit of respectability which may yet linger about his former name is destroyed. He is a vagrant: It is shortened to "Vag." Three letters, two consonants and a vowel, stand between him and the negation of being. He is on the ragged edge of nonentity.

We all know the tramp—that is, we have seen him and talked with him. And what an eyesore he has always been! Perhaps, when hurrying home through the rainy night, all comfortable in mackintosh, umbrella and overshoes, he has dawned upon us like a comet, malignant of aspect. Wet, shivering, and miserable, whining for the price of a bed or a meal, he casts his baleful influence over us: Nor can hastily given largesse or abrupt refusal overcome it. Our comfort seems out of place, actually jars upon us. We are thrown out of our good humor and rudely awakened from the anticipatory dream we have dreamed all day at the office—the snug little home, all cheery, bright and warm; the smiling wife and her affectionate greeting; the laughing children, or perhaps the one little crowing tot, the son and heir. We have met him [the tramp] in the park, always occupying the best benches; on the overland and summer excursions; at the springs and at the seaside: In short, we have met him everywhere, even desecrating the sanctity of our back stoop, where he ate of the crumbs of our table. Still, his land is an unknown region, and we are less conversant with his habits and thoughts than with those of the inhabitants of the Cannibal Islands.

One astonishing thing about Trampland is its population. Variously estimated by equally competent authorities at from 500,000 to 1,500,000 it will be found that 1,000,000 is not far out of the way. A million! It seems impossible, yet is a fact. If a Stanley may be lost in Africa, cannot such a number be lost in the United States? This is rendered easy because of the breadth of country and the evenness of their distribution. Every

town, village, railroad station, watering-tank and siding, has its
proportion; in the great metropolises their numbers mount into
the tens of thousands; while each county and city jail has its
due quota, supported by the taxpayer. It is only when concentrated
that their abundance is manifested. One example will suffice. On
a rainy morning in the spring of '94, an army of then, 2,000
strong, marched out of Council Bluffs. They had, as an organization, already traveled two thousand miles and their numbers
were augmenting at every step. At their head rode their leader
on a handsome black charger, presented him by an enthusiastic
farmer. They were marshalled in divisions and companies and
had staff officers, couriers, aid-de-campes [sic], buglers, banner-
bearers, army physicians and fully equipped medical department, a fife and drum corps, a healthy strong-box, an efficient
police service, a commissary, and above all, the best of discipline.
The stationary Negro population is often called the incubus of
the South; but is not this increasing, shifting, tramp population, not passive like the Negro but full of the indomitability
of the Teuton, equally worthy of consideration, and by the whole
race?

Strange as it may seem, in this outcast world the sharp lines
of caste are as rigorously drawn as in the world from which it
has evolved. There are several prominent divisions. The Simon-
pure tramp, hence professional, calls himself "The Profesh." He
is not the one we meet with so profusely in *Judge* or *Puck*.
The only resemblance lies in that he never works. He does not
carry a tomato-can on a string, wear long hair, or manifest his
calling in his dress. His clothes are almost always good, never
threadbare, torn, and dirty. In fact, with him, the comb, cake of
soap, looking-glass and clothes brush are indispensables. He lives
better and more easily than the average workingman. Having
reduced begging to a fine art, he scorns back stoops and kitchen
tables, patronizes the restaurant, and always has the price of the
drinks about him. His is the class most to be feared. Many
of them have "done time" and are capable and worthy of doing
more. They will commit, under stress of circumstance and favorable opportunity, every crime on the calendar, and then, just a
few more besides. Perhaps the simile is unjust, but they are
looked up to as the aristocracy of their underworld.

The largest class is that of the working tramp. That is, the tramp who looks for work and is not afraid of it when he finds it. He usually carries his blankets and is somewhat akin to his more respectable Australian compatriot, who strikes off into the "bush" with his "swag" and "billy-can." Because of his predilection to carrying his bed with him, he is known in trampland as the "bindle stiff." The etymology of this phrase is simple: Any tramp is a "stiff," and the blanket in a bundle is a "bindle." These are the men, who, in New York, travel into the Genesee country to the hops; in the Dakotas, to the harvests; in Michigan, to the berry-picking; and in California, to the vintage, hops and harvest.

The "Stew Bum" is the most despised of his kind. He is the *Canaille*, the *Sansculotte*, the fourth estate of trampland. Of such stuff are squawmen made. It is he who is the prototype of the individual aforementioned, who graces the pages of our humorous periodicals. He is not supremely wicked nor degraded: deep-sunk in a state of languorous lassitude, he passively exists, viewing the active world with philosophic soul. His one ambition, one dream, one ideal is stew: Hence his only evil trait—an electric affinity which always draws him and chicken roosts into close conjunction.

A curious class, closely connected in career with the Chinatown bum who drinks cheap gin and fills an early grave, is that of the "Alki Stiffs." "Alki" is the argot for alcohol. They travel in gangs and are a close approach to communists,[2] only differing in that they have no community of goods. The reason for this is simple: They have no goods. But the ideal commune could not vie with them in a community of drink. Every penny, begged or stolen, goes to the purchase of their fiery beverage, of which all may drink. The finest mixer of the "cocktail route" cannot approach them in the art of diluting alcohol with water. Too much water and it is spoiled: Too little, and they are spoiled, for then and there is much devastation done to the linings of their stomachs. Masters there are among them, but they have seldom served a long apprenticeship: Death comes too soon for that. In the world, when a man falls, he takes to drink: In trampland, to the

[2] London is not using this word in its current sense.

"white line," as they tritely call it. Somehow, one never meets a gang of these poor devils lying in the grass and wild flowers of the country wayside, sleeping and drowsing in the depths of debauch, without being reminded of Tennyson's *Lotus Eaters*, who swore and kept an oath:—

> In the hollow lotus-land to live and lie reclined
> On the hills like gods together, careless of mankind.

The cripples, usually traveling in pairs, often are to be met with in gangs of twenty or more. A universal custom with such groups is to have two or three of the most brutal of the "profesh" as body guards. These fight their battles, run their errands, handle their money, and take care of them when they are drunk. In return, these mercenaries are given their meal and drink money. It is amusing to witness the meeting of two stranger cripples. Each will solicitously enquire as to how the other lost his limb. Then will follow a detailed account of its amputation, with criticism of the surgeons who officiated and their methods, the conversation usually terminating with an adjournment to some secluded spot, where, with all the fondness of paternal affection, they compare stumps. One touch of amputation makes all cripples kin.

Then there is a transient class, a sort of general miscellany, composed of all kinds of men temporarily down in their luck. Among these, the most interesting character studies may be made. Strikingly diverse and powerful individualities are here found, all bound in a mesh of pathos and ludicrity [sic]. Most of them are men whose money has given out and who are forced to make their way home as best they can. Farmer boys, turning their backs on the city; city-bred men, turning away from the country; men who have been fleeced and are too proud to write or wire for help; others, fleeing from justice; some who have been indiscreet; many who have tried to cut too brilliant a dash; broken down actors, sports and tinhorns; and even some (a small percentage) who, parsimoniously inclined, wish to save their railroad fare. Nearly all of them are possessed of a little money and furnish rich plucking to mean railroad men and the "profesh." They are to be known at a glance. Their ignorance of the customs and unwritten rules of the "road" paint their green-ness as vividly as does the unsophistication and lack of conventionality of our friend the "hayseed," when he comes to town. They are wanderers in a strange land and the scrapes and pitfalls they stumble into, are laughable yet often tragic.

Another division, which is merely a sub-class and closely allied to the "profesh," is that of the "Fakirs." There are tinkers, umbrella menders, locksmiths, tattooers, tooth-pullers, quack doctors, corn doctors, horse doctors—in short, a lengthy list. Some sell trinkets and gew gaws and others, "fakes." These "fakes" are as curious and interesting as they are innumerable. We all remember the Frenchman who made flea powder out of pulverized brick—this is the nature of the "fake." Here is a sample, as simple as it is successful:— The prudent housewife meets at the door a glib young individual, who shows her a piece of tin, so closely perforated with tiny holes that it is almost a gauze. He gives a rambling a very impressive disquisition on the principles of the kerosene lamp, then explains that this tin, fitted to the top of the wick, will give twice the flame, burn less oil, and never burn the wick which will thus last forever. He even volunteers to attach it to her oldest lamp and if she be not convinced it costs her nothing; if convinced, only fifteen cents. She brings from some top shelf an old lamp, long since fallen into disuse. Very business-like, he produces pinchers and snippers and sets to work, volubly chattering all the while. Examining the ancient burner and deftly opening the clogged flues and air vents, he attaches his tin. Then he lights it and the admiring housewife beholds a flame, larger and more luminous than that of her best parlor lamp. After receiving his fifteen cents, he advises her to give it a trial for that night and promises to call next day. He duplicates this operation in the whole neighborhood. In the evening, the wondrous flame is the center of interest in the family circle—"So saving! And so cheap! Father, we must have them on all the lamps." Next day the young man reappears and puts his little "fake" on every burner in the house. He receives anywhere from fifty cents to a dollar for a couple of cents worth of low grade tin, and vanishes for ever, as Carlyle would say, "Into outer darkness." But O, 'tis passing fair! Two days suffice: The tin drops off.

Saddest of all, is the training school of the "Road." Man,

vicious and corrupt, the incarnation of all that is vile and loathsome, is a melancholy object; but how much more, is innocent youth, rapidly becoming so! Modification by environment— O pregnant term! In it lies all the misery and all the joy of mankind, all the purest and all the most degraded soul-developments, all the noblest and foulest attributes and deeds. Man, blindly-groping, with weak, finite conception, personifies these antitheses in the powers of light and darkness: Yet, even to man, poor earthworm, is given the power to qualify these personifications of his, through *modification by environment*. Still, we, Americans, and partakers of the science and culture of our tremendous civilization, cognizant of all this, allow in our midst the annual prostitution of tens of thousands of souls. Boy tramps or "Road-kids" abound in our land. They are children, embryonic souls—the most plastic of fabrics. Flung into existence, ready to tear aside the veil of the future; with the mighty pulse of dawning twentieth century throbbing about him; with the culminated forces of the thousand dead and the one living civilization effervescing in the huge world-caldron; they are cast out, by the cruel society which gave them birth, into a nether world of outlawry and darkness.

But to the "Road-kids." Many are run-aways, who, through romantic dreaming or undue harshness, have left comfortable homes for the stern vicissitudes of tramp life. The romantic always return, but of those who have been cruelly treated, virtually none. These cases may be sad, but there is still a second division —the children, begotten of ignorance, poverty and sin. Uncultivated, with no helping hand to guide their faltering footsteps, with the brand of Cain upon their brows, they raise their moan in silent brute-anguish to a cold world and drift into trampland, the scapegoats of their generation. To become what? "Alki Stiffs" and "Stew Bums"? Perhaps; but almost always to become of the "Profesh" the most professional. Inscrutable scheme of life! Cast out and scourged by society, their mother, they return, the scourge of their mother, society. We have all wept for little Oliver Twist; nor have we failed to reserve a copious draught for Nancy Sykes [sic]—she was a woman; but the artful dodger, who weeps for him?[3] Yet his is the saddest of all.

[3] Characters in Dickens' novel *Oliver Twist*.

Though sometimes journeying in gangs, they often travel with members of the "Profesh." A gang of them, composed of the more intrepid and vicious, is a terrible thing to meet. They are wolves in human guise. Besides committing all sorts of sly and petty depredations, they hunt higher game. "Rolling a stiff," as they call robbing a drunken man, is a mere pastime; but they do not refrain from attacking sober ones. Like wolves, they fly at the throat, giving what is known as the "strong arm." This is applied from behind, the large bone of the wrist and the victim's windpipe coming into painful and dangerous juxtaposition. Those who travel with the "Profesh" are serving their criminal apprenticeship. They are very useful, and in some crimes even indispensable. It is a hard school and they learn rapidly, soon finding the proper field for the exercise of their peculiar talents. The faithfulness of the "Road-kids" for their teachers or "pals" and vice versa, is often pathetic. The self-sacrifice, hardship and punishment they will undergo for each other, is astonishing— a sure index to the latent nobility of soul which lurks within, dwarfed instead of developed. Poor devils! With the hand of society raised against them, it is the only opening through which the shrunken higher parts of their nature may be manifested.

Clothing, eating, and sleeping are not so difficult to obtain in trampland; but of the three, a comfortable place to sleep is the hardest. In the cities and large towns, a goodly portion buy their meals with money begged on the street. Others, not so bold, go from house to house, "slamming gates," as they picturesquely describe it. When at a back door, eatables are given them wrapped in paper, they call it a "poke-out" or "hand-out." This is not prized so highly as a "set-down" (going into the kitchen). Above all the tramp likes his "java" (coffee). Especially in the morning after a cold night, they, all-benumbed, prefer it to all the "hand-outs" in Christendom. As to clothes: Some, being lazy, wait till their very delapidation calls forth a voluntary contribution of cast-off garments; others, possessed with energy and love of neatness, ask for them whenever necessary. Nay, the "Profesh" make many a pretty penny on clothes thus obtained, which they sell to workingmen and Jews.

When out on the "Road," away from cities, the "Profesh" can always be told by their manner of sleeping. Realizing the worth of a good "front" (appearance), it behooves them to take good care of their apparel, so they have recourse to the newspaper blanket: Wherever they may select to sleep, they spread a newspaper or two on which to lie. Sleeping on the "road" in cold weather, the "Bindle Stiff" is the only comfortable tramp. The "Profesh," "Alki Stiffs," "Road-kids," etc. scorn carrying a "bindle" and needs must pay the consequence. But if a warm nook is to be had, trust them to find it. A favorite trick is their method of utilizing a refrigerator car. The walls of such a car are a foot thick, the doors fasten hermetically, and there is little or no ventilation. Once inside with the door closed, they make a bonfire of newspapers. As the heat cannot escape, they sleep comfortably, and in the morning when they open the door, the inner is much warmer than the outer atmosphere.

The circulation of this great mass of human beings is an interesting phenomenon with which few of the upper world are conversant. Every spring the slums of the cities, the jails, poor houses, hospitals—the holes and dens in which the winter has been spent—give up their denizens who take to the "Road." This is the flux. All summer they wander, covering thousands upon thousands of miles, and with fall, crawl back to their holes and dens again—the ebb. Many blow whither they listeth: Many have definite plans. For instance, a tramp winters in New York City; starts out in the spring and travels to the north and west among the mining states; in the fall, goes south to Florida for the winter. Next summer finds him in Canada and the following winter in California. A third summer's wandering through the west and south, concludes with the warm weather of Mexico, where he laughs at winter terrors. This ebb and flow is also noticeable in the rushes to the great catastrophes, such as the Johnstown flood, the Charleston earthquake, the Chicago fire, and the St. Louis cyclone. There is also the periodical rush to the harvests and to the great fairs. At these places, for the "Profesh," is to be found rich loot; for the laboring tramp, work. Most pathetic is the return of the "Bindle Stiffs" from the harvest. They journey up into the Dakotas, and even into Manitoba, by the thousands, paying the brakemen half a dollar a division for the privilege of riding in empty box cars. They are essentially honest, hard-working laborers. All through the harvest they toil from dawn till dark, and at the season's close, are possessed of from one to three hundred dollars. They return in the same manner; but now they encounter the "Profesh," veritable beasts of the jungle. Perhaps half a dozen of them, having tipped the trainmen, are in a box car. Enter one or two "Profesh," who, at the pistol point, rob them of their year's wages. In the good old times, a single "Profesh" has often returned from three weeks of such work with two or three thousand dollars. This form of robbery is still perpetrated, but more rarely and with less remuneration. The resident population has increased, and fewer "Bindle Stiffs" are needed; while those who do earn money, usually send it back by mail or Wells Fargo.

Their *argot* is peculiar study. While in some instances it resembles that of "Chimmie Fadden," in most, it is widely different. Truly has Hugo said of *argot*, "Each accursed race has deposited its stratum, each suffering has dropped its stone, each heart has given its pebble." The sources of much are easily to be traced. *Kibosh* means utter discomfiture, from the Chinook; *galway*—priest—from the Gaelic; *bobbie*—policeman—transplanted from Cockney *argot*; *monica*—cognomen—a distorted version, both in form and meaning, of monogram; *star-route*—a "side jump" away from railroads—can be traced to the asterisks which denote Pony Express stations, and to steering and traveling by the heavenly constellations, when from the latter it is usually called a *star-light*. *Sou-markee* is a distorted combination from two root languages. It is a hyperbolical synonym for the smallest absolute coin and is used thus:— I haven't a *sou-markee*. The derivation is obvious. *Pounding the ear* means to sleep; *gondola*, flat car; *pogy*, poor house; *jerk*, a branch road or one little traveled; *glam*, steal; *gat*, gun; *shiv*, knife; *faune*, false; *crimpy*, cold; *dorse* or *kip*, to sleep; *queens*, women; *punk* or *dummy*, bread. One may understand the ordinary tramp, but it is often impossible to even comprehend the very "Profesh." Attempt to translate this:— *De stem? Nit! Yaeggin's on the sugar train. Hit a fly on the main-drag for a light piece; de bull snared me; got a t'ree hour blin'.* Here is a free version:— The street for begging? It is worthless. On the main street I begged a policeman in citizen's clothes for a small sum, but he (fly) (bull) (policeman) arrested me and the judge gave me three hours in which to leave town.

The tramp problem opens a vast field for study. In our high civilization it is a phenomenon, unique and paradoxical. Cause and cure have received countless explanations; but of one thing we must all be certain; and that, that work is not to be had for them. If they were annihilated, our industries would not suffer—nay, our army of unemployed would still be so large that wages would not rise. Capital being crystallized labor, it is axiomatic that labor produces more than it consumes. Hence, many must be idle; and, since through invention the efficiency of labor is constantly increasing, so must this army of idlers increase—of course, fluctuating as trade fluctuates. Is this true or is it not? Can the tramp be abolished or can he not? Is he an attendant evil on our civilization in certain stages of development or a permanent one? This is the problem: Is it to be solved?

HOUSEKEEPING IN THE KLONDIKE[1]

Jack London left San Francisco by boat on July 25, 1897.[2] According to an unfinished diary, apparently written by a man from Santa Rosa, there were five in the company including Jack London, Mr. Shepard[3] (husband of London's sister, Eliza), Merritt Sloper, Jim Goodman, and the writer. The diary ends abruptly on Monday, October 18, 1897. We know, however, that London and some other prospectors wintered in a cabin in the area of Henderson Creek near the Stewart River. In the Juneau Alaska Empire, *Sunday, November 7, 1965, Dick North of the Alaska-Yukon News Service published an article concerning a cabin believed to be the one in which London lived during the winter of 1897 and 1898. Quoting North, the "cabin was approximately 13 feet by 13 feet. Found inside were a pancake griddle, Yukon Stove, a can of Hopps' gun oil and a shovel. The cabin is located approximately eight miles up the left fork of Henderson Creek and 75 miles from Dawson City." At any rate, London knew firsthand the problems of housekeeping in the Klondike.*

He rarely attempted humorous or facetious articles and when he

[1] *Harper's Bazaar*, September 15, 1900.
[2] According to the diary, the cost of transportation from San Francisco to Juneau, Alaska, "for meals and sleeping accommodations," was twenty-five dollars.
[3] Mr. Shepard returned to Oakland in August because of rheumatism.

did was not often successful in finding publication. Apparently this article was written sometime during the summer of 1899 and probably as a potboiler. While he received what was a fair amount for it at that time, he never included it in any of his collected works.

He also wrote other articles concerning the Klondike including "Economics of the Klondike" published in Review of Reviews, *January 1900; "Thanksgiving on Slav Creek" in* Harper's Bazaar, *November 24, 1900; and some that have not yet been published.*

Housekeeping in the Klondike—that's bad! And by *men*—worse. Reverse the proposition, if you will, yet you will fail to mitigate, even by a hair's-breadth, the woe of it. It is bad, unutterably bad, for a man to keep house, and it is equally bad to keep house in the Klondike. That's the sum and substance of it. Of course men will be men, and especially is this true of the kind who wander off to the frozen rim of the world. The glitter of gold is in their eyes, they are borne along by uplifting ambition, and in their hearts is a great disdain for everything in the culinary department save "grub." "Just so long as it's grub," they say, coming in off trail, gaunt and ravenous, "grub, and piping hot." Nor do they manifest the slightest regard for the genesis of the same; they prefer to begin at "revelations."

Yes, it would seem a pleasant task to cook for such men; but just let them lie around cabin to rest up for a week, and see with what celerity they grow high-stomached and make sarcastic comments on the way you fry the bacon or boil the coffee. And behold how each will spring his own strange and marvelous theory as to how sour-dough bread should be mixed and baked. Each has his own recipe (formulated, mark you, from personal experience only), and to him it is an idol of brass, like unto no other man's, and he'll fight for it—ay, down to the last wee pinch of soda—and if need be, die for it. If you should happen to catch him on trail, completely exhausted, you may blacken his character, his flag, and his ancestral tree with impunity; but breathe the slightest whisper against his sour-dough bread, and he will turn upon and rend you.

From this it may be gathered what an unstable thing sour dough is. Never was coquette so fickle. You cannot depend upon it. Still, it is the simplest thing in the world. Make a batter and place it near the stove (that it may not freeze) till it ferments or sours. Then mix the dough with it, and sweeten with soda to taste—of course replenishing the batter for next time. There it is. Was there ever anything simpler? But, oh, the tribulations of the cook! It is never twice the same. If the batter could only be placed away in an equable temperature, all well and good. If one's comrades did not interfere, much vexation of spirit might be avoided. But this cannot be; for Tom fires up the stove till the cabin is become like the hot-room of a Turkish bath; Dick forgets all about the fire till the place is a refrigerator; then along comes Harry and shoves the sour-dough bucket right against the stove to make way for the drying of his mittens. Now heat is a most potent factor in accelerating the fermentation of flour and water, and hence the unfortunate cook is constantly in disgrace with Tom, Dick, and Harry. Last week his bread was yellow from a plethora of soda; this week it is sour from a prudent lack of the same; and next week—ah, who can tell save the god of the fire-box?

Some cooks aver they have so cultivated their olfactory organs that they can tell to the fraction of a degree just how sour the batter is. Nevertheless they have never been known to bake two batches of bread which were at all alike. But this fact casts not the slightest shadow upon the infallibility of their theory. One and all, they take advantage of circumstances, and meanly crawl out by laying the blame upon the soda, which was dampened "the time the canoe overturned," or upon the flour, which they got in trade from "that half-breed fellow with the dogs."

The pride of the Klondike cook in his bread is something which passes understanding. The highest commendatory degree which can be passed upon a man in that country, and the one which distinguishes him from the tenderfoot, is that of being a "sour-dough boy." Never was a college graduate prouder of his "sheepskin" than the old-timer of this appellation. There is a certain distinction about it, from which the newcomer is invidiously excluded. A tenderfoot with his baking-powder is an inferior creature, a freshman; but a "sour-dough boy" is a man of stability, a post-graduate in that art of arts—bread-making.

Next to bread a Klondike cook strives to achieve distinction by his doughnuts. This may appear frivolous at first glance, and at second, considering the materials with which he works, an impossible feat. But doughnuts are all-important to the man who goes on trail for a journey of any length. Bread freezes easily, and there is less grease and sugar, and hence less heat in it, than in doughnuts. The latter do not solidify except at extremely low temperatures, and they are very handy to carry in the pockets of a Mackinaw jacket and munch as one travels along. They are made much after the manner of their brethren in warmer climes, with the exception that they are cooked in bacon grease—the more grease, the better they are. Sugar is the cook's chief stumbling-block; if it is very scarce, why, add more grease. The men never mind—on trail. In the cabin?—well, that's another matter; besides, bread is good enough for them then.

The cold, the silence, and the darkness somehow seem to be considered the chief woes of the Klondiker. But this is all wrong. There is one woe which overshadows all others—the lack of sugar. Every party which goes north signifies a manly intention to do without sugar, and after it gets there bemoans itself upon its lack of foresight. Man can endure hardship and horror with equanimity, but take from him his sugar, and he raises his lamentations to the stars. And the worst of it is that it all falls back upon the long-suffering cook. Naturally, coffee, and mush, and dried fruit, and rice, eaten without sugar, do not taste exactly as they should. A certain appeal to the palate is missing. Then the cook is blamed for his vile concoctions. Yet, if he be a man of wisdom, he may judiciously escape the major part of this injustice. When he places a pot of mush upon the table, let him see to it that it is accompanied by a pot of stewed dried apples or peaches. This propinquity will suggest the combination to the men, and the flatness of the one will be neutralized by the sharpness of the other. In the distress of a sugar famine, if he be a cook of parts, he will boil rice and fruit together in one pot; and if he cook a dish of rice and prunes properly, of a verity he will cheer up the most melancholy member of the party, and extract from him great gratitude.

Such a cook must indeed be a man of resources. Should his comrades cry out that vinegar be placed upon the beans, and there is no vinegar, he must know how to make it out of water, dried apples, and brown paper. He obtains the last from the bacon-wrappings, and it is usually saturated with grease. But that does not matter. He will early learn that in a land of low temperatures it is impossible for bacon grease to spoil anything. It is to the white man what blubber and seal oil are to the Eskimo. Soul-winning gravies may be made from it by the addition of water and browned flour over the fire. Some cooks base far-reaching fame solely upon their gravy, and their names come to be on the lips of men wherever they forgather at the feast. When the candles give out, the cook fills a sardine-can with bacon grease, manufactures a wick out of the carpenter's sail-twine, and behold! the slush-lamp stands complete. It goes by another and less complimentary name in the vernacular, and, next to sour-dough bread, is responsible for more men's souls than any other single cause of degeneracy in the Klondike.

The ideal cook should also possess a Semitic incline to his soul. Initiative in his art is not the only requisite; he must keep an eye upon the variety of his larder. He must "swap" grub with the gentile understandingly; and woe unto him should the balance of trade be against him. His comrades will thrust it into his teeth every time the bacon is done over the turn, and they will even rouse him from his sleep to remind him of it. For instance, previous to the men going out for a trip on trail, he cooks several gallons of beans in the company of numerous chunks of salt pork and much bacon grease. This mess he then molds into blocks of convenient size and places on the roof, where it freezes into bricks in a couple of hours. Thus the men, after a weary day's travel, have but to chop off chunks with an axe and thaw out in the frying-pan. Now the chances preponderate against more than one party in ten having chili-peppers in their outfits. But the cook, supposing him to be fitted for his position, will ferret out that one party, discover some particular shortage in its grub-supply of which he has plenty, and swap the same for chili-peppers. These in turn he will incorporate in the mess aforementioned, and behond a dish which even the hungry arctic gods may envy. Variety in the grub is as welcome to the men as nuggets. When, after eating dried peaches for months, the cook trades a few cupfuls of the same for apricots, the future at once takes on a more roseate hue. Even a change in the brand of bacon will revivify blasted faith in the country.

It is no sinecure, being cook in the Klondike. Often he must do his work in a cabin measuring ten by twelve on the inside, and occupied by three other men besides himself. When it is considered that these men eat, sleep, lounge, smoke, play cards, and entertain visitors there, and also in that small space house the bulk of their possessions, the size of the cook's orbit may be readily computed. In the morning he sits up in bed, reaches out and strikes the fire, then proceeds to dress. After that the centre of his orbit is the front of the stove, the diameter the length of his arms. Even then his comrades are continually encroaching upon his domain, and he is at constant warfare to prevent territorial grabs. If the men are working hard on the claim, the cook is also expected to find his own wood and water. The former he chops up and sleds into camp, the latter he brings home in a sack—unless he is unusually diligent, in which case he has a ton or so of water piled up before the door. Whenever he is not cooking, he is thawing out ice, and between whiles running out and hoisting on the windlass for his comrades in the shaft. The care of the dogs also devolves upon him, and he carries his life and a long club in his hand every time he feeds them.

But there is one thing the cook does not have to do, nor any man in the Klondike—and that is, make another man's bed. In fact, the beds are never made except when the blankets become unfolded, or when the pine needles have all fallen off the boughs which form the mattress. When the cabin has a dirt floor and the men do their carpenter-work inside, the cook never sweeps it. It is much warmer to let the chips and shavings remain. Whenever he kindles a fire he uses a couple of handfuls of the floor. However, when the deposit becomes so deep that his head is knocking against the roof, he seizes a shovel and removes a foot or so of it.

Nor does he have any windows to wash; but if the carpenter is busy he must make his own windows. This is simple. He saws a hole out of the side of the cabin, inserts a home-made sash, and for panes falls back upon the treasured writing-tablet. A sheet of this paper, rubbed thoroughly with bacon grease, becomes transparent, sheds water when it thaws, and keeps the cold out and the heat in. In cold weather the ice will form upon the inside of it to the thickness of sometimes two or three inches.

When the bulb of the mercurial thermometer has frozen solid, the cook turns to his window, and by the thickness of the icy coating infallibly gauges the outer cold within a couple of degrees.

A certain knowledge of astronomy is required of the Klondike cook, for another task of his is to keep track of the time. Before going to bed he wanders outside and studies the heavens. Having located the Pole Star by means of the Great Bear, he inserts two slender wands in the snow, a couple of yards apart and in line with the North Star. The next day, when the sun on the southern horizon casts the shadows of the wands to the northward and in line, he knows it to be twelve o'clock, noon, and sets his watch and those of his partners accordingly. As stray dogs are constantly knocking his wands out of line with the North Star, it becomes his habit to verify them regularly every night, and thus another burden is laid upon him.

But, after all, while the woes of the man who keeps house and cooks food in the northland are innumerable, there is one redeeming feature in his lot which does not fall to the women housewives of other lands. When things come to a pass with his feminine prototype, she throws her apron over her head and has a good cry. Not so with him, being a man and a Klondiker. He merely cooks a little more atrociously, raises a storm of grumbling, and resigns. After that he takes up his free out-door life again, and exerts himself mightily in making life miserable for the unlucky comrade who takes his place in the management of the household destinies.

THE TERRIBLE AND TRAGIC IN FICTION[1]

London as a young man was interested in all types of writing. In letters between 1897 and 1905 to various friends he discusses different literary genres, including poetry, the novel, the short story, the essay, the drama, and literary criticism. At one time or another in his lifetime he published something in each one of these genres.

As early as October 1900 The Bookman *published "Phenomena of Literary Evolution."*

In 1901 he published, among other things, three book reviews:

[1] *The Critic,* June 1903. An illustrated monthly review of literature, art, and life. January 1881–September 1906.

"Maxim Gorky's Foma Gordyeeff," *"Frank Norris'* The Octopus," *and* "Edwin Markham's Lincoln and Other Poems." *For some reason, however, students of London have never seen him as a literary critic. To our knowledge, a thesis at Utah State University is the first study of this aspect of London's literary career.*[2]

Mrs. Price points out that London has been treated by critics as a novelist, short story writer, essayist, and journalist but never as a literary critic; this aspect she calls the Fifth Dimension.

> I am anxious that your firm should continue to be my publishers, and, if you would be willing to bring out the book, I should be glad to accept the terms which you allowed me before —that is, you receive all profits, and allow me twenty copies for distribution to friends.

So wrote Edgar Allan Poe, on August 13, 1841, to the publishing house of Lee & Blanchard. They replied:

> We very much regret to say that the state of affairs is such as to give little encouragement to new undertakings. . . . We assure you that we regret this on your account as well as our own, as it would give us great pleasure to promote your views in relation to publication.

Five years later, in 1846, Poe wrote to Mr. E. H. Duyckinck:

> For particular reasons I am anxious to have another volume of my tales published before the first of March. Do you think it possible to accomplish it for me? Would not Mr. Wiley give me, say $50, in full for the copyright of the collection I now send?

Measured by the earnings of contemporaneous writers, it is clear that Poe received little or nothing for the stories he wrote. In the autumn of 1900, one of the three extant copies of his "Tamerlane and Other Poems" sold for $2050—a sum greater, perhaps, than he received from the serial and book sales of all his stories and poems.*

On the one hand, he was more poorly rewarded than even the mediocre of his contemporaries; while, on the other hand, he

---

[2] Diane Price, *The Fifth Dimension: Jack London as a Literary Critic.* Utah State University, Logan, Utah, in preparation.

* The manuscript of "The Bells" was sold at auction in Philadelphia on May 6th last for $2100. At the same sale the first edition of "Al Aaraaf, Tamerlane, and Minor Poems" was sold for $1815—Ed. *Critic.*

produced a more powerful effect than the great majority of them and achieved a fame more brilliant and lasting.

Cooke, in a letter to Poe, says:

> "The Valdemar Case" I read in a number of your *Broadway Journal* last winter—as I lay in a Turkey blind, muffled to the eyes in overcoats, &c., and pronounce it without hesitation the most damnable, vraisemblable, horrible, hair-lifting, shocking, ingenious chapter of fiction that any brain ever conceived, or hands treated. That gelatinous, viscous sound of man's voice! there never was such an idea before. That story scared me in broad day, armed with a double-barrel Tyron Turkey gun. What would it have done at midnight in some old ghostly country-house?
>
> I have always found some one remarkable thing in your stories to haunt me long after reading them. The *teeth* of Berenice—the changing eyes of Morella—that red and glaring crack in the House of Usher—the pores of the deck in "The MS. Found in a Bottle"—the visible drops falling into the goblet in "Ligeia," &c.—there is always something of this sort to stick by the mind—by mine at least.

About this time Elizabeth Barrett Browning, then Miss Barrett, wrote to Poe:

> Your "Raven" has produced a sensation, a "fit horror," here in England. . . . I hear of persons haunted by the "Nevermore," and one acquaintance of mine who has the misfortune of possessing a "bust of Pallas" never can bear to look at it in the twilight. . . . Then there is a tale of yours . . . which is going the round of the newspapers, about mesmerism, throwing us all into "most admired disorder," and dreadful doubts as to whether "it can be true," as the children say of ghost stories. The certain thing in the tale in question is the power of the writer, and the faculty he has of making horrible improbabilities seem near and familiar.

Though his stories threw people into "most admired disorders" and scared men in broad day in "Turkey blinds," and though his stories were read, one might say, universally, there seemed at the time a feeling against them which condemned them as a class of stories eminently repulsive and unreadable. The public read Poe's stories, but Poe was not in touch with that public. And when that public spoke to him through the mouths of the magazine editors, it spoke in no uncertain terms; and, rebelliously aspiring, he dreamed of a magazine of his own—no "namby-pamby" magazine, filled with "contemptible pictures, fashion-plates, music, and love-tales," but a magazine which uttered the thing for the thing's sake and told a story because it was a story rather than a hodge-podge which the public might claim it liked.

James E. Heath, writing to Poe concerning the "Fall of the House of Usher," said:

> He [White, editor of the *Southern Literary Messenger*] doubts whether the readers of the *Messenger* have much relish for tales of the German School, although written with great power and ability, and in this opinion, I confess to you frankly, I am strongly inclined to concur. I doubt very much whether tales of the wild, improbable, and terrible class can ever be permanently popular in this country. Charles Dickens it appears to me has given the final death-blow to writings of that description.

Nevertheless, the writer-men of that day, who wrote the popular stories and received readier sales and fatter checks, are dead and forgotten and their stories with them, while Poe and the stories of Poe live on. In a way, this side of Poe's history is a paradoxical tangle. Editors did not like to publish his stories nor people to read them, yet they were read universally and discussed and remembered, and went the round of the foreign newspapers. They earned him little money, yet they have since earned a great deal of money and to this day command a large and steady sale. It was the common belief at the time they appeared that they could never become popular in the United States, yet their steady sales, complete editions, and what-not, which continue to come out, attest a popularity that is, to say the least, enduring. The sombre and terrible "Fall of the House of Usher," "Ligeia," "Black Cat," "Cask of Amontillado," "Berenice," "Pit and the Pendulum," and "Masque of the Red Death" are read to-day with an eagerness as great as ever. And especially is this true of the younger generation which ofttimes places the seal of its approval on things the graybeards have read, approved, forgotten they have approved, and finally censured and condemned.

Yet the conditions which obtained in Poe's time obtain just as inexorably to-day. No self-respecting editor with an eye to the subscription-list can be bribed or bullied into admitting a terrible or tragic story into his magazine; while the reading public, when it does chance upon such stories in one way or another,—and it manages to chance upon them somehow,—says it does not care for them.

A person reads such a story, lays it down with a shudder, and says: "It makes my blood run cold. I never want to read anything like that again." Yet he or she will read something like that again, and again, and yet again, and return and read them over again. Talk with the average man or woman of the reading public and it will be found that they have read all, or nearly all, of the terrible and horrible tales which have been written. Also, they will shiver, express a dislike for such tales, and then proceed to discuss them with a keenness and understanding as remarkable as it is surprising.

When it is considered that so many condemns these tales and continue to read them (as is amply proved by heart-to-heart experience and by the book sales such as Poe's), the question arises: Are folk honest when they shudder and say they do not care for the terrible, the horrible, and the tragic? Do they really not like to be afraid? Or are they afraid that they do like to be afraid?

Deep down in the roots of the race is fear. It came first into the world, and it was the dominant emotion in the primitive world. To-day, for that matter, it remains the most firmly seated of the emotions. But in the primitive world people were uncomplex, not yet self-conscious, and they frankly delighted in terror-inspiring tales and religions. Is it true that the complex, self-conscious people of to-day do not delight in the things which inspire terror? or is it true that they are ashamed to make known their delight?

What is it that lures boys to haunted houses after dark, compelling them to fling rocks and run away with their hearts going so thunderously pit-a-pat as to drown the clatter of their flying feet? What is it that grips a child, forcing it to listen to ghost stories which drive it into ecstasies of fear, and yet forces it to beg for more and more? Is it a baleful thing? a thing his instinct warns him as unhealthy and evil the while his desire leaps out to it? Or, again, what is it that sends the heart fluttering up and quickens the feet of the man or woman who goes alone down a long, dark hall or up a winding stair? Is it a stirring of the savage in them?—of the savage who has slept, but never died, since the time the river-folk crouched over the fires of their squatting-places, or the tree-folk bunched together and chattered in the dark?

Whatever the thing is, and whether it be good or evil, it is a thing and it is real. It is a thing Poe rouses in us, scaring us in broad day and throwing us into "admired disorders." It is rarely that the grown person who is afraid of the dark will make confessions. It does not seem to them proper to be afraid of the dark, and they are ashamed. Perhaps people feel that it is not proper to delight in stories that arouse fear and terror. They may feel instinctively that it is bad and injurious to have such emotions aroused, and because of this are impelled to say that they do not like such stories, while in actuality they do like them.

The great emotion exploited by Dickens was fear, as Mr. Brooks Adams has pointed out, just as courage was the great emotion exploited by Scott. The militant nobility seemed to possess an excess of courage and to respond more readily to things courageous. On the other hand, the rising bourgeoisie, the timid merchant-folk and city-dwellers, fresh from the oppressions and robberies of their rough-handed lords, seemed to possess an excess of fear, and to respond more readily to things fearsome. For this reason they greedily devoured Dickens's writings, for he was as peculiarly their spokesman as Scott was the spokesman of the old and dying nobility.

But since Dickens's day, if we may judge by the editorial attitude and by the dictum of the reading public, a change seems to have taken place. In Dickens's day, the bourgeoisie, as a dominant class being but newly risen, had fear still strong upon it, much as a negro mammy, a couple of generations from Africa, stands in fear of the Voodoo. But to-day it would seem that this same bourgeoisie, firmly seated and triumphant, is ashamed of its old terror, which it remembers dimly, as it might a bad nightmare. When fear was strong upon it, it loved nothing better than fear-exciting things; but with fear far removed, no

longer menaced and harassed, it has become afraid of fear. By
this is meant that the bourgeoisie has become self-conscious,
much in the same fashion that the black slave, freed and conscious of the stigma attached to "black," calls himself a colored
gentleman, though in his heart of hearts he feels himself black
nigger still. So the bourgeoisie may feel in a dim, mysterious way
the stigma attached to the fear of its cowardly days, and, self-
conscious, brands as improper all fear-exciting things, while deep
down in its secret being it delights in them still.

All this, of course, is by the way,—a mere tentative attempt
to account for a bit of contradictory psychology in the make-up
of the reading public. But the facts of the case remain. The
public is afraid of fear-exciting tales and hypocritically continues
to enjoy them. W. W. Jacobs's recent collection of stories, "The
Lady of the Barge," contains his usual inimitable humorous yarns
intersprinkled with several terror-tales. It was asked of a dozen
friends as to which story had affected them the most forcibly,
and the unanimous answer was, "The Monkey's Paw." Now the
"Monkey's Paw" is as perfect a terror-tale as any of its kind. Yet,
without exception, after duly and properly shuddering and dis-
claiming all liking for such tales, they proceeded to discuss it
with a warmth and knowledge which plainly advertised that,
whatever strange sensations it had aroused, they were at any
rate pleasurable sensations.

Long ago, Ambrose Bierce published his *Soldiers and Civilians*,
a book crammed from cover to cover with unmitigated terror
and horror. An editor who dared to publish one of these tales
would be committing financial and professional suicide; and yet,
year after year, people continue to talk about *Soldiers and Civilians*, while the innumerable sweet and wholesome, optimistic,
and happy-ending books are forgotten as rapidly as they leave
the press.

In the rashness of youth before he became converted to
soberer ways, Mr. [W. C.] Morrow was guilty of *The Ape, the
Idiot, and Other People*, wherein are to be found some of the
most horrible horror-stories in the English language. It made his
instant reputation, whereupon he conceived higher notions of his
art, forswore the terrible and the horrible, and wrote other and
totally different books. But these other books are not remem-

bered as readily as is his first one by the people who in the same
breath say they do not like stories such as may be found in
The Ape, the Idiot, and Other People.

Of two collections of tales recently published, each of which
contained one terror-story, nine out of ten reviewers, in each
instance, selected the terror-story as worthy of most praise, and,
after they had praised, five out of the nine of them proceeded to
damn it. Rider Haggard's *She*, which is filled with gruesome terror,
had a long and popular vogue, while the *Strange Case of Dr.
Jekyll and Mr. Hyde* achieved, if anything, a greater success and
brought [R. L.] Stevenson to the front.

Putting the horror-story outside the pale, can any story be
really great, the theme of which is anything but tragic or terrible?
Can the sweet commonplaces of life be made into anything
else than sweetly commonplace stories?

It would not seem so. The great short stories in the world's
literary treasure-house seem all to depend upon the tragic and
terrible for their strength and greatness. Not half of them deal
with love at all; and when they do, they derive their greatness,
not from the love itself, but from the tragic and terrible with
which the love is involved.

In this class may be ranked *Without Benefit of Clergy*,
[R. Kipling] which is fairly typical. The love of John Holden and
Ameera greatens because it is out of caste and precarious, and
is made memorable by the tragic deaths of Tota and Ameera,
the utter obliteration of the facts that they have lived, and the
return of John Holden to his kind. Stress and strain are required
to sound the deeps of human nature, and there is neither stress
nor strain in sweet, optimistic, and placidly happy events. Great
things can be done only under great provocation, and there is
nothing greatly provoking in the sweet and placid round of existence. Romeo and Juliet are not remembered because things
slipped smoothly along, nor are Abélard and Héloïse, Tristram
and Iseult, Paolo and Francesca.

But the majority of the great short stories do not deal with
love. "A Lodging for the Night" [R. L. Stevenson], for instance,
one of the most rounded and perfect stories ever told, not only
has no hint of love in it, but does not contain a hint of one
character whom we would care to meet in life. Beginning with

the murder of Thevenin, running through the fearful night in the streets and the robbing of the dead jade in the porch, and finishing with the old lord of Brisetout, who is not murdered because he possesses seven pieces of plate instead of ten, it contains nothing that is not terrible and repulsive. Yet it is the awfulness of it that makes it great. The play of words in the deserted house between Villon and the feeble lord of Brisetout, which is the story, would be no story at all were the stress and strain taken out of it and the two men placed *vis-à-vis* with a score of retainers at the old lord's back.

The "Fall of the House of Usher" depends upon all that is terrible for its greatness, and there is no more love in it than there is in Guy de Maupassant's "Necklace," or the "Piece of String," or in [R. Kipling] "The Man Who Was," and "Baa Baa, Black Sheep," which last is the most pitiful of all tragedies, a child's.

The editors of the magazines have very good reasons for refusing admission to the terrible and tragic. Their readers say they do not like the terrible and tragic, and that is enough, without going farther. But either their readers prevaricate most shamelessly or delude themselves into believing they tell the truth, or else the people who read the magazines are not the people who continue to buy, say, the works of Poe.

In the circumstances, there being a proved demand for the terrible and tragic, is there not room in the otherwise crowded field for a magazine devoted primarily to the terrible and tragic? A magazine such as Poe dreamed of, about which there shall be nothing namby-pamby, yellowish, or emasculated, and which will print stories that are bids for place and permanence rather than for the largest circulation?

On the face of it two things appear certain: That enough of that portion of the reading public which cares for the tragic and terrible would be sufficiently honest to subscribe; and that the writers of the land would be capable of supplying the stories. The only reason why such stories are not written to-day is that there is no magazine to buy them, and that the writer-folk are busy turning out the stuff, mainly ephemeral, which the magazines will buy. The pity of it is that the writer-folk are writing for bread first and glory after; and that their standard of living goes up as fast as their capacity for winning bread increases,—so that they never get around to glory,—the ephemeral flourishes, and the great stories remain unwritten.

STRANGER THAN FICTION[1]

[*An experience solemnly affirmed to be the truth, the whole truth, and nothing but the truth.*]

I remember frying bacon at a noon halt on the Klondike Trail, some several years back, while I listened incredulously to a Yukon pioneer's tale of woe. There were tears in his voice and a querulous plaint, as he told me of all he had suffered from the mosquitoes. Before his recital reached a close he became angry at the little winged pests, the injuries they had done him waxed colossal, and he cursed them in terms the most uncompromisingly blasphemous I have ever heard.

He was a strong man. He had been seven years in the land. I knew, at that very moment, that he was resting from a tramp of fifty miles which he had covered in the last fifteen hours, and that he intended to cover twenty-five miles more before night came on.

As I say, I knew all this. The man was real. He had done things. He had a reputation. Yet I said to myself: *These mosquito-happenings are impossible things. They cannot be true. The man lies.*

Four months later, two comrades and I, three strong men of us, went down the Yukon two thousand miles in an open boat. Tears came into our voices and remained there, likewise the querulous plaint. We grew irritable and quarrelsome. Instead of talking like men we whined broken-spiritedly, and said that of mosquitoes the half had not been told. And I, for one, marvelled at the restraint and control of the man who had first told me of the mosquito at the noon halt on the Klondike Trail.

Since then, in civilization, I have attempted to tell the story of the mosquito. My friends have listened pityingly, or looked bored, or told me plainly that veracity was evidently not a Klondike product. These things I endured, striving to redeem

[1] *The Critic*, August 1903.

myself with greater earnestness and detail; but, finally, when one fellow said, "That reminds me of a real mosquito story," I dropped the subject for good and all. Since then I have been most exemplary in my conduct and morals, and I still hope that before I totter into the grave I shall succeed in living down my reputation for untruthfulness.

I do not dare to tell the story of the mosquito here. I have merely hinted at it in this somewhat lengthy preamble in order to show that I understand and forgive the editorial mind when certain facts of mine, in fictional garb, are promptly returned to me. For be it known that truth is so much stranger than fiction that it is unreal to editors and readers.

For instance, I knew a girl. Our first meeting was typical. It was up in the rugged Sierras. In the cool of the day she came out of the dark pine woods, in short-skirted costume, her hair down her back, a shotgun across the hollow of her arm. She was hunting rabbits—for her, deer and a Winchester rifle would have been just as likely. She was quite unconventional, and she was straight. She could ride a horse better than the average broncho-buster. She could go down in a diving-bell, scratch off a magazine article (which would sell), or do a Highland fling on the vaudeville stage, for the fun of the thing. On the other hand, she had opened the books. I have at hand now a score of dainty poems by her. She was as close to culture as she was to the wild, free life of the open or of Bohemia. In few words, she was a striking creature.

I toned her down and made a heroine of her. It was for the sake of veracity, and because I remembered the story of the mosquito, that I toned her down. I took away from her realness, diminished the living fact of her, in order that the reader might believe she was real and a living fact. The reviewers swiftly proved to me how signally I had failed. I quote at random: "One cannot believe in her, but one likes her and forgives her culture"; "a projection of the writer's ideal woman upon paper"; "a monster"; "a thing contrary to nature"; "remains at the end of the story utterly incredible and even inconceivable."

From time to time I have written short adventure-stories for a famous juvenile publication. My experience with these stories was practically uniform. Whenever I evolved out of my sheer inner consciousness some boyish adventure, it received the most flattering approval of the editors. Whenever my inner consciousness was not in working order, and I fell back on the facts of my life, wrote adventures I had actually gone through, things I had done with my own hands and head, the editors hummed and hawed. "It is not real," they said. "It is impossible. It could not have happened thus and so."

Once, when they commented in this fashion upon a cliff-climbing story of mine, a literal narrative of a thing I had done, as had thousands of others as well, I flew into rebellion. "I can readily comprehend," I wrote them, though I really didn't at the moment, so befuddled was my reason by my wrath, "I can readily comprehend that the state of consciousness you may achieve on the flat floor of your editorial sanctum concerning a man plastered against the frown [sic] of a cliff is a far different state of consciousness from that a man may achieve who is plastered against the frown of a cliff." They were very nice about it, taking my criticism in better part than I took theirs; and, for that matter, they could afford to, for they were in the right. It is incontrovertible that one cannot do on the printed page what one does in life.

I once wrote a story of a tramp. I intended it to be the first of a series of tramp stories, all of which were to relate the adventures of a single tramp character. I was well fitted to write this series, and for two reasons. First, I had myself tramped ten thousand miles or so through the United States and Canada, begged for my food from door to door, and performed sentences for vagrancy in various jails. Second, my tramp character was a personal friend. Many a time he had shoved his legs under my table or turned into my bed with me. I knew him better than I did my brother. He was a remarkable man, college-educated, qualified to practice law in all the courts, spilling over with the minutest details of every world-philosophy from Zeno to Nietzsche, deeply versed in political economy and sociology, a brilliant lecturer—in short, a genius of extraordinary calibre.

To exploit in fiction this living fact, I not only toned him down, but actually used an experience of his for the *motif* of the first story. I make bold to say that it is one of the best stories I ever wrote, if it is not the best. When nobody is around I sneak it out from the bottom of the box and read it with huge delight, hugging myself the while and feeling great sorrow for the world which is denied my joy.

I need hardly say that this story, to the editorial mind, was an unveracious thing. One editor, only, did it convince. And this is how it was. I know a young writer in Southern California who tramped East for the experience. I shall call him Jones. Well, Jones met this particular editor in New York City and told him divers of his own tramp experiences. Shortly afterward, my tramp story was submitted to this editor. In this fashion he explained his rejection of it: "Had I not known Mr. Jones for some time past, I should have said such a creation as your Tramp was absolutely and utterly impossible, and my reason for rejecting the MS. is that to other people who have not had the opportunity to really understand what a tramp may be, whence he may come, and into what he may be transformed, it might seem too great a tax upon credulity."

Tone down as I would, my Tramp was too real to be true. With the help of Mr. Jones he had convinced but one editor, who, in turn, said very truly that his readers, not having the advantage of Mr. Jones's acquaintance, would remain unconvinced. Suffice it to say, beyond the initial story, the series remains unwritten, and the world little recks of what it has lost.

I had a certain pastoral experience. The effect was cumulative. I had dealings with several hundred different people of all ages, sizes, and sexes, through a long period of time so that the human traits and psychology involved were not extraordinary but merely average human traits and psychology. I sat down and brooded over this pastoral experience. Alas! said I to myself, it would make a bully story, but it is too real to be true.

I should have abandoned it altogether had not a new method of treating it come to me. I pulled up to my desk and started in. First I wrote the title. Underneath the title, in brackets, I wrote, "A True Narrative." Then I wrote the experience as it actually happened, using only the naked facts of it, bringing in for verities, and precisely labelled, my wife, my sister, my nephew, my maid-servant, myself, my house, and my post-office address.

Ah ha! chortled I, as I mailed it East; at last I have circumvented the editorial mind. But it came back. It continued to come back. The editors refused it with phrases complimentary and otherwise, and one and all thanked me for having allowed them the privilege of considering my *story* (!)

At last an editor looked kindly upon it, accepting it with qualifications. He wrote: "It is decidedly good . . . but I shy at the use of the — —. With the ordinary reader this would be considered carrying the matter too far, but I can believe it was necessary in reality." And after indicating the changes he would suggest, he wound up with: "For the *story* (!) I will then pay $—."

Oscar Wilde once proved with fair conclusiveness that Nature imitates Art. I have been forced to conclude that Fact, to be true, must imitate Fiction. The creative imagination is more veracious than the voice of life. Actual events are less true than logical conceits and whimsicalities. And the man who writes fiction have better leave fact alone.

I said to myself that the mosquito-man lied. By innumerable editorial rejections I have been informed that I have lied. And for all that I placed at the head of this narrative, in brackets, a solemn affirmation of its truthfulness I am confident that it will be believed by no one. It is too real to be true.

THE YELLOW PERIL[1]

While "The Yellow Peril" was not one of the series of the Japanese-Russian war correspondence articles, it was written in Manchuria in June of 1904 and published in the San Francisco Examiner *September 25, 1904. London, in spite of Japanese restrictions, went into the battle area, crossed the Yalu River and traveled as far as Antung, China. He wrote about the things that he observed and, in the light of today's situations and events, becomes almost prophetic. From here, he was returned to South Korea by the Japanese Military.*

No more marked contrast appears in passing from our Western land to the paper houses and cherry blossoms of Japan than appears in the passing from Korea to China. To achieve a correct appreciation of the Chinese the traveller should first sojourn amongst the Koreans for several months, and then, one fine day, cross over the Yalu into Manchuria. It would be of ex-

[1] San Francisco *Examiner*, September 25, 1904. Written in Feng-Wang-Cheng, Manchuria, June 1904.

ceptional advantage to the correctness of appreciation did he cross over the Yalu on the heels of a hostile and alien army.

War is to-day the final arbiter in the affairs of men, and it is as yet the final test of the worthwhileness of peoples. Tested thus, the Korean fails. He lacks the nerve to remain when a strange army crosses his land. The few goods and chattels he may have managed to accumulate he puts on his back, along with his doors and windows, and away he heads for his mountain fastnesses. Later he may return, sans goods, chattels, doors, and windows, impelled by insatiable curiosity for a "look see." But it is curiosity merely—a timid, deerlike curiosity. He is prepared to bound away on his long legs at the first hint of danger or trouble.

Northern Korea was a desolate land when the Japanese passed through. Villages and towns were deserted. The fields lay untouched. There was no ploughing nor sowing, no green things growing. Little or nothing was to be purchased. One carried one's own food with him, and food for horses and servants was the anxious problem that waited at the day's end. In many a lonely village not an ounce nor a grain of anything could be bought, and yet there might be standing around scores of white garmented, stalwart Koreans, smoking yard-long pipes and chattering, chattering—ceaselessly chattering. Love, money, or force could not procure from them a horseshoe or a horseshoe nail. "Upso," was their invariable reply. "Upso," cursed word, which means "Have not got."

They had tramped probably forty miles that day, down from their hiding-places, just for a "look see," and forty miles back they would cheerfully tramp, chattering all the way over what they had seen. Shake a stick at them as they stand chattering about your camp-fire, and the gloom of the landscape will be filled with tall, flitting ghosts, bounding like deer, with great springy strides which one cannot but envy. They have splendid vigor and fine bodies, but they are accustomed to being beaten and robbed without protest or resistance by every chance foreigner who enters their country.

From this nerveless, forsaken Korean land I rode down upon the sandy islands of the Yalu. For weeks these islands had been the dread between-the-lines of two fighting armies. The air above had been rent by screaming projectiles. The echoes of the final battle had scarcely died away. The trains of Japanese wounded and Japanese dead were trailing by.

On the conical hill, a quarter of a mile away, the Russian dead were being buried in their trenches and in the shell holes made by the Japanese. And here, in the thick of it all, a man was ploughing. Green things were growing—young onions—and the man who was weeding them paused from his labor long enough to sell me a handful. Near by was the smoke-blackened ruin of the farm-house, fired by the Russians when they retreated from the river-bed. Two men were removing the debris, cleaning the confusion, preparatory to rebuilding. They were clad in blue. Pigtails hung down their backs. I was in China!

I rode to the shore, into the village of Kuel-Ian-Ching. There were no lounging men smoking long pipes and chattering. The previous day the Russians had been there, a bloody battle had been fought, and to-day the Japanese were there—but what was that to talk about? Everybody was busy. Men were offering eggs and chickens and fruit for sale upon the street, and bread, as I live, bread in small round loaves or buns. I rode on into the country. Everywhere a toiling population was in evidence. The houses and walls were strong and substantial. Stone and brick replaced the mud walls of the Korean dwellings. Twilight fell and deepened and still the ploughs went up and down the fields, the sowers following after. Trains of wheelbarrows, heavily loaded, squeaked by, and Pekin carts, drawn by from four to six cows, horses, mules, ponies, or jackasses—cows even with their new-born calves tottering along on puny legs outside the traces. Everybody worked. Everything worked. I saw a man mending the road. I was in China.

I came to the city of Antung, and lodged with a merchant. He was a grain merchant. Corn he had, hundreds of bushels, stored in great bins of stout matting; peas and beans in sacks, and in the back yard his millstones went round and round, grinding out meal. Also, in his back yard, were buildings containing vats sunk into the ground, and here the tanners were at work making leather. I bought a measure of corn from mine host for my horses, and he overcharged me thirty cents. I was in China. Antung was jammed with Japanese troops. It was the thick of war. But it did not matter. The work of Antung went on just the same. The shops were wide open; the streets were lined with peddlers. One could buy anything; get anything made. I dined at a Chinese restaurant, cleansed myself at a public bath in a private tub with a small boy to assist in the scrubbing. I bought condensed milk, butter, canned vegetables, bread, and cake. I repeat it, cake—good cake. I bought knives, forks, and spoons, graniteware dishes and mugs. There were horseshoes and horseshoers. A worker in iron realized for me new designs of mine for my tent poles. My shoes were sent out to be repaired. A barber shampooed my hair. A servant returned with corn-beef in tins, a bottle of port, another of cognac, and beer, blessed beer to wash out from my throat the dust of an army. It was the land of Canaan. I was in China.

The Korean is the perfect type of inefficiency—of utter worthlessness. The Chinese is the perfect type of industry. For sheer work no worker in the world can compare with him. Work is the breath of his nostrils. It is his solution of existence. It is to him what wandering and fighting in far lands and spiritual adventure have been to other peoples. Liberty to him epitomizes itself in access to the means of toil. To till the soil and labor interminably with rude implements and utensils is all he asks for life and of the powers that be. Work is what he desires above all things, and he will work at anything for anybody.

During the taking of the Taku forts he carried scaling ladders at the heads of the storming columns and planted them against the walls. He did this, not from a sense of patriotism, but for the invading foreign devils because they paid him a daily wage of fifty cents. He is not frightened by war. He accepts it as he does rain and sunshine, the changing, of the seasons, and other natural phenomena. He prepares for it, endures it, and survives it, and when the tide of battle sweeps by, the thunder of the guns still reverberating in the distant canyons, he is seen calmly bending to his usual tasks. Nay, war itself bears fruits whereof he may pick. Before the dead are cold or the burial squads have arrived he is out on the field, stripping the mangled bodies, collecting the shrapnel, and ferreting in the shell holes for slivers and fragments of iron.

The Chinese is no coward. He does not carry away his doors

and windows to the mountains, but remains to guard them when alien soldiers occupy his town. He does not hide away his chickens and his eggs, nor any other commodity he possesses. He proceeds at once to offer them for sale. Nor is he to be bullied into lowering his price. What if the purchaser be a soldier and an alien made cocky by victory and confident by overwhelming force? He has two large pears saved over from last year which he will sell for five sen, or for the same price three small pears. What if one soldier persist in taking away with him three large pears? What if there be twenty other soldiers jostling about him? He turns over his sack of fruit to another Chinese and races down the street after his pears and the soldier responsible for their flight, and he does not return till he has wrenched away one large pear from that soldier's grasp.

Nor is the Chinese the type of permanence which he has been so often designated. He is not so ill-disposed toward new ideas and new methods as his history would seem to indicate. True, his forms, customs, and methods have been permanent these many centuries, but this has been due to the fact that his government was in the hands of the learned classes, and that these governing scholars found their salvation lay in suppressing all progressive ideas. The ideas behind the Boxer troubles and the outbreaks over the introduction of railroad and other foreign devil machinations have emanated from the minds of the literati, and been spread by their pamphlets and propagandists. Originality and enterprise have been suppressed in the Chinese for scores of generations. Only has remained to him industry, and in this has he found the supreme expression of his being. On the other hand, his susceptibility to new ideas has been well demonstrated wherever he has escaped beyond the restrictions imposed upon him by his government. So far as the business man is concerned he has grasped far more clearly the Western code of business, the Western ethics of business, than has the Japanese. He has learned, as a matter of course, to keep his word or his bond. As yet, the Japanese business man has failed to understand this. When he has signed a time contract and when changing conditions cause him to lose by it, the Japanese merchant cannot understand why he should live up to his contract. It is beyond his comprehension and repulsive to his common sense that he should live up to his contract and thereby lose money. He firmly believes that the changing conditions themselves absolve him. And in so far adaptable as he has shown himself to be in other respects, he fails to grasp a radically new idea where the Chinese succeeds.

Here we have the Chinese, four hundred millions of him, occupying a vast land of immense natural resources—resources of a twentieth century age, of a machine age; resources of coal and iron, which are the backbone of commercial civilization. He is an indefatigable worker. He is not dead to new ideas, new methods, new systems. Under a capable management he can be made to do anything. Truly would he of himself constitute the much-heralded Yellow Peril were it not for his present management. This management, his government, is set, crystallized. It is what binds him down to building as his fathers built. The governing class, entrenched by the precedent and power of centuries and by the stamp it has put upon his mind, will never free him. It would be the suicide of the governing class, and the governing class knows it.

Comes now the Japanese. On the streets of Antung, of Feng-Wang-Cheng, or of any other Manchurian city, the following is a familiar scene: One is hurrying home through the dark of the unlighted streets when he comes upon a paper lantern resting on the ground. On one side squats a Chinese civilian on his hams, on the other side squats a Japanese soldier. One dips his forefinger in the dust and writes strange, monstrous characters. The other nods understanding, sweeps the dust slate level with his hand, and with his forefinger inscribes similar characters. They are talking. They cannot speak to each other, but they can write. Long ago one borrowed the other's written language, and long before that, untold generations ago, they diverged from a common root, the ancient Mongol stock.

There have been changes, differentiations brought about by diverse conditions and infusions of other blood; but down at the bottom of their being, twisted into the fibres of them, is a heritage in common—a sameness in kind which time has not obliterated. The infusion of other blood, Malay, perhaps, has made the Japanese a race of mastery and power, a fighting race through all its history, a race which has always despised commerce and exalted fighting.

To-day, equipped with the finest machines and systems of destruction the Caucasian mind has devised, handling machines and systems with remarkable and deadly accuracy, this rejuvenescent Japanese race has embarked on a course of conquest, the goal of which no man knows. The head men of Japan are dreaming ambitiously, and the people are dreaming blindly, a Napoleonic dream. And to this dream the Japanese clings and will cling with bull-dog tenacity. The soldier shouting "Nippon, Banzai!" on the walls of Wiju, the widow at home in her paper house committing suicide so that her only son, her sole support, may go to the front, are both expressing the unanimity of the dream.

The late disturbance in the Far East marked the clashing of the dreams, for the Slav, too, is dreaming greatly. Granting that the Japanese can hurl back the Slav and that the two great branches of the Anglo-Saxon race do not despoil him of his spoils, the Japanese dream takes on substantiality. Japan's population is no larger because her people have continually pressed against the means of subsistence. But given poor, empty Korea for a breeding colony and Manchuria for a granary, and at once the Japanese begins to increase by leaps and bounds.

Even so, he would not of himself constitute a Brown Peril. He has not the time in which to grow and realize the dream. He is only forty-five millions, and so fast does the economic exploitation of the planet hurry on the planet's partition amongst the Western peoples that, before he could attain the stature requisite to menace, he would see the Western giants in possession of the very stuff of his dream.

The menace to the Western world lies, not in the little brown man, but in the four hundred millions of yellow men should the little brown man undertake their management. The Chinese is not dead to new ideas; he is an efficient worker; makes a good soldier, and is wealthy in the essential materials of a machine age. Under a capable management he will go far. The Japanese is prepared and fit to undertake this management. Not only has he proved himself an apt imitator of Western material progress, a sturdy worker, and a capable organizer, but he is far more fit to manage the Chinese than are we. The baffling enigma of the

Chinese character is no baffling enigma to him. He understands as we could never school ourselves nor hope to understand. Their mental processes are largely the same. He thinks with the same thought-symbols as does the Chinese, and he thinks in the same peculiar grooves. He goes on where we are balked by the obstacles of incomprehension. He takes the turning which we cannot perceive, twists around the obstacle, and, presto! is out of sight in the ramifications of the Chinese mind where we cannot follow.

The Chinese has been called the type of permanence, and well he has merited it, dozing as he has through the ages. And as truly was the Japanese the type of permanence up to a generation ago, when he suddenly awoke and startled the world with a rejuvenescence the like of which the world had never seen before. The ideas of the West were the leaven powerful enough to quicken the Chinese.

We have had Africa for the Africander, and at no distant day we shall hear "Asia for the Asiatic!" Four hundred million indefatigable workers (deft, intelligent, and unafraid to die), aroused and rejuvenescent, managed and guided by forty-five million additional human beings who are splendid fighting animals, scientific and modern, constitute that menace to the Western world which has been well named the "Yellow Peril." The possibility of race adventure has not passed away. We are in the midst of our own. The Slav is just girding himself up to begin. Why may not the yellow and the brown start out on an adventure as tremendous as our own and more strikingly unique?

The ultimate success of such an adventure the Western mind refuses to consider. It is not the nature of life to believe itself weak. There is such a thing as race egotism as well as creature egotism, and a very good thing it is. In the first place, the Western world will not permit the rise of the yellow peril. It is firmly convinced that it will not permit the yellow and the brown to wax strong and menace its peace and comfort. It advances this idea with persistency, and delivers itself of long arguments showing how and why this menace will not be permitted to arise. To-day, far more voices are engaged in denying the yellow peril than in prophesying it. The Western world is warned, if not armed, against the possibility of it.

In the second place, there is a weakness inherent in the brown man which will bring his adventure to naught. From the West he has borrowed all our material achievement and passed our ethical achievement by. Our engines of production and destruction he has made his. What was once solely ours he now duplicates, rivalling our merchants in the commerce of the East, thrashing the Russian on sea and land. A marvellous imitator truly, but imitating us only in things material. Things spiritual cannot be imitated; they must be felt and lived, woven into the very fabric of life, and here the Japanese fails.

It required no revolution of his nature to learn to calculate the range and fire a field-gun or to march the goose-step. It was a mere matter of training. Our material achievement is the product of our intellect. It is knowledge, and knowledge, like coin, is interchangeable. It is not wrapped up in the heredity of the new-born child, but is something to be acquired afterward. Not so with our soul stuff, which is the product of an evolution which goes back to the raw beginnings of the race. Our soul stuff is not a coin to be pocketed by the first chance comer. The Japanese cannot pocket it any more than he can thrill to short Saxon words or we can thrill to Chinese hieroglyphics. The leopard cannot change its spots, nor can the Japanese, nor can we. We are thumbed by the ages into what we are, and by no conscious inward effort can we in a day rethumb ourselves. Nor can the Japanese in a day, or a generation, rethumb himself in our image.

Back of our own great race adventure, back of our robberies by sea and land, our lusts and violences and all the evil things we have done, there is a certain integrity, a sternness of conscience, a melancholy responsibility of life, a sympathy and comradeship and warm human feel, which is ours, indubitably ours, and which we cannot teach to the Oriental as we would teach logarithms or the trajectory of projectiles. That we have groped for the way of right conduct and agonized over the soul betokens our spiritual endowment. Though we have strayed often and far from right-eousness, the voices of the seers have always been raised, and we have harked back to the bidding of conscience. The colossal fact of our history is that we have made the religion of Jesus Christ our religion. No matter how dark in error and deed, ours has been a history of spiritual struggle and endeavor. We are preeminently a religious race, which is another way of saying that we are a right-seeking race.

"What do you think of the Japanese?" was asked an American woman after she had lived some time in Japan. "It seems to me that they have no soul," was her answer.

This must not be taken to mean that the Japanese is without soul. But it serves to illustrate the enormous difference between their soul and this woman's soul. There was no feel, no speech, no recognition. This Western soul did not dream that the Eastern soul existed, it was so different, so totally different.

Religion, as a battle for the right in our sense of right, as a yearning and a strife for spiritual good and purity, is unknown to the Japanese. Measured by what religion means to us, the Japanese is a race without religion. Yet it has a religion, and who shall say that it is not as great a religion as ours, not as efficacious? As one Japanese has written:—

"Our reflection brought into prominence not so much the moral as the national consciousness of the individual. . . . To us the country is more than land and soil from which to mine gold or reap grain—it is the sacred abode of the gods, the spirits of our forefathers; to us the Emperor is more than the Arch Constable of a Reichsstaat, or even the Patron of a Kulturstaat; he is the bodily representative of heaven on earth, blending in his person its power and its mercy."

The religion of Japan is practically a worship of the State itself. Patriotism is the expression of this worship. The Japanese mind does not split hairs as to whether the Emperor is Heaven incarnate or the State incarnate. So far as the Japanese are concerned, the Emperor lives, is himself deity. The Emperor is the object to live for and to die for. The Japanese is not an individualist. He has developed national consciousness instead of moral consciousness. He is not interested in his own moral welfare except in so far as it is the welfare of the State. The honor of the individual, per se, does not exist. Only exists the honor of the State, which is his honor. He does not look upon himself as a free agent, working out his own personal salvation. Spiritual agonizing is unknown to him. He has a "sense of calm trust in fate, a quiet submission to the inevitable, a stoic composure in sight of danger or calamity, a disdain of life and friendliness with death." He relates himself to the State as, amongst bees, the worker is related to the hive; himself nothing, the State everything; his reasons for existence the exaltation and glorification of the State.

The most admired quality to-day of the Japanese is his patriotism. The Western world is in rhapsodies over it, unwittingly measuring the Japanese patriotism by its own conceptions of patriotism. "For God, my country, and the Czar!" cries the Russian patriot; but in the Japanese mind there is no differentiation between the three. The Emperor is the Emperor, and God and country as well. The patriotism of the Japanese is blind and unswerving loyalty to what is practically an absolutism. The Emperor can do no wrong, nor can the five ambitious great men who have his ear and control the destiny of Japan.

No great race adventure can go far nor endure long which has no deeper foundation than material success, no higher prompting than conquest for conquest's sake and mere race glorification. To go far and to endure, it must have behind it an ethical impulse, a sincerely conceived righteousness. But it must be taken into consideration that the above postulate is itself a product of Western race-egotism, urged by our belief in our own righteousness and fostered by a faith in ourselves which may be as erroneous as are most fond race fancies. So be it. The world is whirling faster to-day than ever before. It has gained impetus. Affairs rush to conclusion. The Far East is the point of contact of the adventuring Western people as well as of the Asiatic. We shall not have to wait for our children's time nor our children's children. We shall ourselves see and largely determine the adventure of the Yellow and the Brown.

THE STORY OF AN EYE-WITNESS[1]

[The San Francisco Earthquake April 18, 1906]

At the time of the San Francisco earthquake London was building The Snark, *in which he hoped to make a seven-year tour of the world. Naturally the earthquake had disrupted business, industry, transportation, and labor in the entire Bay area. On July 16, 1906, he*

[1] Taken from London's holograph copy, Huntington Library, San Marino, California. Published in *Collier's* May 5, 1906.

wrote to Bailey Millard,[2] *editor of the* Cosmopolitan Magazine: *"This damned earthquake is just beginning to show up the delays it caused. There is scarcely a thing we want, that we can buy in the local market." The conditions did not improve and more delays came. On November 11, 1906, he wrote to Arthur T. Vance, the editor of* Woman's Home Companion:

> There are fourteen men at work at the present moment on the boat. The labor conditions are so frightful here that I have taken the building of the boat out of the hands of the shipyard and am going on with it myself, paying a dollar a day extra to each man. Barring accidents, we shall certainly be away by the middle of December. There is the engine, however, that is somewhere in a freight car between New York and San Francisco. If there should be a smash-up on the railroad, and that engine should be destroyed, I should be delayed months, because it took months to build that engine, and would take months to build another like it.

More delays. He had first planned to sail in October 1906, then he planned to leave in December. On March 14, 1907, he again wrote to Arthur T. Vance: ". . . I won't be happy until I get away, and I am going to get away as fast as God, earthquakes and organized labor will let me." He sailed from San Francisco on April 23, 1907. But, in Honolulu, the boat was in need of repairs. On May 28, 1907, he wrote to George F. Brett, editor of The Macmillan Company for an advance on his (book) royalties.

> . . . I just wish to say a word in explanation of my precarious financial situation. The building of the *Snark* has been the cause of it all. I expected to pay about $7,000.00 for the completed boat. Never mind the horrible and monstrous causes. The result is, that at the present moment, the *Snark* has cost me $25,000.00. Naturally, this has absorbed money as fast as I could earn it, and a bit faster. . . .

After his boat was repaired, London left for the South Seas where he spent more than two years. However, during this time he continued to write and, among other things, wrote the novel Martin Eden *and many of his Hawaiian stories, such as "Koolau the Leper," many of his South Sea tales, and his most famous short story, "To Build a Fire."*

The earthquake shook down in San Francisco hundreds of thousands of dollars worth of walls and chimneys. But the con-

[2] London had made arrangements with several magazines to write articles about his voyage. *Cosmopolitan* and *Woman's Home Companion* were two of them. By this means he hoped to pay for the boat and finance the voyage.

flagration that followed burned up hundreds of millions of
dollars worth of property. There is no estimating within hundreds
of millions the actual damage wrought.

Not in history has a modern imperial city been so completely
destroyed. San Francisco is gone. Nothing remains of it but
memories and fringe of dwelling houses on its outskirts. Its industrial section is wiped out. Its business section is wiped out. Its
social and residential section is wiped out. The factories and
warehouses, the great stores and newspaper buildings, the hotels
and the palaces of the nabobs, are all gone. Remains only the
fringe of dwelling houses on the outskirts of what was once San
Francisco.

Within an hour after the earthquake shock, the smoke of San
Francisco's burning was a lurid tower visible a hundred miles
away. And for three days and nights this lurid tower swayed in
the sky, reddening the sun, darkening the day, and filling the
land with smoke.

On Wednesday morning at quarter past five came the earthquake. A minute later the flames were leaping upward. In a dozen
different quarters south of Market Street, in the working class
ghetto and in the factories, fires started. There was no opposing
the flames. There was no organization, no communication. All
the cunning adjustments of a twentieth century city had been
smashed by the earthquake. The streets were humped into ridges
and depressions, and piled with the debris of fallen walls. The
steel rails were twisted into perpendicular and horizontal angles.
The telephone and telegraph systems were disrupted. And the
great water mains had burst. All the shrewd contrivances and
safeguards of man had been thrown out of gear by thirty seconds'
twitching of the earth-crust.

By Wednesday afternoon, inside of twelve hours, half the heart
of the city was gone. At that time I watched the vast conflagration
from out on the bay. It was dead calm. Not a flicker of wind
stirred. Yet from every side wind was pouring in upon the city.
East, west, north, and south, strong winds were blowing upon the
doomed city. The heated air rising made an enormous suck. Thus
did the fire of itself build its own colossal chimney through the
atmosphere. Day and night this dead calm continued, and yet,

near to the flames, the wind was often half a gale, so mighty was the suck.

Wednesday night saw the destruction of the very heart of the city. Dynamite was lavishly used, and many of San Francisco's proudest structures were crumbled by man himself into ruins, but there was no withstanding the onrush of the flames. Time and again successful stands were made by the firefighters, and every time the flames flanked around on either side, or came up from the rear, and turned to defeat the hard won victory.

An enumeration of the buildings destroyed would be a directory of San Francisco. An enumeration of the buildings undestroyed would be a line and several addresses. An enumeration of the deeds of heroism would stock a library and bankrupt the Carnegie medal fund. An enumeration of the dead—will never be made. All vestiges of them were destroyed by the flames. The number of the victims of the earthquake will never be known. South of Market Street, where the loss of life was particularly heavy, was the first to catch fire.

Remarkable as it may seem, Wednesday night, while the whole city crashed and roared into ruin, was a quiet night. There were no crowds. There was no shouting and yelling. There was no hysteria, no disorder. I passed Wednesday night in the path of the advancing flames, and in all those terrible hours I saw not one woman who wept, not one man who was excited, not one person who was in the slightest degree panic-stricken.

Before the flames, throughout the night, fled tens of thousands of homeless ones. Some were wrapped in blankets. Others carried bundles of bedding and dear household treasures. Sometimes a whole family was harnessed to a carriage or delivery wagon that was weighted down with their possessions. Baby-buggies, toy wagons and go-carts were used as trucks, while every other person was dragging a trunk. Yet everybody was gracious. The most perfect courtesy obtained. Never, in all San Francisco's history, were her people so kind and courteous as on this night of terror.

All night these tens of thousands fled before the flames. Many of them, the poor people from the labor ghetto, had fled all day as well. They had left their homes burdened with possessions.

Now and again they lightened up, flinging out upon the street clothing and treasures they had dragged for miles.

They held on longest to their trunks, and over these trunks many a strong man broke his heart that night. The hills of San Francisco are steep, and up these hills, mile after mile, were the trunks dragged. Everywhere were trunks, with across them lying their exhausted owners, men and women. Before the march of the flames were flung picket-lines of soldiers. And a block at a time, as the flames advanced, these pickets retreated. One of their tasks was to keep the trunk-pullers moving. The exhausted creatures stirred on by the menace of bayonets, would arise and struggle up the steep pavements, pausing from weakness every five or ten feet.

Often, after surmounting a heart-breaking hill, they would find another wall of flame advancing upon them at right angles and be compelled to change anew the line of their retreat. In the end, completely played out, after toiling for a dozen hours like giants, thousands of them were compelled to abandon their trunks. Here the shop-keepers and soft members of the middle class were at a disadvantage. But the workingmen dug holes in vacant lots and backyards and buried their trunks.

At nine o'clock Wednesday evening, I walked down through the very heart of the city. I walked through miles and miles of magnificent buildings and towering skyscrapers. Here was no fire. All was in perfect order. The police patrolled the streets. Every building had its watchman at the door. And yet it was doomed, all of it. There was no water. The dynamite was giving out. And at right angles two different conflagrations were sweeping down upon it.

At one o'clock in the morning I walked down through the same section. Everything still stood intact. There was no fire. And yet there was a change. A rain of ashes was falling. The watchmen at the doors were gone. The police had been withdrawn. There were no firemen, no fire-engines, no men fighting with dynamite. The district had been absolutely abandoned.

I stood at the corner of Kearney and Market, in the very innermost heart of San Francisco. Kearney Street was deserted. Half a dozen blocks away it was burning on both sides. The street was a wall of flame. And against this wall of flame, silhouetted sharply, were two United States cavalrymen sitting their horses, calmly watching. That was all. Not another person was in sight. In the intact heart of the city two troopers sat their horses and watched.

Surrender was complete. There was no water. The sewers had long since been pumped dry. There was no dynamite. Another fire had broken out farther up town, and now from three sides conflagrations were sweeping down. The fourth side had been burned earlier in the day. In that direction stood the tottering walls of the *Examiner* Building, the burned out *Call* Building, the smouldering ruins of the Grand Hotel, and the gutted, devastated, dynamited Palace Hotel.

The following will illustrate the sweep of the flames and the inability of men to calculate their spread. At eight o'clock Wednesday evening I passed through Union Square. It was packed with refugees. Thousands of them had gone to bed on the grass. Government tents had been set up, supper was being cooked, and the refugees were lining up for free meals.

At half-past one in the morning three sides of Union Square were in flames. The fourth side, where stood the great St. Francis Hotel, was still holding out. An hour later, ignited from top and sides, the St. Francis was flaming heavenward. Union Square, heaped high with mountains of trunks, was deserted. Troops, refugees, and all had retreated.

It was at Union Square that I saw a man offering a thousand dollars for a team of horses. He was in charge of a truck piled high with trunks from some hotel. It had been hauled here into what was considered safety and the horses had been taken out. The flames were on three sides of the Square, and there were no horses.

Also, at this time, standing beside the truck, I urged a man to seek safety in flight. He was all but hemmed in by several conflagrations. He was an old man and he was on crutches. Said he, "To-day is my birthday. Last night I was worth thirty thousand dollars. I bought five bottles of wine, some delicate fish, and other things for my birthday dinner. I have had no dinner, and all I own are these crutches."

I convinced him of his danger and started him limping on his way. An hour later, from a distance, I saw the truckload of trunks burning merrily in the middle of the street.

On Thursday morning, at quarter past five, just twenty-four hours after the earthquake, I sat on the steps of a small residence on Nob Hill. With me sat Japanese, Italians, Chinese, and Negroes—a bit of the cosmopolitan flotsam of the wreck of the city. All about were the palaces of the Nabob pioneers of forty-nine. To the east and south, at right angles, were advancing two mighty walls of flames.

I went inside with the owner of the house on the steps of which I sat. He was cool and cheerful and hospitable. "Yesterday morning," he said, "I was worth six hundred thousand dollars. This morning this house is all I have left. It will go in fifteen minutes." He pointed to a large cabinet. "That is my wife's collection of China. This rug upon which we stand is a present. It cost fifteen hundred dollars. Try that piano. Listen to its tone. There are few like it. There are no horses. The flames will be here in fifteen minutes."

Outside, the old Mark Hopkins residence, a palace, was just catching fire. The troops were falling back and driving the refugees before them. From every side came the roaring of flames, the crashing of walls, and the detonations of dynamite.

I passed out of the house. Day was trying to dawn through the smoke-pall. A sickly light was creeping over the face of things. Once only the sun broke through the smoke-pall, blood-red and showing quarter its usual size. The smoke-pall itself, viewed from beneath, was a rose-color that pulsed and fluttered with lavender shades. Then it turned to mauve and yellow and dun. There was no sun. And so dawned the second day on stricken San Francisco.

An hour later I was creeping past the shattered dome of the City Hall. Than it, there was no better exhibit of the destructive force of the earthquake. Most of the stone had been shaken from the great dome, leaving standing the naked frame-work of steel. Market Street was piled high with the wreckage, and across the wreckage, lay the overthrown pillars of the City Hall shattered into short crosswise sections.

This section of the city, with the exception of the Mint and the Post Office, was already a waste of smoking ruins. Here and there through the smoke, creeping warily under the shadows of tottering walls, emerged occasional men and women. It was like the meeting of the handful of survivors after the day of the end of the world.

On Mission Street lay a dozen steers, in a neat row stretching across the street, just as they had been struck down by the flying ruins of the earthquake. The fire had passed through afterward and roasted them. The human dead had been carried away before the fire came. At another place on Mission Street I saw a milk wagon. A steel telegraph pole had smashed down sheer through the driver's seat and crushed the front wheels. The milk cans lay scattered around.

All day Thursday and all Thursday night, all day Friday and Friday night, the flames still raged. Friday night saw the flames finally conquered, though not until Russian Hill and Telegraph Hill had been swept and three-quarters of a mile of wharves and docks had been licked up.

The great stand of the firefighters was made Thursday night on Van Ness Avenue. Had they failed here, the comparatively few remaining houses of the city would have been swept. Here were the magnificent residences of the second generation of San Francisco nabobs, and these, in a solid zone, were dynamited down across the path of the fire. Here and there, the flames leaped the zone, but these isolated fires were beaten out, principally by the use of wet blankets and rugs.

San Francisco, at the present time, is like the crater of a volcano, around which are camped tens of thousands of refugees. At the Presidio alone are at least twenty thousand. All the surrounding cities and towns are jammed with the homeless ones, where they are being cared for by the relief committees. The refugees were carried free by the railroads to any point they wished to go, and it is estimated that over one hundred thousand people have left the peninsula on which San Francisco stood. The government has the situation in hand, and, thanks to the immediate relief given by the whole United States, there is not the slightest possibility of a famine. The bankers and business men have already set about making preparations to rebuild San Francisco.

IF JAPAN WAKENS CHINA[1]

After the Londons' return to their home in Glen Ellen on July 24,
1909, London immediately turned his efforts to the development of
the Beauty Ranch and continued his daily output of articles and sto-
ries. One of the problems that had troubled him since his years as a
war correspondent was the question of the Japanese and Chinese de-
velopment. He could not forget the ruthless efficiency of the Japanese
war machine and the threat it posed for world peace.

When one man does not understand another man's mental
processes, how can the one forecast the other's future actions?
This is precisely the situation to-day between the white race and
the Japanese. In spite of all our glib talk to the contrary, we know
nothing (and less than nothing in so far as we think we know
something) of the Japanese. It is a weakness of man to believe
that all the rest of mankind is moulded in his own image, and it
is a weakness of the white race to believe that the Japanese think
as we think, are moved to action as we are moved and have
points of view similar to our own.

Perhaps the one white man in the world best fitted by nature
and opportunity to know the Japanese was Lafcadio Hearn. To
begin with, he was an artist, and he possessed to an extreme
degree the artist's sympathy. By this I mean that his sympathy
was of that order that permits a man to get out of himself and
into the soul of another man, thus enabling him to look at life
out of that man's eyes and from that man's point of view—to
be that man, in short.

Lafcadio Hearn went to Japan. He identified himself with the
Japanese. To all intents and purposes he became a Japanese.
A professor in a Japanese university, he took to himself a Japanese
wife, lived in a Japanese household, and even renounced his own
country and became a Japanese citizen. Being an artist, enthusiastically in touch with his subject, he proceeded to interpret
the Japanese mind to the English-speaking world, turning out the
most wonderful series of books on Japan ever written by an
Occidental. The years passed, and ever he turned out more of his

[1] *Sunset Magazine*, December 1909.

wonderful books, interpreting, explaining, elaborating, formulating every big aspect and minute detail of the Japanese mind.

Just at the beginning of the Russo-Japanese war, full of years and wise with much experience, Lafcadio Hearn died. His last book was in the press, and it appeared shortly afterward. It was entitled *Japan: An Interpretation.* In the foreword Lafcadio Hearn made a confession. He said that after all his years of intimate living with the Japanese, he was at last just on the verge of beginning to understand the Japanese. And he felt justified in this belief, by virtue of the fact that he had taken all those years to find out that he knew nothing of the Japanese. This was a hopeful sign. He had come farther than other white men, who still believed that they did know something, in greater or less degree, of the Japanese.

As for himself, after the many years of thinking, he knew, he frankly confessed, that the Japanese mind baffled him. He told of the Japanese schoolboys with whom he had been in daily contact—of how he had watched their minds unfold and expand as they grew into manhood. And then he sadly explained that now that they were men, Japanese men, out in the world of Japanese men, they were strangers to him. Oh, they greeted him, and shook hands with him and talked with him as of yore; but they were soul-strangers to him. He looked into their faces, but not into their souls. He saw their eyes, but no glimmering could he catch of what went on behind those eyes. Their mental processes were veiled to him. Why they did this or that or some other action was a puzzle to him. He found them actuated by motives he could not guess—motives generated in the labyrinths of their minds where he could not follow the process. Life appeared to them in perspective differently from the way it appeared to him. And he could get no inkling of that perspective. To him it was an inconceivable fourth dimension. And so he wrote that last sad foreword to the last sad book of his, gazing mournfully the while into the mysterious eyes of Asia, which had baffled him as they have baffled the men of the West from the days of Marco Polo to this our day.

The point I have striven to make is that much of the reasoning of the white race anent the Japanese is erroneous, because it is based on fancied knowledge of the stuff and fiber of the Japa-

nese mind. An American lady of my acquaintance, after residing
for months in Japan, in response to a query as to how she liked
the Japanese, said: "They have no souls."

In this she was wrong. The Japanese are just as much possessed of soul as she and the rest of her race. And far be it from
me to infer that the Japanese soul is in the smallest way inferior to the Western soul. It may be even superior. You see, we
do not know the Japanese soul, and what its value may be in the
scheme of things. And yet that American lady's remark but em-
phasizes the point. So different was the Japanese soul from hers,
so unutterably alien, so absolutely without any sort of kinship
or means of communication, that to her there was no slightest
sign of its existence.

Japan, in her remarkable evolution, has repeatedly surprised
the world. Now the element of surprise can be present only when
one is unfamiliar with the data that go to constitute the surprise.
Had we really known the Japanese, we should not have been
surprised. And as she has surprised us in the past, and only the
other day, may she not surprise us to-morrow, and in the days
that are yet to be? And since she may surprise us in the future,
and since ignorance is the meat and wine of surprise, who are we,
and with what second sight are we invested, that we may calmly
say:

"Surprise is all very well, but there is not going to be any
Yellow peril or Japanese peril"?

There are forty-five million Japanese in the world. There are
over four hundred million Chinese. That is to say, if we add together the various branches of the white race, the English, the
French, and the German, the Austrian, the Scandinavian and
the White Russian, the Latins as well, the Americans, the Ca-
nadians, Australians and New Zealanders, the South Africans,
the Anglo-Indians, and all the scattered remnants of us, we shall
find that we are still outnumbered by the combined Japanese
and Chinese.

We understand the Chinese mind no more than we do the
Japanese. What if these two races, as homogeneous as we, should
embark on some vast race-adventure? There have been race-
adventures in the past. We English-speaking peoples are just
now in the midst of our own great adventure. We are dreaming

as all race-adventurers have dreamed. And who will dare to say that in the Japanese mind is not burning some colossal Napoleonic dream? And what if the dreams clash?

Japan is the one unique Asiatic race, in that alone among the races of Asia, she has been able to borrow from us and equip herself with all our material achievement. Our machinery of warfare, of commerce, and of industry, she has made hers. And so well has she done it that we have been surprised. We did not think she had it in her. Next consider China. We of the West have tried, and tried vainly, to awaken her. We have failed to express our material achievement in terms comprehensible to the Chinese mind. We do not know the Chinese mind. But Japan does. She and China spring from the same primitive stock—their languages are rooted in the same primitive tongue; and their mental processes are the same. The Chinese mind may baffle us, but it cannot baffle the Japanese. And what if Japan awakens China—not to our dream, if you please, but to her dream, to Japan's dream? Japan, having taken from us all our material achievement, is alone able to transmute that material achievement in terms intelligible to the Chinese mind.

The Chinese and Japanese are thrifty and industrious. China possesses great natural resources of coal and iron—and coal and iron constitute the backbone of machine civilization. When four hundred and fifty million of the best workers in the world go into manufacturing, a new competitor, and a most ominous and formidable one, will enter the arena where the races struggle for the world-market. Here is race-adventure—the first clashing of the Asiatic dream with ours. It is true, it is only an economic clash, but economic clashes always precede clashes at arms. And what then? Oh, only that will-o'-the-wisp, the Yellow peril. But to the Russian, Japan was only a will-o'-the-wisp until one day, with fire and steel, she smashed the great adventure of the Russian and punctured the bubble-dream he was dreaming.

Of this be sure: If ever the day comes that our dreams clash with that of the Yellow and the Brown, and our particular bubble-dream is punctured, there will be one country at least unsurprised, and that country will be Russia. She was awakened from her dream. We still are dreaming.

NAVIGATING FOUR HORSES NORTH OF THE BAY[1]

The year of 1910 was, for London, a disturbing year. The great dis-
appointment of his life was the death of Charmian's baby girl, who
was born June 19, 1910, but lived only a few hours. Added to this
also was perhaps overwork, both in his writing and in the develop-
ment of the Beauty Ranch. In the spring of 1911, he and Charmian
decided to change their routine and take a four-horse driving trip
along the California coast into Oregon, which began in early June
and ended in early September. Here, as in "Housekeeping in the
Klondike," London shows his ability to handle humorous situations.

"Huh! Drive four horses! I wouldn't sit behind you—not for
a thousand dollars—over them mountain roads."

So said Henry, and he ought to have known, for he drives
four horses himself.

Said another Glen Ellen friend: "What? London? He drive
four horses? Can't drive one!"

And the best of it is that he was right. Even after managing
to get a few hundred miles with my four horses, I don't know
how to drive one. Just the other day, swinging down a steep
mountain road and rounding an abrupt turn, I came full tilt on
a horse and buggy being driven by a woman up the hill. We
could not pass on the narrow road, where was only a foot to
spare, and my horses did not know how to back, especially
uphill. About two hundred yards down the hill was a spot where
we could pass. The driver of the buggy said she didn't dare back
down because she was not sure of the brake. And as I didn't
know how to tackle one horse, I didn't try it. So we unhitched
her horse and backed down by hand. Which was very well,
till it came to hitching the horse to the buggy again. She didn't
know how. I didn't either, and I had depended on her knowledge. It took us about half an hour, with frequent debates and
consultations, though it is an absolute certainty that never in
its life was that horse hitched in that particular way.

No; I can't harness up one horse. But I can four, which compels me to back up again to get to my beginning. Having selected
Sonoma valley for our abiding place, Charmian and I decided

[1] *Sunset Magazine.* September 1911.

it was about time we knew what we had in our own country and the neighboring ones. How to do it, was the first question. Among our many weaknesses is the one of being old-fashioned. We don't mix with gasoline very well. And, as true sailors should, we naturally gravitate toward horses. Being one of those lucky individuals who carries his office under his hat, I should have to take a typewriter and a load of books along. This put saddle-horses out of the running. Charmian suggested driving a span. She had faith in me; besides, she could drive a span herself. But when I thought of the many mountains to cross, and of crossing them for three months with a poor tired span, I vetoed the proposition and said we'd have to come back to gasoline after all. This she vetoed just as emphatically, and a deadlock obtained until I received inspiration.

"Why not drive four horses?" I said.

"But you don't know how to drive four horses" was her objection.

I threw my chest out and my shoulders back. "What man has done, I can do," I proclaimed grandly. "And please don't forget that when we sailed on the *Snark* I knew nothing of navigation, and that I taught myself as I sailed."

"Very well," she said. (And there's faith for you!) "They shall be four saddle-horses, and we'll strap our saddles on behind the rig."

It was my turn to object. "Our saddle-horses are not broken to harness."

"Then break them."

And what I knew about horses, much less about breaking them, and just about as much as any sailor knows. Having been kicked, bucked off, fallen over backward upon, and thrown out and run over, on very numerous occasions, I had a mighty vigorous respect for horses; but a wife's faith must be lived up to, and I went at it.

King was a polo pony from St. Louis, and Prince a many-gaited love-horse from Pasadena. The hardest thing was to get them to dig in and pull. They rollicked along on the levels and galloped down the hills, but when they struck an up-grade and felt the weight of the breaking-cart, they stopped and turned around and looked at me. But I passed them, and my troubles began. Milda was fourteen years old, an unadulterated bronco, and in temperament was a combination of mule and jack-rabbit blended equally. If you pressed your hand on her flank and told her to get over, she lay down on you. If you got her by the head and told her to back, she walked forward over you. And if you got behind her and shoved and told her to "Giddap!" she sat down on you. Also, she wouldn't walk. For endless weary miles I strove with her, but never could I get her to walk a step. Finally, she was a manger-glutton. No matter how near or far from the stable, when six o'clock came around she bolted for home and never missed the directest cross-road. Many times I rejected her.

The fourth and most rejected horse of all was the Outlaw. From the age of three to seven she had defied all horse-breakers and broken a number of them. Then a long lanky cowboy, with a fifty-pound saddle and a Mexican bit, had got her proud goat. I was the next owner. She was my favorite riding-horse. Charmian said I'd have to put her in as a wheeler where I would have more control over her. Now Charmian had a favorite riding mare called Maid. I suggested Maid as a substitute. Charmian pointed out that my mare was a branded range horse, while hers was a thoroughbred, and that the legs of her mare would be ruined forever if she were driven for three months. I acknowledged her mare's thoroughbredness, and at the same time defied her to find any thoroughbred with as small and delicately-viciously pointed ears as my Outlaw. She indicated Maid's exquisitely thin shin-bone. I measured the Outlaw's. It was equally thin, although, I insinuated, possibly more durable. This stabbed Charmian's pride. Of course her thoroughbred Maid, carrying the blood of "Old Lexington, Morella, and a streak of the super-enduring Morgan, could run, walk, and work my unregistered Outlaw into the ground; and that was the very precise reason why such a paragon of a saddle animal should not be degraded by harness.

So it was that Charmian remained obdurate, until, one day, I got her behind the Outlaw for a forty-mile drive. For every inch of those forty miles the Outlaw kicked and jumped, in between the kicks and jumps finding time and space in which to seize its team-mate by the back of the neck and attempt to drag it to the ground. Another trick the Outlaw developed during that drive was suddenly to turn at right angles in the traces and endeavor to butt its team-mate over the grade. Reluctantly and nobly did Charmian give in and consent to the use of Maid. The Outlaw's shoes were pulled off, and she was turned out on the range.

Finally, the four horses were hooked to the rig—a light Studebaker trap. With two hours and a half of practice, in which the excitement was not abated by several jack-poles and numerous kicking matches, I announced myself as ready for the start. Came the morning, and Prince, who was to have been a wheeler with Maid, showed up with a badly kicked shoulder. He did not exactly show up; we had to find him, for he was unable to walk. His leg swelled and continually swelled during the several days we waited for him. Remained only the Outlaw. In from pasture she came, shoes were nailed on, and she was harnessed into the wheel. Friends and relatives strove to press accident policies on me, but Charmian climbed up alongside, and Nakata[2] got into the rear seat with the typewriter—Nakata, who sailed cabin-boy on the *Snark* for two years and who has shown himself afraid of nothing, not even of me and my amateur jamborees in experimenting with new modes of locomotion. And we did very nicely, thank you, especially after the first hour or so, during which time the Outlaw had kicked about fifty various times, chiefly to the damage of her own legs and the paintwork, and after she had bitten a couple of hundred times, to the damage of Maid's neck and Charmian's temper. It was hard enough to have her favorite mare in the harness without also enduring the spectacle of its being eaten alive.

Our leaders were joys. King being a polo pony and Milda a rabbit, they rounded curves beautifully and darted ahead like coyotes out of the way of the wheelers. Milda's besetting weakness was a frantic desire not to have the lead-bar strike her hocks. When this happened, one of three things occurred: either she sat down on the lead-bar, kicked it up in the air until she got her back under it, or exploded in a straight-ahead, harness-disrupting jump. Not until she carried the lead-bar clean away

[2] Nakata later became a dentist and practiced in Honolulu.

and danced a breakdown on it and the traces, did she behave decently. Nakata and I made the repairs with good old-fashioned bale-rope, which is stronger than wrought-iron any time, and we went on our way.

In the meantime I was learning—I shall not say to tool a four-in-hand—but just simply to drive four horses. Now it is all right enough to begin with four work-horses pulling a load of several tons. But to begin with four light horses, all running, and a light rig that seems to outrun them—well, when things happen they happen quickly. My weakness was total ignorance. In particular, my fingers lacked training, and I made the mistake of depending on my eyes to handle the reins. This brought me up against a disastrous optical illusion. The bight of the off lead-line, being longer and heavier than that of the off wheel-line, hung lower. In a moment requiring quick action, I invariably mistook the two lines. Pulling on what I thought was the wheel-line, in order to straighten the team, I would see the leaders swing abruptly around into a jack-pole. Now for sensations of sheer impotence, nothing can compare with a jack-pole, when the horrified driver beholds his leaders prancing gaily up the road and his wheelers jogging steadily down the road, all at the same time and all harnessed together and to the same rig.

I no longer jack-pole, and I don't mind admitting how I got out of the habit. It was my eyes that enslaved my fingers into ill-practices. So I shut my eyes and let the fingers go it alone. Today my fingers are independent of my eyes and work automatically. I do not see what my fingers do. They just do it. All I see is the satisfactory result.

Still we managed to get over the ground that first day—down sunny Sonoma valley to the old town to Sonoma, founded by General Vallejo as the remotest outpost on the northern frontier for the purpose of holding back the Gentiles, as the wild Indians of those days were called. Here history was made. Here the last Spanish mission was reared; here the Bear flag was raised; and here Kit Carson, and Frémont, and all our early adventurers, came and rested in the days before the days of gold.

We swung on over the low rolling hills, through miles of dairy farms and chicken ranches where every blessed hen is white, and down the slopes to Petaluma valley. Here, in 1776, Captain Quiros came up Petaluma creek from San Pablo bay in quest of an outlet to Bodega bay on the coast. And here, later, the Russians, with Alaskan hunters, carried skin boats across from Fort Ross to poach for sea-otters on the Spanish preserve of San Francisco bay. Here, too, still later, General Vallejo built a fort, which still stands—one of the finest examples of Spanish adobe that remain to us. And here, at the old fort, to bring the chronicle up to date, our horses proceeded to make peculiarly personal history with astonishing success and dispatch. King, our peerless polo-pony leader, went lame. So hopelessly lame did he go that no expert, then and afterward, could determine whether the lameness was in his frogs, hoofs, legs, shoulders, or head. Maid picked up a nail and began to limp. Milda, figuring the day already sufficiently spent and maniacal with manger gluttony, began to rabbit-jump. All that held her was the bale-rope. And the Outlaw, game to the last, exceeded all previous exhibitions of skin-removing, paint-marring, and horse-eating.

At Petaluma we rested over while King was returned to the ranch and Prince sent to us. Now Prince had proved himself an excellent wheeler, yet he had to go into the lead and let the Outlaw retain his old place. There is an axiom that a good wheeler is a poor leader. I object to the last adjective. A good wheeler makes an infinitely worse kind of a leader than that. I know . . . now. I ought to know. Since that day I have driven Prince a few hundred miles in the lead. He is neither any better nor any worse than the first mile he ran in the lead; and his worst is even extremely worse than what you are thinking. Not that he is vicious. He is merely a good-natured rogue who shakes hands for sugar, steps on your toes out of sheer excessive friendliness, and just goes on loving you in your harshest moments.

But he won't get out of the way. Also, whenever he is reproved for being in the wrong, he accuses Milda of it and bites the back of her neck. So bad has this become that whenever I yell "Prince!" in a loud voice, Milda immediately rabbit-jumps to the side, straight ahead, or sits down on the lead-bar. All of which is quite disconcerting. Picture it yourself. You are swinging a sharp, down-grade, mountain curve, at a fast trot. The

rock wall is the outside of the curve. The inside of the curve
is a precipice. The continuance of the curve is a narrow un-
railed bridge. You hit the curve, throwing the leaders in against
the wall and making the pole-horse do the work. All is lovely.
The leaders are hugging the wall like nestling doves. But the
moment comes in the evolution when the leaders must shoot
out ahead. They really must shoot, or else they'll hit the wall
and miss the bridge. Also, behind them are the wheelers, and
the rig, and you have just eased the brake in order to put
sufficient snap into the maneuver. If ever team-work is required,
now is the time. Milda tries to shoot. She does her best, but
Prince, bubbling over with roguishness, lags behind. He knows
the trick. Milda is half a length ahead of him. He times it to the
fraction of a second. Maid, in the wheel, over-running him,
naturally bites him. This disturbs the Outlaw, who has been
behaving beautifully, and she immediately reaches across for Maid.
Simultaneously, with a fine display of firm conviction that it's
all Milda's fault, Prince sinks his teeth into the back of Milda's
defenseless neck. The whole thing has occurred in less than a
second. Under the surprise and pain of the bite, Milda either
jumps ahead to the imminent peril of harness and lead-bar, or
smashes into the wall, stops short with the lead-bar over her
back, and emits a couple of hysterical kicks. The Outlaw invariably selects this moment to remove paint. And after things
are untangled and you have had time to appreciate the close
shave, you go up to Prince and reprove him with your choicest
vocabulary. And Prince, gazelle-eyed and tender, offers to shake
hands with you for sugar. I leave it to any one: a boat would
never act that way.

We have some history north of the bay. Nearly three centuries and a half ago, that doughty pirate and explorer, Sir Francis Drake, combing the Pacific for Spanish galleons, anchored
in the bight formed by Point Reyes, on which today is one of
the richest dairy regions in the world. Here, less than two decades
after Drake, Sebastien Carmenon piled up on the rocks with a
silkladen galleon from the Philippines. And in this same bay
of Drake, long afterward, the Russian fur-poachers rendezvous'd
their *bidarkas* and stole in through the Golden Gate to the forbidden waters of San Francisco bay.

Farther up the coast, in Sonoma county, we pilgrimaged to the sites of the Russian settlements. At Bodega bay, south of what today is called Russian River, was their anchorage, while north of the river they built their fort. And much of Fort Ross still stands. Log-bastions, church, and stables hold their own, and so well, with rusty hinges creaking, that we warmed ourselves at the hundred-years-old double fireplace and slept under the hand-hewn roof beams still held together by spikes of hand-wrought iron.

We went to see where history had been made, and we saw scenery as well. One of our stretches in a day's drive was from beautiful Inverness on Tomales bay, down the Olema valley to Bolinas bay, along the eastern shore of that body of water to Willow Camp, and up over the sea-bluffs, around the bastions of Tamalpais, and down to Sausalito. From the head of Bolinas bay to Willow Camp the drive on the edge of the beach, and actually, for half-mile stretches, in the waters of the bay itself, was a delightful experience. The wonderful part was to come. Very few San Franciscans, much less Californians, know of that drive from Willow Camp, to the south and east, along the poppy-blown cliffs, with the sea thundering in the sheer depths hundreds of feet below and the Golden Gate opening up ahead, disclosing smoky San Francisco on her many hills. Far off, blurred on the breast of the sea, can be seen the Farallones, which Sir Francis Drake passed on a southwest course in the thick of a fog that robbed him of the glory of discovering San Francisco bay.

It was on this part of the drive that I decided at last I was learning real mountain-driving. To confess the truth, for delicious titillation of one's nerve, I have since driven over no mountain road that was worse, or better, rather, than that piece.

And then the contrast! From Sausalito, over excellent park-like boulevards, through the splendid redwoods and homes of Mill Valley, across the blossomed hills of Marin county, along the knoll-studded picturesque marshes, past San Rafael resting warmly among her hills, over the divide and up the Petaluma valley, and on to the grassy feet of Sonoma mountain and home. We covered fifty-five miles that day. Not so bad, eh, for Prince the Rogue, the paint-removing Outlaw, the thin-shanked

thoroughbred, and the rabbit-jumper? And they came in cool
and dry, ready for their mangers and the straw.

Oh, we didn't stop. We considered we were just starting,
and that was many weeks ago. We have kept on going over
six counties which are comfortably large, even for California, and
we are still going. We have twisted and doubled, crisscrossed our
tracks, made fascinating and lengthy dives into the interior valleys in the hearts of Napa and Lake counties, traveled the coast
for hundreds of miles on end, and are now in Eureka, on Humboldt bay, which was discovered by accident by the gold-seekers,
who were trying to find their way to and from the Trinity diggings. Even here, the white man's history preceded them, for
dim tradition says that the Russians once anchored here and
hunted sea-otter before the first Yankee trader rounded the
Horn, or the first Rocky mountain trapper thirsted across the
"Great American Desert" and trickled down the snowy Sierra
to the sun-kissed land. No; we are not resting our horses here
on Humboldt bay. We are writing this, gorging on abalones and
mussels, digging clams, and catching record-breaking sea-trout
and rock-cod in the intervals in which we are not sailing, motor-
boating, and swimming in the most temperately equable climate
we have ever experienced.

These comfortably large counties! They are veritable empires.
Take Humboldt, for instance. It is three times as large as Rhode
Island, one and one half times as large as Delaware, almost
as large as Connecticut, and half as large as Massachusetts. The
pioneer has done his work in this north-of-the-bay region, the
foundations are laid, and all is ready for the inevitable inrush
of population and adequate development of resources which so
far have been no more than skimmed, and casually and carelessly skimmed at that. This region of the six counties alone
will some day support a population of millions. In the meanwhile, O you homeseekers, you wealth-seekers, and, above all,
you climate-seekers, now is the time to get in on the ground
floor.

Robert Ingersoll once said that the genial climate of California would in a fairly brief time evolve a race resembling the
Mexicans, and that in two or three generations the Californians
would be seen of a Sunday morning on their way to a cockfight

with a rooster under each arm. Never was made a rasher generalization, based on so absolute an ignorance of facts. It is to laugh. Here is a climate that breeds vigor, with just sufficient geniality to prevent the expenditure of most of that vigor in fighting the elements. Here is a climate where a man can work three hundred and sixty-five days in the year without the slightest hint of enervation, and where for three hundred and sixty-five nights he must perforce sleep under blankets. What more can one say? I consider myself somewhat of a climate expert, having adventured among most of the climates of five out of the six zones. I have not yet been in the Antarctic, but whatever climate obtains there will not deter me from drawing the conclusion that nowhere is there a climate to compare with that of this region. Maybe I am as wrong as Ingersoll was. Nevertheless I take my medicine by continuing to live in this climate. Also, it is the only medicine I ever take.

But to return to the horses. There is some improvement. Milda has actually learned to walk. Maid has proved her thoroughbredness by never tiring on the longest days, and, while being the strongest and highest spirited of all, by never causing any trouble save for an occasional kick at the Outlaw. And the Outlaw rarely gallops, no longer butts, only periodically kicks, comes in to the pole and does her work without attempting to vivisect Maid's medulla oblongata, and—marvel of marvels—is really and truly getting lazy. But Prince remains the same incorrigible, loving and lovable rogue as always.

And the country we've been over! The drives through Napa and Lake counties! One, from Sonoma valley, via Santa Rosa, we could not refrain from taking several ways, and on all the ways we found the roads excellent for machines as well as horses. One route, and a more delightful one for an automobile cannot be found, is out from Santa Rosa, past old Altruria and Mark West Springs, then to the right and across to Calistoga in Napa valley. By keeping to the left, the drive holds on up the Russian river valley, through the miles of the noted Asti vineyards to Cloverdale, and then by way of Pieta, Witter, and Highland Springs to Lakeport. Still another way we took was down Sonoma valley, skirting San Pablo bay, and up the lovely Napa valley. From Napa were side excursions through Pope and Berryessa valleys, on to Aetna Springs, and into Lake county, crossing the famous Langtry ranch.

More valley from Ukiah to Willits, and then we turned westward through the virgin Sherwood forest of magnificent redwood, stopping at Alpine for the night and continuing on through Mendocino county to Fort Bragg and "salt water." We also came to Fort Bragg up the coast from Fort Ross, keeping our coast journey intact from the Golden Gate. The coast weather was cool and delightful, the coast driving superb. Especially in the Fort Ross section did we find the roads thrilling, while all the way along we followed the sea. At every stream the road skirted dizzy cliff-edges, dived down into lush growths of forest and ferns, and climbed out along the cliff-edges again. The way was lined with flowers—wild lilac, wild roses, poppies, and lupins. Such lupins!—giant clumps of them of every lupin-shade and color. And it was along the Mendocino roads that Charmian caused many delays by insisting on getting out to pick the wild blackberries, strawberries and thimbleberries which grew so profusely. And ever we caught peeps, far down, of steam schooners loading lumber in the rocky coves; ever we skirted the cliffs, day after day, crossing stretches of rolling farm lands and passing through thriving villages and saw-mill towns. Memorable was our launch-trip from Mendocino City up Big river, where the stearing gears of the launches work the reverse of anywhere else in the world; where we saw a stream of logs, of six to twelve and fifteen feet in diameter, which filled the river-bed for miles to the obliteration of any sign of water; and where we were told of a white or albino redwood tree. We did not see this last, so cannot vouch for it.

All the streams were filled with trout, and more than once we saw sidehill salmon on the slopes. No, sidehill salmon is not a peripatetic fish; it is a deer out of season. But the trout! At Gualala Charmian caught her first one. Once before in my life I had caught two . . . on angleworms. On occasion I had tried fly and spinner and never got a strike, and I had come to believe that all this talk of fly-fishing was just so much nature-faking. But on the Gualala river I caught trout—a lot of them—on fly and spinner; and I was beginning to feel quite an expert, until Nakata, fishing on bottom with a pellet of bread for bait, caught the biggest trout of all. I now affirm there is nothing in science nor in art. Nevertheless, since that day poles and baskets have been added to our baggage, we tackle every stream we come to, and we no longer are able to remember the grand total of our catch.

At Usal, many hilly and picturesque miles north of Fort Bragg, we turned again into the interior of Mendocino, crossing the ranges and coming out in Humboldt county on the south fork of Eel river at Garberville. Throughout the trip, from Marin county north, we had been warned of "bad roads ahead." Yet we never found those bad roads. We seemed always to be just ahead of them or behind them. The farther we came the better the roads seemed, though this was probably due to the fact that we were learning more and more what four horses and a light rig could do on a road. And thus do I save my face with all the counties. I refuse to make invidious road comparisons. I can add that while, save in rare instances on steep pitches, I have trotted my horses down all the grades, I have never had one horse fall down nor have I had to send the rig to a blacksmith shop for repairs.

Also, I am learning to throw leather. If any tyro thinks it is easy to take a short-handled, long-lashed whip, and throw the end of that lash just where he wants it, let him put on automobile goggles and try it. On reconsideration, I would suggest the substitution of a wire fencing-mask for the goggles. For days I looked at that whip. It fascinated me, and the fascination was composed mostly of fear. At my first attempt, Charmian and Nakata became afflicted with the same fascination, and for a long time afterward, whenever they saw me reach for the whip, they closed their eyes and shielded their heads with their arms.

Here's the problem. Instead of pulling honestly, Prince is lagging back and maneuvering for a bite at Milda's neck. I have four reins in my hands. I must put these four reins into my left hand, properly gather the whip handle and the bight of the lash in my right hand, and throw that lash past Maid without striking her and into Prince. If the lash strikes Maid, her thoroughbredness will go up in the air and I'll have a case of horse hysteria on my hands for the next half hour. But follow. The whole problem is not yet stated. Suppose that I miss Maid and reach

the intended target. The instant the lash cracks, the four horses
jump, Prince most of all, and his jump, with spread wicked teeth,
is for the back of Milda's neck. She jumps to escape—which is
her second jump, for the first one came when the lash exploded.
The Outlaw reaches for Maid's neck, and Maid, who has already
jumped and tried to bolt, tries to bolt harder. And all this
infinitesimal fraction of time I am trying to hold the four animals
with my left hand, while my whip-lash, writhing through the
air, is coming back to me. Three simultaneous things I must
do: keep hold of the four lines with my left hand; slam on the
brake with my foot; and on the rebound catch that flying lash
in the hollow of my right arm and get the bight of it safely
into my right hand. Then I must get two of the four lines
back into my right hand and keep the horses from running
away or going over the grade. Try it some time. You will find
life anything but wearisome. Why, the first time I hit the mark
and made the lash go off like a revolver shot, I was so astounded
and delighted that I was paralyzed. I forgot to do any of the mul-
titudinous other things, tangled the whip-lash in Maid's harness,
and was forced to call upon Charmian for assistance. And now,
confession. I carry a few pebbles handy. They're great for reaching
Prince in a tight place. But just the same I'm learning that whip
every day, and before I get home I hope to discard the pebbles.
And as long as I rely on pebbles, I cannot truthfully speak of
myself as "tooling a four-in-hand."

From Garberville, where we ate eel to repletion and got acquainted with the aborigines, we drove down the Eel river valley for two days through the most unthinkably glorious body
of redwood timber to be seen anywhere in California. From
Dyerville on to Eureka we caught glimpses of railroad construction and of great concrete bridges in the course of building,
which advertised that at last Humboldt county is to be linked
to the rest of the world.

We still consider our trip is just begun. As soon as this is
mailed from Eureka, it's heigh-ho! for the horses and pull on.
We shall continue up the coast, turn in for the Hoopa Reserva-
tion and the gold mines, and shoot down the Trinity and
Klamath rivers in Indian canoes to Requa. After that, we shall
go on through Del Norte county and into Oregon. The trip

so far has justified us in taking the attitude that we won't go home until the winter rains drive us in. And, finally, I am going to try the experiment of putting the Outlaw in the lead and relegating Prince to his old position in the near wheel. I won't need any pebbles then.

OUR GUILTLESS SCAPEGOATS.
THE STRICKEN OF MOLOKAI[1]

London's restless nature once more prevailed in 1912, and this time, instead of four horses and a carriage, the sea enticed him. With Charmian, he took a trip on a windjammer. They left Baltimore in February on the Dirigo *for a trip around Cape Horn and arrived home the following August.*

Also during this year, by the purchase of the Freund ranch, he consolidated the Beauty Ranch and increased its size to thirteen hundred acres.

London had long dreamed of a house he wanted to build and in this year (1912) he began the construction of the "Wolf House." But it was one more disappointment because when it was practically completed in 1913 it was burned, apparently by arsonists.

After his illness in Vera Cruz his health began to decline and in 1915, and again in 1916, he spent several months in Hawaii.

London first visited Hawaii on the cruise of the Snark *in 1907, and at that time was given permission by the authorities to visit the leper colonies at Molokai. While there, he wrote an article entitled "The Lepers of Molokai," which was published in the* Woman's Home Companion *January 1908.*

In 1910 a columnist for the Honolulu Advertiser *wrote a vituperous article about London and his misrepresentation of Hawaii. The columnist, who simply signed himself "Bystander," was particularly disturbed by four of London's stories: "The Lepers of Molokai," "Goodbye Jack," "The Sheriff of Kona," and "Koolau the Leper."*

London defended himself in a letter to the editor of the Honolulu Advertiser. *He wrote:*

> "Bystander" accuses me of having been granted privileges by the authorities to visit the Leper settlement at Molokai, and then having abused those privileges by writing sensational and untrue short-stories about Molokai.
>
> Now, here are the facts: by the consent of the authorities, I visited

[1] *Philadelphia Ledger.* June 21, 1916.

Molokai, and I wrote an article on Molokai that was so satisfactory to the authorities that the stamp of approval was given to it for publication to the world.

In a letter addressed to Lorrin A. Thurston,[2] February 1, 1910, he again defended himself against the charges of the "Bystander." He said to Thurston:

> One other thing: suppose the Irish should object to the telling of funny Irish stories, and that the Jews should object to the telling of funny Jewish stories, and the Dutch, and the Swedes and the English, and the Scotch, and all the rest of the nationalities; immediately would result a paucity of funny racial stories. By the same token, if Hawaii should hold that her most salient characteristics should not be exploited in fiction, and if Ireland and England and South America, and Africa, and Asia, should take a similar stand—well, fiction would go glimmering, that's all. Because, by the same token, every man and woman in every walk of life, trade, or profession, could make a similar objection to having his walk of life, trade, or profession exploited in fiction.

The last four articles published in the year of his death revealed his interest and his love for Hawaii.

I have just come through a happy experience. I am just returned happy from a few days' stay in the Molokai Settlement. Eight years ago, at which time I spent a similar few days in the settlement, there were almost a thousand patients. To-day there are only a trifle over six hundred. I understand that the apprehension and segregation of lepers throughout the Territory is more thorough and rigid than ever. Therefore, there is only one possible conclusion: leprosy, in the Territory of Hawaii is being successfully stamped out.

It is the one way. Europe, in the Middle Ages, was overrun by lepers. And Europe, in the Middle Ages, by the simple policy of segregation, succeeded in stamping out leprosy.

From what history tells me occurred in the Middle Ages, and from what I have observed in my two visits to the Molokai Settlement eight years apart, in which the figures show me a rough diminution of thirty percent of the patients, I can fairly and conservatively say that there is little doubt, fifty years from

[2] Thurston and his wife were friends of London and Charmian from the time of the *Snark* voyage. They all took Hawaiian names. Thurston's name was Kakina; his wife's name was Kakina Wahine; London's name was Lakana; Charmian's, Lakana Wahine.

now, that the Settlement will contain no leper, because no leper will live in the entire Territory of Hawaii. In line with this, I may add that whereas, eight years ago, the steamers conveying patients to Molokai made four trips yearly, to-day they make but one trip yearly.

Out of the foregoing I dare to forecast that fifty years from now the eight thousand rich and beautiful acres of the settlement will be clean for the clean, because all these Islands will be clean—that those eight thousand acres will be inhabited by clean and happy farmer folk, and that Kalaupapa and Kalawao will be happy villages of prosperous farmer folk—and, for the travel-lovers in that day, will be accessible a scenic adventure more wonderful than the world can show anywhere else. I have seen my fair bit of the world, and I assert that I have beheld nothing scenically to compare with the scenery of windward Molokai, from the magnificent descent of the Pali at the back of the Settlement, two thousand feet of it almost in the sheer, to the unbelievably stern and rugged, Doré-esque coast extending from Kalawao across the tremendous faces of the cliffs, and across the rifts of valleys of Pelekunu and Wailau, on to Halawa—sixteen miles of it.

One thing, now, in the immediate present. Governor Pinkham suggested the idea to me, and my mind has reveled in it ever since. The United States has proven itself notoriously, stupidly, and cruelly ignorant in its treatment of its sporadic lepers. Such an unfortunate is a myriad times more horribly treated by the communities in which it happens to be manifest than ever were lepers treated anywhere else in the world. A city of fifty thousand to one hundred thousand inhabitants will discover one leper. It will segregate that one leper in some miserable pest-house in its bleakest suburb, and will pay the salaries of at least two physicians who dare not come within half a mile of the patient, and who will hire some underling to thrust food at it at the end of a long pole. The expense of the community for this one leper is huge, the treatment of the leper is ferocious, and neither community nor leper can possibly be happy over the situation. And now to the idea suggested by Governor Pinkham. Why not let enlightened Molokai receive such sporadic waifs from the mainland, treat them decently and scientifically, as she treats her own unfortunates of the Territory, and let the communities, cities and states of the mainland pay for such treatment of their own outcasts.—This, of course, to obtain only against the time when the last leper shall have ceased to be in the Territory of Hawaii.

I have studied leprosy many years, in the books, in the settlements and lazar houses of the world. I am happier to-day upon the subject of leprosy than ever before. The future stamping out of it is assured. Oh, believe me, I do not minimize the frightfulness of it. I know the frightfulness of it. I accentuate the certain passing of it by means of rigid segregation.

Before I finish, I insist that I must take my hat off in salute to two great, courageous, noble men: Jack McVeigh, Superintendent of the Molokai Settlement, and Dr. Will Goodhue, Resident Physician. My pride is to say that I have had the vast good fortune to know two such men. McVeigh, sitting tight on the purse-strings of the one hundred and fifty thousand dollars a year appropriated by the Territory, sitting up nights as well, begging money from his friends to do additional things for the settlement over and beyond what the Territory finds itself able to-day to appropriate, is the one man in the Territory to-day who could not be replaced by any other man in his job. Dr. Goodhue, the pioneer of leprosy surgery, is a hero who should receive every medal that every individual and every country has ever awarded for courage and life-saving. I say this. I know this. I know of no other place, lazar house or settlement, in the world, where the surgical work is being performed that Dr. Goodhue performs daily. I have watched him operate, many and many times. I have seen him take a patient, who, in any other settlement or lazar house in the world, would from the complications of the disease die horribly in a week, or two weeks or three,— I say, I have seen Dr. Goodhue, many times, operate on such a doomed creature, and give it life, not for weeks, not for months, but for years and years, to the rounded ripeness of three score and ten, and give to it thereby the sun, the ever changing beauty of the Pali, the eternal wine of wind of the northeast trades, the body-comfort, the brain-quickness, the love of man and woman—in short, all the bribes and compensations of existence.

Still another last final word. What is the matter with the United States? What is the matter with the Federal powers that be? What is the matter with the leprosarium built in the Settlement at a cost of three hundred thousand dollars, and which lies idle with not a patient nor a doctor in it year after year? Never was there such a leprosarium in all the world. It is dry-rotting from lack of use. It is fully equipped to the last word in twentieth century hospital equipment. Why not let Jack McVeigh grab the plunder and use it for his people? I have stood beside him in the Federal leprosarium, when he wept over the blankets (hundreds of them stored in the original cases of shipment and stored for years), lying there and deteriorating—to say nothing of the pillows, the iron beds, the washstands, the thousand and one hospital necessaries and comforts, the entire magnificent equipment for the amelioration of hurt and ailing humans, that is dropping into nothingness from lack of use.

And in all solemnity I take our Savior's name, and say, in Christ's sake, why should this immensity of comfort and beneficence be denied our brothers and sisters in Molokai because of Federal politics, because of Federal politicians, because of hopeless and undue red-tape bone-headed bookkeeping, because—my dear and gracious God, because some men, far from Molokai and Hawaii, play the political game to their own good food of belly and swift motion of chauffeur-driven limousine, with all the connotations of such rotund existence, forget, that most of all, we of the clean world, must in utter sacredness serve our unfortunate ones, our guiltless scapegoats of our generation, our brothers and sisters in Molokai.

MY HAWAIIAN ALOHA[1]

Part One

Once upon a time, only the other day, when jovial King Kalakaua established a record for the kings of earth and time, there entered into his Polynesian brain as merry a scheme of international intrigue as ever might have altered the destiny of

[1] Published in three parts in *Cosmopolitan Magazine*, September, October, November 1916.

races and places. The time was 1881; the place of the intrigue, the palace of the Mikado at Tokio. The record must not be omitted, for it was none other than that for the first time in the history of kings and of the world a reigning sovereign, in his own royal person, put a girdle around the earth.

The intrigue? It was certainly as international as any international intrigue could be. Also, it was equally as dark, while it was precisely in alignment with the future conflicting courses of empires. Manifest destiny was more that incidentally concerned. When the manifest destinies of two dynamic races move on ancient and immemorial lines toward each other from east to west and west to east along the same parallels of latitude, there is an inevitable point on the earth's surface where they will collide. In this case, the races were the Anglo-Saxon (represented by the Americans), and the Mongolian (represented by the Japanese). The place was Hawaii, the lovely and lovable, beloved of countless many as "Hawaii Nei."

Kalakaua, despite his merriness, foresaw clearly, either that the United States would absorb Hawaii, or that, allied by closest marital ties to the royal house of the Rising Sun, Hawaii could be a brother kingdom in an empire. That he saw clearly, the situation to-day attests. Hawaii Nei is a territory of the United States. There are more Japanese resident in Hawaii at the present time than are resident other nationalities, not even excepting the native Hawaiians.

The figures are eloquent. In round numbers, there are twenty-five thousand pure Hawaiians, twenty-five thousand various Caucasians, twenty-three thousand Portuguese, twenty-one thousand Chinese, fifteen thousand Filipinos, a sprinkling of many other breeds, an amazing complexity of intermingled breeds, and ninety thousand Japanese. And, most amazingly eloquent of all statistics are those of the race purity of the Japanese mating. In the year 1914, the Registrar-General is authority for the statements that one American male and one Spanish male respectively married Japanese females, that one Japanese male married a Hapa-Haole, or Caucasian-Hawaiian female, and that three Japanese males married pure Hawaiian females. When it comes to an innate antipathy towards mongrelization, the dominant national in Hawaii, the Japanese, proves himself more jealously exclusive by far than any other national. Omitting the records of all the other nationals which go to make up the amazing mongrelization of races in this smelting-pot of the races, let the record of pure-blood Americans be cited. In the same year of 1914, the Registrar-General reports that of American males who intermingled their breed and seed with alien races, eleven married pure Hawaiians, twenty-five married Caucasian-Hawaiians, three married pure Chinese, four married Chinese-Hawaiians, and one married a pure Japanese. To sum the same thing up with a cross-bearing: in the same year 1914, of over eighteen hundred Japanese women who married, only two married outside their race; of over eight hundred pure Caucasian women who married, over two hundred intermingled their breed and seed with races alien to their own. Reduced to decimals, of the females who went over the fence of race to secure fathers for their children, twenty-five hundredths of these pure Caucasian women were guilty; fourteen ten-thousandths of these Japanese women were guilty—in vulgar fraction, one out of four Caucasian women; one out of one thousand Japanese women.

King Kalakaua, at the time he germinated his idea, was the royal guest of the Mikado in a special palace which was all his to lodge in, along with his suite. But Kalakaua was resolved upon an international intrigue which was, to say the least, ethnologically ticklish; while his suite consisted of two Americans, one, Colonel C. H. Judd, his Chamberlain, the other, Mr. William N. Armstrong, his Attorney-General. They represented one of the race manifest destinies, and he knew it would never do for them to know what he had up his kingly sleeve. So, on this day in 1881, he gave them the royal slip, sneaked out of the palace the back way, and hied him to the Mikado's palace.

All of which, between kings, is a very *outre* thing to do. But what was mere etiquette between kings?—Kalakaua reasoned. Besides, Kalakaua was a main-travelled sovereign and a very cosmopolitan through contact with all sorts and conditions of men at the feasting board under the ringing grass-thatched roof of the royal canoe house at Honolulu, while the Mikado had never been off his tight little island. Of course, the Mikado was surprised at this unannounced and entirely unceremonious afternoon call. But not for nothing was he the Son of Heaven,

equipped with all the perfection of gentleness that belongs to a
much longer than a nine-hundred-years-old name. To his dying
day Kalakaua never dreamed of the *faux pas* he committed that
day in 1881.

He went directly to the point, exposited the manifest destinies
moving from east to west and west to east, and proposed no
less than that an imperial prince of the Mikado's line should
espouse the Princess Kaiulani of Hawaii. He assured this delicate, hot-house culture of a man whose civilization was already
a dim and distant achievement at the time Kalakaua's forebears
were on the perilous and savage Polynesian canoe-drift over the
Pacific ere ever they came to colonize Hawaii—this pallid palace
flower of a monarch did he assure that the Princess Kaiulani
was some princess. And in this Kalakaua made no mistake. She
was all that he could say of her, and more. Not alone was she
the most refined and peach-blow blossom of a woman that Hawaii
had ever produced, to whom connoisseurs of beauty and of
spirit like Robert Louis Stevenson had bowed knee and head
and presented with poems and pearls; but she was Kalakaua's
own niece and heir to the throne of Hawaii. Thus, the Americans,
moving westward would be compelled to stop on the far shore
of the Pacific; while Hawaii, taken under Japan's wing, would
become the easterly outpost of Japan.

Kalakaua died without knowing how clearly he foresaw the
trend of events. To-day the United States possesses Hawaii,
which, in turn, is populated by more Japanese than by any other
nationality. Practically every second person in the island is a
Japanese, and the Japanese are breeding true to pure race lines,
while all the others are cross-breeding to an extent that would be
a scandal on any stock farm.

Fortunately for the United States, the Mikado reflected. Because he reflected, Hawaii to-day is not a naval base for Japan,
and a menace to the United States. The *haoles*, or whites, overthrew the Hawaiian Monarchy, formed the Dole Republic, and
shortly thereafter brought their loot in under the sheltering folds
of the Stars and Stripes. There is little use to balk at the word
"loot." The white man is the born looter. And just as the North
American Indian was looted of his continent by the white man,
so was the Hawaiian looted by the white men of his islands.

Such things be. They are morally indefensible. As facts they are irrefragable—as irrefragable as the facts that water drowns, that frost bites, and that fire incinerates.

And let this particular *haole* who writes these lines here and now subscribe his joy and gladness in the Hawaiian loot. Of all places of beauty and joy under the sun—but there, I was born in California, which is no mean place in itself, and it would be more meet to let some of the talking be done by the Hawaii-born, both Polynesian and *haole*. First of all, the Hawaii-born, unlike the Californian, does not talk big. "When you come down to the Islands you must visit us," he will say; "We'll give you a good time." That's all. No swank. Just like an invitation to dinner. And after the visit is accomplished you will confess to yourself that you never knew before what a good time was, and that for the first time you have learned the full alphabet of hospitality. There is nothing like it. The Hawaii-born won't tell you about it. He just does it.

Said Ellis, nearly a century ago, in his *Polynesian Researches:* "On the arrival of strangers, every man endeavoured to obtain one as a friend and carry him off to his own habitation, where he is treated with the greatest kindness by the inhabitants of the district; they place him on a high seat and feed him with abundance of the finest food."

Such was Captain Cook's experience when he discovered Hawaii, and despite what happened to him because of his abuse of so fine hospitality, the same hospitality has persisted in the Hawaiians of this day. Oh, please make no mistake. No longer, as he lands, will the latest beach-comber, whaleship deserter, or tourist, be carried up among the palms by an enthusiastic and loving population and be placed in the high seat. When, in a single week to-day, a dozen steamships land thousands of tourists, the impossibility of such lavishness of hospitality is understandable. It can't be done.

But—the old hospitality holds. Come with your invitations, or letters of introduction, and you will find yourself immediately instated in the high seat of abundance. Or, come uninvited, without credentials, merely stay a real, decent while, and yourself be "good," and make good the good in you—but, oh, softly, and gently, and sweetly, and manly, and womanly—and you will slowly steal into the Hawaiian heart, which is all of softness, and gentleness, and sweetness, and manliness, and womanliness, and one day, to your own vast surprise, you will find yourself seated in a high place of hospitableness than which there is none higher on this earth's surface. You will have loved your way there, and you will find it the abode of love.

Nor is that all. Since I, as an attestant, am doing the talking, let me be forgiven my first-person intrusions. Detesting the tourist route, as a matter of private whim or quirk of temperament, nevertheless I have crossed the tourist route in many places over the world and know thoroughly what I am talking about. And I can and do aver that, in this year 1916, I know of no place where the unheralded and uncredentialed tourist, if he is anything of anything in himself, so quickly finds himself among friends as here in Hawaii. Let me add: I know of no people in any place who have been stung more frequently and deeply by chance visitors than have the people of Hawaii. Yet the old heart and *hale* (house) hospitality holds. The Hawaii-born is like the leopard; spotted for good or ill, neither can change his spots.

Why, only last evening I was talking with an Hawaii matron— how shall I say?—one of the first ladies. Her and her husband's trip to Japan for Cherry Blossom Time was cancelled for a year. Why? She had received a wireless from a steamer which had already sailed from San Francisco, from a girl friend, a new bride, who was coming to partake of generally extended hospitality of several years before. "But why give up your own good time?" I said: "Turn your house and servants over to the young couple and you go on your own trip just the same." "But that would never do," said she. That was all. She had no thought of house and servants. She had once offered her hospitality. She must be there, on the spot, in heart and *hale* and person. And she, island-born, had always travelled east to the States and to Europe, while this was her first and long anticipated journey west to the Orient. But that she should be remiss in the traditional and trained and innate hospitality of Hawaii was unthinkable. Of course she would remain. What else could she do?

Oh, what's the use? I was going to make the Hawaii-born talk. They won't. They can't. I shall have to go on and do all the talking myself. They are poor boosters. They even try to boost, on occasion; but the latest steamship and railroad publicity agent from the mainland will give them cards and spades and talk all around them when it comes to describing what Hawaii so beautifully and charmingly is. Take surf-boarding, for instance. A California real estate agent, with that one asset, could make the burnt, barren heart of Sahara into an oasis for kings. Not only did the Hawaii-born not talk about it, but they forgot about it. Just as the sport was at its dying gasp, along came one, Alexander Ford, from the mainland. And he talked. Surf-boarding was the sport of sports. There was nothing like it anywhere else in the world. They ought to be ashamed for letting it languish. It was one of the island's assets, a drawing card for travellers that would fill their hotels and bring them many permanent residents, etc.

He continued to talk, and the Hawaii-born smiled. "What are you going to do about it?" they said, when he buttonholed them into corners. "This is just talk, you know, just a line of talk."

"I'm not going to do anything except talk," Ford replied. "It's you fellows who've got to do the doing."

And all was as he said. And all of which I know for myself, at first hand, for I lived on Waikiki beach at the time in a tent where stands the Outrigger Club to-day—twelve hundred members, with hundreds more on the waiting list, and with what seems like half a mile of surf-board lockers.

"Oh yes,—there's fishing in the islands," has been the customary manner of the Hawaii-born's talk, when on the mainland or in Europe. "Come down some time and we'll take you fishing." Just the same casual dinner sort of an invitation to take pot luck. And, if encouraged, he will go on and describe with antiquarian detail, how, in the good old days, the natives wove baskets and twisted fish lines that lasted a century from the fibres of a plant that grew only in the spray of the waterfall; or cleared the surface of the water with a spread of the oil of the kukui nut and caught squid with bright cowrie shells tied fast on the end of a string; or, fathoms deep, in the caves of the coral-cliffs, encountered the octopus and bit him to death with their teeth in the soft bone between his eyes above his parrot-beak.

Meanwhile these are the glad young days of new-fangled ways

of fish-catching in which the Hawaii-born's auditor is interested; and meanwhile, from Nova Scotia to Florida and across the Gulf sea shore to the coast of California, a thousand railroads, steamship lines, promotion committees, boards of trade, and real estate agents are booming the tarpon and the tuna that may occasionally be caught in their adjacent waters.

And all the time, though the world is just coming to learn of it, the one unchallengeable paradise for big-game fishing is Hawaii. First of all, there are the fish. And they are all the year round, in amazing variety and profusion. The United States Fish Commission, without completing the task, has already described 447 distinct species, exclusive of the big, deep-sea gamefish. It is a matter of taking any day and any choice, from harpooning sharks to shooting flying-fish—like quail—with shotguns, or taking a stab at a whale, or trapping a lobster. One can fish with barbless hooks and a six-pound sinker at the end of a drop-line off Molokai in forty fathoms of water and catch at a single session, a miscellany as generous as to include: the six- or eight-pound *moelua*, the fifteen-pound *upakapaka*, the ten-pound *lehe*, the *kawelea* which is first cousin to the "Barricoot," the *hapuupuu*, the *awaa*, and say, maybe, the toothsome and gamy *kahala makulaie*. And the bait one will use on his forty-fathom line will be the fish called the *opelu*, which, in turn, is caught with a bait of crushed pumpkin.

But let not the light-tackle sportsman be dismayed by the foregoing description of such crass, gross ways of catching unthinkable and unpronounceable fish. Let him take a six-ounce tip and a nine-thread line and essay one of Hawaii's black sea bass. They catch them here weighing over six hundred pounds, and they certainly do run bigger than do those in the kelp beds off Southern California. Does the light-tackle man want tarpon? He will find them here as gamy and as large as in Florida, and they will leap in the air—ware slack!—like range mustangs to fling the hook clear.

Nor has the tale begun. Of the barracuda, Hawaiian waters boast twenty species, sharp-toothed, voracious, running to a fathom and even more in length, and, unlike the Florida barracuda, travelling in schools. There are the albacore and the dolphin—no mean fish for light tackle; to say nothing of the ocean bonita and the California bonita. There is the *ulua*, pound for pound the gamest salt-water fish that ever tried a rod; and there is the *ono*, half-way a swordfish, called by the ancient Hawaiians the father of the mackerel. Also, there is the swordfish, at which light-tackle men have never been known to sneer—after they had once hooked one. The swordfish of Hawaii, known by its immemorial native name of *a'u*, averages from three to four hundred pounds, although they have been caught between six and seven hundred pounds, sporting swords five feet and more in length. And not least are those two cousins of the amber jack of Florida, the yellow tail and the amber fish, named by Holder as the fish of Southern California *par excellence* and by him described for their beauty and desperateness in putting up a fight.

And the tuna must not be omitted, or, at any rate, the *thunnus thynnus*, the *thunnus alalonsa*, and the *thunnus macrapterus*, so called by the scientists, but known by the Hawaiians under the generic name of *ahi*, and, by light-tackle men as the leaping tuna, the long-fin tuna, and the yellow-fin tuna. In the past two months, Messrs. Jump, Burnham and Morris, from the mainland, seem to have broken every world record in the tuna line. They had to come to Hawaii to do it; but, once here, they did it easily, even if Morris did break a few ribs in the doing of it. Just the other day, on their last trip, Mr. Jump landed a sixty-seven pound yellow-fin on a nine-thread line, and Mr. Morris similarly a fifty-five pound one. The record for Catalina is fifty-one pounds. Pshaw! Let this writer from California talk big, after the manner of his home state, and still keep within the truth. A yellow-fin tuna, recently landed out of Hawaiian waters and sold on the Honolulu market, weighed two hundred and eighty-seven pounds.

Part Two

Hawaii is the home of shanghaied men and women, and of the descendants of shanghaied men and women. They never intended to be here at all. Very rarely, since the first whites came, has one, with the deliberate plan of coming to remain, remained. Somehow, the love of the Islands, like the love of a woman, just happens. One cannot determine in advance to love a particular woman, nor can one so determine to love Hawaii. One sees, and one loves or does not love. With Hawaii it seems always to be love at first sight. Those for whom the Islands were made, or who were made for the Islands, are swept off their feet in the first moments of meeting, embrace, and are embraced.

I remember a dear friend who resolved to come to Hawaii and make it his home forever. He packed up his wife, all his belongings including his garden hose and rake and hoe, said "Goodbye, proud Calfornia," and departed. Now he was a poet, with an eye and soul for beauty, and it was only to be expected that he would lose his heart to Hawaii as Mark Twain and Stevenson and Stoddard had before him. So he came, with his wife and garden hose and rake and hoe. Heaven alone knows what preconceptions he must have entertained. But the fact remains that he found naught of beauty and charm and delight. His stay in Hawaii, brief as it was, was a hideous nightmare. In no time he was back in California. To this day he speaks with plaintive bitterness of his experience, although he never mentions what became of his garden hose and rake and hoe. Surely the soil could not have proved niggardly to him!

Otherwise was it with Mark Twain, who wrote of Hawaii long after his visit: "No alien land in all the world has any deep, strong charm for me but that one; no other land could so longingly and beseechingly haunt me sleeping and waking, through half a lifetime, as that one has done. Other things leave me, but it abides; other things change, but it remains the same. For me its balmy airs are always blowing, its summer seas flashing in the sun; the pulsing of its surf-beat is in my ears; I can see its garlanded crags, its leaping cascades, its plumy palms drowsing by the shore, its remote summits floating like islands above the cloudrack; I can feel the spirit of its woodland solitudes; I can hear the plash of its brooks; in my nostrils still lives the breath of flowers that perished twenty years ago."

One reads of the first Chief Justice under the Kamehamehas, that he was on his way around the Horn to Oregon when he was persuaded to remain in Hawaii. Truly, Hawaii is a woman beautiful and vastly more persuasive and seductive than her sister sirens of the sea.

The sailor boy, Archibald Scott Cleghorn, had no intention of leaving his ship; but he looked upon the Princess Likelike, the Princess Likelike looked on him, and he remained to become the father of the Princess Kaiulani and to dignify a place of honor through long years. He was not the first sailor boy to leave his ship, nor the last. One of the recent ones, whom I know well, arrived several years ago on a yacht in a yacht race from the mainland. So brief was his permitted vacation from his bank cashiership that he had planned to return by fast steamer. He is still here. The outlook is that his children and his grandchildren after him will be here.

Another erstwhile bank cashier is Louis von Tempsky, the son of the last British officer killed in the Maori War. His New Zealand bank gave him a year's vacation. The one place he wanted to see above all others was California. He departed. His ship stopped at Hawaii. It was the same old story. The ship sailed on without him. His New Zealand bank never saw him again, and many years passed ere ever he saw California. But she had no charms for him. And to-day, his sons and daughters about him, he looks down on half a world and all of Maui from the rolling grasslands of the Haleakala Ranch.

There were the Gays and Robinsons. Scotch pioneers over the world in the good old days when families were large and patriarchial, they had settled in New Zealand. After a time they decided to migrate to British Columbia. Among their possessions was a full-rigged ship, of which one of their sons was master. Like my poet friend from California, they packed all their property on board. But in place of his garden hose and rake and hoe, they took their plows and harrows and all their agricultural machinery. Also, they took their horses and their cattle and their sheep. When they arrived in British Columbia they would be in shape to settle immediately, break the soil, and not miss a harvest. But the ship, as was the custom in the sailing-ship days, stopped at Hawaii for water and fruit and vegetables. The Gays and Robinsons are still here, or, rather, their venerable children, and younger grandchildren and great grandchildren; for Hawaii, like the Princess Likelike, put her arms around them, and it was love at first sight. They took up land on Kauai and Niihau,

the ninety-seven square miles of the latter remaining intact in
their possession to this day.

I doubt that not even the missionaries, windjamming around
the Horn from New England a century ago, had the remotest
thought of living out all their days in Hawaii. This is not the
way of missionaries over the world. They have always gone
forth to far places with the resolve to devote their lives to the
glory of God and the redemption of the heathen, but with the
determination, at the end of it all, to return to spend their
declining years in their own country. But Hawaii can seduce
missionaries just as readily as she can seduce sailorboys and bank
cashiers, and this particular lot of missionaries was so enamored
of her charms that they did not return when old age came upon
them. Their bones lie here in the land they came to love better
than their own; and they, and their sons and daughters after
them, have been, and are, powerful forces in the development
of Hawaii.

In missionary annals, such unanimous and eager adoption of
a new land is unique. Yet another thing, equally unique in
missionary history, must be noted in passing. Never did missionaries, the very first, go out to rescue a heathen land from
its idols, and on arrival find it already rescued, self-rescued, while
they were on the journey. In 1819, all Hawaii was groaning
under the harsh rule of the ancient idols, whose mouthpieces
were the priests and whose utterances were the frightfully cruel
and unjust taboos. In 1819, the first missionaries assembled in
Boston and sailed away on the long voyage around the Horn.
In 1819, the Hawaiians, of themselves, without outside counsel or suggestion, overthrew their idols and abolished the taboos.
In 1820, the missionaries completed their long voyage and
landed in Hawaii to find a country and a people without gods
and without religion, ready and ripe for instruction.

But to return. Hawaii is the home of shanghaied men and
women, who were induced to remain, not by a blow with a
club over the head or a doped bottle of whiskey, but by love.
Hawaii and the Hawaiians are a land and a people loving and
lovable. By their language may ye know them, and in what
other land save this one is the commonest form of greeting,
not "Good day," nor "How d'ye do," but "Love"? That greet-

ing is *Aloha*—love, I love you, my love to you. Good day—what is it more than an impersonal remark about the weather? How do you do—it is personal in a merely casual interrogative sort of way. But *Aloha!* It is a positive affirmation of the warmth of one's own heart-giving. My love to you! I love you! Aloha!

Well, then, try to imagine a land that is as lovely and loving as such a people. Hawaii is all of this. Not strictly tropical, but sub-tropical, rather, in the heel of the Northeast Trades (which is a very wine of wind), with altitudes rising from palm-fronded coral beaches to snow-capped summits fourteen thousand feet in the air, there was never so much climate gathered together in one place on earth. The custom of the dwellers is as it was of old time, only better, namely: to have a town house, a seaside house, and a mountain house. All three homes, by automobile, can be within half an hour's run of one another; yet, in difference of climate and scenery, they are the equivalent of a house on Fifth Avenue or the Riverside Drive, of an Adirondack camp, and of a Florida winter bungalow, plus a twelve-months' cycle of seasons crammed into each and every day.

Let me try to make this clearer. The New York dweller must wait till summer for the Adirondacks, till winter for the Florida beach. But in Hawaii, say on the island of Oahu, the Honolulu dweller can decide each day what climate and what season he desires to spend the day in. It is his to pick and choose. Yes, and further: he may awake in his Adirondacks, lunch and shop and go to the club in his city, spend his afternoon and dine at his Palm Beach, and return to sleep in the shrewd coolness of his Adirondack camp.

And what is true of Oahu, is true of all the other large islands of the group. Climate and season are to be had for the picking and choosing, with countless surprising variations thrown in for good measure. Suppose one be an invalid, seeking an invalid's climate. A night's run from Honolulu on a steamer will land him on the leeward coast of the big island of Hawaii. There, amongst the coffee on the slopes of Kona, a thousand feet above Kailua and the wrinkled sea, he will find the perfect invalid-climate. It is the land of the morning calm, the afternoon shower, and the evening tranquility. Harsh winds never blow. Once in a year or two a stiff wind of twenty-four to forty-eight hours will blow from the south. This is the Kona wind. Otherwise there is no wind, at least no air-draughts of sufficient force to be so dignified. They are not even breezes. They are air-fans, alternating by day and by night beween the sea and the land. Under the sun, the land warms and draws to it the mild sea air. In the night, the land radiating its heat more quickly, the sea remains the warmer and draws to it the mountain air faintly drenched with the perfume of flowers.

Such is the climate of Kona, where nobody ever dreams of looking at a thermometer, where each afternoon there falls a refreshing spring shower, and where neither frost nor sunstroke has ever been known. All of which is made possible by the towering bulks of Mauna Kea and Mauna Loa. Beyond them, on the windward slopes of the Big Island, along the Hamakun Coast, the trade wind will as often as not be blustering at forty miles an hour. Should an Oregon web-foot become homesick for the habitual wet of his native clime, he will find easement and a soaking on the windward coasts of Hawaii and Maui, from Hilo in the south with its average annual rainfall of one hundred and fifty inches to the Nahiku country to the north beyond Hana which has known a downpour of four hundred and twenty inches in a single twelve-month. In the matter of rain it is again pick and choose—from two hundred inches to twenty, or five, or one. Nay, further, forty miles away from the Nahiku, on the leeward slopes of the House of the Sun, which is the mightiest extinct volcano in the world, rain may not fall once in a dozen years. Cattle live their lives without ever seeing a puddle, and horses brought from that region shy at running water or try to eat it with their teeth.

One can multiply the foregoing examples indefinitely, and to the proposition that never was so much climate gathered together in one place, can be added that never was so much landscape gathered together in one place. The diversification is endless, from the lava shores of South Puna to the barking sands of Kauai. On every island break-neck mountain climbing abounds. One can shiver above timber-line on the snow-caps of Mauna Kea or Mauna Loa, swelter under the banyan at sleepy old Lahaina, swim in clear ocean water that effervesces like champagne on ten thousand beaches, or sleep under blankets every night in the upland pastures of the great cattle ranges and awaken each morning to the song of skylarks and the crisp, snappy air of spring. But never, never, go where he will in Hawaii Nei, will he experience a hurricane, a tornado, a blizzard, a fog, or ninety degrees in the shade. Such discomforts are meteorologically impossible, and so the meteorologists affirm. When Hawaii was named the Paradise of the Pacific, it was inadequately named. The rest of the Seven Seas and the islands in the midst thereof should have been included along with the Pacific. "See Naples and die"—they spell it differently here: *see Hawaii and live.*

Nor is Hawaii niggardly toward the sportsman. Good hunting abounds. As I write these lines on Puuweawaa Ranch, from every side arises the love-call of the quail, which are breaking up their coveys as the mating proceeds. They are California quail, yet never in California have I seen quail as thick as here. Yesterday I saw more doves—variously called turtle doves and mourning doves—than I ever saw before in any single day of my life. Day before yesterday I was out with the cowboys roping wild pig in the pastures.

Of birds, in addition to quail and doves, in place and season may be hunted wild duck, wild turkey, rice birds, Chinese and Japanese pheasants, pea fowl, guinea fowl, wild chicken (which is a mongrel cross of the indigenous moa and the haole chicken), and, not least, the delicious golden plover fat and recuperated after its long flight from Alaska and the arctic shores. Then there are the spotted deer of Molokai. Increasing from several introduced pair, they so flourished in their new habitat that they threatened the pastures and forests, and some years ago the government was compelled to employ professional hunters to reduce their numbers. Of course there is pig-sticking, and for real hunting few things can out-thrill the roping, after cowboy fashion, of the wild bulls of the upper ranges. Also are there to be had wild goats, wild sheep—yes, and wild dogs, running in packs and dragging down calves and cows, that may even prove perilous to the solitary hunter. And as for adventure and exploration, among many things, one can tackle Rabbit Island, inaccessible to all but the most intrepid and most fortunate, or seek for the secret and taboo burial places of the ancient kings.

Indeed, Hawaii is a loving land. Just as it welcomed the spotted deer to the near destruction of its forests, so has it welcomed many other inimical aliens to its shores. In the United States, in greenhouses and old fashioned gardens, grows a potted flowering shrub called lantana; in India dwells a very noisy and quarrelsome bird known as the mynah. Both were introduced into Hawaii, the bird to feed upon the cutworm of a certain moth called *spodoptera mauritia;* the flower to gladden with old associations the heart of a flower-loving missionary. But the land loved the lantana. From a small flower that grew in a pot, the lantana took to itself feet and walked out of the pot into the missionary's garden. Here it flourished and increased mightily in size and constitution. From over the garden wall came the love-call of all Hawaii, and the lantana responded to the call, climbed over the wall, and went a-roving and a-loving in the wild woods.

And just as the lantana had taken to itself feet, by the seduction of its seed it added to itself the wings of the mynah, who distributed its seed over every island in the group. Like the creatures Mr. Wells writes of who ate of the food of the gods and became giants, so the lantana. From a delicate, hand-manicured, potted plant of the greenhouse, it shot up into a tough and belligerent swashbuckler a fathom tall, that marched in serried ranks over the landscape, crushing beneath it and choking to death all the sweet native grasses, shrubs, and flowers. In the lower forests it became jungle. In the open it became jungle only more so. It was practically impenetrable to man. It filled and blotted out the pastures by tens of thousands of acres. The cattlemen wailed and vainly fought with it. It grew faster and spread faster than they could grub it out.

Like the invading whites who dispossessed the native Hawaiians of their land, so did the lantana to the native vegetation. Nay, it did worse. It threatened to dispossess the whites of the land they had won. And battle royal was on. Unable to cope directly with it, the whites called in the aid of the hosts of mercenaries. They sent out their agents to recruit armies from the insect world and from the world of micro-organisms. Of these doughty warriors let the name of but one, as a sample, be given— *cremastobombycia lantanella.* Prominent among these recruits were the lantana seed-fly, the lantana plume-moth, the lantana butterfly, the lantana leaf-miner, the lantana leaf-bug, the lantana gall-fly. Quite by accident the Maui blight or scale was enlisted.

Some of these predaceous enemies of the lantana ate and sucked and sapped. Others made incubators out of the stems, tunneled and undermined the flower clusters, hatched maggots in the hearts of the seeds, or coated the leaves with suffocating fungoid growths. Thus simultaneously attacked in front and rear flank, above and below, inside and out, the all-conquering swashbuckler recoiled. To-day the battle is almost over, and what remains of the lantana is putting up a sickly and losing fight. Unfortunately, one of the mercenaries has mutinied. This is the accidentally introduced Maui blight, which is now waging unholy war upon garden flowers and ornamental plants, and against which some other army of mercenaries must be turned.

Hawaii has been most generous in her hospitality, most promiscuous in her loving. Her welcome has been impartial. To her warm heart she has enfolded all manner of hurtful, stinging things, including some humans. Mosquitos, centipedes and rats made the long voyages, landed, and have flourished ever since. There was none of these here before the *haole* came. So, also, were introduced measles, smallpox, and many similar germ afflictions of man. The elder generations lived and loved and fought and went down into the pit with their war weapons and flower garlands laid under their heads, unvexed by whooping cough, and mumps, and influenza. Some alien good, and much of alien ill, has Hawaii embraced and loved. Yet to this day no snake, poisonous or otherwise, exists in her forests and jungles; while the centipede is not deadly, its bite being scarcely more discomforting than the sting of a bee or wasp. Some snakes did arrive, once. A showman brought them for exhibition. In passing quarantine they had to be fumigated. By some mischance they were all suffocated, and it is whispered that the quarantine officials might have more to say of that mischance than appeared in their official report.

And, oh, there is the mongoose. Originally introduced from India via Jamaica to wage war on that earlier introduction, the rat, that was destroying the sugar cane plantations, the mongoose multiplied beyond all guestly bounds and followed the lantana into the plains and forests. And in the plains and forests it has well nigh destroyed many of the indigenous species of ground-nesting birds, made serious inroads on the ground-nesting imported birds, and compelled all raisers of domestic fowls to build mongoose-proof chicken yards. In the meantime the rats have changed their nesting habits and taken to the trees. Some of the pessimistic farmers even aver that, like the haole chickens which went wild in the woods and crossed with the moa, the mongoose has climbed the trees, made friends with and mated with the rats, and has produced a permanent hybrid of omnivorous appetite that eats sugar cane, birds eggs, and farmyard chickens indiscriminately and voraciously. But further deponent sayeth not.

Part Three

Hawaii is a great experimental laboratory, not merely in agriculture but in ethnology and sociology. Remote in the heart of the Pacific, more hospitable to all forms of life than any other land, it has received an immigration of alien vegetable, insect, animal, and human life more varied and giving rise to more complicated problems than any other land has received. And right intelligently and whole-heartedly have the people of Hawaii taken hold of these problems and striven to wrestle them to solution.

A melting-pot is what Hawaii is. In a single school, at one time, I have observed pupils of as many as twenty-three different nationalities and mixed nationalities. First of all, is the original Hawaiian stock of pure Polynesian. These were the people whom Captain Cook discovered, the first pioneers who voyaged in double canoes from the South Pacific and colonized Hawaii at what is estimated, from their traditions, as some fifteen hundred years ago. Next, from Captain Cook's time to this day, has drifted in the *haole*, or Caucasian—Yankee, Scotch, Irish, English, Welsh, French, German, Scandinavian. Every Caucasian country of Europe and every Caucasian colony of the world have contributed their quota. And not least to be reckoned with are the deliberate importations of unskilled labor for the purpose of working the sugar plantations. First of these was a heavy wave of

Chinese coolies. But the Chinese Exclusion Act put a stop to their coming. In the same way, King Sugar has introduced definite migrations of Japanese, Koreans, Russians, Portuguese, Spanish, Porto Ricans, and Filipinos. With the exception of the Japanese, who are jealously exclusive in the matter of race, all these other races insist and persist in intermarrying, and the situation here should afford much valuable data for the ethnologist.

Of the original Hawaiians, one thing is certain: They are doomed to extinction. Year by year, the total number of the pure Hawaiians decreases. Marrying with the other races as they do, they could persist as hybrids if—*if fresh effusions of them came in from outside sources equivalent to such continued effusions that do come in of the other races*. But no effusions of Polynesian come in or have ever come in. Steadily, since Captain Cook's time, they have faded away. Today, the representatives of practically all the old chief-stocks and royal stocks are half-whites, three-quarters whites, and seven-eighths whites. And they and their children continue to marry whites, or seven-eighths and three-quarters whites like themselves, so that the Hawaiian strain grows thinner and thinner against the day when it will vanish in thin air. All of which is a pity, for the world can ill afford to lose so splendid and lovable a race.

No better opportunity could be found for observing this medley of all the human world than that afforded by the Mid-Pacific Carnival last February, when the population turned out and held festival for a week. Nowhere within the territory of the United States could so exotic a spectacle be witnessed. And unforgettable were the flower-garlanded Hawaiians, the women *pa-u* riders on their lively steeds, with flowing costumes that swept the ground, toddling Japanese boys and girls, lantern processions straight out of old Japan, colossal dragons from the Flowery Empire, and Chinese schoolgirls, parading two by two in long, winding columns, bareheaded, their demure black braids down their backs, slimly graceful in the white costumes of their foremothers. At the same time, while the streets stormed with confetti and serpentines tossed by the laughing races of all the world, in the throne-room of the old palace (now the Executive Building) was occurring an event as bizarre in its own way and equally impressive. Here, side by side, the two high representatives of the old order and the new held reception. Seated, was the aged Queen Liliuokalani, the last reigning sovereign of Hawaii; standing beside her was Lucius E. Pinkham, New England born, the governor of Hawaii. A quarter of a century before, his brothers had dispossessed her of her kingdom; and quite a feather was it in his cap for him to have her beside him that night, for it was the first time in that quarter of a century that anyone had succeeded in winning her to enter the throne-room.

Hawaii is a paradise—and I can never cease proclaiming it; but I must append one word of qualification: *Hawaii is a paradise for the well-to-do*. It is not a paradise for the unskilled laborer or for the person without capital from the mainland. The one great industry of the islands is sugar. The unskilled labor for the plantations is already here. Even the skilled laborer is needed only in small, definite numbers.

For the person without capital, dreaming to start on a shoe-string and become a capitalist, Hawaii is the last place in the world. The shoe-string days are past. The land and industries of Hawaii are owned by old families and large corporations.

But the homesteader may object, saying that he has read the reports of the millions of acres of government land in Hawaii which are his for the homesteading. But he must remember that the vastly larger portion of this government land is naked lava rock and not worth ten cents a square mile to a homesteader, and that much of the remaining land, while rich in soil values, is worthless because it is without water. The small portion of good government land is leased by the plantations. Of course, when these leases expire, they may be homesteaded. It has been done in the past. But such homesteaders, after making good their titles, almost invariably sell out their holdings to the plantations. There is a reason for it. There are various reasons for it.

For, be it understood, that Hawaii is patriarchal rather than democratic. Economically, it is owned and operated in a fashion that is a combination of twentieth century, machine-civilization methods and of medieval feudal methods. Its rich lands, devoted to sugar, are farmed scientifically. The last word in machinery is vocal here, the last word in fertilizing and agronomy, and the last word in scientific expertness.

The Sugar Planters' Association and the several sugar factors or financial agencies control sugar, and, since sugar is king, control the destiny and welfare of the Islands. And they are able to do this, under the peculiar conditions that obtain, far more efficiently than it could be done by the population of Hawaii were it a democratic commonwealth, which it essentially is not. Much of the stock in these corporations is owned in small lots by members of the small business and professional classes. The larger blocks are held by families who, earlier in the game, ran their small plantations for themselves, but who learned that they could not do it so well and so profitably as the corporations, which, with centralized management, could hire far better brains for the entire operation of the industry. As a result, absentee ownership or landlordship has come about. Finding the work done better for them than they could do it themselves, they prefer to live in their Honolulu and seaside and mountain homes, to travel much, and to develop a cosmopolitanism and culture that never misses shocking the traveler or newcomer with surprise. Of course there are notable exceptions to this practice of absentee landlordism, and such men are active as sugar factors and in the management of the Planters' Association.

Yet will I dare to assert that no owning class on the mainland is so conscious of its social responsibility as is this owning class of Hawaii, and especially that portion of it which has descended out of the old missionary stock. Its charities, missions, social settlements, schools, hospitals, and other philanthropic enterprises are many; and some of its members contribute from twenty-five to fifty percent of their incomes to work for the general good.

But all the foregoing, it must be remembered, is not democratic or communal, but is distinctly feudal. The coolie and peasant labor possess no vote, while Hawaii is, after all, only a territory, its governor appointed by the President of the United States, its one delegate sitting in Congress at Washington but denied the right to vote. Under such conditions, it is patent that the small class of large landowners finds it not too difficult to control the small vote in local politics.

Interesting, even menacing, problems loom large for Hawaii in the not distant future. Let but one of these be considered, namely, the Japanese and citizenship. Granting that no Japanese immigrant can ever become naturalized, nevertheless remains the irrefragable law and fact that every male Japanese, Hawaii-born, by his birth is automatically a citizen of the United States. Since practically every other person in all Hawaii is Japanese, it is merely a matter of time when the Hawaii-born Japanese vote will not only be larger than any other Hawaiian vote but will be practically equal to all other votes combined. When such time comes, it looks as if the Japanese will have the dominant say in local politics. If Hawaii should get statehood, a Japanese governor of the state of Hawaii would be not merely probable but very possible.

In passing, it may be significantly noted that while the Chinese, Filipinos, and Portuguese flock enthusiastically into the national guard, the Japanese do not. There are no Japanese in the national guard.

But a truce to far troubles. This is my Hawaiian *aloha*—my love for Hawaii; and I cannot finish it without stating a dear hope for a degree of honor that may some day be mine before I die. I have had several degrees in the past of which I am well proud. When I had barely turned sixteen, I was named "Prince of the Oyster Pirates," by my fellow pirates. Since they were all men grown and a hard-bitten lot, and since the term was applied in anything but derision, my lad's pride in it was justly great. Not long after, another mighty degree was given me by a shipping commissioner in San Francisco, who signed me on the ship's articles as A. B. Think of it—able-bodied! I was not a landlubber or an ordinary seaman, but an A. B. An able-bodied seaman before the mast! No higher could one go—before the mast. And in those youthful days of romance and adventure, I would far rather have been an able-bodied seaman before the mast than a captain aft of it.

When I went over Chilokot Pass in the first Klondike Rush, I was called a *chechaquo*. This was equivalent to newcomer, greenhorn, tenderfoot, short horn, or new chum, and as such I looked reverently up to the men who were sour-doughs. It was a custom of the country to call an old-timer a sour-dough. A sour-dough was a man who had seen the Yukon freeze and break, traveled under the midnight sun, and been in the country long enough to get over the frivolities of baking-powder and yeast in the making of bread, and to content himself with bread raised from sour dough.

I am very proud of my sour-dough degree. A few years ago I received another degree. It was in the West South Pacific. A kinky-headed, asymmetrical, apelike, head-hunting cannibal climbed out of his canoe and over the rail and gave it to me. He wore no clothes. On his chest, from around his neck, was suspended a broken white-china plate. Through a hole in one ear was thrust a short clay pipe. Through diverse holes in the other ear were thrust a freshly-severed pig's tail and several rifle-cartridges. A bone bodkin four inches long was shoved through the dividing wall of his nose. And he addressed me as "skipper." Owner and master I was, the only navigator on board; but it was the first time I had been called "skipper," and I was mighty proud of it.

I'd rather possess these several degrees of able seaman, sourdough, and skipper than all university degrees from bachelor of arts to doctor of philosophy. But there is yet one degree I should like to receive, than which there is no other in the wide world for which I have so great a desire. It is *kamaaina*.

Kamaaina is Hawaiian. It contains five vowels, which, with the three consonants, compose five syllables. No syllable is accented; all syllables are pronounced, the vowels having precisely the same values as the French vowels. *Kamaaina* means not exactly old-timer or pioneer. Its original meaning is "a child of the soil," one who is indigenous. But its meaning has changed, so that it stands to-day for "one who belongs"—to Hawaii, of course. It is not merely a degree of time or length of residence. It applies to the heart and the spirit. A man may live in Hawaii for twenty years and yet not be recognized as a *kamaaina*. He has remained alien in heart-warmth and spirit-understanding.

Nor can one assume this degree for oneself.

Kamaaina must be given to one. He must be so named by the ones who do belong and who are best fitted to judge whether or not he belongs. *Kamaaina* is the proudest accolade I know that any people can lay with the love-warm steel of its approval on an alien's back.

Pshaw! Were it a matter of time, I could almost be reckoned a *kamaaina* myself. Nearly a quarter of a century ago—to be precise, twenty-four years ago—I first saw these fair islands rise out of the sea. I have been back here numerous times. As the years pass, I return with increasing frequency and for longer stays.

Some day, some one of Hawaii may slap me on the shoulder and say, "Hello, old *kamaaina*." And some other day, I may chance to overhear some one else of Hawaii speaking of me and saying, "Oh, he's a *kamaaina*." And this may grow and grow until I am generally so spoken of and until I may at last say of myself: "I am a *kamaaina*. I belong." And this is my Hawaiian *aloha*:

Aloha nui oe, Hawaii Nei!

INDEX